4

THE GUIDE AT A GLANCE

The book is carefully structured both to convey an understanding of Hong Kong and its culture and to guide readers through its attractions and activities:

◆ The Best Of section at the front of the book helps you to prioritise. The first spread contains all the Top Sights, while Editor's Choice details unique experiences, the best buys or other recommendations.

◆ To understand Hong Kong, you need to know something of its past. Its unique history and culture are described in authoritative essays written by special-

ists in their fields who have lived in and documented the territory for many years.

◆ The Places section details all the attractions worth seeing. The main places of interest are coordinated by number with the maps.

◆ A list of recommended restaurants and bars is included at the end of each chapter.

◆ Photographs throughout the book are chosen not only to illustrate geography and buildings, but also to convey the moods of Hong Kong and the life of its people.

◆ The Travel Tips section includes all the practical information you will need, divided into six key sections: transport, accommodation, activities (including events, tours and sports), shopping, an A–Z of practical tips, and language. Information may be located quickly by using the index on the back cover flap of the book.

◆ Two detailed street atlases are included at the back of the book, complete with a full index. On the second one, you will find all the restaurants and hotels plotted for your convenience.

PLACES & SIGHTS

Colour-coding at the top of every page makes it easy to find each neighbourhood in the book. These are coordinated by specific area on the orientation map on pages 94–95.

A locator map pinpoints the specific area covered in each chapter. The page reference at the top indicates where to find a detailed map of the area highlighted in red.

Margin tips provide extra little snippets of information, whether it's a practical tip, a whimsical quote, an historical fact or advice on shopping and eating.

A four-colour map provides a bird's-eye view of the area covered in the chapter, with the main attractions coordinated by number with the main text.

INSIGHT ON... / PICTURE STORIES

Picture stories provide magazine-style visual coverage of some of Hong Kong's major cultural themes and attractions. Topics covered include dim sum, Chinese beliefs and superstitions, theme parks, nature, festivals, shopping, modern architecture, horse-racing and the Star Ferry.

RESTAURANT LISTINGS

Restaurant listings feature the best establishments within each area, giving the address, phone number, opening times and price category followed by a useful review. The grid reference refers to the atlas at the back of the book.

platters from around the planet dished up in chic surroundings.

Lucy's
3 Shamian Nanjie, Shamian Island ☎ 020 8121 5106.
$$
A menu that embraces the world, and smiles

TRAVEL TIPS

border at Lo Wu, then catch an MTR train south to Kowloon once you have cleared customs.

By Sea
Numerous cities in Guangdong province are connected by sea with Hong Kong, and it is also ...ble to take a ferry fro...

Advice-packed Travel Tips provide all the practical knowledge you'll need before and during your trip: how to get there, getting around, where to stay and what to do. The A–Z section is a handy summary of practical information, arranged alphabetically.

Contents

Maps

THE BEST OF HONG KONG: TOP SIGHTS

With its vibrant Chinese culture, superb food, exciting nightlife, shopping and one of the world's most dramatic settings, there is an awful lot to see and do in Hong Kong. This brief introduction sketches out some of the highlights

△ **The Star Ferry** Take in the superb harbour views aboard one of these appealingly old-fashioned vessels. At HK$2.20 for the first-class upper deck, this is one of the world's great travel bargains, and a must for all visitors to Hong Kong. *See pages 122–123*

◁ **Tsim Sha Tsui and Yau Ma Tei** Quintessential Hong Kong: shops, restaurants, crowds, and neon everywhere. Temple Street Night Market (pictured) is a great place to get acquainted with the local vibe, but watch out for fake merchandise! *See pages 151–162*

▽ **The Outlying Islands** In complete contrast to the crowded urban areas, Hong Kong's 230 Outlying Islands – such as Lamma (pictured) – are largely rural, and lack buildings over three storeys tall. Most also lack roads. There are some beautiful beaches and great hiking. *See pages 202–211*

▽ **Hong Kong Island views**
Like nowhere else on earth, the urban strip along the north coast of the island is a mass of skyscrapers wedged against tall green mountains. *See pages 99–111 (Central District), 153 (views from across the harbour)*

▽ **Man Mo Temple** Hong Kong's most atmospheric temple – all clouds of pungent incense and mysterious statues looming out of the darkness. *See page 110*

△ **Wan Chai and Causeway Bay** Two of Hong Kong's most dynamic and colourful neighbourhoods, crammed full of bars, restaurants and shops. *See pages 125–135*

△ **Po Lin Monastery**
A (relatively) peaceful escape high in the mountains of Lantau. The Big Buddha statue draws the crowds, and the area can be accessed by cable car from Tung Chung. *See pages 203–204*

△ **The Peak** Gaze down from these wooded heights and take in one of the world's greatest vistas, accessed from Central by the Peak Tram – an attraction in itself. There are some wonderful walks from the tram terminus. *See pages 114–117*

▷ **Hiking in the hills** A surprisingly high proportion of Hong Kong is covered by country parks, largely uninhabited tracts of land consisting of big grassy hills and patches of woodland. The Sai Kung area in the eastern New Territories is one of the most attractive, and is well-endowed with fabulous hiking trails. *See pages 188, 192–3*

THE BEST OF HONG KONG: EDITOR'S CHOICE

An overview of the best family attractions, festivals, walks and other free highlights, plus the Hong Kong essentials – eating, shopping and nightlife – as selected by our editor

ONLY IN HONG KONG

- **Light fantastic** The nightime view from the Peak, a gaudy celebration of the power of neon lighting. *See page 115*
- **Red sails in the sunset** Catch a ride on the *Aqua Luna* junk, which crosses the harbour every afternoon *(see page 280)*. For a budget option, grab a drink-to-go from a convenience store and take a ride on the Star Ferry. *See pages 122–3*

- **Cultural insights** The Hong Kong Tourist Board (HKTB) runs free talks and tours where local experts share their knowledge on subjects ranging from Chinese medicine and feng shui to t'ai chi. Most require advance booking. *See pages 280, 288*
- **Escape the city** Few cities in the world have such easy access to beautiful, empty countryside with lofty hills and good beaches. *See pages 188, 193, 200, 202*

ABOVE: the view from the top of the IFC2 tower.
LEFT: Bruce Lee sculpture on the Kowloon waterfront.
RIGHT: dim sum.

BEST DINING

- **Seafood feast** Take a ferry over to Lamma or Cheung Chau and gorge yourself on delectable seafood at one of the islands' open-air restaurants. *See page 211*
- **Dim Sum** Don't miss out on this Hong Kong speciality. *See pages 64–65*
- **Be adventurous** Try some of the more

unusual local delicacies, such as snake soup or the un-appetising-sounding "thousand-year eggs". *See pages 58–61*
- **Cosmopolitan choice** Hong Kong is hard to beat for sheer quantity and choice of restaurants from all corners of the globe. Quality is generally high. *See page 63*

BEST FOR FAMILIES

- **Ocean Park** is always a hit with families. Attractions include rides for all ages – there is a thrilling rollercoaster – plus aquariums and performing dolphins. *See pages 144, 212–213*
- **Disneyland** opened in 2005 and has naturally become a must-visit for kids. *See pages 206, 212–213*
- **The Peak** appeals to visitors of all ages. The Peak Tram is exciting, the views are amazing (best after

dark for kids), and then there is always Madame Tussaud's to enjoy. *See pages 114–117*
- Visit an **Outlying Island** – the ferry ride, the seafood and the beaches make for an enjoyable day out. *See pages 202–210*
- **The Science Museum** has the usual hands-on interactive exhibits to entertain and educate. Nearby is the **Space Museum** with its IMAX cinema. *See pages 153, 159*
- A trip to Aberdeen's **Jumbo Kingdom floating restaurant** always seems to go down well with children. *See page 142*
- The **Ngong Ping 360** cable car is great for children, and, once at the top, the Big Buddha won't disappoint either. *See page 205*

TOP: the Ocean Park cable car and (**LEFT**) welcoming zebras. **ABOVE RIGHT:** Cat Street merchandise. **RIGHT:** New Year dragon dance.

BEST SHOPPING

- **Smart shopping malls** For seeking out Armani, Dior and co. *See page 270*
- **Grimy markets** At the other end of the scale, Hong Kong's street markets are worth a visit for local colour and, of course, that fake Rolex you have always promised yourself. *See pages 111, 161, 163, 170, 270*
- **Antiques** Don't expect bargains, but the shops along Hollywood Road are full of interesting chinoiserie. *See pages 110, 270*

- **Electronics** People tend to think of Nathan Road's "Golden Mile", but while there is no denying the abundance, prices can be keener elsewhere. *See pages 271–272*
- **Clothing bargains** Hong Kong has everything from 5-star luxury to factory outlet stores – and obliging tailors. *See page 271*

For shopping overviews, see pages 168–171, 269–273

BEST FESTIVALS

- **Chinese New Year** is the time to see dragon dances, firecrackers and a truly breathtaking firework display over the harbour. *See page 179*
- **The Bun Festival** on Cheung Chau features stilt-walkers and colourful costumes. *See pages 207–8*
- **The Dragon Boat Festival** takes place in early summer, with dragon boat races at locations around Hong Kong. *See page 178*
- **The Mid-Autumn Festival**, with its lantern parades and moon cakes, is best

experienced at Victoria Park. *See page 178*

For an overview of local festivals, see pages 178–179

1 2

Best Walks – Urban and Non-Urban

- **Kowloon waterfront to Kowloon Park** Admire the famous skyline, then head north via subways to the heart of Tsim Sha Tsui – Nathan, Peking, Hankow roads and Kowloon Park. *See page 153*
- **Star Ferry Pier (Central) to Lan Kwai Fong** *(see pages 100–105)*
- **Central/Western back streets** Explore the area around Staunton Street, hub of the lively SoHo nightlife area, then return downhill to the authentic Chinese atmosphere around Gage, Graham and Peel streets. *See pages 107–109*
- **The Peak Trail** Along Lugard and Harlech roads is a gentle but rewarding stroll. Some more strenuous hikes can also be enjoyed from here. *See pages 116-7*
- **MacLehose Trail** Take your pick of walks along this 100-km (62-mile) trail running across the New Territories. Highlights are Tai Long Wan, a beautiful beach at the eastern extremity, and Tai Mo Shan, the SAR's highest peak. *See pages 188, 193*
- **Tai Po Kau** One of the largest remaining forests in the New Territories. Watch out for monkeys. *See page 186*
- **Lantau** To escape the Big Buddha crowds, follow any of several trails leading into the peaceful grassy hills around. *See pages 202–203*

Hong Kong for Free (or Almost Free)

- **Junk trip** $50 to all foreign passport holders, take a trip around the harbour on an old Chinese junk. *See page 280*
- **Free museums on Wednesdays** All day Wednesday, every Wednesday. Applies to most major museums in Hong Kong.
- **HK Magazine** Good, free listings magazine, available in most cafés and bars. *See pages 274, 286*
- **Internet access** Several cafés (Pacific Coffee, etc) have free internet access for customers. Major post offices also offer this service, as do public libraries. *See page 285*
- **Local phone calls** are free in Hong Kong (mobile calls are very cheap). If you need to make a local call you can ask in a shop and they will probably let you use their phone. *(See also Moneysaving Tips, opposite.)*
- **Horse racing at Happy Valley** Admission fee is a nominal HK$10, great value for what can be an exhilarating night out – although of course it can work out very expensive… *See pages 136–137*

Top Left: HKTB offers free junk trips around the harbour. **Above Left:** painting at the Tang Chung Ling Ancestral Hall in the New Territories. **Above:** an exhilarating walk. **Left:** the Sha Tin races. **Below:** the view from Lamma Island across to the south shore of Hong Kong Island.

HONG KONG MISCELLANEA

- With 7,684 **high-rise buildings** (over 13 storeys), Hong Kong has more skyscrapers than any city in the world, easily beating New York's 5,861, Sao Paulo's 5,662 and Singapore's 4,363. The new ICC is Hong Kong's tallest building.
- Always lively Hong Kong is actually one of the fastest ageing cities in the world. The proportion of the population aged 65 and over is projected to rise from 13 percent in 2009 to 26 percent in 2036, when the city's population is expected to reach 8.6 million.
- Ongoing **reclamation work** has halved the size of Hong Kong's harbour in the last 100 years. The scarcity of flat land and high values mean that land sales account for a large proportion of government revenue.
- A 2008 survey by the University of Hong Kong revealed that employees are becoming concerned about their **work-life balance.** While the government is promoting a five-day week (working Saturday mornings is growing less common), average working hours are still 49.6 hours per week (down from 55.2 hours in 2004), reflecting the fact that 52 percent of employees work late into the evening.

BEST NIGHTLIFE

- **SoHo (SOuth of HOllywood Road)** This area adjoining Lan Kwai Fong has really taken off over the past few years. Lots of trendy bars, clubs and restaurants. *See pages 108–109, 121*
- **Wan Chai** More down to earth than the Central nightspots. The main hub is focused on Lockhart and Jaffe roads. *See pages 126, 135*
- **Lan Kwai Fong** Long-established nightlife hub in the heart of Central, with a wide range of restaurants and bars – packed at weekends. *See pages 105, 121*
- **Tsim Sha Tsui** A mix of touristy and local bars and restaurants, with clusters in the streets between Peking and Haiphong roads, and on Knutsford Terrace. A new nightlife zone is developing around Minden Avenue east of Nathan Road. *See page 167*

ABOVE LEFT: SoHo nightlife.
LEFT: Aberdeen's Jumbo Floating Restaurant.
BELOW: Octopus card.

MONEY-SAVING TIPS

Octopus Card
Recommended to anyone who is staying more than a day or so, this stored-value card costs HK$150 (which includes a refundable $50 deposit. Unused credit is also refundable). It can be used on almost all forms of transport, as well as to buy museum tickets, and even items in convenience stores. You can top up the credit (up to HK$1000) at MTR stations and convenience stores. Tel: 2266 2222 or visit www.octopuscards.com.

Museum Pass
Available from HKTB visitor centres and participating museums; gains the holder open access to Hong Kong's main museums. The 6-month pass costs only HK$50 ($25 for kids) and will pay for itself with just a few museum trips, and also entitles you to 10 percent off purchases at museum shops and cafés.

Mobile Phones and Phone Cards
If you are staying for a few days and need to make local calls on your mobile, invest in a SIM for your phone, sold in 7-11 convenience stores for around HK$100. Another worthwhile purchase if you are calling abroad from Hong Kong is a phone card – the kind that gives you an access number. These can provide you with up to 5 hours calling time to the UK and US for only HK$50, and can also be used on your mobile.

Miscellaneous
In restaurants, ask for filtered tap water rather than bottled mineral water. Taxis are quite cheap, but costs can add up quickly – try to avoid rush hours and cross-harbour tunnel routes as far as possible.

HONG KONG, CHINA

Few cities ignite the senses as does Hong Kong, and the appeal is as strong as ever more than a decade after the return to Chinese sovereignty

Hong Kong pulsates with the visual energy of a fireworks display. It resonates to the din of a dim sum restaurant's peak hour. Polymesmeric, at times chaotic, intriguing, puzzling, endlessly exciting and in parts possessed of an astounding alternative beauty, Hong Kong is a place that precipitates the strongest emotions. More than one visitor has noted that this must be one of the Earth's acupuncture points.

Hong Kong is fuelled and inspired by constant immigration, from mainland China, from elsewhere in Asia and from the four corners of the world, with 7 million souls simultaneously focused on top dollar and bottom line in an area rather smaller than the English county of Berkshire and less than half the size of the American state of Rhode Island. Cosmopolitan yet integrally Chinese, Hong Kong's inhabitants are defined by what's written on their business cards. Off duty, they may go shopping, play tennis and basketball on courts perched atop skyscrapers, or pinball their way between the bars and clubs crammed hugger-mugger in the numerous nightlife zones; everyone here is all too aware that Time's winged chariot doesn't so much hurry near as overtake on the inside lane.

Hong Kong took an extended bath in the limelight at the end of the 20th century, with a dignified return to Chinese sovereignty in 1997 which marked the end of a colony, an era and an empire. It's all history now. Hong Kong is a Special Administrative Region (SAR) of China, with a key role to play in the spectacular growth of the Chinese economy, although it remains markedly different from the mainland: the "one country two systems" pledge is clearly working, despite concerns and protests over certain issues. Within this framework, Hong Kong's peculiar, cosmopolitan blend of Chinese and Western, and its prosperity, continue to thrive.

For the first time, though, it is facing real competition from its neighbours. The economic revolution in the Pearl River Delta has catapulted entire new cities like Shenzhen onto the world map. And Macau's lackadaisical ambience has been given a makeover with the arrival of a clutch of casinos which are being dubbed the "Las Vegas of the East". Does the former Crown colony have the stamina to keep up? The smart money is saying: you bet. ❑

PRECEDING PAGES: the glittering harbour from the Tsim Sha Tsui promenade; the bustle of Wan Chai. **LEFT:** Hong Kong's urban areas have the world's highest population densities.

HONG KONG'S PEOPLE

Outsiders may see Hong Kong's people as materialistic
and sometimes brusque. But there are reasons
for this, including an obsession with success

The people of Hong Kong are variously described as being the most business-minded, materialistic, competitive and restless population on the planet. Few other cities have such a complex, unsettled history. It is a place that moves at lightning speed because time is money, and every minute costs. Love it or hate it, life in Hong Kong is addictive, and even those who have escaped to more peaceful places – vowing never to return – have been drawn back like iron filings to a magnet. Even the most jaded visitor usually finds something seductive about it.

Hong Kong's 7 million people are packed into just 1,103 sq km (426 sq miles), and certain areas have some of the world's highest population densities. During rush hour, overwhelming crowds of commuters squeeze themselves into trains and buses. Lunch hour is a feeding frenzy, as thousands of office workers dash for restaurants, jostling and barging their way into tiny noodle shops and delicatessens. Elbowing strangers, jumping queues and honking horns in traffic jams (often complemented by deafening construction sites and roadworks) are unavoidable features of daily life here.

As a major trading port situated on the fertile Pearl River Delta, Hong Kong has long been a magnet for immigrants in search of a better life. New arrivals continue to flood in from China and overseas, all sharing one dream: to make money quickly and to enjoy

spending it. This continual injection of new blood is part of what gives Hong Kong its excitement and intensity.

For those seeking a settled, peaceful existence, Hong Kong will be a hard slap in the face. This place resounds with rags-to-riches tales of entrepreneurs who built up their business empires from scratch, and this promise of success is in the minds of almost every immigrant who heads here.

Local identity

Hong Kong is, and always has been, Chinese. In spite of more than 150 years of colonial rule, the Chinese, who make up 95 percent of

---

LEFT: Hong Kongers love their dogs.
RIGHT: mah-jong is a popular, sociable game.

the population, never had a sense of allegiance to the British Crown. Those of the older generation, who originated from elsewhere, often identified with their home provinces or towns in China rather than Hong Kong.

On the whole, however, local Chinese are more inclined to view themselves as Hong Kong citizens rather than Han Chinese. This sense of identity has increased in the post-handover years, along with what could be termed an embryonic civic pride – Hong Kongers no longer regard their city simply as somewhere to live and make money, with an eye to moving on somewhere else as needs dictate. Greater political and even environmental awareness – examples include the campaign to halt further reclamation of the harbour – are symptoms of a maturing city growing in confidence and sophistication. It is in part due to the fact that the local population is ever more likely to have been born and raised here, and that they are part of what is likely to become the world's largest economy within a generation.

Ethnic groups

Hong Kong's original inhabitants *(see page 35)* settled in what is now the New Territories and outlying islands. Sometimes referred to as the Punti "people of the earth", they were mainly

farmers. In the 13th century, Kublai Khan's Mongol hordes swept south into China, destroying the Song dynasty and pushing Han Chinese farmers southwards from the mainland into Hong Kong. The Tang clan settled in the fertile Shek Kong Valley, where they established a cluster of walled villages including Kat Hing Wai in Kam Tin *(see page 197)*. They were followed over the centuries by various other families, forming the so-called "Five Great Clans": the Tang, Hau, Pang, Liu and Man. These people developed trade in salt, pearls, ceramics and fishing, and farmed the fertile river valleys.

Meanwhile, the **Hakka** ("guest people") migrated southwards in waves from central China. As later arrivals they made the best of the more hilly land in the eastern New Territories.

For centuries a sprinkling of **Tanka** "boat people" have lived on junks in places like Tai O and Aberdeen, harvesting pearls and making salt. Legend has it that the Tanka are the descendants of the 5th-century general, Lu Tsun, who revolted against the emperor; after his death, his people were persecuted and deemed unworthy to live on land.

The Tanka's boat-based communities also attracted the **Hoklo** people, who originate from the area around Fuzhou (Fujian province) and were traditionally fishermen and manual labourers. Today all fishing communities celebrate the sea goddess Tin Hau's birthday on the 23rd day of the third moon, sailing in elaborately decorated fishing boats to her temples to pray for protection at sea.

TOP LEFT: shopping is a Hong Kong obsession.
ABOVE: grandmother and granddaughter, Central Market. **LEFT:** Hakka woman in the New Territories.
ABOVE RIGHT: a crowded street in Mong Kok.

These ethnic groups remained remote from the Chinese, and later British, imperial authorities all the way through to the 1950s

The Cantonese

This mix of "indigenous" people is now comprehensively outnumbered by the Cantonese, who trace their roots back to other areas of Guangdong province. Traditionally regarded as a rebellious, ungovernable people given to spontaneous action if angered, they have always been mistrusted by emperors and regimes. The Nationalist revolution, which toppled the Qing dynasty in 1912, was instigated by a Cantonese, Dr Sun Yat-sen, and

Guangzhou became the centre for the Nationalist Party, the first modern political party in China. The Chinese Communist Party founded the Peasant Movement Training Institute, their first school, in Guangzhou in 1922, and Mao Zedong is said to have developed his theory of peasant revolution while working in the city.

> With British domination of local business brought to an end by World War II, Chinese entrepreneurs – both Hong Kong-born and newly arrived – were quick to seize opportunities.

THE CANTONESE LANGUAGE

The Cantonese language often sounds harsh and argumentative to unaccustomed ears, but its humour, slang and interspersed English words make for lively conversation. Cantonese is also centuries older than Mandarin (putonghua), the official language of China, which evolved later in the courts of Mongol emperors during the Yuan dynasty (1271–1368). Therefore, the original rhythms and sounds of classical Tang- and Song-dynasty poetry are probably closer to modern-day Cantonese. On a day-to-day level Cantonese is a bawdy language: quite innocent-looking individuals swear like troopers, and people are often brutal when commenting on other people's appearance and delight in puns and double entendres.

For over a hundred years, from the latter part of the 19th century to the present day, the port of Hong Kong has been the destination of migrants, some of whom stayed in the farming villages of the New Territories or the urban centres of Kowloon or Central and Western. Many headed further afield to the US, Australia or Southeast Asia. Never was the push and pull of migration more evident than during and after the Japanese Occupation and following the end of the Chinese Civil War. Arrivals from Guangdong remained the majority, but in the late 1940s large numbers of refugees from Shanghai, the former commercial centre of China, fled

to Hong Kong when the communists took over. Many foreign firms also relocated their Chinese headquarters to Hong Kong. The Shanghainese community settled in North Point on Hong Kong Island, and the businessmen among them were quick to use their capital, know-how and pool of labour to set up factories.

In 2008, when it was revealed that five out of eight new civil service political appointees also held a foreign passport, critics said they were unpatriotic. Many locals see a second passport as insurance in case China "turns nasty".

The Chiu Chow (Shantou) people from further up the Guangdong coast, also renowned for their business acumen, clung together in powerful clan networks, and settled in Sai Ying Pun and Kowloon City.

Population explosion

For much of the 1950s, '60s and '70s, illegal immigrants continued to outwit the battalions of the People's Liberation Army (PLA) and Chinese coastal gunboats, which cooperated with Hong Kong's security forces. By 1980 this influx, combined with a high birth rate, had

pushed Hong Kong's population to 4 million *(see panel, page 41)*.

These decades of population growth coincided with Hong Kong's rapid industrialisation, a time when factories were desperate for labour. During the early 1950s many people lived in squatter huts, then later in newly built government housing blocks in Kowloon, which preceded the vast New Town developments (today more than half of Hong Kong's citizens live in New Towns in the New Territories).

In the New Territories, farming was in decline, unable to provide sufficient employment for the typically large families living there. Throughout the 1950s, the UK's policy to

POPULATION FACTS AND FIGURES

Hong Kong's population passed the 7 million mark in 2009, which means that each square kilometre of its territory is home to some 6,300 people (16,000 per sq mile) – making the SAR one of the world's most crowded places. Locally born residents form the majority of the population (60 percent), with 33 percent having been born elsewhere in China. Cantonese is spoken by 96 percent, but 45 percent can speak English and 40 percent Mandarin. There are also over 200,000 speakers each of Hakka, Chiu Chow, Hokkien (Fukien) and Shanghainese. At 82.4 years, life expectancy is the second-highest in the world, while infant mortality rates are among the lowest.

recruit unskilled workers from its colonies drew thousands of young men from these rural communities. Many of the founders of British Chinese takeaway restaurants were part of this exodus.

The Right of Abode

As China opened up in the 1980s, a growing number of Hong Kong men, typically new migrants, married mainland Chinese women, creating a new social problem of divided families. Dad lived and worked in Hong Kong while Mum and the kids stayed in Guangdong, visiting only occasionally. After 1997 many of these dependent children, now grown up, sought to claim Right of Abode in Hong Kong, causing fierce debate over residency rights. Initially the Hong Kong Court ruled in their favour, but with Hong Kong concerned that this would instantly grant residency to around 300,000 mainland Chinese, the government in Beijing was asked to rule on the matter, and the interpretation of the Right of Abode was subsequently altered.

Since then, anyone from mainland China who is coming to Hong Kong from China to reunite families is given priority in the quota of new arrivals allowed. Nowadays, the number of mainlanders allowed to settle has been increasing – from 25,000 a year in the late 1980s to 55,000 in 2008. However, 25,000 Hong Kong men married mainland women in 2006, and in the same year, 26,000 pregnant mainland women arrived, unannounced, at Hong Kong maternity wards in the advanced stages of labour. This stretched the city's obstetrics wards to breaking point and caused resentment from local residents.

ABOVE LEFT: the MTR makes getting around easy.
ABOVE: commuters in Kowloon.
RIGHT: lighting incense in a temple.

Most mothers were married to Hong Kong men and were determined to gain a Hong Kong ID card for their offspring. Imposing an advance fee of US$5,000 did something to reduce numbers. Most plan to send the children to Hong Kong for schooling to live with their fathers, while they remain working in Guangdong; this is creating a new range of social problems and difficulty in adjustment. Today, many new arrivals from the mainland

---

DUAL IDENTITY

After the 1984 Sino-British agreement to return Hong Kong to China, and the events in Tiananmen Square in 1989, a new type of migration emerged in the territory. Between 1990 and 1997 some 300,000 are thought to have left Hong Kong to secure foreign passports, travelling mainly to Canada, Australia and the United States. The price of such security meant sacrificing businesses, family and friends, and starting from scratch in an alien country. Many of the émigrés then returned to Hong Kong after establishing permanent residence overseas, shuttling back and forth annually to retain their status in both places. In theory, Beijing insists that all ethnic Chinese Hong Kong residents are Chinese nationals; therefore, they are not entitled to foreign consular protection. However, many wealthier Hong Kong residents enter the SAR with their Hong Kong ID card, and find it easier to travel on a foreign passport.

---

are still derided as *ah tsan* (country bumpkins) and are the butt of jokes in soap operas, despite the fact that they share the same heritage as most Hong Kong residents.

Expatriates in Hong Kong

Hong Kong's cultural diversity is largely a result of the many different foreign nationals who have made their home here, either temporarily or permanently. Indeed, the 5 percent of the population that is not Chinese have made valuable contributions to cuisine, arts, culture and religion in Hong Kong, while assimilating local customs and traditions. Hong Kong grants permanent residency and the right to vote (albeit for a limited number

of seats in Legco) to all – with the exception of domestic helpers – who have lived here legally for seven years continuously, but only those with Chinese parentage will be granted a Hong Kong SAR passport.

American, Australian, Canadian, South African, British and other European expatriates – *gweilo* ("ghost person" or "foreign devil") as they are known in Cantonese – make up the majority of the foreign business community, numbering around 36,000 in 2008. (It is worth noting that the term *gweilo* is in such common use that it is not generally taken to be offensive. However Cantonese slang for people from the mainland, and anyone with a darker skin, *is* generally derogatory.) During British rule, expatriates were often given preferential treatment in the workplace, commanding much higher salaries than the Chinese. Today, these inequalities are less apparent. Nonetheless, in recent years Hong Kong has tried to focus on attracting skilled professionals through various schemes. It grants working visas to more than 210,000 non-Chinese professionals each year, and has a special scheme targeting mainland professionals.

There are increasing numbers of Asian expatriates and overseas-born Chinese living as expatriates in Hong Kong. The Japanese business community has played a quiet but important role in commerce in Hong Kong and China, and there are some 2,000 Japanese companies and more than 20,000 Japanese residents in the SAR.

One of the more established foreign communities in Hong Kong comprises the descendants of early merchant traders and soldiers who followed the Union Jack from the Indian subcontinent to Hong Kong: **Indians** – including many **Sikhs** and **Parsees**, as well as **Sri Lankans, Pakistanis** and **Bangladeshis**. Their descendants, many of whom speak fluent Cantonese can only be granted HKSAR passports if they can prove Chinese blood or jump through a tough series of hoops. Up to 8,000 were granted British passports in a last-minute ruling in 1996. A few thousand ex-Gurkha troops, who once served in the British army, are now working as security guards in Hong Kong, and many of their locally-born offspring use their right to permanent residency to work in Hong Kong too.

Hong Kong's largest ethnic groups are Filipina and Indonesian domestic helpers. Over 200,000 a year enter on strict employment visas that stipulate they must live-in with their employers and work six days a week. Payment is set at around US$480 per month. This enables both parents in many Hong Kong families to work full time and care for children and elderly relatives.

Most domestic helpers remit the bulk of their pay home to support their own children through schooling and to provide for their extended families. Come Sundays and public holidays, thousands of Filipina helpers gather in Central to meet friends, while the growing Indonesian community tends to gather near Victoria Park in Causeway Bay. ❏

ABOVE LEFT: Hong Kong has a lively clubbing scene. **LEFT:** fan-assisted t'ai chi in the park. **ABOVE:** the South Asian community numbers around 45,000. **ABOVE RIGHT:** traditional medicine vendor in Western District.

CULTURE AND SOCIETY

Hong Kongers are proud of their Chinese culture, one which emphasises hard work, the role of the family and – not least – the pursuit of financial success. As a thoroughly international city, Hong Kong is also open to influences which have produced some unique cultural quirks

F or all its modernity and dynamism, Hong Kong's culture and society are underpinned by a strong foundation of traditional Chinese values and beliefs. The Confucian concepts of humility, perseverance, reverence for ancestors and respect for elders have been adapted to its modern, capitalist society. Confucius said that a person should always examine motives carefully before acting, since all individuals are directly responsible for their fate. As the teachings of the great sage permeated into Chinese society over the centuries, this has led to a belief that anything can be achieved through sheer will and hard work. The attitude is, "If you don't have any money, then go out and earn some!" rather than relying on government support or charity to provide financial assistance.

With this work ethic in mind, many parents work at least nine or ten hours a day, six days a week to provide for their children who will, one day, look after them in old age. Most of the family budget goes towards children's clothing, healthcare and education, so that they may enjoy what their parents never had in their youth. Children are expected to support their elderly parents and to honour the memory of deceased parents by regularly visiting their graves and making offerings.

Family values are very strong, and parents dote on their children by spending time and money on them. On Sundays and holidays, parents take the whole family, with grandparents in tow, for Western-style buffets or dim sum. After lunch, families wander around the streets and shopping malls, buying new toys and clothes for the children.

Money and status

Successive famines, wars and political upheaval in China have taught the Hong Kong Chinese not to be complacent about financial security. They are eagle-eyed at spotting opportunities for making money; here "filthy lucre" really does seem to buy happiness, since material security is vital to one's sense of well-being.

LEFT: Central MTR station. **TOP RIGHT:** entertainers at Ocean Park. **ABOVE RIGHT:** worship at Wong Tai Sin Temple. **ABOVE FAR RIGHT:** a Lantau windsurfer downs a beer. **RIGHT:** pollution is a serious problem.

There is no other place in the world where people, rich or poor, are as business-minded and clued-up about property, stocks and horse-racing. It's no coincidence that *kung hei fat choi* – literally "congratulations on your wealth" – is a common greeting at Lunar New Year. As in most places in the world, of course, the quest for wealth is also motivated by self-respect or "face". Wearing designer labels and buying expensive dishes in a restaurant, such as lobster, abalone and shark's fin, are all ways of showing you have wealth. At the end of a meal, diners will fight to pay the bill, since generosity also gains face. Face and *guanxi* – life-long obligations of mutual assistance – are crucial to relationships. That's why the Chinese prefer to give business to family and friends rather than deal with strangers, who might prove to be unreliable. In friends there is certainty.

The public persona

Many foreigners visiting Hong Kong have complained that the people are sometimes

POLLUTION AND THE ENVIRONMENT IN HONG KONG

Most visitors to Hong Kong are likely to notice the appalling quality of the air. Hazing out the views from The Peak, on bad days even making it difficult to see across the harbour, the pollution is frequently cited by residents as the worst single aspect of the SAR. Some of the smog is home-grown, but a good proportion is imported – a photo-chemical cloud drifting down on the northeast winds from the industrial zones of Guangdong. These winds are at their most persistent during the October–April period; pollution levels are usually lower between May and September as the wind blows in from the south and east, and heavy rain washes out the dust. Meanwhile, the waters are also filthy, and this and over-fishing has reduced local fish stocks by 80 percent.

In the past few years, these environmental problems have become a hot topic in Hong Kong, and some progress is being made on local emissions – some taxis and buses running on LPG gas, for example. Yet despite a great deal of debate (and protest), there is a lack of will-power from the authorities to do anything about it – partly as a result of a powerful business lobby reluctant to sanction anything likely to cut profit margins.

brusque to the point of rudeness. This has often been a result of cultural misunderstandings, but not always. Hong Kong does not yet have the "have a nice day" culture, and chitchat about the weather seems unnecessary when there's business to be done. Even so, there has been a campaign to improve politeness to meet tourists' expectations. The customer service in many of Hong Kong's hotels and restaurants is second to none.

Property and the cost of living

For financial reasons, Hong Kongers often marry later than mainland Chinese – for women, 29 is a typical age, for men, 31. Because of high property prices, most people,

even married couples, have no choice but to live with their parents until they have saved enough money. Cramped living conditions, however, make life difficult for would-be lovers. Moments alone are rare, and the prying eyes of relatives are not conducive to romance. People often socialise in large mixed groups; parks are few and far between, so busy anonymous places such as malls or large theme parks offer a chance to to be alone.

This is a capitalist society where Darwin's theory of the "survival of the fittest" predominates. Local tax laws give residents incentive to be among those that not only survive, but thrive. Residents keep most of what they earn – the highest income-tax rate is 15 percent, and only around 2 percent of the working population pays this, with over half paying no income tax at all.

However, Hong Kong has a high cost of living due to rising inflation, limited land, the expense of importing raw materials and food, and high duties imposed on petrol and cars. On the other hand, there is no sales tax, and public transport is cheap. Luxury goods score

LACK OF SPACE

Hong Kong is one of the world's most crowded environments, with correspondingly expensive property and often cramped living conditions. Over half of Hong Kong's population lives in public housing, where families benefit from low rents (the average monthly rent for public housing is HK$1,390) as well as shared income from family members, and are thus relatively well-off compared to low-income families in other parts of the world. However, lower-middle-class families are often caught: they do not qualify for public housing, and most property prices are way beyond their budget. The average apartment is just 500 sq ft (48 sq metres), enough for a living area, small kitchen and one, sometimes two, small bedrooms.

high points in the "face" game, and some people will gladly blow all their disposable income on a Louis Vuitton bag even if they can't then afford much else.

Land prices have always been high, a result of the shortage of suitable terrain for construction. The government makes huge profits on land sales – a situation which fuels the desire for more and more land to be reclaimed from the sea. The largest and most successful Hong Kong compa-

> *Hong Kong has steadily expanded in area as a total of 70 sq km (27 sq miles) has been reclaimed from the sea. Around 70 percent of this has taken place since 1980.*

nies, such as Cheung Kong and Sun Hung Kai, have built their fortunes upon this system.

Social welfare and health

Hong Kong may be one of the world's wealthiest cities, but not all share in its prosperity. An estimated 150,000, mostly elderly people, live in inadequate housing, with the worst-off in shacks or so-called "cages" (with room for a bed and nothing else, and usually packed several to a room – as pictured above), or out on the streets. There is a welfare system for the elderly, with payments of HK\$2,590–3,140 per month. The Mandatory Provident Fund introduced in 1999, forces employees to invest up to 5 percent of their salary for retirement when the fund can be withdrawn as a lump sum.

Primary medical care is largely taken care of by private GPs in Hong Kong, while 90 percent of hospital admissions are at government-subsidised hospitals. The problem of over-crowded public wards and long waiting lists has drawn a great deal of criticism, however, and this has led to substantial growth in private medical insurance funded by both companies and individuals. Many employers offer health insurance to subsidise private healthcare.

Affordable government medical care is currently assured for the entire population through public funds and private donations, but the administration is considering making private health insurance mandatory.

Crime

Hong Kong's over-the-top action movies often give the impression of a crime-ridden city which is a perpetual hunting ground for

TOP FAR LEFT: Filipinas form the largest foreign community. **ABOVE LEFT:** tailor at work. **LEFT:** housing block in Kowloon. Apartments are typically comprised of only four small rooms. **ABOVE:** martial arts practice session. **ABOVE RIGHT:** a cage-dweller. **RIGHT:** Cantopop celebrity Aaron Kwok, with Ferrari.

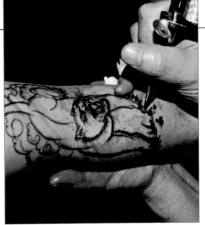

chopper-wielding tattooed thugs and armed robbers. In reality, one of the pleasures of Hong Kong is its lack of crime – the streets are safe at any time, and the chances of being mugged or pickpocketed are significantly lower than almost anywhere in Europe or America. This is often mentioned as a major quality of life benefit, one that encourages expats to live in Hong Kong.

Organised crime does exist, though. The triad crime syndicates rely on a hierarchical structure, with ranks denoted by numbers that begin with four, representing the four elements, compass points and seas. The highest-profile gangs are "14K" and "San Yee On", whose illegal activities include loan-sharking, gambling, narcotics, prostitution, smuggling and extortion.

Hong Kong has an estimated 14,000 drug abusers: 52 percent of them are heroin addicts, 35 percent use methamphetamine and 11 percent ketamine. The government takes a tough stance on narcotics. Possession of marijuana carries the same penalties as hard drugs: a criminal record and possible imprisonment. Still, Hong Kong's "work hard, play hard" culture, coupled with its affluence, has meant that recreational drugs are readily available.

Education

Hong Kong's educational system is every bit as competitive as its business community. Children suffer great pressure to get into prestigious schools. The most sought-after are English or bilingual schools – English is widely used in business, medicine and law. As elsewhere in the world, some students commit suicide each year if they fail an important exam. Parental pressure often proves too much for children, who spend much of their time cramming for exams and studying foreign languages for overseas study. Tutors are hired to prepare toddlers for kindergarten entrance exams, an ordeal that sometimes requires two hours of testing to determine a child's Chinese, English and arithmetic skills.

The government regularly carries out studies to ascertain the standard of English spoken by

---

WHAT'S IN A NAME

One of Hong Kong's odder cultural quirks is the range of eccentric English nicknames chosen by the Hong Kong Chinese: Biscuit, Photosynthesis, Frandie, Wealthy, Xerox, Tweetie… This is in part the result of a desire to embrace the English-speaking world, and in part a way of identifying with a particular respected figure, a hobby or interest.

Emulation of the famous and successful accounts for the plethora of Jackie Chans in the territory, and may also explain some of the Wilsons – after the colony's penultimate British governor. Seemingly gaudy names such as Lucky or Wealthy or the no-nonsense Money represent the aspirations of a people who have only enjoyed prosperity for a couple of generations.

Humour is apparent with names that echo the individual's Chinese name, leaving the glorious Winky Winky Wong Wing-kee. Sometimes the name puns on the family name, as in Gypsy Lee or Ivan Ho. Hobbies or interests can play a role, scientific processes clearly being of fascination to Photosynthesis Wong. Fandie, Ankie and Banda represent a desire to be the only person in the entire world to have a certain name. And then there are the downright peculiar but memorable, such as Onions, Squash or Catherine (a man).

teachers, to ensure that students get every opportunity to become confidently bilingual. The core competency remains Chinese, English and maths, but an overseas education is seen as a passport to a higher salary.

Political awareness

Now that Hong Kong is into its second decade of "one country two systems", its residents seem to be developing a clearer identity. They are proud of what the city has achieved, and nostalgic about the tough years when they or their parents helped create the economic miracle. There is also an inner conflict between pride in being Chinese and lingering unease at Beijing's rule.

Self-censorship in some sections of the media is a concern, but locals do voice freely their criticism of the Hong Kong government. There is some frustration amongst ordinary people that certain groups within society wield more influ-

> *A 2008 survey shows that Hong Kong men are now spending more time each day surfing the internet than watching TV. Those aged 10–29 had the heaviest internet usage, at 2.9 hours a day, 5.5 days a week.*

ence than others, in particular the tycoons who control the property sector and monopolies. The mess of urban planning, and the issues of harbour reclamation, pollution and a lack of public spaces only adds to public vexation. Yet at the same time these very same tycoons, who have the ear of Beijing, are widely admired for their business acumen and sheer volume of wealth.

In the last few years, political awareness has developed, and street protests have become a regular feature as local people have grown increasingly frustrated with the SAR government's decisions. There is a keen sense of injustice, yet by and large, people do not appear to associate this with the lack of accountability of a largely appointed administration.

The future

Hong Kong's economic success can be credited above all to one thing: its industrious people. As Beijing is well aware, any attempts to restrict freedoms could result in an exodus of a talented, highly educated workforce, with disastrous consequences for China. Most China-watchers believe that for Hong Kong to continue to thrive, it is here that China's economic reforms must coincide with the advance of democracy rather than its suppression. The concern that Shanghai could take over Hong Kong's privileged position as the gateway to China is voiced less often now, and some influential groups look to a future where Hong Kong forms a giant megalopolis with Shenzhen. ❑

HOU Q: THE CUTE OBSESSION

In tandem with much of the rest of Asia, Hong Kong is in thrall to Japanese pop culture and its obsession with all things cute – what is termed in Japan as *kawaii*, in Hong Kong as *hou Q*. The epitome of this is "Hello Kitty", the ubiquitous cat created by the Japanese company Sanrio which adorns over 20,000 products, from clothing to stationery. Sociologists say the fascination with Japanese style is fuelled by Asians' need to find a modern image of themselves, to form their own popular culture rather than borrow from the West. Or, as an 18-year-old Hong Konger expressed it: "Japanese society is very fast-paced and always changing. Everything is very cute and stylish."

TOP FAR LEFT: Lord Buddha's Festival at Po Lin Monastery. **TOP LEFT:** triad tattoo. **ABOVE RIGHT:** Hong Kong's education system is highly regarded. **RIGHT:** "Hello Kitty" is everywhere in Hong Kong.

THE STORY OF HONG KONG

Initially regarded by the British as an ill-chosen gain of limited value, Hong Kong soon became an important part of the Empire – and one that was only reluctantly relinquished

To most people, Hong Kong's history starts with the Opium Wars in the 1840s. However, archaeological studies have uncovered evidence of human habitation along this stretch of the southern Chinese coast dating back some 6,000 years.

Most of the excavated stone tools, pottery and other artefacts have been found preserved in coastal areas, suggesting a strong dependence on the sea. Bronze appeared in the middle of the second millennium BC, and weapons and tools such as axes and fish hooks have been excavated from local sites. There is evidence, too, in the form of stone moulds from the islands of Chek Lap Kok, Lantau and Lamma, that the metal was worked locally. Rock carvings, most of which are geometric in style, have also been discovered around Hong Kong Island and on some of the smaller islands.

An increasing number of people from the mainland came to settle in the region during the Qin (221–206 BC) and Han (206 BC–AD 220) dynasties. Coins of the Han period have been found in Hong Kong, and a brick tomb was uncovered at Kowloon's Lei Cheng Uk (see page 177) with a collection of typical Han tomb furniture. Other findings included pottery and iron implements. Little has been discovered from the next 1,000 years, but engraved writings, coins and celadon pottery suggest strong links with the Chinese Song dynasty during the 13th century. The many Ming-style blue-and-

white porcelain works discovered on Lantau suggest increasing contact with the mainland during the Ming (1368–1644) and Qing (1644–1911) dynasties.

The coming of the Europeans

The West began to show an interest in China and Asia during the 15th and 16th centuries due to the increased trade in products such as silk and tea. The Portuguese were the first to arrive, trading with China at various points along the coast and establishing a settlement at Macau in 1557. The British, on the other hand, did not appear in force until the latter part of the 17th century.

LEFT: houses on The Peak; this picture was taken in 1937, before the reforestation programme.
RIGHT: early colonial buildings on the harbour, 1856.

In 1685, Emperor Kangxi, who reigned when the Qing dynasty was at the peak of its power, opened Guangzhou for limited trade. Ships began arriving from the British East India Company stations on the Indian coast, and soon Hong Kong, with its deep-water harbour, began to establish itself as a trading hub. Fifteen years later the Company, the world's largest commercial organisation, received permission to build a storage warehouse outside Guangzhou.

EARLY TRADE WITH EUROPEANS

To begin with, in the early 18th century, trade with Western countries was in China's favour. Traders paid huge amounts of silver for fine Chinese tea and silk products, for which there was great demand in Europe. Tough terms were imposed on foreign traders, considered to be barbarians. They could only live in restricted areas in Guangzhou. They could not bring in arms, warships or women. Learning the Chinese language was forbidden, and traders also had to put up with the Chinese system of royalties, bribes and fees. Local merchants were appointed by the emperor to keep an eye on foreigners.

The opium trade

After more than a century of trading with China, the East India Company tried to balance its increasingly expensive purchases by developing its profitable sale of opium to the Chinese, mostly shipped from their colonies in Bengal. By the beginning of the 19th century there were already millions of addicts in China, and the country was paying for its spiralling drug habit with silver specie, disastrously depleting the national treasury. Clearly, from a Qing perspective, something had to be done.

Alarmed at the increasing outflow of silver, the emperor Jiaqing banned the drug trade completely in 1799. In 1810 he went further, announcing: "Opium is a poison, undermining our good customs and morality. Its use is prohibited by law." But neither foreigners nor Guangdong merchants were willing to give up the profitable business, and they resorted to smuggling. By 1820, the trade had grown to 30,000 chests annually.

Jiaqing's son, Daoguang, continued to issue edicts after he came to the dragon throne in 1820, but to no avail – the British weren't listening, and nor, apparently, were the opium addicts. Accordingly, in 1838 Daoguang dispatched Lin Zexu, the formidable Governor-

General of Henan and Hubei, as his commissioner to impose Qing anti-opium legislation on the unruly foreign traders in Guangzhou. To the fury of the Westerners – at whose head stood the British – Lin confiscated and destroyed more than 20,000 chests of opium and blockaded the port to foreign shipping. Lin also wrote to Queen Victoria, asking why the British prohibited opium imports into their own country, but forced it on China. "Was this a morally correct position?", the commissioner asked rhetorically.

Lin's letter was never delivered to the queen, although it was published in *The Times*. And while it may have given liberal anti-opium campaigners in Great Britain pause for thought, it raised no sympathy at all with the opium merchants of India and Canton, who loudly demanded compensation for their lost opium, and pressed for military retaliation. This came in 1840, with the arrival of warships and soldiers from India. European military superiority ensured the First Opium War (1840–42) was short, sharp and one-sided. The British seized control of Guangzhou. Intimidated, the Qing commissioner, Qi Shan, who had replaced Lin, agreed in January 1841 to the Convention of Chuen Pi, which ceded Hong Kong Island to Britain. On 26 January

1841, the British flag was raised at Possession Point on Hong Kong Island, and the island was officially occupied. Five months later, British officials began selling plots of land and the colonisation of Hong Kong began.

Neither China nor Britain was happy with the terms of the Chuen Pi agreement, however. The Chinese government and its people saw the loss of a part of its territory as an unbearable humiliation, and Qi Shan was ordered to Beijing in chains. The British government, particularly Lord Palmerston, the irascible

> The name "Hong Kong" is derived from the Cantonese Heung Gong, which means "fragrant harbour". In the past, sandalwood incense was produced around what is now Aberdeen, and the scent drifted out to sea.

Foreign Secretary, was unhappy with Hong Kong, which he contemptuously – and famously – described as "a barren island with barely a house upon it", and refused to accept it as an alternative to a commercial treaty.

Blaming Captain Charles Elliot of the Royal Navy for failing to make full use of the troops sent to China, Palmerston replaced him with Sir Henry Pottinger, Hong Kong's first governor, in August 1841. Pottinger soon realised Hong Kong's potential future, even though

ABOVE LEFT: 19th-century opium addicts. **LEFT:** a foreign envoy at the Qing court. **ABOVE:** the British demand the opening of China's ports.

Britain had treated it as just another pawn in ongoing negotiations with the Chinese. He encouraged long-term building projects and awarded land grants.

After Shanghai fell in 1842, the Qing authorities sued for peace, and the Treaty of Nanking was signed in August, formally trans-

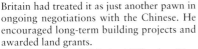

Hong Kong became a British colony in three stages: Hong Kong Island (1841–2) was followed by the Kowloon peninsula (1860), then New Kowloon and the New Territories were leased for 99 years (1898).

ferring Hong Kong Island to the British "in perpetuity" (the Chuen Pi Convention of the previous year had not been signed and so was never accepted as an official agreement by the British). As well as awarding the British 21 million ounces of silver in compensation for the opium seized three years earlier, the treaty also opened five "Treaty Ports" to foreign shipping and residence including Guangzhou, Xiamen and Fuzhou, Ningbo and Shanghai.

Suddenly China was exposed to a new and troublesome "enemy at the gate". Subsequently, with the silting of Macau's harbour and the weakening of Portuguese power in Asia, Hong Kong began its growth into one of the greatest port cities the world had ever seen.

The early colonial period

In its early days, the new British colony grew slowly, but further Anglo-Chinese conflict was soon to change this. In 1856 a dispute over the interpretation of the earlier treaty led to the outbreak of the Second Opium War, and during the two-year conflict, many companies in Guangzhou transferred their offices to Hong Kong, considerably strengthening the fledgling colony. China, weak with a corrupt government, lost again. By the summer of 1858, allied British and French troops had advanced far to the north, forcing the Chinese government to sign the Treaties of Tianjin (Tientsin). The terms gave foreigners the right to send diplomatic representatives to China and travel freely throughout the land.

Hostilities were renewed the following year when Chinese soldiers fired on the first British envoy to China as he made his way to the

court in Beijing. Fighting continued until 1860. The British consul in Guangzhou secured the perpetual lease of the Kowloon peninsula all the way north to what is now Boundary Street, including Stonecutter's Island.

By this time, other countries – Russia, France, Germany and Japan – were waking up to the importance of having easy access to China. Not to be outdone by the British, they began to make similar incursions to secure footholds all along the Chinese coastline. In 1862, a Sino-Portuguese treaty gave Macau a colonial status similar to that of Hong Kong. A second treaty in 1887 confirmed it as a Portuguese colony in perpetuity.

The British were concerned that their territory in Hong Kong was vulnerable to attack from the north, and wished to gain control of the mountainous area north of Kowloon as far as the Shenzhen River. In 1898 they got their way, securing the lease of what became known as the New Territories (as well as some 230

islands) for a period of 99 years. There was later regret at having signed this treaty, which only leased the land, while Hong Kong Island and the Kowloon peninsula were British in perpetuity. (It would later be impractical for Britain to keep Hong Kong Island and Kowloon when the New Territories lease ran out in 1997.)

At first, Chinese warships were allowed to use the wharf at Kowloon City, and Chinese officials were permitted to remain in office. However, a year later, the British took over the city completely. The New Territories was declared a part of Hong Kong, although it kept

ABOVE LEFT: storming the fortress at Xiamen (Amoy) in 1841. **ABOVE:** a panorama of Victoria Harbour from 1860. **RIGHT:** a military parade at the former Queen's Monument, 1870.

Turbulent times

From the beginning of the 20th century, China experienced a series of political upheavals. In 1900, a peasant uprising known as the Boxer Rebellion seriously challenged the authority of the creaky and corrupt Qing government, which collapsed for good a few years later. In 1911 Sun Yat-sen established the Republic of China. (Although Sun Yat-sen travelled to Hong Kong many times to enlist support for his cause, his revolution did not have much impact on the British colony.)

a separate administrative body from the urban area. Under a laissez-faire style of British rule, Hong Kong people were left alone to concentrate on their businesses.

During the late 19th and early 20th centuries, the colony developed rapidly, becoming a magnet for immigrants and a centre of trade with Chinese communities abroad. Several public-service companies were established, including the Hong Kong and China Gas Company in 1861, the Peak Tram in 1885 and the 137-km (85-mile) Kowloon-Canton Railway (KCR) in 1910. The paucity of land for building due to the steep terrain meant that land-reclamation projects got under way as early as

Between 1920 and the late 1940s life in China was dominated by conflict. The long-running civil war between Mao Zedong's Communist Party (founded in 1921) and the Nationalists (Guomintang), led by Chiang Kaishek, divided the country. The Japanese invasion in 1937, and World War II, brought terrible suffering. In December 1941 Japanese troops attacked Hong Kong from the north; Allied forces withdrew from the New Territories and Kowloon to Hong Kong Island. After 18 days of fighting, the British forces surrendered on Christmas Day. The Japanese Occupation lasted for three years and eight months, during which time all British and Allied nationals were interned in camps and two-thirds of Hong Kong's Chinese population fled to China.

> *The divide between the British colonial administrative and business districts (Central) and the Chinese commercial "bazaar" areas (Western) were well established by the 1860s and can still be discerned today.*

1851. In 1904, the first land reclamation was completed in what is now the area of Chater, Connaught and Des Voeux roads. In 1929, another reclamation project was completed in Wan Chai. Today around 6 per cent of Hong Kong's land has been reclaimed from the sea.

ABOVE LEFT: street scene in the 1860s. **ABOVE:** the Prince of Wales is carried in a Chinese litter through the streets en route to Government House, 1922. **ABOVE RIGHT:** Western District in the late 1950s. **RIGHT:** refugees fleeing famine-hit China at the border, 1960.

During the occupation, Hong Kong's trade virtually stopped, the currency lost its value and food supplies were limited. Chinese guerrillas fought against the invaders in the New Territories, and villagers helped foreigners to escape. Under an agreement between Japan and Portugal, Macau became neutral territory, and some Europeans found refuge here during the war.

In August 1945, after the Japanese surrender, the Royal Navy arrived in Hong Kong to re-establish British rule over a battered colony with a population of just 600,000.

Post-war Hong Kong

After the war, Hong Kong Chinese who had escaped to those mainland areas beyond Japanese control returned in large numbers. China's civil war, which resurfaced in 1946 soon after the Japanese surrender, drove more people – including affluent Shanghai entrepreneurs, shipping magnates and property tycoons – into the British territory. By 1949, the population had swelled to 2 million.

In October 1949, Mao Zedong declared the establishment of the People's Republic of China, and the defeated Nationalists fled to Taiwan. The United Nations imposed an embargo on trade with China, with serious consequences for Hong Kong's economy. A shift to manufacturing proved its saviour, with the hundreds of thousands of refugees providing cheap labour for textile factories set up by Chinese entrepreneurs.

With hundreds of thousands of people living in squatter camps, a series of fires culminated in the1953 Shek Kip Mei fire, which left 53,000 homeless and led the colonial government to fast-track its public housing policy.

Soon the first high-rise New Towns were being planned and developed.

By the 1960s the textile and garment industries accounted for more than half of the colony's exports. The manufacture of plastic toys also became important. At the same time, the situation in China was becoming ever more desperate, with famine bringing another wave of immigrants to Hong Kong. This time the numbers were alarming, and the colonial government tried desperately to keep them out. For most of the Hong Kong population, the standard of living continued to rise during the 1960s, in stark contrast to their relatives on the mainland.

REFUGEES AND MIGRANTS

For much of the 20th century, Hong Kong was a place of refuge from the chaos in China. The civil war of the 1930s brought large numbers of refugees from southern areas, but this paled in comparison with the influx that took place between 1945 and 1950, when more than 1.5 million Chinese flooded south. A significant number of émigrés were savvy businessmen, notably from Shanghai: their arrival, combined with an enlarged supply of cheap labour, proved to be a big boost to Hong Kong's ailing economy.

After 1950, regulations were introduced to limit numbers, yet throughout the 1960s and '70s people continued to arrive at the Lo Wu border post, desperate to escape poverty. Some succeeded, but after numbers shot up between 1978 and 1980, the door was firmly shut. The focus then switched to the Vietnamese boat people, arriving by sea and housed in refugee camps until forced repatriation in the 1990s. Post-1997, movement between the PRC and the SAR is controlled, but fluid. *For more on immigration, see pages 23–26.*

China's trading partner. This was made possible by greater stability in China, and the rapid economic advance there due to Deng Xiaoping's pragmatic policies. Hong Kong began to play a vital role as China's window to the world and the world's gateway to China. An increasing number of local businesses began investing in factories in the PRC, where labour and raw materials were cheaper.

To keep pace with economic development, infrastructure was improved, and the territory was transformed into a modern, efficient and cosmopolitan city. The government increased its investment in education, housing and other social welfare projects. An efficient civil service system introduced by the British government played a major role in the economic boom, aided by the Independent Commission Against Corruption (ICAC), set up in 1974.

By the 1980s, the Hong Kong government enjoyed near-complete autonomy from London, and even had the power to conclude certain negotiations with foreign powers. The colony regularly negotiated its own economic agreements with other countries, and was admitted into several international financial institutions, such as the Asian Development Bank.

During the Vietnam War in the late 1960s and early 1970s, US Navy vessels, en route to or from Vietnam, were a familiar sight in Victoria Harbour, and American soldiers headed to bars and nightclubs of the Wan Chai and Tsim Sha Tsui for R&R.

At this time, China was ravaged by the Cultural Revolution, and the turmoil drifted into Hong Kong, where tensions erupted into a series of disturbances in the mid-1960s, and also to Macau where Red Guards waged a propaganda war with posters and slogans, calling on the Chinese residents to start a revolution *(pictured above)*. The chaos almost paralysed the economy, but by the end of 1967, the unrest had been more or less quelled.

1970s and '80s

Starting in the late 1970s and continuing through the 1980s, Hong Kong's economy developed at an amazing pace, as it expanded its role as an entrepôt with its neighbours and as

Anxieties and the build-up to dialogue with China

Amid all the prosperity, however, was an inescapable anxiety over the future, with the 1997 expiry of the 99-year lease on the New Territories looming large. By the early 1980s, life in Hong Kong was dominated by the issue of its return to China. Most of the local population would have preferred to stay under British rule rather than embrace the communist regime. Although they were unhappy with the fact that British companies and expatriates had enjoyed privileges in business and in government positions, people appreciated being able to compete in a free market. Having escaped extreme poverty or, in some cases, political persecution, they feared going back to the

ABOVE LEFT: the ultimate clash of cultures – English colonels playing cricket against a backdrop of Mao posters draped on the old Bank of China Building during the 1967 pro-communist riots. **LEFT:** immigration control on the border, 1950. **ABOVE RIGHT:** Margaret Thatcher takes tea on a resettlement estate during her 1982 visit.

communist system. But their destiny was not in their own hands.

China had always maintained its stance that it would take back Hong Kong when the time was "ripe". By the early 1980s, the moment

Although China refused Portugal's offer to return Macau in the mid-1970s for fear of destabilising Hong Kong, circumstances had changed by the 1980s. Now China's leaders began thinking about getting Hong Kong back.

seemed to have arrived, and Beijing became intent on expunging 150 years of humiliation.

Negotiating the return

Margaret Thatcher's visit to Beijing in 1982 formally launched the discussion on what would happen to Hong Kong after the 99-year lease on the New Territories, nine-tenths of the colony, expired in 1997. The reaction to the news that the colony's future was being negotiated was typical of Hong Kong – the local stock market nosedived.

In September 1984, after two years of often acrimonious negotiations, Britain and China came to an agreement, the Joint Declaration, which formally agreed the return of the colony to China in 1997. The Declaration stipulated that Hong Kong's way of life would remain unchanged for 50 years, that the territory would become a Special Administrative Region (SAR) and continue to enjoy a "high degree of autonomy" – except in foreign affairs and defence – and that China's socialist system and policies would not be imposed. As Deng Xiaoping put it, "Horses will keep racing, and nightclub dancing will continue."

Plans were drawn up for Hong Kong's administration in the years running up to 1997. Key points included elections to the Legislative Council (Legco), the District Boards and new Regional Councils. Beijing soon appointed a committee of 59 members, only 23 of whom were from Hong Kong, to draft the mini-constitution – known as the Basic Law – for the SAR. In military matters, Britain announced it would phase out its garrison, while China said the People's Liberation Army (PLA) would be stationed in Hong Kong after the handover.

During Hong Kong's first Legco elections in 1985, initiated by the British, 24 of the 56 members took their places through indirect elections. Out of a total population of 5.5 million at the time, only 70,000 people were eligible to vote under Hong Kong's restricted system of indirect elections. Of that number, only 47,000 registered to vote and only 25,000 actually went to the polls. Nevertheless, this election started a debate about whether the Hong Kong government would allow open elections to take place in 1988, as had been promised.

The democracy question and the brain drain

By the late 1980s, China was beginning to worry about the territory's fledgling attempts at democracy. Beijing's top man in the territory, Lu Ping, insisted that Britain was deviating from the Joint Declaration and arousing fear and anxiety amongst Hong Kong's people. Amid the political tension, however, Hong Kong's economy continued to thrive.

The British government wanted direct elections to be held before 1997. Increasingly irritated, Beijing eventually declared that political changes not consistent with the Basic Law would be nullified in 1997. Deng Xiaoping added that universal suffrage might not be beneficial for Hong Kong.

In June 1989, the Chinese government crushed a pro-democracy demonstration centred in Beijing's Tiananmen Square. Horrified by the brutality, 1 million people took to the streets in Hong Kong to protest.

The massacre exacerbated the Hong Kong brain drain, with large numbers leaving the territory annually in the next few years. At the end of 1989, Britain said it would grant British citizenship to just 225,000 Hong Kong Chinese before Hong Kong reverted to China. In 1990, about 60,000 of Hong Kong's most accomplished professionals moved overseas (often to secure passports), mainly to Canada and Australia. Britain called on its allies to accept Hong Kong immigrants; the United States amended its immigration laws to increase Hong Kong's quota to 10,000 annually until 1994 and 20,000 thereafter. The Hongkong & Shanghai Bank (HSBC), the ter-

FUNDING THE NEW AIRPORT

At the start of the 1990s it seemed that barely a day went by without some wrangling between Britain, Hong Kong and China over who was to foot the bill for the hugely expensive new airport under construction at Chek Lap Kok, off the coast of Lantau Island.

To boost the economy and restore confidence battered by the Tiananmen Square massacre, the Hong Kong government announced it would build a new airport, scheduled for completion in early 1997 at an estimated cost of HK$78 billion. China attacked the scheme, insisting that it should be consulted because its future SAR government might be saddled with debt.

Government representatives paid many visits to Beijing to win approval for the project, all the time trying not to appear as if they were grovelling. China was unrelenting. Finally, in 1991, Beijing and London announced that an understanding had been reached, although – like the 1984 Sino-British Agreement – its conclusion was without Hong Kong's participation. China gave its support for the airport in exchange for fiscal guarantees and a place on the airport authority's board.

Almost two decades on, it all appears to have been worthwhile – Chek Lap Kok is universally acclaimed as one of the world's most efficient airports, and plays a large part in Hong Kong's continuing success.

ritory's largest, moved its HQ to Britain, generally seen as reflecting the company's lack of confidence in Hong Kong's future.

Direct elections

London tried to keep earlier promises of democratic reform without provoking China's displeasure at free elections for Legco. Pushed by budding political awareness among its citizens, the Hong Kong government agreed to speed up the process, saying it would put 18 seats up for direct elections in 1991.

After numerous consultations, the two governments agreed in early 1990 that members elected to Legco in 1995 would serve until their term ended in 1999, two years after the handover, and that they would be among the 400 people who would select Hong Kong's first post-1997 handover Chief Executive. China later reneged on the agreement after Governor Chris Patten carried out electoral reforms against Beijing's wishes; China replaced the elected Legco with a Beijing-appointed provisional legislature.

In June 1991, Hong Kong's new Bill of Rights backing the "rights and freedoms" guaranteed in the 1984 Sino-British Agreement became law, despite China's insistence that the move was against the principles stated in the Basic Law, Hong Kong's post-handover constitution.

The first direct elections in Legco's 150-year history took place in September 1991. For the first time, the incumbent government faced opposition and the potential of legislative

defeats from the opposition under barrister Martin Lee. China, in a not-too-subtle move, advised voters to take candidates' "attitudes toward the mainland" into account when casting their votes. The comment was widely interpreted as a call to vote for the pro-Beijing candidates and not those of the pro-democracy camp represented by Lee's United Democrats. Unimpressed, voters demonstrated their independence by giving 15 of the 18 seats up for direct election to pro-democracy candidates.

Patten and the handover

In April 1992, Britain's Conservative Party chairman Chris Patten was named Hong Kong's last governor – the first time a politician instead of a diplomat had been given the post.

Patten's arrival heralded the most tense period in relations between Britain and China. Championing the democratic rights of Hong Kong people put him unerringly onto a collision course with Beijing. A low point was reached when the Chinese government declared that all contracts, leases and agreements signed or ratified by the British Hong Kong administration without the approval of China would not be honoured after 30 June

ABOVE LEFT: Vietnamese refugees. **LEFT:** the airport at Chek Lap Kok. **ABOVE:** Martin Lee, pro-democracy politician. **ABOVE RIGHT:** street demonstrations following the deaths at Tiananmen Square in 1989.

The Last Governor

Chris Patten, Hong Kong's last governor for the five turbulent years leading up to the handover, took over from David Wilson in 1992 with the avowed aim of protecting the interests of the Hong Kong people. Unlike his predecessors, who had arrived decked out in full ceremonial dress (plumed helmet and all), Patten wore a dark business suit – discreetly modernising the image of the office of governor in Hong Kong in the process. Despite, or perhaps because of some of his unorthodox ways,

Patten soon proved to be a popular leader. Instead of sitting in his office, he went out into the streets to meet ordinary people, listened to their opinions, and held question-and-answer sessions in public during which he addressed politically sensitive issues with a candid, sometimes controversial attitude.

Patten announced various proposals for increased spending on welfare, health, housing and the environment. The most controversial move, however, was his proposal to reform the political system. China wanted no such shift towards greater democracy, and openly attacked Patten's political reforms.

As a result, the Hang Seng Index dropped about 5 percent in October 1992, and brokers warned that unless Patten made a U-turn on his push for greater democracy, the stock market could suffer further.

In 1994, Legco passed Patten's proposed electoral reforms by a narrow margin, inviting strong condemnation from China. The reforms were a halfway point between full direct elections for all members of the legislature and a more muted electoral plan. Legco remained far from being a directly elected legislature, but the change was still enough to draw more criticism from China.

The electoral reform was Patten's last major act in office. As China began to play an increasingly important role in Hong Kong society and the business sectors competed with each other to get on Beijing's good side, Patten was sidelined. Beijing simply refused to talk to him, making it difficult for him to take any further action.

Despite the many humiliating insults the Chinese leaders threw his way during his five years in office, Patten's political reforms and personal charisma won him the respect of Hong Kong's residents. At the British farewell ceremony on the night of 30 June 1997, Patten's forceful farewell speech received long applause from the crowd, and people shouted "We will miss you" as he and Prince Charles boarded the royal yacht *Britannia* for England.

Over a decade on, it all seems like ancient history. The handover was followed, coincidentally, by an economic downturn, but prosperity has since returned and Hong Kong has moved forward. Patten must approve of the clear rise in political awareness and civic pride over the past few years.   ❏

LEFT: Patten speaking at a Legco assembly. **ABOVE:** at the ceremony marking the departure from Government House, 30 June 1997. **ABOVE RIGHT:** lowering the Union Jack. **RIGHT:** getting into the party spirit on the night of the handover.

1997, the last day of Britain's rule. Beijing also pointed its accusing finger at the private sector, including the British company Jardines, which it accused of supporting Patten's political agenda and damaging the international community's confidence in Hong Kong's future. *For more on Patten and the handover, see panel, opposite.*

A loophole in the Right of Abode section of the Basic Law led to many mainland relatives of Hong Kong citizens trying to be in Hong Kong by 1 July to claim residency. Migration became blurred as Hong Kong companies sought out talented professionals from the mainland, and Hong Kongers moved to China, or travelled there frequently, to take advantage of business opportunities in the new booming China.

Several opinion polls taken shortly before the handover showed that most Hong Kong people would have preferred to remain under British rule if they could control their own destiny, although it was deemed politically correct to say they loved the motherland. And although many were sceptical that Beijing would keep its promise to let Hong Kong's political system continue for another 50 years, most people had decided to accept the reality and adapt, aware that their future economic success was inextricably tied to China.

Finally, the day arrived: journalists from all over the world flew in to cover the events, while there was fevered last-minute activity to complete the Convention Centre in time for the ceremony. A slightly surreal party atmosphere, building over the preceding weeks, took over *(see panel, right).*

Tung – along with his Chief Secretary Anson Chan and Financial Secretary Donald Tsang – had previously been a member of the colonial government appointed by Patten.

Legco was dismantled on 1 July 1997, and replaced with a Beijing-appointed provisional legislature. After taking office, Tung announced a new voting system for Hong Kong's first

Post-handover

The SAR's first chief executive was selected by a Beijing-appointed committee at the beginning of 1997 from a choice of three candidates. Tung Chee-hwa, a Shanghai-born shipping tycoon who had received financial help from China in his earlier business days, was the obvious candidate from early on.

END OF EMPIRE

The handover of Hong Kong back to China on 30 June 1997 saw more parties, spontaneous street celebrations and fireworks in one night than at any other time in the territory's history. Most Hong Kongers, Chinese and Western residents alike, forgot the political implications for the night and celebrated the historic occasion with a festive spirit. At midnight, all major figures who either had, or were to have, a hand in Hong Kong's future gathered in the Hong Kong Convention and Exhibition Centre, although one was conspicuously missing – Deng Xiaoping having died months earlier.

Just before midnight, the Union Jack made its slow descent down the flagpole as the British military band played "God Save the Queen". The Chinese flag was raised. Chris Patten shook hands with the crowds of people near the pier in Central before boarding the royal yacht. Inside the Convention Centre, Hong Kong civil servants swore allegiance to the People's Republic of China in Mandarin.

In the early morning of 1 July, People's Liberation Army troops crossed over the border, welcomed by villagers lining the roads.

legislative election, set for May 1998, that gave the biggest say to business groups, a move believed to have been designed to sideline the most popular party, the Democrats.

Economic downturn and recovery

Before the handover, a popular view was that Hong Kong under communist China would undergo political changes, while remaining stable and prosperous economically. What happened in the months after the handover was just the opposite. There were few political confrontations, apart from some dissent concerning the make-up of the SAR's first legislative body, and the PLA kept a low profile in its bar-

racks. However, in late 1997 and through 1998 Hong Kong experienced a major economic crisis, as did many Asian countries. The Hang Seng Index dropped 6,000 points – about 40 percent.

A slow recovery began in 1999, but even by 2003 the economy was still in the doldrums, unemployment had soared and, in an ironic reversal of history, many locals began seeking work on the mainland. From March to May 2003 the SARS virus epidemic caused panic across the region – the Hong Kong public wore surgical masks and plastic gloves outdoors, and tourist numbers dried to a trickle.

As the city recovered, a growing frustration with the government's handling of the SARS outbreak and in particular its proposal to introduce controversial anti-subversion laws brought more than 500,000 peaceful demonstrators onto the streets to protest against the plans on 1 July 2003. The plans were shelved and the minister responsible, Regina Ip, resigned within the month.

Hong Kong's improving economic fortunes are largely thanks to the double-digit growth in China's economy, and increased Chinese tourist arrivals. Yet this success did little to help the Chief Executive. Unable to regain the

public's confidence, Tung Chee-hwa stepped down in early 2005.

His replacement, appointed by Beijing, was Donald Tsang, a devout Catholic and career civil servant. Born in Hong Kong, Tsang is more comfortable dealing with press and public than his predecessor. While his popularity remains relatively high, Tsang hasn't avoided controversy. His political reform package attracted vociferous pro-democracy demonstrations, which demanded that a date was set for electing Legco by universal suffrage by 2008 or 2012. Tsang himself was re-elected as Chief Executive until 2012, by an 800-strong election committee.

One country, two systems?

In 2007 Hong Kong celebrated the tenth anniversary of the establishment of the SAR, and four years of economic prosperity. Ten years into the 50 years of "one country two systems", the Chinese national anthem plays at the start of the day's television broadcast, the PRC flag flies alongside the Hong Kong Bauhinia, and the school curriculum has changed to include the Basic Law and Putonghua. Cantonese has replaced English as the language of instruction in most schools, in a much-criticised attempt to improve education standards.

Beijing has, nonetheless, largely kept its promise not to interfere in Hong Kong's internal affairs. After Tsang's re-election in December 2007, the Standing Committee of the National People's Congress (NPC), China's parliament,

issued a ruling that the earliest possible date for direct elections for Hong Kong's Chief Executive is 2017, and 2020 for Legco. While local democracy campaigners were deeply disappointed, many Hong Kongers take the pragmatic view that at least a date (that's acceptable for Beijing) to work towards has been set.

Mandarin is heard more on the streets of Hong Kong now, in part because over 14.5 million Chinese tourists visit each year.

Analysts say 'three flows from China' are now driving Hong Kong's economy – goods, visitors and capital. In 2010 the move back to Hong Kong from London of HSBC's CEO was seen as highly symbolic of the shift in the world's economic centre of gravity to China.

A generation that cannot remember Hong Kong as anything but part of China is coming of age, as a growing sense of civic identity is expressed through issues such as heritage conservation and the preservation of street markets. There is also increased concern about the environment, in particular what can be done to reduce pollution in a city whose haze obscures its iconic views all too often, and where roadside pollution reaches dangerously high levels.

The new generation are also sufficiently confident, and savvy in their use of the internet and social media, to co-ordinate large-scale political protests. The July 1 marches are seen as an established annual event, with changing targets. ❑

ABOVE LEFT AND ABOVE: free speech (anti-Article 23) protests, July 2003. **LEFT:** the Falun Gong movement has been suppressed by the Chinese government. **ABOVE RIGHT:** Donald Tsang.

DECISIVE DATES

c.4000 BC
The first stone-age settlements are established on the south China coast.

1557
Portuguese traders establish a colony at Macau.

1685
Emperor Kangxi allows limited trade in Guangzhou (Canton). Ships begin arriving from the British East India Company.

1773
British traders unload 1,000 chests of opium in Guangzhou.

1799
China's opium consumption reaches 2,000 chests a year, forcing Beijing to ban the drug, which then drives the trade underground.

1834
The British East India Company loses its monopoly on the opium trade to other European nations.

1839
China appoints the anti-opium viceroy, Lin Zexu, to clean up drugs in Guangzhou. He confiscates some 20,000 chests of opium from the British. Hostilities mount until November, when British ships blow up four Chinese

junks, sparking the first Anglo-Chinese War, which became known as the First Opium War.

1840–1
Negotiations between China and Britain break down, and the British fleet attacks Guangzhou and

occupies the city's forts. The two sides agree on a preliminary resolution (the Convention of Chuen Pi), which cedes the island of Hong Kong (population 5,000) to the British. But neither government is happy with the terms and both refuse to ratify it.

1842
The Opium War ends and British possession of Hong Kong is confirmed by the Treaty of Nanjing, which

---

TOP LEFT: Emperor Kangxi.
ABOVE: Hong Kong harbour in 1800. **LEFT:** the Nanking Treaty of 1842. **RIGHT:** Sir Henry Pottinger, the first governor. **MIDDLE RIGHT:** Sun Yat-sen. **TOP RIGHT:** the Japanese arrive, 1941.

cedes Hong Kong Island to Britain "in perpetuity". Sir Henry Pottinger becomes the first British governor of Hong Kong.

Colonial period
1856–60
The Chinese cede Kowloon and Stonecutter's Island "in perpetuity" to Britain. But hostilities continue, culminating in the Second Opium War.

1862
A Sino-Portuguese treaty grants Macau colonial status similar to Hong Kong's.

1898
Britain forces China to lease the New Territories, including the outlying islands, for 99 years.

1911
Dr Sun Yat-sen overthrows the Qing dynasty and establishes the Republic of China.

1912
Emperor Puyi abdicates, signalling the end of Imperial China.

1932
The Chinese Communists declare war on Japan.

1941
On Christmas Day the British surrender Hong Kong to the Japanese.

1945
World War II ends and the British resume control of Hong Kong. China's civil war between the Commu-

nists and the Nationalists (Guomintang) resumes.

1949
The Nationalists are defeated and flee to Taiwan. The Communists found the People's Republic of China (PRC).

1953
With tens of thousands of people arriving each month, Hong Kong's population hits 2.2 million, but many are living in squatter camps. The Shek Kip Mei fire leaves 53,000 homeless. Public housing policy is fast-tracked.

1966
Cultural Revolution begins in China, spilling over into Hong Kong with riots over a price increase in the first-class Star Ferry fare.

1971
Sir Murray MacLehose becomes the first Hong Kong governor to be appointed from the British diplomatic corps.

1972
Opening of the first cross-harbour tunnel. Hong Kong population hits 4 million.

1973
The first New Town, Tuen Mun, is completed.

1974
The Independent Commission Against Corruption (ICAC) is set up to stamp out crime and corruption.

1976
Death of Mao ushers in a new era for China.

1978
Under Deng Xiaoping, China starts to reform its economy and open its doors to the world.

first election for the Legislative Council (Legco), drawing criticism from China, which insists that any political changes not accepted by Beijing will not be respected after the handover.

1988
The proposed Basic Law, Hong Kong's post-handover constitution, is published.

1989
One million people take to the streets to protest against the Tiananmen Square massacre. Forced repatriation of Vietnamese boat people begins.

1979
Hong Kong's US$1 billion Mass Transit Railway (MTR) opens.

1982
British Prime Minister Margaret Thatcher visits Beijing and Hong Kong to begin discussions on Hong Kong's future. China decides to develop Shenzhen, a small town on Hong Kong's northern border, into a Special Economic Zone (SEZ).

Handover countdown
1983
China reveals its plan for Hong Kong to become a Special Administrative Region (SAR) after 1997. Under the proposed terms, Hong Kong will keep its own capitalist system, judiciary and police, and the leading official will be a Hong Kong Chinese. The Hong Kong dollar is pegged to the US dollar at a rate of 7.8.

1984
The British Ambassador to China and the Chinese Vice Foreign Minister initial "A Draft Agreement on the Future of Hong Kong", ending two years of acrimony. The Hong Kong government starts to plan for the territory's administration in the years running up to 1997.

1985
Britain and China ratify the Sino-British Joint Declaration. The colony holds its

1991
Beijing and London announce an agreement regarding the new airport.

1992
Hong Kong's 28th and last British governor, Chris Patten, arrives in the territory and proposes political reform. The move draws attacks from Beijing.

1994
Legco passes Patten's proposed electoral reforms.

China and UK continue to squabble.

1997

China resumes sovereignty on 1 July, Tung Chee-hwa is appointed chief executive (CE) and Hong Kong becomes an SAR. The stock market dives in response to the Asian economic crisis.

Post-handover

1998

Voters go to the polls to select a third of the seats on Legco. Hong Kong International Airport at Chek Lap Kok opens. Asian economic crisis worsens. First known human case of bird flu virus kills six people.

1999

The rule of law is undermined as government asks Beijing to overturn the Court of Final Appeal's ruling on

TOP LEFT: waxwork at Madame Tussaud's of the Deng/Thatcher talks, 1984. **LEFT:** a sombre Chris Patten at the Handover ceremony in 1997. **TOP:** street protests after Tiananmen Square, 1989. **ABOVE RIGHT:** the SARS outbreak caused panic in 2003. **RIGHT:** the ICC tower became Hong Kong's tallest building in 2010.

the right of abode. Typhoon York kills two and injures over 500. China resumes sovereignty of Macau.

2003

The deadly SARS virus spreads to Hong Kong, killing 299. Economic recovery stumbles. On 1 July, over half a million people join a march to protest against proposals for national security laws ("Article 23"). The government

backs down and shelves the plans indefinitely.

2004

Mainland tourist arrivals boom and economic recovery begins. Up to half a million protestors again march on 1 July, calling for more democracy and local control.

2005

Tung Chee-hwa resigns and is succeeded by Donald Tsang, a career civil servant with a finance background.

2006

As travel restrictions on the mainland continue to ease, Chinese visitor arrivals hits 13.6 million.

2007

An election committee appoints Donald Tsang as CE until 2012.

2008

Hong Kong hosts equestrian events for the Beijing Olympics. In September, SAR-wide elections are held for half the seats on Legco.

2009–10

Buoyed by China's continued economic growth, Hong Kong emerges from a brief recession in mid-2009, with the economy returning to normal by mid-2010.

WHERE FOOD IS AN ART

Cantonese cuisine has been exported around the world for decades. Much of what makes it unique, however, is rarely found outside southern China

I t has been said that when the Chinese are confronted with something they have never seen before or do not understand, their first impulse is to try eating it. This folk philosophy has helped inspire one of the greatest cuisines the world has known.

Each region of China naturally evolved a distinctive cooking style that reflected its topography, climate, flora and fauna, the temperament of its people and their contact with outsiders. Foods of northern and western China developed separately from those of the southern and eastern coastal "rice bowl". Southern Chinese (mainly the Cantonese, but also sub-groups such as the Hunanese, Chiu Chow and Hakka people) like to complain that Beijing-based food lacks smoothness and subtlety. Beijing folks, meanwhile, argue that southerners grind, chop and dilute the flavour out of their food.

Whatever their regional biases, Chinese everywhere talk about their food the way foreigners might talk about art. This is probably because Chinese cuisine is regarded as an art form. And even if they aren't conscious of their food as a major cultural accomplishment, no Chinese can ever avoid talking about it. The most common Cantonese greeting, for example, is *sik tzo fan mei* – meaning "Have you eaten?" Every dialect is rich in food symbolism. "You are breaking my rice bowl", wails

the Chinese whose livelihood is threatened.

Even to learn simply how to say rice in Chinese requires an annotated dictionary. Consider the linguistic variables of Cantonese: plain rice is *mai*; cooked rice is *faan*; rice porridge (commonly called congee) is *juk*; and harvested but unhusked rice is *guk*.

The traditional Chinese concept of a meal is very much a communal affair and one that provides strong sensory impact. Dishes are chosen with both taste and texture in mind – a stomach-pleasing succession of sweet-sour, sharp-bland, hot-cool and crunchy-smooth.

In a land that has experienced recurrent famine and natural disasters, wastage is not

PRECEDING PAGES: preparing dim sum at a Central District restaurant. **LEFT:** the elegant simplicity of dim sum. **RIGHT:** lunchtime noodles at a neighbourhood *dai pai dong*.

acceptable. Children are warned by their parents that if they leave any rice in their bowls, they will marry a pock-marked spouse – and the more grains left in the bowl, the more pock-marked the partner will be.

In spite of traditional poverty and privation, the Chinese nearly always insist on fresh food. Many Chinese still shop every day for fresh meat and vegetables. Cooks do not start with

> Integral to Chinese cooking is the yin-yang philosophy of the correct balance of "hot" and "cold" ingredients. A hot (yang) item such as snake or chicken requires a compensating cool (yin) "partner" – such as cabbage or tofu.

a particular dish in mind, but rather go to the market to buy what's fresh and in season, then create the meal.

To many outsiders, some Chinese foods seem bizarre, if not downright repulsive. The search for rare delicacies is common to all Chinese, but the Cantonese have pushed it to the extreme. Among them are monkey's brain,

bear's paw, snake, dog, frog, sparrow, shark's fin, bird's nest and lizard. Unfortunately for the average Hong Kong Chinese who savours such outlandish fare, many of these delicacies are either illegal or virtually impossible to obtain. Hence, many are rare and expensive.

Cantonese cuisine

The Cantonese live to eat and, at its most refined level, their gastronomy achieves a finicky discrimination that borders on cultism. In the Cantonese method of preparation, food is cooked quickly and lightly, usually stir-fried in shallow water or an oil base in a wok. The flavour of the foods is thus preserved, not cooked away in preparation. Many dishes, particularly vegetables or fish, are steamed. This discourages overcooking and preserves a food's delicate and natural flavours (as well as its vitamins). Sauces are used to enhance – and usually contain contrasting ingredients

TOP LEFT: choi sum. **TOP:** noodles. **ABOVE:** thousand-year eggs. **ABOVE RIGHT:** photo call at the Cathay Pacific Worldwide Chinese Chef workshop. **RIGHT:** a typical bilingual menu in a Cantonese restaurant.

such as vinegar and sugar, or ginger and onion.

The Cantonese are very fond of seafood – as anyone who has visited one of Hong Kong's outlying islands will attest *(see page 211)*. Fish is typically steamed whole with fresh ginger and spring onions and sprinkled with a little soy sauce and sesame oil, and fish eyes and lips are considered delicacies. Prawns and crabs – steamed or in a black-bean sauce – are very popular. The term "jumping prawns" signifies that they are alive, but it doesn't mean you are expected to eat them that way. Other seafood favourites include squid, in various forms including a delectable deep-fried version, octopus and crab. Shark's fin soup – golden threads of gelatinous-like shark's fin in a broth – is the centrepiece of Cantonese banquets, despite mounting ecological concerns *(see page 70)*.

Vegetable dishes are ubiquitous, featuring leafy greens such as box choi and choi sum, gently steamed and often liberally flavoured with garlic. Tofu, a versatile ingredient made from pressed bean curd, is another staple – either steamed or deep-fried.

Chicken is commonplace and, in keeping with the Chinese sense of economy and variety, a single bird is often used to prepare several dishes. Chicken blood, for example, is cooked and solidified for soup, and the liver is used in a marvellous speciality called Gold

FAUX CHINESE

Overseas visitors who are familiar with Chinese food in Western countries soon learn the authentic cuisine often has little to do with what they have been served in Chinese restaurants abroad. Take, for example, two supposed Cantonese dishes: sweet-and-sour pork is said to have been invented by the ever-resourceful inhabitants of Guangzhou solely for sweet-toothed foreigners. And chop suey was reportedly invented in San Francisco when a customer entered a restaurant at closing time, and the cooks threw their leftovers into a pot, served it up and in quiet jest called this oriental goulash "chop suey". Also, despite the Chinese preoccupation with luck and superstitions, American-style fortune cookies do not exist here.

Coin Chicken. The livers are skewered between pieces of pork fat and red-roasted until the fat becomes crisp and the liver soft and succulent. The delicacy is then eaten with wafers of orange-flavoured bread. Cantonese chicken dishes can be awkwardly bony for chopstick novices, although lemon chicken is prepared boneless with the skin coated in a crisp batter and served in a lemon sauce flavoured with onions, ginger and sugar.

For starters, choose something from the display of barbecued meats in the restaurant's display window. Cantonese barbecuing methods are unrivalled. Try goose, duck or, best of all, tender slices of pork with a golden and honeyed skin served on a bed of anise-flavoured preserved beans.

Also experience the taste sensation of double-boiled soups with duck, mushroom and tangerine peel, and a winter speciality called Monk Jumping over the Wall. This is a blend of abalone, chicken, ham, mushrooms and herbs so irresistible that monks are said to break their vows of vegetarianism once they smell it.

Snake is a traditional winter dish, often served as an energy-enhancing soup. Dog meat

TOOLS AND TECHNIQUES

Many foreigners struggle with chopsticks (*faai jee* in Cantonese), with small, loose rice grains a particular menace. Thankfully, it's perfectly acceptable to raise the rice bowl to your lips and shovel the elusive morsels into your mouth. Scraping and slurping are not considered a faux pas.

Chopsticks are thought to have been adopted for eating because of a traditional Confucian distaste for knives – potentially dangerous weapons – on the dining table. If they prove impossible to handle, it is perfectly acceptable to use the porcelain spoon provided for soups as a scoop for other courses. And no one minds if you make a mess – it is even permissible to wipe your hands on the edge of the tablecloth.

A typical meal starts with a cold dish, which is followed by several main courses. Soup – usually clear, light broth – may be eaten after the heavier entrées to aid digestion. However, a thick and full-bodied soup may be served as a main dish, and a sweet soup often serves as a dessert at the meal's end. There are no rules when it comes to ordering your meal. The main thing is to enjoy the food.

One mistake some foreigners make is swamping their rice with soy sauce, a crude act that robs it of its character and function. A Chinese meal should include enough spicy and savoury dishes to make the relative blandness of steamed rice an essential balancing agent.

is also a winter dish but is illegal in Hong Kong: there are special tours across the border specifically to eat dog meat. Another Cantonese winter warmer to sample is a casserole of chicken and Chinese smoked pork sausage. These sausages are sold in pairs and are usually served steamed on a bed of rice. In autumn, restaurants serve rice birds – culled from paddy fields at harvest time. These are quite often eaten together with succulent Shanghai hairy crabs. Frogs are also found in the rice paddies, and these "field chickens" are often served at banquets in southern China. In Hong Kong markets they are sold live in plastic bags, and restaurants prepare them in many delicious ways, including deep-fried frog's legs cooked in a crunchy batter mixed with crushed almonds and served with sweet-and-sour sauce.

Probably the single most famous Cantonese culinary phenomenon is dim sum, a superbly tasty treat and a must on every Hong Kong tourist's itinerary – see pages 64–65.

Other Chinese cooking styles

Cantonese restaurants dominate in Hong Kong, but other distinctive forms of Chinese cooking – the subtle flavours of Chiu Chow and Shanghai, the spicy dishes of Sichuan and Hunan, northern specialities such as Peking Duck and Mongolian hotpot – are also well represented.

Chiu Chow cuisine is also known as Swatow food because this type of cooking originated around the city of Swatow in eastern Guangdong province. Seafood addicts enjoy such dishes as oysters fried in egg batter

and clams served in a spicy sauce of black beans and chillies. Grey mullet is a favourite cold dish, and pomfret smoked over tea leaves and freshwater eel stewed in brown sauce are

> The Chinese penchant for bizarre culinary innovation reaches its apogee with bird's nest soup, for which the dried saliva lining a swiftlet's nest provides the base.

other highly recommended seafood wonders.

A Chiu Chow restaurant is also an appropriate place to try banquet-style food such as shark's fin soup and bird's nest soup. The owner of one restaurant in Hong Kong reputedly rents a mountain in Thailand that is said to harbour the finest collection of swiftlet nests in Southeast Asia. The nest itself is virtually tasteless, but its nourishing saliva linings are believed to rejuvenate the old. This delicacy is also eaten as a dessert flavoured with coconut milk or almonds. Another unusual avian meal is minced quail, cooked with water chestnuts and eaten wrapped in crisp lettuce leaves

---

LEFT: cleaning up at the local *dai pai dong*. **ABOVE:** Shanghai hairy crabs are a seasonal delicacy in autumn. **RIGHT:** a favourite winter warmer, snake soup *(se gung)*.

spiked with a dollop of plum sauce.

After Cantonese, the emphatically flavoured cuisine of the central province of Sichuan is perhaps the most familiar Chinese food to foreigners. Hunanese food is similar but even spicier. Much of the emphasis comes from chillies, which appear in many guises: dried and fried in chunks, together with other ingredients; ground into a paste with a touch of added oil; as chilli oil; and crushed to a powder. Other ingredients important to Sichuanese cuisine are Sichuan "pepper" (the dried berry of the prickly ash or fagara), garlic, ginger and fermented soybean. Popular dishes include *mala doufu* (spicy tofu) and *gongbao* chicken (with chilli and peanuts).

A typical Sichuan eating experience is hotpot, or *huo guo*. Diners sit around a table with a pot of seasoned broth heated by a gas fire (charcoal was used in the past). Each diner adds bits and pieces of prepared vegetable, meat, fish and beancurd. The food cooks very quickly and can be fished out of the broth using chopsticks or a special strainer, then dipped in sesame oil, peanut sauce or a beaten egg.

The cuisine of the lower reaches of the Yangzi River, especially around Huaian and Yangzhou, gave rise to the term *huaiyang* to describe the food of China's eastern seaboard. This fertile area, known as the land of fish and rice, produces a wide range of crops as well as abundant fish, prawns, crab and eel. Huaiyang cooks often steam or gently simmer their food, rather than using the faster deep-frying style. Signature dishes include pork steamed in lotus leaves, Duck with Eight Ingredients, and Lion's Head Meatballs. For the most part, the cooking of Shanghai, Jiangsu and Zhejiang is usually regarded as being part of Huaiyang cuisine.

Over the centuries, culinary elements from all over eastern Asia have been liberally adapted and absorbed into Chinese cuisine, and it's difficult to trace the origins of some dishes. Peking Duck, prepared by roasting the duck over an open charcoal fire and slowly basting it with syrup until the skin is a deep, crispy brown, was originally Mongolian. Mongolian hotpot, called "steamboat" in Singapore and Malaysia, is in fact of central Chinese Muslim origins. It is probably the second best-known of the northern dishes, and as a winter food, is served between November and March in northern-style restaurants.

A surprise for many at their first northern Chinese meal is that rice is not served unless specially requested. Wheat is the common grain staple in the north, so northerners traditionally eat steamed bread *(pao)* or tasty onion cakes instead of rice. One of the spectacular treats at a northern Chinese meal is

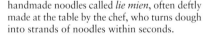

handmade noodles called *lie mien*, often deftly made at the table by the chef, who turns dough into strands of noodles within seconds.

Eating in Hong Kong today

Nowadays, while Cantonese and other Chinese cuisine predominates in Hong Kong, there is a vast array of other fare on offer. Stand beneath the escalator in Cochrane Street in Central, and within spitting distance you'll find a modern British gastropub, Russian, Indian and Thai restaurants, and a scarlet-hued sushi joint with platters humming round the bar on a conveyor belt.

Food hawkers still ply their trade on street corners – although officialdom is seeking to eradicate them – and a browse round a 7-Eleven or Circle K convenience store leads past microwaveable dim sum and pot noodles, packets of dried fish and fruit, as well as boxed drinks that might be mistaken for medicine.

The budget-minded can feast for a few score dollars on seafood noodles at a seaside restaurant on one of the outer islands, or you can splurge in a five-star hotel, diving in and out of cosmopolitan buffets or settling down to a lengthy repast with maître d' and sommelier shimmering discreetly in the shadows.

Hong Kong's long-established Indian community has resulted in a good supply of curry houses all over the main urban areas, notably in Tsim Sha Tsui's Chungking Mansions *(see page 157)*. Also very easy to find and usually excellent are the numerous Thai restaurants, as well as plenty of other Southeast Asian cuisine – not just Malaysian and Singaporean but Vietnamese and Burmese, too. Japanese food is also very well represented. As in any large cosmopolitan city, there is no shortage of European (mainly French and Italian) and American restaurants (McDonald's outlets are everywhere, and extremely cheap), as well as other cuisines ranging from Egyptian to Argentinian. ❑

HONG KONG'S BAKERIES

Bakeries occupy a special place in Hong Kong hearts, dispensing breakfast and snacks from the ubiquitous egg-custard tarts *(daan taht)*, doughnuts and doughy sausage buns to a wide range of colourful celebratory cakes and pastries. Young parents take their offspring to the same bakery they patronised when they were children, and after a spell overseas, Hong Kongers drop by their friendly neighbourhood cake shop, a reflex reaction which confirms their homecoming. And when a rent hike forced the closure of the famed Tai Cheung Bakery on Lyndhurst Terrace (Central) after 51 years of business, people took to the streets in (futile) protest.

TOP LEFT: dumplings at a street stall in Guangzhou.
LEFT: ingredients are chopped into small pieces for stir-frying. **ABOVE:** Cantonese chef shows off his speciality dish. **ABOVE RIGHT:** colourful lotus-paste cakes.
RIGHT: egg-custard tarts, a Hong Kong bakery staple.

DIM SUM

Perhaps the most famous Cantonese culinary phenomenon, dim sum is one of Hong Kong's traditional delicacies and goes down a treat with visitors

From sunrise through to lunchtime people all over Hong Kong enjoy *yum cha* ("drink tea"), catching up with friends and eating dim sum ("little hearts"), small portions of Cantonese dishes and dumplings often served in bamboo baskets. To share the experience, head to a dim sum restaurant and join in the noise and enjoyment of this tasty Hong Kong tradition.

In Hong Kong (and neighbouring Guangdong province) people eat dim sum for breakfast or brunch, congregating in bustling, informal eateries that often open at the crack of dawn. In those traditional establishments where menus have not yet taken over, self-service trolleys stacked with small plates and steamer baskets are wheeled past. Steamed, pan-fried, deep-fried or congee (a rice-based, soupy dish) are the traditional categories for dim sum, although a few varieties are baked. Most common are the delicate steamed dumplings, which come with a range of fillings. Dessert dim sum is also available.

Novices often start with *siu mai* (shrimp and pork dumplings), *ha gow* (shrimp dumplings) and *cha siu bau* (steamed barbecue pork buns) – these three are probably the most popular dishes.

ABOVE: in a traditional dim sum restaurant, diners replenish from the ever-circulating trolley rather than ordering everything in one go.

LEFT: varieties of Chiu Chow dumplings *(chiu-chau fun guo)*, variously containing pork, shrimp, peanuts and chives.

BELOW: chicken's feet *(foong jao)*, chewy and not popular with Westerners, are usually marinated in a black bean sauce.

LEFT: dim sum is kept in traditional wicker baskets.

INFORMATION FOR NOVICES

A dim sum restaurant can be daunting for foreigners with no experience of Chinese etiquette, so here are some pointers to follow.

At the table you will be presented with a bowl, plate, chopsticks and a small teacup. Tea is the first thing to order, after which you will be presented with the all-important "card", which resembles a large lottery ticket. Each time you order something the item will be ticked by the waiting staff. A few restaurants have English menus, but on the whole be prepared simply to look and point and try new things. Older establishments still have vendors wheeling trolleys around, each carrying a different special-ity. If you can't see what it is they are selling, stop the trolley, with a polite but loud *ng goi* (excuse me). Sometimes there's a counter, so walk up with your card, open the baskets and point at what you want. When your teapot is empty, simply flip the lid over and someone will appear and top it up with hot water. When your bowl is empty it's time to sample another bamboo basket.

RIGHT: *ha gow*, a succulent shrimp dumpling, is one of the most popular varieties of dim sum.

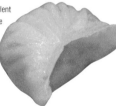

BELOW: *siu mai* come in several varieties, usually filled with pork and shrimp.

ABOVE: *cha siu so*, barbecued pork pastries, one of the few baked varieties.

RIGHT: *cha siu bao* are barbecued pork dumplings – filling and delicious, but watch out for scalding hot fillings and peel the rice paper off the base before eating.

CHINESE MEDICINE

Chinese remedies have been practised for 4,000 years and, aided by the international popularity of acupuncture, have been gaining recognition around the world

Traditional Chinese medicine is based on an array of theories and practices from both foreign and native sources. It was during the Zhou period (11th century–221 BC) that many of these theories first emerged. This stage of Chinese history, marked by near-continuous fighting and misery, lasted several centuries. Against the background of this constant state of turmoil, many ideas took root that were to colour all aspects of life in China for the next 2,000 years – including medicine, which itself was influenced by the teachings of Confucianism and Daoism.

Holism – the idea that parts of a human body form an integral, connected and inseparable whole – is one of the distinguishing features of Chinese medicine. Whereas Western medicine tends to treat symptoms in a direct fashion, Chinese medicine examines illnesses in the context of the whole person.

Yin-yang philosophy and the theory of five elements form a system of categories that explain the complex relationships between parts of the body and the environment. *Yin* and *yang* represent two opposite sides in nature such as hot and cold or light and dark. Each of the different organs is said to have *yin* or *yang* characteristics, and balance between the two is vital for maintaining health. Likewise, each organ is linked directly to a particular element: fire for the heart, earth for the spleen, water for the kidneys, metal for the lungs and wood for the liver. The way in

which they interact affects a person's health, so, for example, the kidneys (water) nourish the liver (wood).

Traditional versus modern

The mention of traditional Chinese medicine often conjures up images of magical needles, aromatic herbs and strange animal parts. Yet, despite the exotic stereotype, it is increasingly gaining respect from both scientists and the general public in Europe and the US, particularly with regard to the alleviation of pain.

In China, scepticism and debate arose as to the value of traditional medicine during the first half of the 20th century, with progressive

LEFT: a typical Chinese medicine shop in Western.
RIGHT: ingredients come from all kinds of animals.

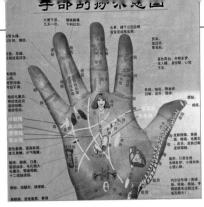

they are seriously ill and need to be treated quickly. If the problem is not too serious or urgent, the patient may seek out a traditional doctor to restore harmony to the body and thus provide a long-term cure.

The pharmacy

Chinese pharmacies tend to have a unique odour, a mixture of 1,001 scents. There are all sorts of exotic animals, insects and vegetables, all of which appear in the pages of the *Encyclopaedia of the Traditional Chinese Pharmacopoeia*, a weighty tome published in 1977, running to 2,700 pages and listing some 5,767 substances with medicinal or preventative properties. Have a look around the pharmacies in Western District and you will see birds' eggs, snakes wound up in spirals, toads, tortoises, centipedes, grasshoppers, dried fish, deers' antlers and the genitalia of various

intellectual and political groups particularly hostile. After the founding of the People's Republic of China, competition between Western and Chinese medicine was eradicated for practical as well as ideological reasons, with an attempt to integrate the two systems.

This integrated approach has persisted, and today, medical care in China often consists of a mixture of both Western and traditional Chinese medicine, although the former, or *xiyi*, tends to be dominant. Large public hospitals *(renmin yiyuan)* in cities across the country offer both the traditional Chinese and Western approaches to medical treatment. Hospitals dealing exclusively with traditional Chinese medicine (TCM), or *zhongyi*, tend to be smaller, less well equipped and harder to find. In Hong Kong, the Chinese Medicine Council of Hong Kong (www.cmchk.org.hk) has been regulating the industry since 1999, and while there are no full-scale TCM hospitals, there are several places in Central and Sheung Wan that offer a basic consultation (an example is the Good Spring Company on the corner of Stanley Street, beside the Mid-Levels escalator).

The Chinese will usually visit a doctor trained in Western medicine if they feel that

FINDING THE RIGHT BALANCE

Traditional Chinese medicine entails more than just acupuncture: the knowledge of remedies *(zhongyao)* is an important factor. Patients are treated with different kinds of massage and chiropractics *(tuina)*, as well as breathing and movement therapies, such as *taijiquan* (shadow-boxing) and *qigong* (breathing therapy). While Hong Kong's main hotels offer extensive Western-style health treatments, it's worth re-establishing your inner harmony the local way. Start off with the familiar: a relaxing toe rub to boost circulation and free the flow of *qi*, or a full body massage: the Sunny Paradise Sauna (341 Lockhart Road, Wan Chai; tel: 2831 0123) is a typical venue.

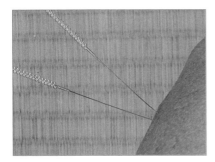

unfortunate – and often endangered – animals *(see page 70)*. And then there are the myriad herbs, blossoms, roots, berries, mushrooms and fruits – dried and preserved. All traditional Chinese pharmacies are well stocked with ginseng roots, often shaped like a human figure – in fact, the character for ginseng contains the sign *ren*, which means person.

Traditional cures are not only available from pharmacies. Wandering around a Hong Kong market, one may see herbs and produce for sale which are used as remedies rather than food.

Acupuncture

One effect of acupuncture that is undisputed and valued by a billion Chinese is the relief of pain. While others rely on drugs to moderate physical pain, the Chinese go to the acupuncturist. Cases of acute back pain, for example, can be cured by sticking just one needle in the *renzhong* point between the top lip and nose.

A new form of painless acupuncture, which does not use needles, is administered by ear. Small, round seed kernels are stuck onto certain points of the ear and massaged by the patient from time to time. This method is not only very successful in treating pain, but is also said to relieve such allergies as hay fever.

When entering an acupuncture clinic, you will notice one of the dominant aromas of the Chinese pharmacy – that of the *moxa* herb, which is the same thing as Artemisia, or mugwort. It is considered especially helpful in

FAR LEFT: varieties of Chinese tea. **ABOVE LEFT:** diagram of pressure points. **LEFT:** a Wan Chai sauna. **ABOVE:** acupuncture needles. **ABOVE RIGHT:** Muay Thai boxers on Tsim Sha Tsui promenade.

treating illnesses that, in Chinese medical terminology, are classified as "cold" – for example, stomach and digestive complaints without fever, certain rheumatic illnesses, chronic pains in the back and cramped neck and shoulders. The mugwort is placed onto the acupuncture point or on the end of the acupuncture needle, or moulded into the shape of a cigar and rolled back and forth over the skin.

> *Increasingly accepted by many physicians, acupuncture was in 1997 approved as a legitimate – and insurable – treatment for pain by medical authorities in the United States.*

Exercise

At some stage while in Hong Kong, visit a public park at dawn to witness the Chinese exercise arts of *taijiquan* and *qigong*. *Taijiquan* is the most common type of exercise, so-called shadow-boxing. *Qigong* is often translated in the West as breathing therapy.

Both exercises are based on the belief that the human body is endowed with the life energy, *qi*. If this can be harnessed and controlled, a person can influence the course of

The Animal Parts Trade

The Chinese have been using animal parts for medicinal purposes for well over 1,000 years. Yet for all its growing appeal across the world as people look for alternatives to Western drugs, there is a darker side. Wildlife, under pressure from intensive industrial and economic development in recent decades, is now being pushed to the brink of extinction by the increased demand for body parts.

The demand for tigers, for example, is forcing these magnificent creatures ever

closer to extinction (recent studies estimate that there are only 30 to 80 South China tigers, 150 to 200 Siberian tigers and 600 to 650 Sumatran tigers left in the wild). Various tiger parts are used in Chinese medicine: eyeballs to treat epilepsy, the tail for various skin diseases, bile for convulsions in children, whiskers for toothaches, the penis for male impotence and the brain to combat laziness and pimples. Yet of all tiger parts, it is the bones that are most valued – used to treat rheumatism, weakness, stiffness and even paralysis.

Rhinoceros, bear and shark populations are also rapidly shrinking. Rhinoceros horn

is reputed to be an aphrodisiac. Only about 12,500 rhinos remain in the wild, with another 1,000 in captivity. About half of these are white rhinos and the remaining half consists of four other species. Without assistance, these could soon be extinct. Also greatly threatened by Chinese demand, bears from as far away as North America are cruelly farmed for their bile, used to treat a variety of ailments, and paws, which are used in soup.

Like bear's paw, shark's fin, though not used exclusively for medicine, is a delicacy. Served most commonly as shark's fin soup, this broth is believed to benefit the internal organs. Sharks are caught and their top fin sliced off. They are then tossed back into the ocean, alive, to drown. In some areas, the shark population – essential to the ecosystem, as the shark is the top predator – is declining.

In recent years, human populations and expendable incomes have increased dramatically in Asia, along with a resurgence of interest in traditional cures. Use of traditional medicines is seen as a status symbol and also as a way to hold on to traditional customs amidst rapid social and economic changes.

While the effectiveness of these endangered animal products in medicine is still disputed, researchers confirm the benefits of the active ingredients present in a considerable number of Chinese prescriptions.

As endangered animal populations plummet, the use of their parts to feed an ever-growing demand is no longer sustainable. One way or another, the trade in endangered animal parts for medicine must stop. This means finding an alternative to alternative medicine. ❏

LEFT: tigers are threatened by the Chinese medicine industry. **ABOVE:** shark's fin.

certain ailments that afflict the body. Body and breathing exercises are thus preventative forms of "medicine".

During the Cultural Revolution in China, *qigong* was banned because it was said to be too close to superstition. But in 1980, new *qigong* groups sprang up, and soon gained a large following. Some forms involve hardly any movement: breathing and "sinking into oneself" are of prime importance. Other forms, like the "wild goose" variety, entail a great deal of movement and are aesthetically appealing.

In both *taijiquan* and *qigong*, changes in mental and emotional states follow a certain pattern of movement. The most extreme of these is the "crane *qigong*", which involves violent, sometimes cathartic emotional outbursts. Practitioners may scream, cry, laugh, dance or jump around as they experience *fagong*, abandoning oneself to spontaneous movements.

It's in the diet

The Chinese have little doubt of the efficacy of different foods for treating ailments and healing certain parts of the body. Consider three traditional delicacies: shark's fin, abalone and bird's nest. These are exquisite parts of an extensive cuisine, eaten for their sensory delights. Yet each is claimed to have medicinal value. Shark's fin and abalone are said to benefit internal organs, including the heart and kidneys. Abalone also regulates the liver and reduces dizziness and high blood pressure. Bird's nest, usually taken as a soup, allegedly cleanses the blood and the complexion.

Verifying such claims is difficult. The scientific method, which involves controlled experiments using known values and quantities, doesn't lend itself well to the analysis of claims that a food item can help cure physical illnesses. Moreover, to be valid, a result must be independently verifiable. Consideration must also be given to the placebo effect, where a valid result occurs because one believes in something's efficacy. Many say the success of Chinese cures is simply a question of mind over matter. However, recent research on the health effects of soybeans and green tea, for example, suggests that components in these two items have substantive medicinal value, possibly against some forms of cancer.

> For much of China's history, herbalists have attributed medicinal value to various foods. At times, the distinction between food and treatment can blur.

Herbal remedies have gradually gained respect around the world. Western nutritionists have always stressed that certain foods provide necessary vitamins and minerals that are good for the body – carrots for good eyesight, calcium for strong bones. Traditional Chinese medicinal foods simply take these scientific remedies one level further. ❏

ABOVE: solitary and communal morning exercises.

BELIEFS AND SUPERSTITIONS

Ancient beliefs such as fortune-telling and feng shui, as well as more traditional religions, continue to colour daily life in Hong Kong

Few modern-day city residents take their traditional beliefs more seriously than the Hong Kong Chinese. A constant undercurrent, counterpoint to the brash, modern metropolis, these values have been formed over the centuries through an interaction of the three primary Chinese religions or philosophies – Buddhism, Daoism and Confucianism – overlayed with elements of animism, superstition and folk tradition. Adding further to this esoteric mix is the Chinese tradition of ancestor worship. Some aspects of the core beliefs overlap with each other (for example, many temples are both Buddhist and Daoist).

These religions are complemented by the more overtly superstitious beliefs so important in Hong Kong. Feng Shui *(see page 74)* is based around the central Chinese concept of *qi* (the energy, life force or spirit that is believed to exist in nature and all living creatures) – an underlying principle in Chinese medicine *(see page 69)*. Numerology *(see page 75)* is a more straightforward superstition. Throughout, two themes are universal – the desire for prosperity and longevity.

Yet it is often said that Hong Kongers worship one thing and one thing only: money. And it is true that the almost evangelical pursuit of personal wealth seems to be hard-wired into much of the population. Deity worship is often used in the pursuit of worldly gains – including advice on stock-market and horse-racing tips (witness the large number of offerings to the god of good fortune, Wong Tai Sin, at his temple).

ABOVE: busy Wong Tai Sin Temple, dedicated to the Daoist god of healing and good fortune, is famous for its fortune-tellers *(see page 174)*.

ABOVE: a typical Chinese temple entrance features a spirit wall inside the main doorway to block the path of evil spirits. The red lanterns also offer protection, as well as symbolising well-being and happiness.

LEFT: fish represent harmony and prosperity to the Chinese: this stylised example crowns the Tin Hau Temple in Causeway Bay.

ABOVE: ancestors' ashes are stored at Man Mo Temple. Ancestor worship is an ancient Chinese tradition. When someone dies, his or her soul is thought to enter the underworld and come under the threat of evil spirits. Offerings are made and "spirit money" burnt to protect the ancestor, who will in return offer protection to his or her descendants. It is also considered important to keep the grave clean. Eventually the remains are dug up and cremated.

BELOW: Daoism is China's only true native religion, founded in the sixth century by Laozi (pictured), a semi-mythical philosopher. Chinese "popular" religions are often a blend of elements taken from Daoism, Buddhism and Confucianism.

ABOVE: temples in Hong Kong are dedicated to a particular deity, generally from the Daoist pantheon. The god of war, Mo – also known as Kuan Ti or Kuan Kung – is pictured here at Man Mo Temple (the temple is co-dedicated to Man, the god of literature). One of the most popular deities is Tin Hau, goddess of the sea and worshipped throughout coastal China, where she is variously known as Tianhou (in Mandarin Chinese), A-Ma (in Macau) or Matsu (in Taiwan). *(See page 178 for details of the Tin Hau Festival.)*

FENG SHUI

Most people agree that I.M. Pei's iconic Bank of China Tower is an impressive and attractive structure, but there is one negative aspect: its strikingly sharp angles channel bad feng shui onto its neighbours. Feng shui ("wind and water") is an ancient Chinese form of geomancy, and an important consideration when a new tower block is being planned – a feng shui master *(pictured above)* will advise on which direction it should face and where desks, beds or even a vase should be placed to attract the best luck and prevent bad fortune. A sheltered position, facing the water and away from a hillside, is considered auspicious, but although the Bank of China was built with these principles in mind, the fact that its aggressive angles arrowed hostile energy towards, amongst others, Government House and the HSBC Building, was not considered. The construction of the Cheung Kong Centre, at an angle askew to the Bank and between it and the HSBC, and a strategically placed willow tree at Government House, have improved neighbourly relations.

ABOVE & BELOW: paper money is burnt so that ancestors can benefit in the other world, in which they need money and consumer goods (cars, flats, TVs, etc. are all made in paper form for this purpose). Offerings of incense and food are also considered to be important.

RIGHT: fortune-telling can be a lucrative business in Hong Kong. Clairvoyants, usually in residence at a temple, read palms or the feet or face to predict the future. Other methods include using *chim* sticks (at temples such as Wong Tai Sin), or game-like activities such as throwing coins or other objects at a target – an example being the Wishing Tree near Tai Po *(see page 187)*. Following a fortune-teller's advice to the letter can impinge on daily life. In order to appease the fortune god, it may be deemed necessary to shave off all one's hair skinhead-style, or to wear a bright-red belt at all times.

LEFT: a roadside shrine in the New Territories.

LUCKY NUMBERS

Hong Kong may be the only place in the world where someone would pay US$1.7 million for a vehicle licence plate. In 1994, local tycoon Albert Yeung did just that – investing in a licence plate bearing the single digit nine, considered lucky because the Cantonese word for "nine" sounds like the word for "eternity", "longevity" or "perpetuity".

Other lucky numbers include two, which stands for "easy", three for "living or giving birth", six for "longevity" and eight for "prosperity". But it is the combinations that are in most demand. For example, 163 means "live for ever" or "give birth non-stop", 168 equals "prosperity all the way", and 162 "easy all the way". Lucky licence-plate numbers became so much in demand that, in 1973, the government's transport department began auctioning them off to the highest bidders. The number eight has consistently drawn the highest bid. Today, all licence-plate numbers considered lucky in Cantonese are reserved and available only through auctions where they attract high prices.

The superstition over numbers also applies to street, apartment and telephone numbers. For example, the price for an apartment on the 14th floor can be 20 percent cheaper than that for the same flat on the 18th floor, because 14 in Cantonese means "definitely dies", while 18 means "definitely prospers". Some buildings get around this problem by simply omitting a 14th floor, going straight from the 13th to the 15th.

ABOVE: *taijiquan* balls (also known as healthy balls) are moved around the hand to massage the acupressure points and circulate *qi* energy through the entire body.

THE PERFORMING ARTS

Spend any time in Hong Kong and one will encounter a diverse catalogue of performing arts, including traditional opera, lion dances and Cantopop

Although Chinese opera is no longer the most popular performance art in Hong Kong and China, it remains an integral part of Chinese entertainment and culture. Originating from China's earliest folk music and dances, modern-day Chinese opera – a story put to music and dance – emerged during the Song dynasty (960–1279). Although Chinese opera came to be associated with festivals and state occasions at the 18th-century imperial court in Beijing, it was also popular among the common people.

In Hong Kong, a performance of Chinese opera is customary during important festivals in the Chinese calendar. Performances are usually held in bamboo-and-mat theatres temporarily erected in public areas. Chinese opera has many cultural and regional variations. Cantonese operas, which are naturally the most popular in Hong Kong, are quite different from Chiu Chow operas. Beijing operas are performed in the court's official dialect, Mandarin.

The repertoire is drawn from folklore, legends and historical events. The backbone of the performance is the actor-singer. In the same way as their Western counterparts, Chinese operatic singers undergo many years of intensive training to achieve a properly pitched falsetto. Singing artists are often accompanied by a traditional Chinese orchestra. Percussionists occupy one side of the stage, while the wind-and-string section sits opposite, leaving the main area of the stage clear for the primary performers. To foreign ears, the sounds of a Chinese opera seem bizarre and discordant, with the high-pitched dialogue, deafening gongs and drums echoing from the music pit.

There were no actresses during Chinese opera's early development, because women were not allowed to make public appearances, so male actors took the female roles. As in Western opera, however, that tradition has died.

Make-up, movements, props and specific costume colours identify an actor's age, sex and personality the moment he or she appears on stage. Actors in Beijing operas wear extremely heavy make-up, a cosmetic style derived from

LEFT: the painted mask is critical in Chinese opera.
RIGHT: colours of the face identify the character.

the use of painted masks in older operatic forms. A white patch on the nose indicates a comic character of low rank; a completely white face suggests evil and treachery; a red face identifies a courageous but dim-witted man; and a black-faced actor is an ordinary person. There are 18 types of opera beards, each symbolising a different personality.

Chinese operas also incorporate mime, dance, swordplay and acrobatics. For the principal artists, gesture, movement and attitude are all as important as their spoken lines.

Headdresses are also a vital part of Chinese opera costume; the more important the character, the more elaborate the headdress. Costumes are exaggerated in style to achieve as great a theatrical effect as possible. Each colour identifies the rank, status and personality of the different operatic roles: purple for barbarians, yellow for emperors. Props are usually minimal, the idea being to leave as much as possible to the audience's imagination.

It is perfectly acceptable for audiences to arrive late for a performance, leave early, walk around and chat, or even eat during a show, which may run from three hours to a whole day. When an actor sings especially well, the audience is expected to respond by shouting out praise and applauding.

Most of the traditional opera performances in Hong Kong are called *sumkung* (god's eulogy), as they are performed to celebrate special festivals or the birthdays of different gods. Many of these performances are related to Daoism and Buddhism. For example, during the Ghost Festival, operas are staged together with other activities to expiate the sins of the dead. On each occasion, performances can last up to five days.

To revive the popularity of Chinese operas, some artists have taken measures to rejuvenate both form and content. The most active reformer in Hong Kong is veteran Leung Hon-wai, who has formed his own operatic group and employed writers to produce new scripts, while a symphony orchestra was introduced to bring a more modern tempo.

Ironically, the first major reform of Chinese opera was started on the mainland by the late Chinese leader Mao Zedong's wife, who persecuted intellectuals during the Cultural Revolution. Under her instructions, traditional opera troupes put on "revolutionary model plays". They sang the praises of the Communist Party and condemned the evils of capitalism. Delicate young girls yearning for love were replaced by iron ladies sweating away in the fields. Symphonic music was introduced to add a stronger mood, while Western opera-singing techniques were applied to make revolutionary leaders stand out.

Rigid political propaganda aside, these revolutionary plays introduced modern elements to traditional Chinese operas and convinced veteran artists that new stories could work.

Lion and dragon dances

A lion dance, in which two performers wear and manipulate a lion costume, is also an integral part of festive occasions. This *qongfu*-related entertainment form is usually performed at festivals, or on special occasions such as the opening of a new business or a corporate anniversary.

Since the lion is considered a holy animal and seen as a spirit that has its own importance in Chinese mythology, lion dances are believed to bring good luck. Sometimes performances are accompanied by firecrackers to scare away evil spirits. There may also be a dragon dance to accompany the lion. The difference between the two dances is simple: the dragon is held aloft by a group of performers, who move the giant puppet from outside. They walk in set patterns to make the dragon look like it is flying. But the lion dance has a crew of only two, who move the large cloth or paper puppet from within. Also, in the lion dance performers can move the head in various ways, as well as the eyes, mouth and ears.

There are generally two types of Chinese lions – northern and southern. The differences are in their appearance and the way they move. While the northern lion has a furry yellow coat and a semi-rigid mouth, the southern version has a movable mouth and a more colourful body, but no long hair for fur.

Music and film

Despite efforts to adapt to modern times, interest in traditional arts has been replaced by pop music and movies. Mainland Chinese immigrants in the 1950s and 1960s brought to Hong Kong not only money and entrepreneurial skills, but also arts, culture and the Mandarin language. During the 1950s and 1960s, most of the well-known artists in Hong Kong were from Shanghai. In the 1970s, when contact between Hong Kong and Taiwan increased, Hong Kong's music scene was dominated by Taiwanese songs, mostly written by

WHERE TO SEE PERFORMING ARTS

Hong Kong's flagship venue is the Cultural Centre in Tsim Sha Tsui. Home to the Hong Kong Philharmonic Orchestra, the centre also plays host to many visiting artists and touring productions of hit musicals. The Hong Kong Arts Centre in Wan Chai is the place to go for theatre and the occasional concert, while City Hall (Central) is synonymous with dance and Chinese opera. The Academy for Performing Arts, close to the Arts Centre in Wan Chai, contains the Lyric Theatre and organises concerts by its own students and international musicians. The annual Hong Kong Arts Festival (Feb–Mar) brings together local talent and leading international performers. *For listings, see pages 274–277.*

TOP LEFT AND LEFT: resplendent costumes embellish the operatic performance. **ABOVE AND ABOVE RIGHT:** New Year dragon dances. **RIGHT:** outside the Arts Centre.

Chinese Arts and Crafts

Chinese arts and crafts have a long history. Traditional forms include porcelain, embroidery, brocade, carpets, jade products, carvings (wood, bamboo and ivory) and paper decorations called "scissors-cuts" – all with different styles and regional influences – as well as brush painting and calligraphy. In Hong Kong, the most reliable places to buy these items are the China Arts and Crafts shops and the Chinese Products department stores on Hong Kong Island and

Kowloon. For antiques, look no further than Hollywood Road and neighbouring Upper Lascar Row (more commonly known as Cat Street; *see page 111*).

Chinese **embroidery and brocade** have had a reputation for excellent quality since the days of trade on the Silk Road. The best silk products come from eastern regions where the climate is suitable for raising silkworms, while the dry northwestern regions of the country produce fine-quality cashmere.

Silk embroidery from Suzhou, near Shanghai in eastern China, is especially well known for its fine workmanship and venerable history stretching back over 2,000 years. **Drawn work** from Shantou in eastern Guangdong also enjoys a good reputation overseas.

Scissors-cut is traditionally a product of rural China, where various kinds of colourful designs are created to decorate windows before Chinese New Year. Patterns include animals, fruit, flowers and characters from ancient Chinese folk tales or operas, often with themes of good harvests, prosperity and happiness.

Carvings of jade, ivory, wood, bone, rock and bamboo are a familiar sight in China. The best-known are jade carvings from Beijing, an art form that dates back to the Ming dynasty (1368–1644); ivory balls featuring legendary Chinese figures from Guangzhou; stone carvings from Shoushan in Fujian province; bamboo carvings from Huangyan in Zhejiang province; and high-quality ink-slabs made in Duanxi and Zhaoqing in Guangdong.

The Chinese invented **porcelain** in the 7th century AD, a good 1,000 years before Europeans managed to unlock the secret. The best variety comes from Jingdezhen County in Jiangxi province – fine, smooth and reminiscent of the ceramics made during the Yuan dynasty. Closer to Hong Kong, the ceramics produced at Shiwan *(see page 244)* are renowned for their quality.

Chinese landscape painting and **calligraphy** are generally mounted on a hanging scroll. In days gone by, the scroll was rolled up, stored away, and brought out on special occasions to be slowly unfurled, revealing only parts of a scene, subtly drawing the observer into the picture. **Miniature paintings** on shells, feathers, tree bark, deer horns and even thin strands of wheat straw are also popular souvenirs and gifts.   ❏

LEFT: a large and complicated jade carving.
ABOVE: embroided silk.

college students on the island ruled by the Guomintang (Nationalist) Party.

In the mid-1970s, some Hong Kong-born singers with a clear local identity started a movement to promote Cantonese pop songs, and by the early 1980s the first generation of Cantonese pop stars – dubbed "Cantopop" by the local press – appeared. Since the late 1980s, this local scene has been dominated by teen idols – young male and female singers in their late teens or early twenties – whose popularity depends more on their looks than their voices. In the 1990s, the biggest local pop stars were described as "emperors" and "empresses", with the most famous performers called the "four heavenly emperors" – singers Leon Lai, Jackie Cheung, Andy Lau and Aaron Kwok. Each developed his own loyal legion of fans who zealously track their idol's every public appearance. When heart-throb singer/actor Leslie Cheung died – a suicide jump from the top floor of the Mandarin Oriental hotel in 2003 – the city was practically paralysed by grief. Tribute websites continue on the Internet, and fans still parade wreaths in public.

Life for the more traditional professional artists has got tougher, since the local society is so commercially oriented that people do not have much time for serious art. However, as the city gets more affluent, the government and its citizens are beginning to appreciate the high-quality arts.

There are eight professional performance companies in Hong Kong and hundreds of amateur groups. The most prominent players include the Hong Kong Philharmonic Orchestra, Hong Kong Repertory Theatre, Hong Kong Chinese Orchestra and the Hong Kong Dance Company. Founded in 1985, the Academy for Performing Arts in Wan Chai is one of the top performing-arts schools in Asia. Major cultural events include the annual Hong Kong Arts Festival and the Fringe Festival.

The profile of Chinese cinema has risen considerably in recent years. Hong Kong films are gaining international attention, and local film

> *The top 5 highest-grossing films in HK are: Titanic HK$114,930,000, Jurassic Park $161,900,000, Kung Fu Hustle $161,280,000, Shaolin Soccer $160,260,000 and Jurassic Park 2 $58,230,000.*

talent has become more influential following the achievements in Hollywood of director John Woo, actor Chow Yun-fat and action-star Jackie Chan, as well as the highly acclaimed, idiosyncratic work of director Wong Kar-wai. Hong Kong remains one of only a handful of places in the world where locally made films (mainly action and romance) can still outsell Hollywood. ❑

ABOVE: a scene from local director Wong Kar-wai's acclaimed *Chungking Express* (1994).
ABOVE RIGHT: Cantopop star Andy Lau.

MONEY IS EVERYTHING. OF COURSE

Making money is Hong Kong's *raison d'être*: the fast buck is revered and the tycoon's status stops just short of beatification

US$21.3 billion (his initial fortune was created by manufacturing plastic flowers in the 1950s). The post-2008 global recession affected Hong Kong far less than most developed economies.

Hong Kong is a city riddled with contradictions. It continues to top lists of the world's "freest economies", yet there is no competition law and the property-rich cartels dominate major sectors of the economy. Half the working population earns less than HK$130,000 (US$16,700) per year, and the wealth gap has increased in recent years with about a tenth of households surviving on an annual income of less than HK$48,000 (US$6,160).

An economic success story

An excellent deep-water harbour and a strategic location on China's doorstep – the factors which brought the British here in the first place – have long encouraged Hong Kong's shipping and trading business. Today it is the world's second-busiest air cargo hub and third-busiest container port.

For the first century of British rule, Hong Kong developed as a trading port through which China did business with the rest of the world, but this entrepôt role rapidly diminished after World War II, as communist China became increasingly isolated. In a short time, the economy switched its focus to manufacturing. A large number of mainland entrepreneurs fled here after the Communist Party came to power in 1949. Bringing capital and business skills, they re-established themselves by setting up factories making textiles and toys. A sizeable workforce was on hand to provide the labour.

Even with its limited resources and space, prosperity and affluence are among the first impressions a visitor gets after arriving in Hong Kong. At HK$229,329 (US$30,000), per capita GDP is one of the highest in the world, although this is skewed by a small elite of super-rich residents – the median total household income held steady at HK$207,000 (US$26,600) between 1996 and 2006. According to Forbes, in 2009 Hong Kong's 40 richest individuals were all billionaires and the city is thought to have the highest concentration of millionaires in the world. Li Ka Shing, known locally as "Superman", is the richest of all: in 2010 Forbes estimated his personal wealth at

Manufacturing gradually diversified into electronics, printing, publishing, machinery, fabricated-metal products, plastic products (the famous "made in Hong Kong" cheap toys), watches and jewellery. But this proved to be a relatively short-lived stage in Hong Kong's economic history.

Since the late 1980s, most companies have moved their processing operations to China, where labour is considerably cheaper. Hong Kong companies own half of 400,000 or so factories in the Pearl River Delta. By 2006 the manufacturing sector accounted for just 3.6 percent of GDP, down from 24 percent in 1984. Today many companies have an office in Hong Kong that coordinates with overseas clients looking to have goods manufactured in China or elsewhere in Asia. If they don't have a factory of their own, they source one in China or Asia. The Hong Kong offices coordinate payments and shipping, and may also provide design services, quality control and production services. For the moment, most buyers are more confident to deal with Hong Kong-based companies, governed as they are by Hong Kong law.

As well as local success stories, Hong Kong is maintaining its role as a major international commercial and financial centre (a position it has held since the mid-1980s). In 2007, 3,800 international companies had regional offices in the city. Tourism is important too, and Hong Kong welcomed over 29.6 million visitors in 2009.

In January 2010, Hong Kong's foreign currency assets stood at US$257 billion, making it the world's ninth-largest holder of foreign currency reserves.

> Hong Kong is rich with the stories of tycoons who have ascended to the summit, fallen into the financial abyss, then climbed to the top once more, attaining legendary status.

Links with China

The single most important factor in Hong Kong's current prosperity has been the opening up of China to foreign trade.

Until the late 1970s, the Hong Kong business sector was dominated by British companies, known as *hongs* by the Cantonese. The four leading British *hongs* were Jardine Matheson, Wheelock Marden, Hutchison Whampoa and

LEFT: gold has an appeal in Hong Kong.
ABOVE: the trading floor at a large financial institution.

the Swire Group. But in the last few decades, energetic and ambitious Hong Kong Chinese groups, with investments in shipping, property and the textile industry, have built new empires and taken over some of the British-founded concerns. Considering mainland China to be the biggest market in the world, Hong Kong entrepreneurs – with their blood and emotional ties to the mainland and their knowledge of the Chinese way of doing business – naturally edged out their British rivals.

> Hong Kongers have a sharp eye for business. As soon as they have saved enough money by working for other people, many of them venture into their own businesses.

With the advent of Deng Xiaoping's economic reforms in the late 1970s, Hong Kong's strategic position as the international community's gateway to China, and China's trade window to the outside world, suddenly became far more important. Both China and HK benefited hugely from their fast-developing economic ties.

These days China accounts for nearly half of Hong Kong's total trade in goods, making the mainland its largest trading partner. In 2010 just under 50 percent of all Hong Kong exports went to China, and just over half of all imported goods came from China. Hong Kong remains the largest investor in China; its companies employ an estimated 12 million people there and about 240,000 HK residents work in China. Being part of a motherland with a market of 1.3 billion people just across the border means HK businesses are ideally placed to target consumers in China and to help international companies tap into the vast opportunities there.

Currency control

To provide a stable currency, the government introduced a linked exchange-rate system in 1983 that pegged Hong Kong's currency to the US dollar. The system was designed to align interest rates with those in the USA's then stable economy. The exchange rate was fixed at HK$7.8 to US$1. However, during the 1997 financial crisis that spread through Asia, many people questioned the wisdom of linking Hong Kong's currency to the US dollar so rigidly, and there is still periodic doubt as to whether the "peg" should remain, as it overvalues the HK dollar. The Renminbi is now pegged to a basket of currencies and China is under pressure to allow it to trade freely, something that will not happen overnight. In the longer term, the Renminbi could become Asia's regional currency.

The peg still exists, but is coming under increasing pressure as the US economy slips into recession, or worse. On the other hand, the current US dollar slide has indirectly made Hong Kong's currency more competitive.

Further reasons for success

The global economic crisis meant Hong Kong's economy shrank by 2.5 percent in 2009, but was back to 4 or 5 percent growth in 2010 and trade

has increased by two-thirds since 1997. The government is quick to point out it likes to keep business people happy, with its low and simple tax regime: profits tax is capped at 16.5 percent, and salaries tax at 15 percent. There is no capital gains tax, estate duty, VAT and sales tax.

The government's long-standing policy of minimum interference and maximum support for business has been a key factor in its prosperity. A sound legal and financial framework, a convertible and secure currency, a highly efficient network of transport and communication, a skilled workforce, the enterprising spirit of locals, a high degree of internationalisation and cultural openness all help, too. Hong Kong's financial markets have a high degree of liquidity and transparent regulations – the founding of the Independent Commission Against Corruption (ICAC) in 1974 effectively stamped out a serious corruption problem that was stifling growth, and has been of enormous benefit to Hong Kong (though it is still kept busy). There are few places in the world where it is easier to

set up and register a business. On the other hand, local companies are increasingly competing with mainland companies, as the pool of skilled labour begins to extend into China.

For the moment, Hong Kong's position as gateway to China seems assured, but financial commentators suggest it will inevitably be overtaken by Shanghai, which is tipped to become one of the world's top three centres of commerce within the next 20 years. ❑

STOCK MARKET GAMBLING

Hong Kong's Hang Seng Index, which tracks the value of stocks and shares on the Hong Kong stock market, was set up in 1969 and is considered the key indicator of the SAR's economic health. Unsurprisingly for a place so obsessed with money, it appears, prominently, everywhere in the city – on gigantic screens in Central, in taxi cabs and outer-island ferries, in elevators, hotel lobbies and shopping centres. Recent jitters in the global economy emanating from the now notorious US "sub-prime" mortgage difficulties have bucked the trend of solid growth in recent years (with a record high attained in October 2007).

Hong Kong's other form of gambling involves horses (see pages 136–7), the "Mark 6" lottery and trips to Macau.

FAR LEFT: Hong Kong has the world's highest proportion of über-expensive cars. **ABOVE LEFT:** at work in the HSBC Building. **ABOVE:** casino gambling is only allowed offshore in Hong Kong, but is hugely important in Macau. **RIGHT:** the ubiquitous Hang Seng Index.

MODERN ARCHITECTURE

Few of the world's cities confront the visitor with their architecture as dramatically as Hong Kong, with its constantly shifting skyline

Hong Kong is a city that likes to flaunt its wealth, and nowhere is this more apparent than in its architecture. The acute scarcity of land, particularly on the dense urban strip of Hong Kong Island, and subsequent high prices have pushed buildings ever higher into the polluted skies. In fact there are more tall structures (over 13 storeys) here than anywhere else on the planet. Showpiece buildings vie for the prime spot and the most eye-catching design, augmented by gaudy night-time light displays.

This being Hong Kong, nothing stays still for long. At one time St John's Cathedral was the tallest building. In the early 1960s, the Mandarin Oriental Hotel took over the mantle, to be usurped by Jardine House (1973), the Hopewell Centre (1980), the Bank of China (1990), Central Plaza (1992), IFC2 (2003), and Kowloon's ICC Tower (2010).

But height isn't everything. With money to play with, architects have been able to produce some truly exciting designs. Prime examples are Norman Foster's widely admired HSBC Hongkong Headquarters, the Convention and Exhibition Centre, and I.M. Pei's elegant Bank of China Tower.

LEFT: the IFC2 tower is currently the world's tenth-tallest structure.

ABOVE: Hong Kong Island's constantly evolving skyline never fails to captivate, with the glass and steel towers framed against the forested backdrop of Victoria Peak.

BELOW: old and new side by side, Flagstaff House is dwarfed by the Lippo Centre towers.

HIGH DEMAND, HIGH PRICES

The construction industry is big business in Hong Kong, and the government draws much of its revenue from the sale of land (income taxes are low). With supply exhausted and demand as high as ever, land has to be reclaimed from the sea, with construction companies willing to fork out staggering sums for the right to build on the new plots.

In contrast to the high-tech buildings themselves, the giant webs of scaffolding used in their construction are made entirely of bamboo (pictured above). Extremely strong and durable, bamboo goes up four times faster than steel – no nails or screws are used – and withstands typhoons better. There are around 250 experienced bamboo scaffolders in Hong Kong, who clamber about barefoot hundreds of feet above the streets. Few use proper safety equipment, however, and there are several deaths each year.

Hong Kong Island has long held a monopoly on these super-tall glass-and-steel towers, but Kowloon is catching up. With the end of height restrictions following the closure of Kai Tak Airport, development is rapid – and the ICC Tower (on the West Kowloon reclamation; *see page 162)* that has now taken over from IFC2 as the tallest building in town. The New Territories are also getting in on the act, with the completion of the 319-metre (1,046-ft) Nina Tower at Tsuen Wan.

ABOVE: the Convention and Exhibition Centre was extended, at great expense, for the handover ceremony in 1997. The result is unusual and spectacular.

BELOW LEFT: much of urban Hong Kong is characterised by run-of-the-mill 1950s, '60s and '70s apartment blocks such as here in Mongkok. The typical living space is cramped, around 45–65 sq. metres (500–700 sq. ft).

PLACES

A detailed guide to Hong Kong, Macau,
Shenzhen and Guangzhou, with principal sites
clearly cross-referenced by number to the maps

Today's Hong Kong can be divided into four parts: Hong Kong Island, the Kowloon peninsula, the New Territories and the numerous outlying islands. Hong Kong Island is 75 sq km (29 sq miles) of topsy-turvy real estate. The earliest British settlements were established here; it is now dominated by great banks, enormous futuristic buildings, opulent hotels, splendid residences on the Peak, surprisingly restful beaches and the territory's oldest Chinese communities. Across the Harbour – by the Mass Transit Railway, Star Ferry or via one of three tunnels – is Kowloon, with its millions of people packed into just a few square kilometres. Tsim Sha Tsui District, the site of many hotels, bars and shops, is changing as fast as anywhere in Hong Kong, with massive developments above and below ground.

Beyond the mountains which ring Kowloon to the north lie the anachronistically named New Territories, leased by the British for 99 years and handed back to China, together with the rest of Hong Kong, in 1997. A mix of empty hillsides, bucolic landscapes and bustling developments, it's a very different side of the SAR. A further step into the outfield is granted by the 230-plus outlying islands, some changing for ever – Walt Disney's second Asian theme park opened on Lantau in 2005 – and others uninhabited and unaltered since the day the Union Jack was first planted. To the west across the silt-laden waters of the Pearl River mouth is the former

Portuguese enclave of Macau, busily reinventing itself as East Asia's leisure capital. Across the border, the Pearl River Delta, anchored by the ever-expanding cities of Shenzhen and Guangzhou, is well on its way to becoming one of the great financial powerhouses of Asia. ❏

PRECEDING PAGES: high-rise Wan Chai; looking south from the Dragon's Back, Hong Kong Island. **LEFT:** Man Mo Temple. **ABOVE LEFT:** city streets at night. **ABOVE RIGHT:** Shek O.

HONG KONG TOP SIGHTS

The Star Ferry
pages 122–123

Tsim Sha Tsui and Yau Ma Tei
pages 151–162

Hong Kong Island and views
pages 99–107, 153

Man Mo Temple
page 110

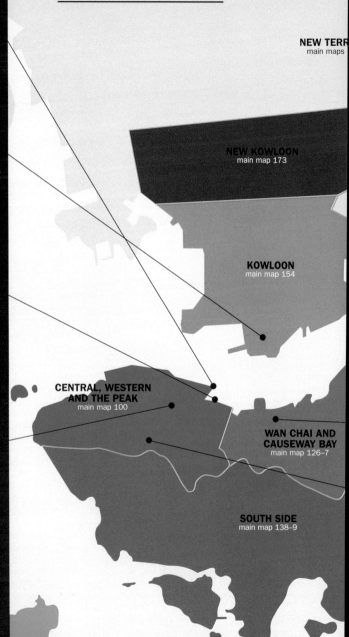

NEW TERR
main maps

NEW KOWLOON
main map 173

KOWLOON
main map 154

CENTRAL, WESTERN AND THE PEAK
main map 100

WAN CHAI AND CAUSEWAY BAY
main map 126–7

SOUTH SIDE
main map 138–9

NEW TERRITORIES
main maps 184, 195

OUTLYING ISLANDS
main map
96–7

Po Lin Monastery
pages 203–204

*Hiking in the
New Territories*
pages 188, 193

The Outlying Islands
pages 202–211

*Wan Chai and
Causeway Bay*
pages 125–132

The Peak
pages 114–117

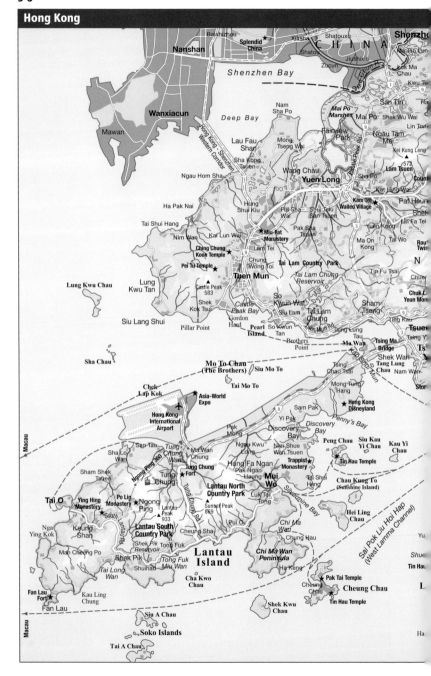

SOUTH

CHINA

SEA

N

| 0 | | 3 km |
| 0 | | 3 miles |

Recommended Restaurants, Bars, Pubs & Cafés on pages 118–121

CENTRAL, WESTERN AND THE PEAK

With its mass of skyscrapers wedged against precipitous slopes, the world of business and finance dominates Central District. In stark contrast, the traditional Chinese way of life still thrives in neighbouring Western District. Gaze down at it all from the rarefied heights of The Peak

Central District – Chung Wan in Cantonese – is Hong Kong's business and financial hub, at the heart of the incredible cliff-face of high-rise buildings that extends along the north shore of Hong Kong Island. Wedged between the harbour and the precipitous slopes of Victoria Peak, this is where the money is, the financial powerhouses, the glamorous high-end shopping malls, overlooked by the multi-millionaires' mansions up on The Peak.

To the west, Sheung Wan and Western District retain more elements of Hong Kong's past; this was the area that the British established as Victoria City in the 1840s, and from here the city has expanded and grown in every direction, including upwards. It all adds up to one of the most fascinating areas of modern Hong Kong.

Yet, like the rest of Hong Kong, there is little in the way of conventional tourist sights here: despite the efforts of the tourist board to highlight the past with such innovations as the Sun Yat-sen Trail, most of the "landmarks" en route are simply plaques recording some building or other that has long since disappeared. Instead, the fascination is in

the contemporary, the everyday life of the place, the drama of the architecture, the amazing contrasts of scale and the sheer energy that emanates from the crowded streets.

And although most of the pedestrians on Central's streets are attired for business, and giant video screens flash the latest news and financial figures from around the world to passers-by, there are still strong elements of former days, with wayside hawkers selling novelties and knock-offs, incense sticks smouldering by

Main attractions

STAR FERRY
HSBC BUILDING
BANK OF CHINA TOWER
THE LANES
LAN KWAI FONG AND SOHO
HOLLYWOOD ROAD
MAN MO TEMPLE
THE PEAK TRAM
THE PEAK (WALKS AND VIEWS)

LEFT: the bright lights of Central.
RIGHT: clothing stalls on the steps of Pottinger Street.

A familar presence at the old (pre-2006) Star Ferry Pier, the anachronistic bright-red rickshaws – largely redundant for decades – finally succumbed to the inevitable and disappeared from the scene.

tiny shrines, and delivery boys serenely pedalling through red lights with a cargo of fresh meat balanced in their bike's cast-iron basket.

THE FINANCIAL CENTRE

The **Central Ferry Pier ❶**, the new terminal for the Star Ferry on Hong Kong Island, is as good a place as any to begin exploring Central. With reclamation continually narrowing the harbour, the Star Ferry has been forced to relocate to a new site next door to the outlying island ferry piers. It features Edwardian-style embellishments and is more user-friendly than its predecesor, with plenty of places to grab a snack. Having been in business since the 19th century, the company has taken the upheaval in its stride. *(For more on the Star Ferry, see pages 122–3.)*

The prosaically named **International Finance Centre (IFC) ❷**, a combination of smart shopping mall and offices, sits atop the Airport Express Central terminal. Just to the north in front of the ferry piers, and part of the same complex, is the **International Finance Centre Two (IFC2) ❸**. It stands at 420 metres (1,378 ft), which makes it currently the 10th-tallest building in the world (fully 39 metres/128 ft higher than the Empire State Building), and is capped by a mass of curving spires. When it was finished in 2003, IFC2 became the tallest of Hong Kong's 7,500-odd high-rise buildings, but in 2010 that title passed to the International

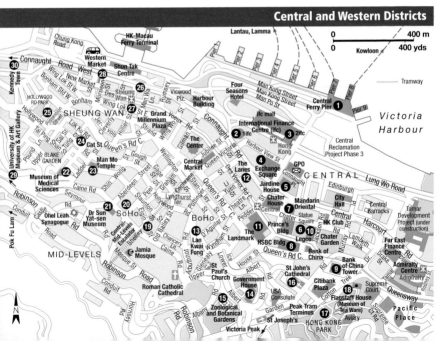

Central and Western Districts

Commerce Centre (ICC) across the harbour in West Kowloon *(see page 152)*. Unfortunately people are not normally allowed up to the 88th floor to admire the views. There is, however, a pleasant outside terrace (fifth floor) with bars and restaurants above the Lane Crawford department store. The tower block on the west side of the IFC houses the super-luxury **Four Seasons Hotel**.

Walkways connect the IFC to the rest of Central via **Exchange Square 4**, home of the Hong Kong Stock Exchange. On the first floor of One and Two Exchange Square, a new **Exchange Exhibition Hall** (open trading days 9.30am–5pm, last admission 3.30pm; charge) allows visitors to view the Trading Hall in action and to learn about the development of Hong Kong's financial markets.

Head east along the walkway to **Jardine House 5**, whose distinctive 1,700-plus round windows have inspired the nickname "House of a Thousand Orifices". Opened in 1973 (when it was known as the Connaught Centre), it was for many years the tallest building in Hong Kong. Just behind is the **General Post Office** (GPO), and beyond that City Hall, which lost its waterfront position in 2008 when the (supposed) final part of the Central Wan Chai reclamation was built.

It's possible to get a good overview of all the current reclamation and proposals at the **Hong Kong Planning and Infrastructure Exhibition Gallery** (Wed–Mon 10am–6pm) on Murray Road. The main feature is an 18.5-metre (60-ft) model of the city, while computer animations and other exhibits showcase the planners' vision of the new Hong Kong. **City Hall** itself not only houses administrative offices, but a concert hall, theatre,

Exchange Square is enlivened by a fine crop of sculptures by Henry Moore and Ju Ming.

ABOVE LEFT: a tram trundles through Central.
BELOW: looking south from Statue Square.

TIP

To get the most out of a walking tour of Central District, visit on a weekday during working hours, as (Lan Kwai Fong/SoHo apart) this is not one of Hong Kong's after-hours locations – unlike Tsim Sha Tsui and Causeway Bay, many shops close by 7pm. Shops are open on Saturdays, but the energised atmosphere of the working week is lacking. Sundays are quiet, with shops shut, although the weekly Filipina get-together (see opposite) is in full swing.

ABOVE RIGHT:
Central's most famous five-star hotel. **BELOW:**
buses, trams and people at rush hour on Des Voeux Road.

marriage registry and three restaurants, including the popular Maxim's Palace (for dim sum).

East to Statue Square

Between City Hall and the GPO, an underpass will take you to **Statue Square** ⑥ and Chater Road. On Sundays, throngs of Filipina maids gather here on their day off in a festive outdoor party. The 138,000 Philippine nationals, most of whom work here as maids, now form the second largest foreign community living in Hong Kong – over double the number of British, Canadian, Australian and American passport-holders, who total around 70,000 in all. Indonesian nationals, also working as domestic helpers, are now the largest foreign community with 141,000, and tend to meet up in Causeway Bay.

Statue Square was once graced with a statue of Queen Victoria, long transplanted to Causeway Bay, and replaced by a statue of Sir Thomas Jackson, an Irishman who managed the Hongkong and Shanghai Banking Corporation for 30 years around the end of the 19th century. Chinese

and expatriate victims of World Wars I and II are commemorated at the **Cenotaph**, and Hong Kong's war veterans gather here on Remembrance Day every November.

The **Mandarin Oriental** ⑦ is one of the oldest and grandest hotels in Hong Kong. It's unusual to mention the Mandarin without the accompanying adjective "venerable", and at four decades old it's something of a treasure. Hong Kong's tallest building when it opened in 1963, the hotel had a US$140 million facelift in 2006 to keep up with the new wave of rivals.

This part of Central District is the financial hub of Hong Kong, home to the HQ of several major banks. Facing Statue Square is Norman Foster's striking US$1 billion **HSBC Building** ⑧, the most expensive building in the world when it was completed in 1985. A short way along Des Voeux

Road, is the Cheung Kong Center, its dull 1999 design prompting the nickname the "box the Bank of China came in". The height of 283 metres (927ft) is said to have been determined by drawing a line between the Bank of China and the HSBC Building. Asia's richest man, Li Ka-Shing is Cheung Kong's CEO and has offices on the top floor between the financial giants.

The dramatic 368-metre (1,209-ft) **Bank of China Tower ❾**, designed by the American-Chinese architect I.M. Pei, is one of Hong Kong's most famous buildings. Opened in 1990, its bold design and sharp angles make "cutting-edge" an unusually apt description – and these angles, pointing directly at other financial institutions, are blamed for channelling bad feng shui to them *(see page 74)*. The 43rd-floor observation area is open to the public (Mon–Fri 9am–6pm, Sat 9am–1pm; free). Behind it is **Citibank Plaza**, another ultra-modern tower.

The Legco Building

East of Statue Square is the colonial-style former Supreme Court Building, home to the **Legislative Council (Legco) Building ❿** until 2012 when it moves to the new government HQ on the harbour front. Built in 1912, it is topped by a statue of the Greek goddess Themis, and its Edwardian dome shows up brilliantly against the Bank of China Tower. The building was used as a torture chamber by Japanese police during World War II, and wartime shrapnel damage can still be seen on the eastern wall. Across Jackson Road, **Chater Garden** is a rare (but not especially pleasant) open space that may host demonstrators, dancing off-duty maids or munching office workers on their lunch break. Until the 1970s, the site was occupied by the Hong Kong Cricket Club *(see picture, page 42)*.

Inland to Des Voeux and Queen's roads

Heading inland from the GPO, pedestrian thoroughfares take you over Connaught Road Central to **Des Voeux Road**, named after Sir George William Des Voeux,

Hong Kong's taxis are cheap and plentiful, and available if the sign is lit (for details see page 259).

BELOW LEFT: Filipinas congregate at Statue Square on Sundays.
BELOW: the "chopsticks" atop the Bank of China Tower.

A rare historic presence in Central District, the former Supreme Court Building currently home to Legco.

Hong Kong's most successful home-grown fashion stores. British-Chinese entrepreneur David Tang, who first brought the territory the exclusive China Club, then Cuban cigars, turned his attention to making Chinese fashion chic. Across the street **The Landmark** is a prestigious shopping mall with enormous stand-alone stores dedicated to luxury brands, a four-floor Harvey Nichols department store and The Landmark Mandarin Oriental hotel. Five floors surround a vast 6,000-sq metre (20,000-sq ft) atrium. Walkways connect the floors around the atrium with neighbouring buildings: **Chater House** which has more than half a dozen Georgio Armani shops and an Armani bar; and **Prince's Building**, with a further abundance of marble and upmarket shops.

governor from 1887 to 1891. The tram stop here, at the junction with Pedder Street, is a blur of traffic on weekdays. Parallel to Des Voeux, **Queen's Road Central** was the area's original "Main Street" – until a little footpath was turned into Des Voeux Road, which eventually upstaged it. These days both are very busy, although Queen's Road has more in the way of shops.

Shopping lanes and Shopping malls

Some of the side streets connecting Queen's and Des Voeux roads are well worth exploring. On **Pedder Street**, Shanghai Tang is one of

By way of contrast, **Li Yuen Street East** and **Li Yuen Street West**, generally known collectively as **The Lanes** , are narrow alleyways lined with stalls and shops that sell clothing, fabrics and counterfeit designer fashion accessories. Bargaining is still expected, and the atmosphere is

BELOW & BELOW RIGHT: pedestrian walkways in Central.

Walking through Central

Central's streets tend to be busy and sweaty for much of the year; they are more easily navigated via the walkways which run from the GPO (first floor) past Exchange Square and the IFC to the Macau Ferry Terminal, and via Chater House and adjacent buildings as far as the bottom of Lan Kwai Fong. Numerous (slightly world-weary) security guards en route are very obliging with directions. In the hot months, at least for those from cooler climes, it is quite an experience to walk through Central on these walkways – one minute you are

perspiring in the unbelievable heat and humidity of a Hong Kong summer, the next you are instantly cool as the walkway passes into an air-conditioned mall; then, suddenly, you are out in the open again and the wall of damp heat washes over you like a wave. The contrast is heightened by the decibel level – soft piped muzak in the malls, traffic and piledriver din on the streets.

Recommended Restaurants, Bars, Pubs & Cafés on pages 118–121

completely different from that of the surrounding shops and malls.

Party Central

Behind Queen's Road Central, which was the waterfront road before land reclamation began in the 1850s, the terrain rises steeply. D'Aguilar Street leads up to the nightlife centre of **Lan Kwai Fong** ⑬, which together with nearby Wyndham St and SoHo *(see page 108)* is the prime partying area for Hong Kong's young and trendy. Modern cuisine, funky bars, clubs, English pubs and tiny snack shops generate dollars and hangovers in equal measure, and late-night revellers

can get everything from pizza to sushi in the wee hours. At weekends many bars stay open until 5am *(see page 121 for listings of bars and clubs).*

Colonial relics

At the top of Lan Kwai Fong, **Wyndham Street** marks a boundary of the commercial and residential areas. Uphill from here are the tower blocks of the Mid-Levels, with desirable and expensive apartments.

Glenealy snakes steeply uphill and eastward onto Upper Albert Road and **Government House** ⑭, the grand home of the former colonial leaders of Hong Kong. After a spell as a state guesthouse during the Tung Chee-hwa administration, it is now the official residence of the Chief Executive of the HKSAR. The mansion dates from the 1850s but was remodelled by the Japanese during World War II, who added a tower with a vague Shinto look. There is a clear view of the building through the wrought-iron gates, which are opened to the public only a couple of times a year, usually in spring and autumn (no set dates).

People usually assume that the dark-green forested backdrop to the famous view across Victoria Harbour is "natural". In fact, the hillsides were stripped of their original forest cover over the centuries, and it wasn't until the 1940s and '50s that replanting took place. Early photographs (see page 34) clearly show the absence of trees, altering the scene almost as dramatically as the lack of buildings.

ABOVE LEFT: silk jackets, scarves and accessories for sale on Li Yuen Street East.
BELOW: in the heart of Lan Kwai Fong.

The surrounding area is one of the few remaining parts of Hong Kong that retains a genuinely colonial feel. If you go any further up, the pocket of exotic greenery is quickly invaded by the high-rises of the Mid-Levels; lower down, the area is engulfed by banks and office towers.

Opposite Government House are the **Zoological and Botanical Gardens** ⑮ (open daily 6am–7pm; free), a lush tropical area worthy of any urban retreat. The small zoo houses a variety of exotic wildlife, including an impressive collection of red-cheeked gibbons. It opened in 1864 and still retains elements of its original Victorian gentility, with the added Eastern spirituality of elderly Chinese practising their t'ai chi each morning.

St John's Cathedral

Tucked away opposite the Citibank Plaza on Battery Path Road, and just below Government House, the Victorian Gothic **St John's Cathedral** ⑯ was consecrated in 1849 and is the city's oldest Anglican church. Note that **Battery Path** itself is a pleasant walk, beginning at the HSBC Building and leading past the cathedral to Hong Kong Park. The red-brick **French Mission Building**, behind the Cheung Kong Center, is more than 150 years old and now serves as the Court of Final Appeal.

Hong Kong Park

Follow Battery Path to the east of the cathedral along the footbridge to Citibank Plaza to reach the lush, green expanse of **Hong Kong Park** ⑰ (daily 6am–11pm; free). As Central's only large open space, it is busy all day long, with t'ai chi practitioners first thing in the morning, joggers and office workers, and bridal parties posing against a backdrop of waterfalls and shrubs. The **aviary** (daily 9am–5pm; charge) is home to over 90 different species of birds from the rainforests of Southeast Asia, including various barbets, shamas, fairy bluebirds and bulbuls. Walk through a giant mesh up to 30 metres (100ft) high on a one-way elevated wooden walkway (enter near the Kennedy Road entrance).

The park is also home to one of Hong Kong's best examples of bespoke architecture – **Flagstaff House**, home to the **Museum of Tea Ware** ⑱ (Wed–Mon 10am–5pm; tel: 2869 0690; free). The building – of more interest than the museum –

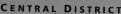
Recommended Restaurants, Bars, Pubs & Cafés on pages 118–121

neighbourhood. The unique **Central–Mid-Levels Escalator** ⑲ runs through the heart of this transitional zone between Central and Western District, which in recent years has become a lively nightlife centre.

The remarkable escalator itself was completed in 1993, at a cost of HK\$245 million. Comprising 20 separate sections, at 800 metres (2,625 feet) it is the world's longest outdoor escalator system. It was built partly to ease traffic congestion in the narrow streets below, but the most significant effect has been to revive the areas alongside it. Around 54,000 pedestrians use it each day, double the original estimate.

An exhibit at the Museum of Tea Ware in Flagstaff House.

was completed in 1846 and is reputedly the SAR's oldest surviving colonial structure. It once functioned as the residence of the commander-in-chief of the British forces, when the area was Victoria Barracks.

AROUND THE ESCALATOR AND SOHO

The character of Central begins to change as one walks westwards along Queen's Road Central away from the banks, shiny malls and shops and into an older, Chinese

The escalator starts at 100 Queen's Road Central next to the erstwhile wet market (Central Market) established here in 1842, to ascend the steep hillside, passing above Cochrane Street, across Hollywood Road to Shelley Street and then on to Conduit Road, up in the Mid-Levels. From early morning to

BELOW LEFT: Hong Kong Park with Citibank Plaza and the Bank of China Tower beyond.
BELOW: the aviary.

Old Bailey Street leads steeply uphill to Caine Road from Hollywood Road, on the fringe of the SoHo area. On the left is part of the old Central Police Station, slated for redevelopment as a leisure complex.

ABOVE RIGHT: high-rise blocks. **BELOW:** the Central–Mid-Levels escalator.

sunset, canny shoppers pack **Gage Street** where stalls selling fresh meat, live fish and more line the street in front of noodle shops, roast meat shops and hardware emporiums. It's worth descending to ground level on **Graham Street** to witness the market stalls displaying an astounding array of fresh fruit, vegetables and herbs.

Walk back up the hill to rejoin the escalator at **Hollywood Road**, famous for its antiques shops *(see page 110)*.

SoHo ⑳

Before the escalator was built, the area to the southwest of this part of Hollywood Road – Staunton Street, Shelley and Elgin streets – was rather run-down and seldom visited by outsiders. Now, as the hub of a nightlife

area that has become known as SoHo (SOuth of HOllywood Road), these narrow streets are home to over 100 cafés, restaurants and bars, offering an ever-changing mix of venues with cuisines from all over the world, plus boutiques selling young designers' clothes, jewellery and trendy gifts.

With the escalator providing easy access for people from the financial and business district, and the upmarket Mid-Levels residential area, SoHo is busy every night of the week and an easy place for the out-of-town visitor to feel comfortable and not be tagged as a tourist. Its cosmopolitan vibe and eateries have now spread in all directions in the streets near the escalator. Restaurateurs are also setting up shop in

Gough Street as well as along Peel, Cochrane and Aberdeen streets. This area is sometimes called NoHo, because it lies to the north of Hollywood Road.

Old Bailey Street has a typically SoHo eclectic mix of outlets that includes Hong Kong's New Age Shop and overlooks the now closed Victoria Prison. The prison is part of a complex that includes **Central Police Station** and Hong Kong Magistracy, built between 1841 and 1925 by the early colonists. Currently closed, there are plans to redevelop the attractive old complex as a dining and retail area.

Below the Former Central Police Station, **Wyndham Street**, which connects with Hollywood Road, is also lined with restaurants, with a few art galleries interspersed. It connects neatly with the bijou SoHo bistros with the boisterous Lan Kwai Fong nightlife area *(see page 105; and page 121 for listings of bars and clubs in both areas).*

Above SoHo

Uphill from SoHo, between Caine Road and Conduit Road, the only site of note among the apartment towers is the Jamia Masjid Mosque, which was first built in 1890 and is Hong Kong's oldest mosque.

If you exit the escalator at Caine Road and walk for five minutes you will discover the Dr Sun Yat-sen Museum and – a few minutes' walk further along – the Museum of Medical Sciences.

Dr Sun Yat-sen Museum

✉ 7 Castle Road, Central
www.hk.drsunyatsen.museum
☎ 2367 6373 🕒 Mon–Wed, Fri–Sat 10am–6pm, Sun 10am–7pm
💲 charge, but free on Wed 🚇 MTR Central

Housed in a beautifully preserved mansion built in 1914, the **Dr Sun Yat-sen Museum ㉑** tells the story of the Father of Modern China, and his time as a medical student in Hong Kong, exploring the colony's role in shaping his ideas about the modernisation of China – which led to revolution. While Sun never set foot in the hall, it is a useful starting point for painting a picture of the places along the **Sun Yat-sen Historical Trail**, which guides visitors through 12 significant sites in the Central and Western districts.

Museum of Medical Sciences

The Old Pathological Institute, built in 1906 to step up the fight against the plague and infectious diseases in Hong Kong, is today home to the **Museum of Medical Sciences ㉒**

With its numerous small bars and restaurants, SoHo is the preferred nightlife centre for many locals.

ABOVE LEFT: Sun Yat-sen.
BELOW: expensive furniture on Hollywood Road.

TIP

The streets of SoHo are known for their bars and restaurants, but there are also a lot of good shops, mostly clustered on Staunton Street. If you're looking for non-mainstream fashion or accessories, this is one of the best places in Hong Kong.

(Tue–Sat 10am–5pm, Sun 1–5pm; charge; www.hkmms.org.hk). The small galleries include a reconstruction of an early 20th-century pharmacy, an autopsy room, and the contrasts between Western and Chinese medicine. A chance to take a break in its small Chinese herbal medicine garden warrants a detour on the way down Caine Road or up from Hollywood Road.

Hollywood Road to Western

West of the escalator, Hollywood Road itself is well known for its abundance of shops selling all manner of Chinese (and other Asian) antiques – notably furniture, art and ornaments. Prices can be quite high, and – as always – it's best to shop around and look out for the logo of the HKTB's Quality Tourism Services Scheme (QTS; *see page 269*).

Man Mo Temple

✉ 126 Hollywood Road, Central
📞 2540 0350 🕐 daily 8am–6pm
🆓 free 🚇 MTR Sheung Wan

ABOVE RIGHT: helpful signposts. **BELOW:** sizing up the antiques.

Follow Hollywood Road west to the corner of Ladder Street and the wonderfully dark and atmospheric **Man Mo Temple ㉓**, built around 1842 on what must have been a little dirt track at that time. Tourists regularly throng Man Mo, but this doesn't inhibit the temple's regular worshippers from visiting to fill the temple with thick clouds of smoke from their joss sticks. The immense incense spirals hanging from the ceiling can burn for weeks.

Man is the god of civil servants and of literature, and in Mandarin society, civil servants were the best-educated and most sophisticated group. Mo is the god of martial arts and war, and is more popularly known by his worshippers as Kuan Ti or Kuan Kung. Statues of the legendary Eight Immortals stand guard outside the temple; inside, two solid-brass deer (representing longevity) adorn the main chamber. Near the altar, there are two sedan chairs encased in glass. Years ago, when the icons of Man and Mo were paraded through Western on festival days, they were transported on these chairs.

Ladder Street and Cat Street

These small streets are two of the most quirky of all local thoroughfares. **Ladder Street**'s 19th-century stone slab steps zigzag down steeply from Caine Road past the Museum of Medical Sciences to Hollywood Road and onto Queen's Road.

Just off this last stretch of Ladder Street below Hollywood Road is the street officially called Upper Lascar

Recommended Restaurants, Bars, Pubs & Cafés on pages 118–121

Row but much more commonly known as **Cat Street** ㉔, because the odds and ends you can buy here are known in popular Chinese as

"mouse goods", and those who trade in them are known as "cats". The lanes are filled with bric-a-brac, real and fake antiques, set out on myriad stalls. Bargaining is the rule here – whether for a safety pin, a shoelace, or, if you should be so lucky, a Tang-dynasty porcelain horse. The area was once famous for seamen's lodging houses and brothels, and it was a hang-out for criminals and low-life characters of all kinds. In nearby Lok Ku Road are the **Cat Street Galleries**, which are devoted

to artwork and antique reproductions from all over Asia.

Continue west to **Possession Street** ㉕, so called because it was here that Captain Sir Edward Belcher landed in January 1841 to plant the Union Jack and take possession of Hong Kong for Britain. No monument marks the exact spot where the British flag was planted. The only memento to the HMS *Sulphur*, whose crew was the first to step ashore, is Belcher Street, west of Possession Street.

WESTERN DISTRICT

Western District is located just to the west of Central, but is worlds away from the ultra-modern financial district. Ironically, considering its name, this is one of the least Westernised areas of Hong Kong, and provides a rare hint of the old city. The area begins officially at Possession Street and sprawls west to Kennedy Town.

One of Western's charms is that it is packed with shops and merchants trading in traditional goods, tea, rice and ingredients for herbal medicine. Find the Chinese herbalist, with his

The antiques shops along Hollywood Road sell a large range of replicas and reproductions of ancient Chinese art.

ABOVE LEFT: 1950s road sign. **BELOW:** inside Man Mo Temple.

aromatic concoctions of snake musk, herbs, ginseng and powdered lizards, all part of pharmacopoeial potions dating back 4,000 years.

Sheung Wan

A buffer zone between the steel-and-glass skyscrapers of the financial district, Sheung Wan is the gateway to the more traditional, and residential, districts of Sai Ying Pun and Kennedy Town. Until recently development here was on a building-by-building basis, so it is not unusual to find modern buildings poking up between older tenement buildings.

Heading inland from the urban expressway of Connaught Road, **Man Wa Lane** ㉖ is lined with the chop-makers who carve elaborate name stamps from blocks of stone. These chops are not only practical instruments (formal documents in Hong Kong require a "chop", used as a signature), but works of ancient Chinese craftsmanship. Perhaps only the Arabs have as much respect for calligraphy as the Chinese. Watching a Man Wa chop-carver sculpt a customer's name out of a small block of

stone, ivory, jade or wood is an interesting experience. There are male and female chop styles: when background material is carved out, the chop is male; when the characters are carved out, it's female. The chop is also important in other Asian countries, particularly Japan.

The heart of Western

As Queen's Road Central becomes **Queen's Road West**, the architecture becomes more traditional with a few open-fronted "shop-houses", where traditional wholesale trading houses and shops overflow onto the pavements with a unique Hong Kong mix of everything from daily neces-

Western was the first district to be settled by the British when they arrived in Hong Kong in 1841, although malaria soon scared them away, leaving this part of Hong Kong Island to the Chinese immigrants who arrived in the early 1850s.

ABOVE RIGHT: typical food stall in Western. **BELOW:** a small shop in Western. **BELOW RIGHT:** all kinds of odds and ends can be found along Hollywood Road and Cat Street.

Recommended Restaurants, Bars, Pubs & Cafés on pages 118–121

sities to traditional Chinese medicine, money from the "Bank of Hell" and funerary items to burn at graves and handmade cake moulds and dim sum baskets.

West from Ma Wa Lane are some of the most aromatic streets in Hong Kong. **Wing Lok Street** ㉗, **Bonham Street** and **Des Voeux Road West** are the centre of the Chinese medicine trade in Hong Kong. Shops here specialise in selling herbs, ancient remedies, dried extracts of plants and animal parts. Specialists in delicacies such as bird's nest abound, as do stores selling a pungent range of dried seafoods, including abalone, sea cucumber and – more controversially – shark's fin. Hong Kong is a major centre for the world's trade in shark's fin. Once a regional delicacy, eaten occasionally by wealthy Chinese families in a few areas of southern China, shark's fin soup has become extremely popular throughout Greater China as a prestigious treat at banquets. With increasing wealth in the region, many species of shark are facing extinction.

One block inland on **Hillier Street** and **Jervois Street** is a mix of small teashops, cafés, print shops and merchants selling wholesale goods. It is a great neighbourhood to explore on foot, for poking into little alleys and for getting lost in the web of side streets. Look for the tea merchants, noodle specialists, Chinese sweets and preserved nuts, as well as stores selling traditional Chinese pots, pans

and bamboo steamers. On the cross-streets, minuscule stalls and workshops can often occupy less than 6 sq m (20 sq ft) of space.

On Morrison Street, close to the harbour, stands **Western Market** ㉘, a red-brick Edwardian-style structure. It was opened in 1906 and served for more than 80 years as a food market. Recognised as a historical landmark, its elegant architectural features were preserved and restored, and in 1991 it was converted into a shopping complex. It offers a diversity of handicrafts, fabric and souvenir stalls, as well as a Chinese restaurant on the top floor, enlivened by afternoon "tea dances".

From Western Market you can take a walkway across Connaught Road West to the Shun Tak Centre, which houses the Macau Ferry Terminal. Now you are in Western proper: the name of this neighbourhood, **Sai Ying Pun**, means "Western military camp", named after the first British camps were established here in the 1840s. The steep steps of Centre Street connect Bonham Road with Queen's Road

Chops are Chinese name stamps, and make good souvenirs. Chop-carvers carve your name into the marble, and thus personalised, your chop is sold complete with an ink pad and an attractive small box.

BELOW: delivery from Central Market.

Traffic on Queensway. In the background, The Center is a 73-storey building that comes alive at night in a hypnotic display. Bars of neon, girdling the whole structure, pulse through a wave of gradually changing colours.

BELOW: admiring the view on the Peak Tram.

West, and the architecture betrays the historical boundaries. The Chinese were not allowed to live above High Street in the 19th century and the area retains a flavour of an older Hong Kong, with small earth-god shrines outside each shop. Above High Street, European architecture reappears, especially around Hong Kong University, which was founded in 1911.

Further west

From Western it is possible to walk up towards the residential district of Pok Fu Lam. The hilly upper part of Western (which is actually part of the Mid-Levels) is quite different. Here the architecture is more Portuguese colonial than traditional Chinese – with tiled pitch roofs, stucco walls and projecting balconies. The **University of Hong Kong** has its campus here. The **University Museum and Art Gallery** ㉙ (Mon–Sat 9.30am–6pm, Sun 1.30–5.30pm; free; bus 3B, 23, 40, 40M or 103) at 94 Bonham Road is worth a look. Housed in

the 1930s Fung Ping Shan Building, it contains an interesting collection of pottery and porcelain dating back to the 7th century, although the most prized possession is the world's largest collection of bronzeware from the Yuan; contemporary art is exhibited in the adjoining T.T. Tsui Building. It also has a welcoming Tea Gallery where you can pause over a cup of Chinese tea.

Beyond the university is the residential district of Pok Fu Lam, while down by the harbour, **Kennedy Town** ㉚ is one of Hong Kong's oldest Chinese settlements, and one of the cheapest places to live on Hong Kong Island. Also here is the result of another huge land-reclamation project – the new **Western Harbour Crossing**, Hong Kong's third cross-harbour tunnel to Kowloon.

THE PEAK

The Peak, properly though rarely called **Victoria Peak** ㉛ (Shan Teng in Cantonese), is Hong Kong's most notable natural landmark, the resi-

Recommended Restaurants, Bars, Pubs & Cafés on pages 118–121

Once the **Peak Tramway** *(see panel, below)* was opened in 1888, the area quickly developed into one of the most sought-after places to live in Hong Kong – and has remained so ever since.

The upper terminus of the Peak Tram is the **Peak Tower** ㉜. Shaped like a wok, this is for many people one of the ugliest buildings in Hong Kong. Of course, the main reason for coming up to The Peak is to marvel at one of the world's finest vistas, which on Hong Kong's increasingly rare clear days should include a view all the way to mainland China. Many find the nighttime views even more incredible, a vast glittering swathe of electric light, most spectacular immediately below in Central and Wan Chai as the buildings attempt to outdo each other in their eye-catching displays. The Peak Tower was renovated in 2006, adding new shops, restaurants, and significantly more windows to make the most of the views. Best of all, the viewing platform was raised 30 metres (100ft) to the top of

dential aspiration of most of the population and goal of more than 7 million visitors a year.

Yet it wasn't always regarded with such awe. A travel writer once described it as "beautiful in the distance, but sterile and unpromising upon more close examination" (although that this was before reforestation took place – *see margin, page 105)*, and during the first six years of Hong Kong's history, hardly anybody travelled to its inhospitable heights. But as Hong Kong developed as a colony, the British sought out a hill resort away from the hot, malaria-infested lower elevations.

The Peak Tower is something of a tourist trap, full of overpriced souvenir shops.

ABOVE LEFT: the Peak Tower. **BELOW:** ascending on the Peak Tram.

The Peak Tram

The vertiginous Peak Tram – actually a funicular railway – is more than just a transport facility. Rising to 396 metres (1,299ft) above sea level in just seven minutes up gradients as steep as 27 degrees (1 in 2), the tram runs from 7am to midnight, and hasn't had a single accident since it began operation in 1888. It still has only two cars, each carrying 72 passengers and one driver, and is pulled up and lowered by 1,500-metre (5,000-ft) steel cables wound on drums. Eight minutes from the Garden Road terminus (which can be accessed by free open-top double-decker bus from Central Pier), the upper terminus at the Peak Tower is reached. The Peak Tram is also used by commuters.

Before the tram, sedan chairs transported privileged colonials to the top. Such coolie-powered transportation disappeared long ago, but palanquins are still used during charity races once a year.

The Sky Terrace on top of the Peak Tower. For the clearest views, summer mornings after heavy rain has washed the polluted haze out of the air are the best bet – July is often the clearest month of the year. Early mornings are better than later in the day, although the Sky Terrace itself doesn't open until 10am.

the "wok". Now renamed the **Sky Terrace** (daily Mon–Fri 10am–11pm Sat, Sun 8am–11pm, charge), you can enjoy a superb 360-degree panorama and, if you are really lucky and visibility is good, see all the way to mainland China. There is also a Sky Gallery with regular outdoor exhibitions.

For indoor entertainment, the Peak Tower has its very own **Madame Tussaud's** (open daily 10am–10pm; charge; www.madame-tussauds.com.hk), with over 100 waxworks of Asian and international celebrities that delight photo-op-crazed visitors. For gamers, the

EA Experience lets you try out the latest interactive games and virtual worlds free of charge (Mon–Fri noon–9pm, Sat–Sun 10am–10pm).

Peak walks

There are a variety of superb walks from the Peak Tower. **The Peak Trail** follows Lugard and Harlech roads to complete a circuit of Victoria Peak, affording magnificent views across the harbour and Kowloon to the north, Cheung Chau and Lantau to the west, and the great masses of junks and sampans at Aberdeen to the south, with Lamma Island beyond. This gentle 3-km (2-mile) walk, well signposted and shaded from the sun, takes about 50–60 minutes round-trip from the Peak Tower.

The area around the Peak Tower is in fact **Victoria Gap**, whereas the summit of Victoria Peak itself (552 metres/1,811 ft) lies to the west. Follow the Peak Trail until you reach Mount Austin Road, which winds up to the attractive **Victoria Peak Gardens**. The summit itself, with its pair of radio towers, is out of bounds.

It is possible to walk back down

Recommended Restaurants, Bars, Pubs & Cafés on pages 118–121

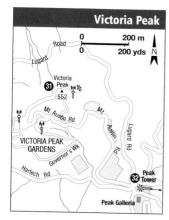

Victoria Peak

In the exclusive residential streets that meander around the Peak's wooded heights, flats and houses are rented by banks and corporate giants for their top executives at astronomical sums. In 2010 a 4-bed (3,600 sq ft) apartment rented for HK$200,000 (US$ 25,700) a month. A 5-bed (5,500 sq ft) house on The Peak cost HK$260 million (US$ 33.4 million) to buy.

to Central and indulge in some of the finer views and footpaths through The Peak's wooded slopes. The **Central Green Trail** – marked by 14 bilingual signboards highlighting points of interest – winds its way down from Barker Road, across May Road and then via paths named Clovelly, Brewin and Tramway back to the Garden Road terminus. Another short, steep route through the forest, sign-posted to the Mid-Levels, descends northwards from Findlay Road (just below the Peak Tower) to the beginning of the Old Peak Road. A popular longer walk descends westwards through Pokfulam Country Park, and constitutes Stage 1 of the **Hong Kong Trail**. For more ambitious hikers, the rest of the trail heads east for some 50km (30 miles) all the way to Tai Tam and on to Shek O *(see page 148)*. Nature-lovers can wander through forests of bamboo and fern, stunted Chinese pines, hibiscus and vines of wonderful, writhing beauty. Ornithologists log sightings of birds such as blue magpies and crested goshawks.   ❑

ABOVE LEFT: high on the Hong Kong Trail at Jardine's Lookout.
BELOW: an unusually clear day allows a truly spectacular view from The Peak.

BEST RESTAURANTS, BARS, PUBS, CLUBS AND CAFÉS

Restaurants

Prices for a three-course dinner per person with one beer or glass of house wine:
$ = under HK$150
$$ = HK$150–300
$$$ = HK$300–500
$$$$ = over HK$500

Central's main restaurant and bar areas are in the streets in and around Lan Kwai Fong and SoHo. The Peak has a choice of cafés for a snack and smart bar-restaurants. In Western, try the streets between Western Market and Grand Millennium Plaza for good lunch deals.

Cantonese

City Hall Chinese Restaurant
5–7 Edinburgh Place ☎ 2921 2840 ⓒ L & D daily. **$$** [p307, D2]
A raucous Cantonese institution, serving good dim sum from old-fashioned trolleys wheeled around by uniformed staff. A vast, well-lit space with views out across the harbour.

The Grand Stage
2/F, Western Market, 323 Des Voeux Rd, Sheung Wan ☎ 2815 2311 ⓒ L & D daily. **$$** [p306, B1]
On the top floor of this restored four-storey colonial building, the high ceilings and white tablecloths set the scene for something different, although the menu is familiar – dim sum and Cantonese favourites.

Luk Yu Teahouse
24–26 Stanley St ☎ 2523 1970 ⓒ L & D daily. **$$** [p307, C2]
Established in 1933, this traditional Cantonese teahouse in the heart of Central is legendary for its bad-mannered management. Despite that, chauffeurs tend the lined-up Mercs outside while tycoons and criminal kingpins in dark glasses take their yum cha. Tourists take second place, but the food can be excellent.

Mak's Noodles
77 Wellington St ☎ 2854 3810 ⓒ L & D (closes 8pm) daily. **$** [p306, C2]
If wonton noodle soup is Hong Kong's national dish, this is the place to sample it. Pale-pink, prawn-filled pillows of pastry float on a nest of noodles in a beef tendon broth tinged with fermented shrimp paste. Better by far than its imitative neighbours.

Ser Wong Fun
30 Cochrane St ☎ 2543 1032 ⓒ L & D daily. **$** [p306, C2]
A good example of a traditional family-run restaurant with an emphasis on seasonal Cantonese cuisine. A great place to try snake soup in winter.

Tim's Kitchen
93 Jervois St, Sheung Wan ☎ 2543 5919 ⓒ L & D daily. **$$** [p306, B1]
Lunch-time offerings are simple-but-excellent Cantonese dishes designed to satisfy office crowds, while the dinner menu reveals why such a modest restaurant has a Michelin star. Highlights include crab claw with winter melon and pomelo skin with shrimp roe.

Yung Kee
32–40 Wellington St ☎ 2522 1624 ⓒ L & D daily. **$$** [p306–7, C2]
Visiting the Yung Kee is like taking a 1970s time warp. A true Hong Kong institution, with a rags-to-riches history spanning almost 70 years. Justly famous for its roast goose and the obligatory thousand-year-old eggs. Also great for dim sum.

Other Chinese

Bistro Manchu
33 Elgin St ☎ 2536 9218 ⓒ L & D daily. **$$** [p306, B2]
Authentic northern Chinese cooking with an emphasis on dumplings and a variety of intriguing vegetarian and "healthy" options. Clean, comfortable and well decorated.

Yellow Door
6/F, 37 Cochrane St ☎ 2858 6555 ⓒ L & D Mon–Fri, D only Sat. **$$** [p306, C2]
Hard to find, but worth

Café chains in Hong Kong

Like almost every city these days (including Macau, Shenzhen and Guangzhou), Hong Kong has its fair share of **Starbucks** dotted around the urban area. The main local competitor is **Pacific Coffee**, which offers a similar choice of drinks from lattes to ice teas, a more varied menu of food, and plush armchairs. **Mix** has a dozen outlets, mainly on Hong Kong Island, and promises vitality with its smoothies, fresh juices, wheatgrass drinks, salads and wraps. As well as drinks, **Cafe O** offers light meals, pizza-by-the-metre, and is also licensed. Its outlets in Central and Wan Chai are open 24 hours.

Almost all cafés have wireless Internet and many provide PCs, but this is not consistent across all outlets.

the effort, Yellow Door is owned by one of Hong Kong's best-known artists – obvious from the simple but inventive interior. High-quality, authentic Sichuanese and Shanghainese menus are served at lunch and dinner respectively.

European

Ola European Cuisine
22 Ying Wo St, Sheung Wan
☏ 2851 0012 ☏ L & D daily. $ [p306, C1]
Hidden gem with back-street French bistro vibe. Owner, host and chef David Chiu cooked in five-star hotels before setting up this family business. Browse the quirky collection of vinyl and spin a 33 while awaiting your order.

Indian

Massala
10 Mercer St, Sheung Wan
☏ 2581 9777
☏ L & D. $ [p306, B1]
Friendly family-run Indian restaurant with an extensive choice of favourites. Standouts include bhindi masala, fish madras, tarka dhal and tandoori chicken. The set menus are excellent value.

Tandoor
1/F, Lyndhurst Tower, 1 Lyndhurst Terr ☏ 2845 2262 ☏ L & D daily. $$ [p306, C2]
Hong Kong's top Indian eatery features life-sized

Sikh guards cast in solid silver at the door, with big-screen Bollywood and live Indian music in the first-floor dining room. A top-notch buffet is served for lunch.

International

Dot Cod Seafood Restaurant & Oyster Bar
B4 Basement, Prince's Building, 10 Chater Rd
☏ 2810 6988 ☏ B, L & D daily. $$$ [p307, D2]
Extensive options for seafood-lovers, including a "green" menu of sustainably sourced fish and shellfish at this smart fish restaurant on Statue Square. Lunch is packed out with business types, but there are reasonably priced sets and happy hours, too.

Café Grey Deluxe
Level 49, The Upper House, Pacific Place, 88 Queensway. ☏ 3968 1106 ☏ B, L & D daily. $$–$$$ [p307, E1]
Chef Gray Kunz has returned from New York to share his unique style of European classics. Open for breakfast, lunch and dinner, all represent remarkable value for this world-renowned chef's creations.

Harvester
G/F, Shop A–B, Yardley Commercial Building, 3 Connaught Rd, Sheung Wan
☏ 2542 4788 ☏ L & D daily. $ [p306, B1]
Close to Western Market,

Harvester is a healthy-eating option that serves a mix of Chinese and Western vegetarian cuisine buffet-style. The kitchen closes at 9pm.

La Pampa
32 Staunton St, SoHo
☏ 2868 6959 ☏ L & D daily, D only Sat & Sun. $$$ [p306, C2]
Meat-lovers in the know head to this intimate restaurant for some of the best steaks in town. Aside from tender South American beef, there's an interesting selection of Argentinian dishes and wines, but – as you'd expect – there is little on offer for vegetarians.

Life
10 Shelley St ☏ 2810 9777 ☏ L & D daily. $ [p306, C2]
Popular vegetarian restaurant right next to

the Mid-Levels Escalator. Attracts dreadlocks and gym-toned executives who munch on flapjacks and alfalfa between sips of passion fruit and carrot juice.

Peak Lookout
121 Peak Rd ☏ 2849 1000 ☏ L & D daily. $$ [off p306, B4]
This historic stand-alone building in its own grounds on Victoria Peak is like an Alpine hunting lodge transported to the tropics. Offers great views over the south side of Hong Kong Island. Vivid, lively and colourful, with a very international menu.

RED Bar & Restaurant
Podium Level 4, IFC Mall
☏ 8129 8882 ☏ L&D daily (bar open until 3am Fri & Sat). $$$ [p307, D1]
A glitch in the licensing laws means RED can't

RIGHT: Cantonese food is served as fresh as possible.

Prices for a three-course dinner per person with one beer or glass of house wine:

$ = under HK$150
$$ = HK$150–300
$$$ = HK$300–500
$$$$ = over HK$500

serve you drinks outside, but you can fetch them yourself to enjoy the coolest harbour view in town. As part of the PURE fitness group, there's plenty of light Californian cuisine mixed in with substantial burgers, a variety of home-made pasta and Cajun food.

Watermark

Central Pier No.7 (Star Ferry) ℂ 2167 7251 ℂ L & D daily. $$$ [p307, D1]
Located at Level P at the Star Ferry Pier, with its huge windows and harbour views, Watermark is an elegant, and welcome, addition to the waterfront scene. Cuisine is "contemporary continental", and includes a user-friendly wine list. It's best to book ahead to make the most of the panoramic 270° views.

Italian
Di Vino

73 Wyndham St ℂ 2167 8883 ℂ L & D Mon–Fri, D only Sat. $$ [p307, C3]
Smooth and savvy wine bar and restaurant operated by a trio of charming Italians. Always has an interesting menu, and serves tapas-style appetisers gratis to guests.

Pizza Express

21 Lyndhurst Terrace ℂ 2850 7898 ℂ L & D daily. $$ [p306, C2]
This Far East franchise of the famous chain serves well-prepared pizza and pasta from a straightforward menu.

Japanese
Tokio Joe

16 Lan Kwai Fong ℂ 2525 1889 ℂ L & D daily. $$ [p307, C3]
Japanese-style cuisine is becoming increasingly influential in Hong Kong, and this lively sushi restaurant offers a youthful take on formal traditions in the heart of Lan Kwai Fong. Well known for its comprehensive selection of sake.

Korean
Korea House

G/F, 119–121 Connaught Rd, Sheung Wan ℂ 2544 0007 ℂ L & D daily. $$ [p306, B1]
Established in 1965 as a focus for Hong Kong's Korean community. This off-the-beaten-track eatery serves authentic bulgogi and kimchee.

Malaysian
CoCo Nut Curry House

8 Wing Wah Lane ℂ 2523 9611 ℂ L & D daily. $$ [p306, C2]
The best of a bunch of great little restaurants, whose fold-up tables and chairs overflow all over this side street just off Lan Kwai Fong. Watch the chef make fresh roti and enjoy with Malay favourites like beef rendang.

Middle Eastern
Habibi Cafe

112–114 Wellington St ℂ 2544 3886 ℂ L & D daily. $$ [p306, C2]
With Egyptian black-and-white movies playing in the background, and authentic cuisine, this small nook is ideal for an informal meal of tasty Middle Eastern cuisine. For more sumptuous surroundings visit Habibi Restaurant next door.

Olive

32 Elgin St ℂ 2521 160 ℂ L & D daily. $$$ [p306, B2]

Very popular Maghreb and Middle East-inspired restaurant. The menu features contemporised classics like *bastilla*, a rich pigeon pie seasoned with cinnamon, and Fatima's fingers, stuffed cigar-like tubes of crisp filled pastry. The long, slim dining room has the air of a Moroccan souk.

Thai
Lime

14 Hau Wo St, Kennedy Town ℂ 2581 9992 ℂ D only. $-$$ [off p306, A1]
There's no chance of missing this neon-lime restaurant, which is drawing diners out west to Kennedy Town with its authentic Thai flavours. *Laab* – spicy minced meat wrapped in lettuce leaves – is a must-try, along with papaya salad and delicious *tom yum goong*.

Vietnamese
Nha Trang

88–90 Wellington St ℂ 2581 9992 ℂ L & D daily. $ [p306, C2]
Deservedly popular restaurant serving dishes such as *bun*, beef and chicken *pho*, grilled prawn rice paper rolls, and beef and watercress salad. Food is always fresh and fast and queues are common, so perhaps the grumpy waiting staff are just exhausted.

LEFT: noodles in Central. **ABOVE RIGHT:** Lan Kwai Fong on a Friday evening.

Bars, Pubs and Clubs

Baby B, G/F, Wo On Lane, Lan Kwai Fong. Tel: 2167 7244. Incense coils add to the vibe of this tiny bar next to a Taoist earth god shrine. 6m until late.

Barco, 42 Staunton St, SoHo. Tel: 2857 4478. Small stylish bar with a courtyard lounge area tucked away at the back.

Bex, 4/F, SoHo Square, 21 Lyndhurst Terrace, Tel: 3102 2066. Compact but cool bar for reasonably priced quiet early evening drinks on a balcony near the escalator. Fills up after 10pm.

The Captain's Bar, Mandarin Oriental Hong Kong, 5 Connaught Rd Central. Tel: 2522 0111. More a place to find captains of industry than seafarers, this Mandarin Oriental bar is now an institution in itself. Dress as if you mean business.

Club 71, B/F, 67 Hollywood Rd. Tel: 2858 7071. Friendly bar, tucked down an alley, behind Hollywood Rd. Named after Hong Kong's 1 July protests and attracts a low-key media crowd and politically minded locals.

Club 97, 9 Lan Kwai Fong. Tel: 2810 9333. One of the longest-running but still one of the hippest clubs. Friday night is gay night.

Club Feather Boa, 38 Staunton St, SoHo. Tel: 2857 7156. Like a regency drawing room; eclectic and so SoHo.

Dragon-i, The Centrium, 60 Wyndham St. Tel: 3110 1222. Operates a guest-list-only entrance policy, but you may call in advance to request entry. One of the "to be seen" places for minor and would-be celebs.

Dublin Jack, 1/F, 40 D'Aguilar St. Tel: 2543 0081. Lively Irish bar in Lan Kwai Fong. Plenty of Irish-style comfort food, Guinness and screens for sports.

The Fringe Club, 2 Lower Albert Rd. Tel: 2521 7485. Live bands downstairs, or a relaxing beer garden on the roof – a rare gem.

Frites, 1/F, Queen's Pl, 74 Queen's Rd Central. Tel: 2179 5179. Classy place with Belgian beer on draught, plenty of bottled choices and tasty fare to soak it all up.

Hei Hei Club, 3/F, On Hing Terrace, Wyndham St. Tel: 2899 2068. Two open-air balconies with comfy seating around jacuzzis and a pool plus dance floor.

Le Jardin, 1/F, 10 Wing Wah Lane. Tel: 2877 1100. The best outdoor bar in Central/ Lan Kwai Fong. Laid-back atmosphere with a good mix of people.

Linq, G/F, 35 Pottinger St. Tel: 2971 0680. Describes itself as a pre-club bar, but stays open until 2am on weekdays and later at weekends. Laid-back.

Makumba Africa Bar, G/F Garley Building, 48 Peel St, SoHo. Tel 2522 0544. Frequent live music acts and Afro beats provide the soundtrack at this vast bar. African-inspired food and drinks too.

Nu, Winly Building, 1–5 Elgin St, SoHo. Tel: 2549 8386. Smooth lounge club, takes its music seriously. Occasionally hosts speed-dating and tarot-card parties.

Pickled Pelican, 43 Wyndham St. Tel: 2868 6026. English-style pub, HK-style prices. Pub grub and TV sports.

Pier 7, 7 Viewing Deck, Central Pier 7. Tel: 2167 8377. Located on top of the Central Star Ferry terminal, Pier 7's outdoor deck faces the Central skyscrapers. There's a long wine list and happy hour from 6–9pm, with free nibbles while they last.

Soda, 79 Wyndham St. Tel: 2522 8118. Australian-style lounge bar, attracts young crowd.

Staunton's, 10 Staunton St, SoHo. Tel: 2973 6611. Long-running trendy bar.

V-13 Vodka Bar, 13 Old Bailey St, SoHo. Tel: 2525 1513. Unpretentious bar, with decent prices, plus movie nights and quirky promotions.

Yumla, Lower Basement, Harilela House, 79 Wyndham St. Tel: 2147 2382. Packed little dance club with great music.

THE STAR FERRY

Costing just a couple of Hong Kong dollars, the crossing of Victoria Harbour aboard one of the Star Ferries is a visual feast that is over in just eight minutes

From ancient to modern, from Rolls-Royce to rickshaw, Hong Kong offers every mode of conveyance for rich and poor. But the territory's quintessential transport is the Star Ferry. Shunting back and forth across Victoria Harbour, these green-and-white ferries link the community together in a way that is both symbolic and endlessly practical.

The fleet would win few prizes for glamorous design. Even the grandly named *Celestial Star* (other names include *Morning Star*, *Meridian Star*, *Shining Star* and *Twinkling Star)* is just one of a dozen juddering, smoke-belching people-movers. Yet the clanking gangways, weather-beaten coxswains and solid wooden decks have a timeless character.

The first of the current "Star" fleet made their maiden voyages in 1898, although earlier ferries began operating a quarter of a century before that. Until Hong Kong Island was connected to Kowloon by road tunnel in 1972 and the Mass Transit Railway (MTR) in 1979, the Star Ferry was the prime way to cross the harbour – these days it is generally quicker to use the MTR unless you are travelling between points close to the piers.

BELOW: not all Star Ferries are green and white – some feature (temporary) custom paint-jobs. The main route is between Central and Tsim Sha Tsui, but there are also Wan Chai to Tsim Sha Tsui and Hung Hom to Central and Wan Chai services.

LEFT: the top deck is more expensive and gives slightly better views. Seat backs can be moved back and forth, depending upon which way the ferry and the view are headed. Tourists, local or otherwise, are easy to spot on the Star Ferry – they are looking at the scenery. Commuters, on the other hand, will be looking at the horse-racing news or reading a novel, looking up only when the ferry eases to the gate.

HONG KONG'S TRAMS

A kind of double act with the Star Ferry, Hong Kong's fleet of electric trams was introduced in 1904, and has remained virtually unchanged since 1925, when the familiar double-decker cars came into service. There are plans, however, to modernise the fleet – a handful of vehicles have new seats and air-conditioning, although it is unclear if the old-style trams are to be phased out entirely.

As with the Star Ferry, riding the tram is not only one of the city's best bargains (a flat fare of HK$2 however far you go) but also a great way to sightsee – as long as you can get a seat on the top deck, preferably at the front where the views are accompanied by a refreshing breeze. It's a great vantage point from which to observe the city go about its business. A seat at the rear of the top deck is also good, and gives wonderful photo opportunities.

Redecorated annually according to advertising-agency whim, the trams – known locally as the "ding-ding" for the bells that announce their arrival – run daily from 6am until midnight. The line runs right along the north coast of Hong Kong Island: from Kennedy Town in the west to the heart of the city at Des Voeux Road Central, from where the route proceeds along Queensway and through the middle of Wan Chai and Causeway Bay before continuing past Victoria Park to North Point or Shau Kei Wan in the east. A branch leads off to Happy Valley and the terminus south of the famous racecourse. Vintage-style trams can also be hired out for private parties.

ABOVE: as reclamation continues to narrow the harbour, the Star Ferry Pier in Central moved northwards in 2006. The new location is next to the Outlying Islands ferry piers in front of the IFC2 tower. The distance across to Kowloon is now shorter than ever, but journey times remain the same, as choppier waters prolong docking manoeuvres.

RIGHT: Central District's new Star Ferry Pier has an Edwardian-style clock tower and overall retro appearance, replacing the functional 1950s design of its predecessor.

LEFT: Star Ferries only ply between Hong Kong Island and Kowloon, but ferries to Lantau and elsewhere offer deck-top views and longer cruises. If you want a view, avoid the fast ferries, or – best of all – take a harbour cruise (these can be arranged via the HKTB: see page 280).

Recommended Restaurants, Bars, Pubs and Clubs on pages 133–5

WAN CHAI AND CAUSEWAY BAY

Wan Chai and Causeway Bay offer an authentic taste of modern Hong Kong, with some of the SAR's best shopping and nightlife

CHINA

Hong Kong

East of Central lie two crowded, vibrant districts that wholeheartedly embrace the local passion for eating, drinking and shopping. Home to almost 200,000 people, Wan Chai and Causeway Bay have a great deal to offer anyone wishing to sample the authentic flavour of modern Hong Kong. The tramline (which was on the waterfront when it was built at the beginning of the 20th century) runs right the way through these districts, and provides cheap and convenient transportation as well as numerous photo opportunities from the top deck.

Admiralty

Admiralty ❶, bridging Central and Wan Chai, used to be the site of a British naval station. These days it is an agglomeration of gleaming office towers and smart shopping malls.

When the British first came to Hong Kong, they were unable to find a suitable site for a naval garrison, so HMS *Tamar* was moored offshore just east of Central (or "Victoria" as it was then known). Many years later, after the Japanese occupation in World War II, the Tamar naval compound was moved ashore. After

the handover, the compound was turned over to the Chinese People's Liberation Army. Following more than a century of reclamation projects, the shoreline is fixed and – after years as a building site – will soon be developed. The Hong Kong Central Government Complex, Tamar is likely to be completed in 2013 to the west of the garrison of the People's Liberation Army, formerly known as the Prince of Wales Building.

The epicentre of Admiralty is **Pacific Place**, one of Hong Kong's

Main attractions
HONG KONG CONVENTION AND
  EXHIBITION CENTRE
NIGHTLIFE AROUND
  LOCKHART ROAD
HAPPY VALLEY HORSE-RACING
CAUSEWAY BAY SHOPPING

LEFT: on the tramlines, Johnston Road.
RIGHT: the air-conditioned glitz of Pacific Place shopping mall.

The Hong Kong Convention and Exhibition Centre is used for regular events from trade fairs to pop concerts.

ABOVE RIGHT: Wan Chai's urban jungle.

ritziest malls, showcasing the top names in fashion and housing three of Hong Kong's best hotels: the Conrad, Marriott and Island Shangri-La.

WAN CHAI

From Admiralty, it is just a few minutes' walk to Wan Chai, which has long elicited knowing nudges from residents because of its reputation as a red-light district – although over the past years most of the girlie bars have been replaced by a lively mix of bars and pubs. By day, it is a regular business district where locals head for less expensive shopping and dining.

Wan Chai's multi-faceted character builds up in layers, starting with the older area between the hillside and the tramline, which segues into the lively nightlife district around Hennessy and Lockhart roads, and finally the smart waterfront area.

Close to the waterfront (north of multi-lane Gloucester Road), in an area sometimes known as Wan Chai

North, are the **Academy for Performing Arts ❷** and the **Hong Kong Arts Centre ❸**, two popular venues for theatrical and cultural performances. The Arts Centre also has galleries, rehearsal rooms and a café with views of the harbour.

Jutting out into the harbour is the futuristic **Hong Kong Convention and Exhibition Centre ❹**, which underwent a HK$4.8 billion extension in order to serve as the venue for the formal handover ceremony in 1997 – the

Wan Chai and Causeway Bay

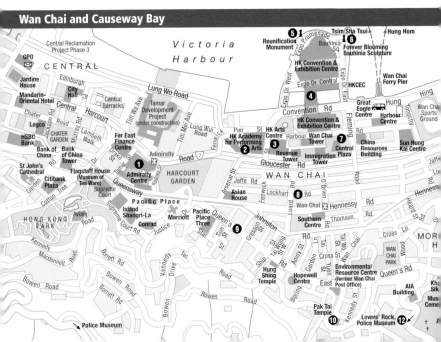

Recommended Restaurants, Bars, Pubs and Clubs on pages 133–5

obelisk is the **Reunification Monument ⑤**, which was erected to commemorate the handover and signed in gold by former Chinese President Jiang Zemin. Close by is the gaudy, golden **Forever Blooming Bauhinia Sculpture ⑥**. The bauhinia flower is indigenous to Hong Kong and, as the SAR's emblem, its five petals are printed on the Hong Kong flag. Further on past the tourist cruise operators is Wan Chai's own Star Ferry pier, with ferries to Tsim Sha Tsui.

building work was completed days (some say hours) before the ceremony. Over a decade on, the Convention Centre attracts over 3.3 million visitors a year to its exhibitions, conferences, trade shows and concerts.

The complex is adjacent to the svelte Grand Hyatt and the Renaissance Harbour View Hotel, and fringed on the harbourside by a waterfront **promenade**. At its northernmost point are two rather odd-looking statues. The tall black

The heart of Wan Chai

Elevated walkways lead south from the Convention Centre to the 78-storey **Central Plaza ⑦** office tower, currently Hong Kong's second highest building at 374 metres (1,227 ft), and on into the heart of Wan Chai around the MTR station and **Lockhart Road ⑧**.

From here westwards is a lively neighbourhood with numerous bars and restaurants housed beneath age-

The Bauhinia Sculpture, and neighbouring Reunification Monument, are well established as a favourite photo-stop for patriotic tourists from mainland China. There is a flag-raising ceremony here at 7.50 each morning.

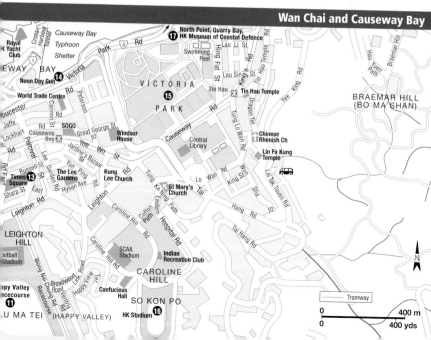

Wan Chai and Causeway Bay

Royal Yacht Club
Cross Harbour Tunnel
Causeway Bay Typhoon Shelter
Park Rd
North Point, Quarry Bay, **⑰** HK Museum of Coastal Defence
Lau Li St
Swimming Pool
Hau Yuen Path
Braemar Hill

EWAY BAY
Noon Day Gun **⑭**
Victoria Rd
World Trade Centre
Gloucester Rd
Jaffe Rd
Cannon St
Peterson St
Lau Sing St
Hing Fat St
Tin Hau
Tin Hau Temple Rd
Dragon Ter
VICTORIA ⑮ PARK
Tung Lo Wan Rd
Yee King Rd
BRAEMAR HILL (BO MA SHAN)

Lockhart Rd
Percival St
SOGO
Great George St
Jardine's Bazaar
Yun Ping Rd
Yee Wo St
Windsor House
Causeway Rd
Central Library
Chinese Rhenish Ch
Lin Fa Kung Temple

Russell St
Times Square ⑬
Sharp St East
Lee Garden Rd
The Lee Gardens
Hysan Ave
Kung Lee Church
Tung Ka Eastern Path
Lo Wan
St Mary's Church
King St
Wun Sha St
Lan Tak Tsuen Rd

LEIGHTON HILL
Leighton Rd
Caroline Hill
Cotton Path
Hospital Rd
Hang Rd
Tai Hang Rd

otball Stadium
Caroline Hill Rd
SCAA Stadium
Indian Recreation Club
CAROLINE HILL

ppy Valley acecourse
Wong Nai Chung Rd
Broadwood Rd
Link Road
Ventris Rd
Happy View Rd
Racecourse
Confucius Hall
SO KON PO
U MA TEI (HAPPY VALLEY)
HK Stadium **⑯**

Tramway

0 — 400 m
0 — 400 yds

N

Lockhart Road is the neon-lit hub of Wan Chai's restaurant and bar scene.

ing office buildings. During the 1960s, Wan Chai was a favourite rest-and-recreation destination for tens of thousands of troops fighting in the Vietnam War. It was during this period that the area earned its reputation as a tawdry but thriving red-light district, captured in the famous film *The World of Suzie Wong*. Four decades on, a few diehard girlie bars on Lockhart Road remain and can be easily identified by their black-curtained doors. Today's Wan Chai is a mix of bars and all-night establishments that pull in a varied mix of expats, locals and out-of-towners, who start off in more expensive areas like Lan Kwai Fong and SoHo, then gravitate to Wan Chai to let rip.

There are a few rather anachronistic British-style pubs in the area, but international-style bars – with sports and music on plasma screens and a young clientele – are the more typical after-hours offering.

ABOVE RIGHT: shrine at Hung Shing Temple. **BELOW:** still from the classic 1960 film *The World of Suzie Wong,* set in the Wan Chai red-light district.

Queen's Road East

Two blocks inland from Lockhart Road, cross the tram tracks on Johnston Road and take a walk through Wan Chai Street Market. Wan Chai's huge urban regeneration project has seen some shophouses *(tong lau)* torn down in favour of offices – but others have been preserved, for instance the four elegantly restored tenement buildings at 60–66 Johnston Road *(see Pawn restaurant, page 134).*

Beyond the market, **Queen's Road East ❾** is the place to track down home furnishings of all kinds, from cool, modern designer shops to Chinese traditional rosewood furniture.

This neighbourhood also has two traditional Chinese temples that provide a glimpse of the old way of life in stark contrast to their modern surroundings. On Queen's Road East next to a narrow lane of steps leading up towards the Mid-Levels is the tiny, dark **Hung Shing Temple**. Legend has it that this temple, built on top of huge boulders, was named after a Tang-dynasty official who was renowned for his extreme virtue and his ability to make predictions that proved to be of great value to traders. Perhaps by coincidence, several small banks in the neighbourhood are filled with groups of elderly "traders" who stare at computer screens to follow the share-price movements of the stock market.

Much more impressive is the **Pak Tai Temple** ❿ at the top of Stone Nullah Lane, a triple-halled temple noted for its 400-year-old, 3-metre (10-ft) statue of the deity Pak Tai, who assures harmony on earth. The temple itself was not built until 1863. There are usually old men and women pottering around in the dark recesses of the temple, lighting incense sticks or laying out offerings.

Back on Queen's Road East, the former **Wan Chai Post Office** (1912), on the corner of Wan Chai Gap Road, now houses the **Environmental Resource Centr**e (Wed–Mon 10am–

5pm). Take a look inside at the original wooden counter and red postboxes; nature-lovers can pick up a leaflet on the 1.5-km (1-mile) **Wan Chai Green Trail**, which starts beside the 80-year-old mango tree and giant candlenut tree just outside.

Take a turn up 19th-century Ship Street to discover the shiny new Wan Chai on Star Street with lounge bars, teashops, restaurants and Pacific Place Three office tower.

Happy Valley

At the eastern end of Queen's Road East is one of the oldest settlements on Hong Kong Island, developed after early colonial settlers abandoned Western District due to malaria. This second settlement was named **Happy Valley**, reportedly because a cartographer's girlfriend accepted his proposal of marriage there. It was far enough from the sea, somewhat deserted and, importantly, didn't have malaria-ridden rice farms in its vicinity.

Shortly after settling in Happy Valley, the colony's residents created the greensward and edifice that has made the area world-famous amongst

TIP

The circular, 66-storey Hopewell Centre on Queen's Road East was once Hong Kong's tallest building. Take the glass-fronted elevator up to the 62nd floor and R66 – a revolving restaurant with an inspiring view of the city. Built close to the steep mountainside to its south, the Hopewell also provides a neat short cut to the Mid-Levels – take the elevator to the 17th floor and step out of the building onto Kennedy Road.

ABOVE LEFT: the Hopewell Centre's circular tower.
BELOW: gridlock on Gloucester Road.

On the hillside above Happy Valley, the 4-km (2½-mile) Bowen Road walk (accessed via Stubbs Road) is one of Hong Kong's best urban strolls. Along the route you'll come to Lovers' Rock, where locals flock on the 6th, 12th and 26th days of each lunar month to light joss sticks, hang wine bottles on the tree opposite the rock, and pray for harmonious marriages.

ABOVE RIGHT AND BELOW: at the Wednesday evening races, Happy Valley.

horse racing fans: the Hong Kong Jockey Club's **Happy Valley Racecourse** ⓫. During the September to July season, races are held here most Wednesday nights – as well as at Sha Tin Racecourse at the weekend. A night out at the Happy Valley track is a quintessential Hong Kong experience and less expensive than most (*see pages 136–7*).

If you can't make it to the actual races, visit the **Hong Kong Racing Museum** (Tue–Sun 10am–5pm; free), at the Happy Valley Stand inside the racecourse. The museum has eight galleries and a video presentation that tell the history of horse-racing in Hong Kong, and

the locals' all-consuming obsession with it.

Above the valley

For panoramic views, head up to leafy Bowen Road and Lovers' Rock (*see margin, left*). For more good views of the harbour, branch off uphill to the left at Wan Chai Gap Road for the **Police Museum** ⓬ (Tue 2–5pm, Wed–Sun 9am–5pm; free). The museum traces the history of the Hong Kong police force, packed with information on illegal narcotics, triads and occasional oddities such as the stuffed head of a tiger shot in 1915 after it killed a policeman.

CAUSEWAY BAY

Beyond Canal Road to the east of Wan Chai is **Causeway Bay** (Tung Lo Wan), one of Hong Kong's premier shopping areas and a hive of activity from early morning until late at night.

Causeway Bay's modern history began in 1972 when the Cross-Harbour Tunnel opened to link Hong Kong Island and Kowloon by road for the first time. There are now three cross-harbour tunnels,

but this one is still the busiest. It transformed the neighbourhood into a thriving urban area, these days best-known as a place where you can shop and dine late into the night and where retail space is some of the most expensive on the planet. The streets are often crowded to the point of being uncomfortable, even by Hong Kong standards, and pollution levels are notoriously bad, exacerbated at times by the "canyon effect" of its narrow streets and tall buildings, which trap exhaust fumes.

Times Square , a few blocks south of the crossroads near Sogo Department Store in Causeway Bay, is the area's biggest mall, with 14 floors of shops and restaurants, plus a cinema. The streets around include an exhaustive mix of factory outlets, designer boutiques, high-end fashion chains and other malls like the elegant Lee Gardens on tree-lined Hysan Avenue.

On the waterfront

The bay here was spanned by a causeway before it disappeared into a great land-reclamation project in the 1950s; the former coastline is traced by Tung Lo Wan Road, while the present-day "bay" is occupied by the **Royal Hong Kong Yacht Club** (nostalgic members voted to keep the club's royal title, although the Chinese translation makes no allusion to the House of Windsor) and the Typhoon Shelter.

This part of Hong Kong's waterfront also features a unique genuflection to the musical genius of Noël Coward: the **Noonday Gun** ⑭. Nobody knows for sure why the gun is fired at noon every day, but the story goes that the ritual dates back to the mid-19th century (although the present cannon was installed in 1982), when one of the Jardine's opium ships sailed into the harbour and an over-excited minion gave the vessel a 21-gun salute. The egotisti-

cal governor was incensed that a mere trader should receive the same greeting as himself, so, as penance, he ordered that the gun be fired at noon every day in perpetuity. Despite the demise of the colonial era, the (Jardine-owned) tradition looks likely to continue just as long as Jardine keeps trading.

Victoria Park

Causeway Bay is bounded on the east by **Victoria Park** ⑮, named after Queen Victoria, whose statue (moved here from Statue Square in Central after World War II) can be seen surveying the activities of her former subjects. One of the less loyal daubed her with red paint, and traces

> *In Hong Kong*
> *They strike a gong*
> *And fire off a*
> *noonday gun*
> *To reprimand each*
> *inmate who's in late.*
>
> Noël Coward
> *Mad Dogs and Englishmen*

ABOVE: the noonday gun ritual has survived.
BELOW: Wan Chai and Causeway Bay are good places to look for a tailor-made suit.

are still visible despite the efforts of cleaning staff. This welcome swathe of parkland has a swimming pool, jogging tracks and tennis courts and is popular with t'ai chi devotees in the early morning. Tens of thousands of people gather here on special occasions, such as Chinese New Year (when flower markets dominate) and, notably, during the Mid-Autumn Festival, when the park is illuminated with lanterns.

At the southernmost reach of Causeway Bay, the striking form of the 40,000-seat **Hong Kong Stadium** ⑯ is the SAR's largest outdoor venue, and host to the annual Rugby Sevens (see panel, below).

During the Mid-Autumn Festival, Victoria Park is illuminated by colourful lanterns – a beautiful sight.

ABOVE RIGHT: Hong Kong Stadium. **BELOW:** getting into the spirit of the Rugby Sevens.

North Point and beyond

Beyond Victoria Park, the urban strip continues more or less unbroken all the way to Shau Kei Wan. If you have the time, it is interesting to take a tram through these residential areas (you can then return westwards more rapidly by MTR). You'll pass through the old Shanghainese residential neighbourhood of **North Point** to the newly emerging bars and restaurants

of **Quarry Bay**, and the shopping extravaganza of **Tai Koo Shing**.

Further east at Shau Kei Wan, the well-interpreted **Hong Kong Museum**

of **Coastal Defence** ⑰ (Fri–Wed 10am–5pm; charge, but free on Wed), details HK maritime military history. The museum is housed in a 19th-century fort, 15 minutes' walk from Shau Kei Wan MTR station. The **Hong Kong Film Archive** (Fri–Wed, 10am–8pm, or 15 minutes after last screening; www.filmarchive.gov.hk) near Sai Wan Ho MTR is also well worth a look, while the up-and-coming strip of bars and restaurants at **Lei King Wan** (aka SoHo East) is just around the corner. ❑

The Rugby Sevens

The Hong Kong Rugby Sevens is one of the biggest parties in the city. Twenty-four national teams take part at the Hong Kong Stadium in Causeway Bay, and the atmosphere and festivities, plus the fast and furious game, make for an exciting event. The South Stand is infamous as the place where elaborate fancy dress and heavy drinking are the order of the day.

Held on the third weekend in March, tickets sell out quickly (www.hksevens. com). If you miss out, you can share some of the atmosphere in the marquees at the Sevens Village, next door in the grounds of the Indian Recreation Club. Matches are shown live on a huge plasma screen with handy bar access, and the party goes on into the night.

BEST RESTAURANTS, BARS, PUBS AND CLUBS

Restaurants

Prices for a three-course dinner per person with one beer or glass of house wine:

$ = under HK$150
$$ = HK$150–300
$$$ = HK$300–500
$$$$ = over HK$500

Wan Chai has a diverse selection of restaurants and cuisines, with the main focus around Lockhart and Jaffe roads. In Causeway Bay, Times Square and the surrounding streets have some of the best choices.

Cantonese

Dim Sum

63 Sing Woo Rd, Happy Valley 🄲 2834 8893 🄲 L & D daily. **$$** [off p308, B-C4]
Crowded little eatery in a sleepy neighbourhood that is widely appreciated for its well-above-average dim sum. A clean and efficient operation housed in a decadent Shanghai-style teahouse.

Dynasty

3/F, Renaissance Harbour View Hotel, 1 Harbour Rd, Wan Chai 🄲 2802 8888 🄲 L & D daily. **$$$** [p308, B2]
Dynasty's palatial dining hall is a long-standing Hong Kong institution. The chef is a highly

regarded barbecue expert, but the kitchen excels in all areas. Look for seasonal delicacies like snake soup.

Farmhouse

I/F Ming An Plaza, 8 Sunning Rd, Causeway Bay 🄲 2881 1331 🄲 L & D daily. **$$$** [p309, D3]
Farmhouse aims to resurrect "home-style" Cantonese cooking, which puts emphasis on natural flavours and textures. Specialities include stuffed chicken wings and simply steamed grouper.

Forum

485 Lockhart Rd, Causeway Bay 🄲 2891 2516 🄲 L & D daily. **$$$$** [p309, C2]
Celebrity owner Yeung Koon Yat is the Bao Yu king. Bao Yu are preserved abalone from Japan, and Yeung is acknowledged as the undisputed master of their lengthy and complicated preparation. These dehydrated shellfish are bank-breakingly expensive, but other Cantonese dishes are, by contrast, surprisingly reasonable. The opulent kitsch decor features photos of Yeung pressing palms with an endless procession of dignitaries, celebrities and politicians.

Tai Woo

27 Percival St, Causeway Bay 🄲 2893 0822 🄲 L & D daily. **$$** [p309, C2]
Little-known and well off the tourist trail, Tai Woo is very highly regarded by locals. With its exemplary service and its highly creative yet respectful menu, it is an example to restaurants everywhere. Check out the spare ribs in strawberry sauce or the hairy crab dumplings served in individual bamboo steamers.

Victoria City

2/F, Sun Hung Kai Centre, 30 Harbour Rd, Wan Chai 🄲 2827 9938 🄲 D daily. **$$** [p308, B2]
Seafood heaven for

local Cantonese. Seen as one of the best for daily dim sum and well worth the trip. The highlight is steamed grouper. The open bright room can get very noisy when busy.

Other Chinese

Chuen Cheung Kui

108–120 Percival St, Causeway Bay 🄲 2577 3833 🄲 L & D daily. **$$** [p309, D3]
Long-standing Hakka specialist famous for chicken cooked in salt and served with a pungent garlic and scallion sauce. The ground-floor dining room offers congee, noodles and snacks, but the main event is up the stairs on the first floor.

RIGHT: vegetarian food at Kung Tak Lam restaurant.

Prices for a three-course dinner per person with one beer or glass of house wine:

$ = under HK$150
$$ = HK$150–300
$$$ = HK$300–500
$$$$ = over HK$500

Kung Tak Lam

10/F World Trade Centre, Causeway Bay, ☎ 2890 3127. Ⓒ L&D. **$** [p309, D2]
This outstanding vegetarian restaurant has views of the typhoon shelter and harbour. The extensive choice of dishes include Buddhist-style meat "look alike" dishes and Shanghainese classics like *xiao long bao*.

Quan Ju De Roast Duck Restaurant

4/F, China Resources Building, 26 Harbour Rd, Wan Chai ☎ 2884 9088 Ⓒ L & D daily. **$$** [p308, B2]
A Hong Kong branch of the legendary Peking Duck restaurant in Beijing. Pancakes, shredded scallions and dabs of hoi sin sauce. Highly organised and efficient.

Red Pepper

G/F, 7 Lan Fong Rd, Causeway Bay ☎ 2577 3811 Ⓒ L & D daily. **$$$** [p309, D2]
This long-established Sichuanese restaurant serves up authentic fiery dishes. For the cautious the menu has helpful chilli symbols to indicate heat, and for fans of spicy food, Red Pepper's sizzling chilli prawns are a must. No faux retro here, decor is much as it was in the 1970s.

Ye Shanghai

L3, Pacific Place, Admiralty ☎ 2918 9833 Ⓒ L & D daily. **$$** [p307, E3]
Cool and sophisticated with views over the hustle and bustle of Admiralty, this modern Shanghainese restaurant serves traditional dishes like *xiao long bao* (steamed dumplings stuffed with pork), drunken chicken and steamed hairy crab to appreciative diners.

Burmese

Golden Myanmar

379–389 Jaffe Rd, Wan Chai ☎ 2838 9305 Ⓒ L Mon–Fri, D daily. **$** [p308, C2]
A tiny hidden gem serving wonderful and very inexpensive Burmese cuisine. Stunning pickled tea salad or pork and preserved mango curry are to die for.

Indian

Curry Pot One

1/F, 68–70 Lockhart Rd, Wan Chai ☎ 2865 6099 Ⓒ L & D daily. **$** [p308, A3]
Classic Indian dishes in a cosy but bright venue, with cute two-table balcony. Lunch buffet is under HK$100, and the set "feasts" are excellent value, too.

Indonesian

Indonesia 1968

G/F, 28 Leighton Rd, Causeway Bay ☎ 2577 9981 Ⓒ L & D daily. **$** [p309, C3]
Serving up favourites like *gado gado*, *sambal rending* and *nasi goreng* since 1968, Indonesia has smartened up its decor to meet the high quality of its food – but remains good value.

International

Duetto

2/F, Sun Hung Kai Centre, 30 Harbour Rd ☎ 2827 7777 Ⓒ L & D daily. **$$$** [p308, B2]
Open daily from noon to 3pm and 6 to 11pm. Duetto's owners have combined two successful venues, and cuisines, to make one enormous restaurant. Choose from the outstanding Indian or Italian cuisine and enjoy panoramic harbour views from an outdoor terrace. It also hosts the monthly Punchline Comedy Club featuring some fine international comedians.

Lawry's Prime Rib

4/F, The Lee Gardens, 33 Hysan Ave, Causeway Bay ☎ 2907 2218 Ⓒ L & D daily. **$$$** [p309, D2–3]
When nothing but classic American-style prime rib roast beef with Yorkshire pudding will do, head to Lawry's. Prawn cocktails and English trifle are equally comforting and delicious.

The Pawn

62 Johnston Rd ☎ 2866 3444 Ⓒ L & D daily. **$$$$** [p308, A3]
This restored 19th-century pawn shop was an instant hit when it opened in 2008. The second-floor "Dining Room" serves Modern British cuisine, and

LEFT: cool decor at Wasabisabi. **RIGHT:** a well-stocked bar.

there's also a lounge bar and rooftop garden to enjoy.

Slim's
1 Wing Fung St, Wan Chai
☎ 2528 1661 ⓒ
L &D daily. **$$$**
[p308, A3]

One of Star Street's great little secrets, Slim's serves up great burgers and much more in a smart, but very narrow, space. It also has a decent range of tasty micro-brews and ales to choose from.

Thai
Simply Thai
11/F Times Square, Matheson St, Causeway Bay
☎ 2506 1212 ⓒ L
Mon–Fri, D daily. **$$$**
[p308, C2]
Beautifully presented dishes with some fresh

twists on traditional Thai cuisine inspired by the flavours of Northern Thailand. Persevere with the Times Square lift queues to enjoy this contemporary, spacious and relaxing dining experience.

Bars, Pubs and Clubs

Beer Garden & Innside Out, 10 Hysan Ave, Causeway Bay. Tel: 2895 2900. Unpretentious bar with outdoor seating, big-screen sports, peanuts on demand – shells must be thrown on the floor – big glasses of Hoegaarden and a wide range of other beers.

Canny Man, Basement, 57–73 Lockhart Rd, Wan Chai. Tel: 2861 1936. Run by a Scot, the spacious Canny Man is the place to head for leather sofas, deer heads on the wall, tartan touches and a choice of beers, whisky and Irn Bru.

Carnegie's, 53–55 Lockhart Rd, Wan Chai. Tel: 2866 6289. A rowdy, rocky two-tier bar that is packed and boisterous at weekends and fun most nights. Hosts live-music events.

Champagne Bar, Grand Hyatt, Wan Chai. Tel: 2588 1234. Intimate, opulent bar for expensive after-work entertaining.

Club JJs, Grand Hyatt Hong Kong, 1 Harbour Rd, Wan Chai. Tel: 2584 7662. Dress up to visit JJs, an upmarket bar and club with a decent house band. The place also serves excellent though fairly expensive home-style Thai cuisine.

Delaney's, One Capital Place, 18 Luard Rd, Wan Chai. Tel: 2804 2880. This is a very popular Irish theme pub with good food.

Joe Banana's, 23 Luard Rd, Wan Chai. Tel: 2529 1811. This bar/club has been running for years, with a reputation as something of a meat market for expatriates. There is a smart-casual dress code.

Joe's Billiards and Bar, 2/F King's Hotel, 303 Jaffe Rd, Wan Chai. Tel: 3188 1470.
All-night pool hall with billiards and snooker. Eight tournament-quality pool tables, plus challenge tables. A decent range of bar snacks will sustain you for hours.

Mes Amis, 83 Lockhart Rd, Wan Chai. Tel: 2527 6680. Open-front bar on the corner of Luard and Lockhart roads for both relaxed early-evening people-watching and late-night dancing.

Nuevo 1/5, 9 Star St, Wan Chai. Tel: 2529 2300. Chill out on plush red suede at this über-cool lounge bar with Spanish vibe and late night music.

R66, Revolving Restaurant, 62/F, Hopewell Centre, 183 Queen's Rd East, Wan Chai. Tel: 2862 6166. Skip the food and have a drink with great city views of Hong Kong. You'll find that there's just enough time to down a couple of cocktails and do one complete circuit.

Rockschool, 2/F, 21-25 Luard Rd, Wan Chai. Tel: 2510 7339. By music lovers, for music lovers. This roomy venue provides a stage for local bands and aspiring artists.

Opens as a pub during the day, so drop in for lunch or a drink and find out what's on.

S, 8 Yiu Wa St, Causeway Bay. Tel: 2838 0044. A fashionable and funky jet-black wine bar with a great range of chill-out music.

Skitz Sports Bar, 5/F, 21–25 Luard Rd. Tel: 2866 3277. There are pool tables, dart boards, and sports from all over the world on screen.

TOTT's Asian Grill and Bar, 281 Gloucester Rd, Causeway Bay. Tel: 2894 8888. This chic restaurant at the top of the Excelsior is a popular nightspot after dinner.

HORSE-RACING

The Wednesday evening races under floodlights at Happy Valley are one of the most enjoyable nights out in Hong Kong, with a great atmosphere and excitement

From September to July, there's a buzz in the air most Wednesdays on Hong Kong Island, as form guides and newspaper pundits are carefully studied ahead of the floodlit night races on turf at Happy Valley race track. Most visitors who attend say that this is one of the most enjoyable experiences of their time in Hong Kong.

Take a tram to Happy Valley or catch a taxi (ask your driver for a racing tip – you can then of course tip him to return the favour), pay HK$10 at the public entrance and then wander between the trackside beer garden, open-air or air-conditioned stands. Dress code is casual and refreshments are cheap, with good-quality pizza slices and meat skewers costing just HK$40, and jugs of beer starting at HK$125. There are up to eight races between 7.15pm and 11pm.

The HKTB operates a Come Horseracing Tour that will pick you up from your hotel and provide seats in the Visitors' Box, with a buffet and open bar for HK$600 per person.

ABOVE: the weekend races at Sha Tin see even larger crowds (with far fewer tourists). The track hosted the equestrian events at the 2008 Olympics. **BELOW:** the quality of the horses and racing is high. Annual cup races attract international racing fans and thoroughbreds from all over the world.

BELOW: bring your passport, pay HK$150 for a Tourist Badge, and you can enter the members' enclosure (no shorts or flip-flops!).

HOW TO BET: A NOVICES' GUIDE

Even if you are a complete beginner at the horses, it is very easy to join in. The Jockey Club produces a guide in English for the Wednesday night races that clearly details the form, trainer, owner, jockey, etc, of each horse, and lets you at least pretend you are making an informed choice. Counter staff mostly speak good English and are patient with non-gambling foreigners having a flutter.

The simplest punt is for a Win. Opt for a Place and your horse has to come first or second if less than seven horses start, or in the top three if seven or more start. For a Quinella you choose three horses, and if any two of them finish in the top three you're a winner. For a Trio you bet on which horses will come in the first three places, but in any order, while a Tierce is the same but must be in the correct order. Minimum bet is HK$10. There are leaflets available to explain all bets.

LEFT: racing at Happy Valley dates back to 1846, and typically attracts over 50,000 punters each Wednesday evening – the amount

of money gambled is extraordinary, and contributes around 12 percent of Hong Kong's tax revenue.

RIGHT: horse-racing is entrenched in local culture, as seen in this float at the Cheung Chau Bun Festival.

BELOW: the most popular horse in Hong Kong racing history, Silent Witness retired in 2007 after 18 wins.

Hong Kong Island

KOWLOON

Sulphur Channel

S u l p h u r   C h a n n e l

Lantau

Green Island

Little Green Island

Shek Tong Tsui

Sai Ying Pun

Hong Kong University ★

★ Man Mo Temple

Victoria Harbour

Sheung Wan

Central Station

Hong Kong Station

Central

Central

Caus

Macau

Kennedy Town

Mount Davis 269 ▲

Wan Chai

Admiralty ✚ Wan Chai

Causeway

Pau M (Happy)

Victoria Peak 552 ▲

★ Hong Kong Park

Happy Valley Racecourse

Pok Fu Lam

Victoria Peak Garden ★

★ Peak Tram

Central

Magazine Gap

P o k   F u   L a m

Peak Tower

Mt Gough 479 ▲

Kong Sin Wan

C o u n t r y   P a r k

Mt Cameron 439 ▲

Cyberport

Pok Fu Lam Reservoir

Mount Kellett 501 ▲

A b e r d e e n

C o u n t r y   P a r k

H o n g

K

Pokfulam Rd

Wah Fu

Chinese Permanent Cemetery ★

★ Tin Hau Temple

Aberdeen Reservoir

Shous Hill

Aberdeen (Heung Gong Tsai) ❶

★ Wholesale Fish Market

Wong Chuk Hang

Aberdeen Harbour

Jumbo Kingdom

❸ Ocean Park

Aberdeen Channel

South Horizons

Fo Yeuk Chau

Boulder Point

▲ 138

Pak Kok San Tsuen

Luk Chau Wan

❷

Ap Lei Chau (Duck's Tongue Island)

Horizon Plaza

Ocean Park

T u n g   P o k   L i u   H o i   H a p

(E a s t   L a m m a   C h a n n e l)

❸

Cable Car

Ocean Theatre ★

★ Atoll Reef

Mid Isla

D W b

Yung Shue Wan

Ap Lei Pa

Sham Shui Kok

Ko Long

Tin Hau Temple ★

Luk Chau (George Island)

Lo Tik Wan

Power Station

Hung Shing Ye

Hung Shing Ye Beach ★

L a m m a

Luk Chau Tsuen

S o k   K w u   W a n

(P i c n i c   B a y)

Re Is

Lo So Shing Beach ★

Lo So Shing

Sok Kwu Wan

Ling Kok Shan

Mo Tat

H a   M e i   W a n

I s l a n d

Mount Stenhouse 353 ▲

Tung O Wan

Tung O

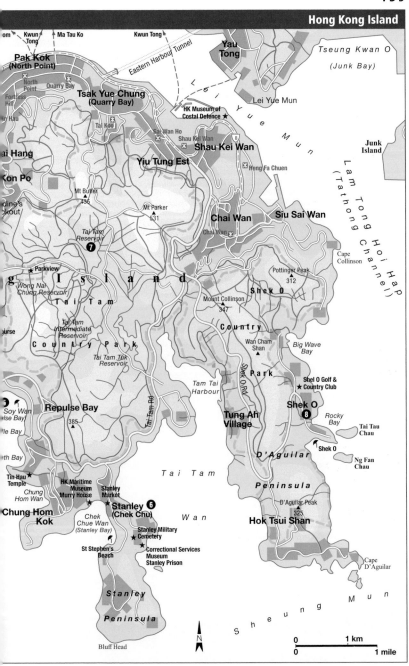

om Kwun Tong
Ma Tau Ko
Kwun Tong
Yau Tong
Tseung Kwan O
(Junk Bay)

Pak Kok
(North Point)
North Point
Quarry Bay
Fortress Hill
n Hau
Lei Yue Mun

Tsak Yue Chung
(Quarry Bay)
Tai Koo
HK Museum of
Costal Defence ★

ai Hang
Sai Wan Ho
Shau Kei Wan
Shau Kei Wan
8

Yiu Tung Est
Heng Fa Chuen

Kon Po
Mt Butler
436
Mt Parker
531
Chai Wan
Chai Wan
Siu Sai Wan

dine's
kout

Tai Tam
Reservoir ❼

★ Parkview
Wong Nai
Chung Reservoir
Tai Tam
Junk Island

Cape
Collinson

Pottinger Peak
312
Shek O

Mount Collinson
347
Country

g i s l a n d

Tai Tam
Intermediate
Reservoir
urse
C o u n t r y   P a r k
Tai Tam Tuk
Reservoir
Wan Cham
Shan ▲
Big Wave
Bay

P a r k

Shek O Golf &
★ Country Club

Tam Tai
Harbour
Shek O ❽
Rocky
Bay
Tung Ah
Village
Shek O Rd
Tai Tau
Chau

Shek O

Repulse Bay
385 ▲

Soy Wan
lse Bay)
le Bay

th Bay

D'Aguilar
Ng Fan
Chau

P e n i n s u l a

Tin Hau ★
Temple
Chung
Hom Wan
HK Maritime
Museum Stanley
Murry House Market
Stanley ❻
(Chek Chu)

Tai Tam

D'Aguilar Peak
325
Hok Tsui Shan

Chung Hom
Kok
Chek
Chue Wan
(Stanley Bay)
St Stephen's
Beach
Stanley Military
Cemetery
Correctional Services
Museum
Stanley Prison
W a n

Cape
D'Aguilar

Stanley

Peninsula

Bluff Head

S h e u n g   *M u n*

N

0   1 km
0   1 mile

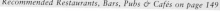
THE SOUTH SIDE

The southern part of Hong Kong Island acts as alter ego to the commercial north. Except for the busy spots of Aberdeen and Stanley, much of the coast here is relatively unspoiled and uncrowded

In contrast to the northern coast of Hong Kong Island, which has changed almost beyond recognition in recent times with successive land-reclamation projects, the rocky southern shoreline remains more or less as nature intended. Much of the area is green – there are four country parks here – but also, somehow, 290,000 people, some in the most sought-after real estate in the SAR. With its sweeping views of the South China Sea and outlying islands, this is the easiest place to escape the heavily urbanised strip on the other side of the mountains. Ocean Park's pandas, dolphins and hair-raising rides are a major draw, while elsewhere there are some good beaches, challenging walks and pleasant villages to discover.

ABERDEEN

The harbour town of **Aberdeen** (Heung Gong Tsai) ❶ is the only place on the south coast with an urban feel. It can be reached by road from Kennedy Town through the residential district of Pok Fu Lam and past the new Cyberport development, although most visitors take a more direct route south from Wan Chai through the Aberdeen Tunnel

along Stubbs Road and Magazine Gap Road.

Named after the earl who was Secretary of State for the Colonies in 1848, Aberdeen is chiefly notable for the huge numbers of vessels bobbing in the water along its shoreline, and the over-the-top Jumbo Kingdom's floating restaurants *(see panel, page 142)*. No longer a fishing village, the main town is now all high-rises and concrete, but the natural typhoon shelter is packed with boats of all kinds, from wooden fishing boats

Main attractions
ABERDEEN
OCEAN PARK
REPULSE BAY BEACH
STANLEY MARKET
MARITIME MUSEUM
BIG WAVE BAY AND SHEK O

LEFT: a verdant scene at Ocean Park.
RIGHT: the Jumbo Floating Restaurant.

TIP

Buses from Central (Exchange Square) to the southern parts of Hong Kong Island include: nos. 66 and 260 which run to Stanley and Repulse Bay *(see also margin tip, page 147)*; nos. 629 and 629S to Ocean Park; no. 309 to Shek O. For Aberdeen take buses nos. 7, 71, 91 or 94.

and *kaidos* (small cargo boats) to ferries, junks, sampans and yachts. A floating population of around 20,000 people once lived in boats in Aberdeen harbour, but today most of their descendants have opted for re-settlement in high-rise accommodation on dry land. With fish stocks down 80 percent since the 1950s, Hong Kong's fishing industry is in decline, hard hit by overfishing and pollution. While a few people are living in relative luxury on modern junks in the harbour, most of Hong Kong's "boat people" are from two main ethnic groups: the Tanka (literally, the egg people, so called because they used to pay taxes with eggs rather than cash) and the Hoklo, originally from Fujian province.

A ride through the harbour is an interesting experience. Eager sampan drivers, often persistent elderly women, are usually on the lookout for tourists and will offer rides (you will probably have to bargain for a price: HK$60–80 for 20 minutes is about right). Alternatively, look out for the Jumbo signs on the harbourfront, and you can hop on the free shuttle boat for a five-minute ride to the flamboyant floating restaurants *(see panel, below)*. Opposite the Jumbo the sleek white yachts are owned by members of the Aberdeen Marina Club, which is one of the most exclusive and expensive private clubs in the SAR. This area is also home to some of Hong Kong's last boat-builders and repairers.

Tin Hau Temple

Back on dry land, the **Tin Hau Temple** on Aberdeen Main Road is rather shabby for most of the year, but comes alive during the Tin Hau Festival in April or May, when thousands of boats converge on Aberdeen's shores and the temple is decorated with paper shrines and lanterns. Lion dances are performed

ABOVE RIGHT: Tanka people and their floating home. **BELOW:** Aberdeen's famed floating restaurant, Jumbo Kingdom. **BELOW RIGHT:** one of the restaurant piers.

Jumbo Dining

Irresistibly kitsch, the pagoda-shaped Jumbo and Tai Pak floating restaurants have been part of the Aberdeen scenery for over 30 years. The Jumbo is one of the world's largest floating restaurants, with seats for over 4,000, and after a multi-million dollar refurbishment in 2007, the dragons that greet you at the entrance are a tad gaudier and the fairy lights are twinkling all the brighter in the harbour. Now called the Jumbo Kingdom, it is building on its appeal as a tourist attraction in itself.

There is a free shuttle from two clearly marked piers on Aberdeen waterfront. Hop on and take a look around the fish tanks and the tea shop. The food in the indoor restaurants has improved, but isn't the best in Hong Kong. That said, the former rooftop storage area has been converted to a bar restaurant, The Top Deck at the Jumbo, and is a great place for a drink or a light meal, with outdoor seating and panoramic views across the harbour sampans and luxury cruisers in the typhoon shelter.

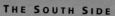
outside – an event that's charged with atmosphere and highly photogenic.

Along the promenade

The Aberdeen promenade has been brightened up in recent years and now features plaques telling the story of the town and the boat-dwellers. At its western end, the **Aberdeen Wholesale Fish Market** is at its busiest in the morning, when customers turn up to select and collect the best produce for seafood-loving Hong Kong diners.

Up on the steep hillside above the fish market is the quaintly named **Chinese Permanent Cemetery**, entered through a pagoda-style gate. From the cemetery there is an excellent view across Aberdeen; higher still is the starting point for various hikes in the Aberdeen Country Park.

Plans are afoot to develop the shoreline around the Aberdeen Typhoon Shelter that connects the town's waterfront with nearby Ocean Park. The revitalisation programme will include a promenade, dubbed Fisherman's Wharf, and three hotels. By 2015 the new South Island MTR line should reach this area.

Further west along the coast is the controversial **Cyberport** development, which has singularly failed to become Hong Kong's hi-tech centre.

Ap Lei Chau

Across the harbour from the bumper-to-bumper fishing boats, the high-rise towers of **Ap Lei Chau** (Duck's Tongue Island) ❷ pack in almost 90,000 people. The main reason to detour here is to visit Horizon Plaza, on Lee Wing Street, a former warehouse now packed with 28 floors of shops. As well as floor after floor of contemporary, antique and reproduction furniture stores, carpet stores, gourmet food and wine outlets, Horizon Plaza also has designer fashion discount 'warehouses'.

The Ocean Park cable car connects the two sections of the site.

BELOW: inside the Jumbo Kingdom Restaurant. The traditional Chinese preference for *re nao* (hot and noisy) – a loud, boisterous atmosphere – is satisfied here.

The sea-lion tank at Ocean Park. Despite fears for its survival following the opening of Disneyland in 2005, Hong Kong's original theme park has flourished in recent years, and has added new areas and attractions.

BELOW: Repulse Bay has one of Hong Kong's best sandy beaches.

Ocean Park ❸

✉ Wong Chuk Hang ☎ 2552 0291; www.oceanpark.com.hk 🅒 daily 10am–6pm 🅢 charge 🚌 629 Ocean Park Citybus from Central piers and Admiralty; 6A, 6X, 70, 75, 90, 97, 260 from Central, 973 from Tsim Sha Tsui (Star Ferry)

From Aberdeen, go east past the Police Training School at Wong Chuk Hang to one of Hong Kong's biggest home-grown attractions. Opened in 1977 at a cost of HK$150 million, Ocean Park is a combination of theme park and oceanarium. The complex is divided into two sections, a lowland site and a headland site, linked by a 1.4-km (1-mile) cable-car. *For more on Ocean Park see pages 212–213.*

East to Repulse Bay

Beyond Ocean Park to the east is a region of rocky coasts and smooth white sands – home to 12 of Hong Kong's 40 gazetted beaches *(see panel, page 146)*. On summer weekends it can seem as if half the population of Hong Kong have made their way here. A few locations, such as Rocky Bay on the road to Shek O, have virtually no public facilities, but offer unparalleled views and un-crowded stretches of sand and sea. Others, like Repulse Bay, attract bus-loads of tourists, fast-food restaurants and, at weekends, about as much peace and quiet as a carnival. Repulse Bay, Stanley, Tai Tam and Shek O are also home to several residential developments that command some of the highest real-estate prices and rents in the world.

Deep Water Bay ❹, the first beach beyond Aberdeen and Ocean Park, has some beautiful mansions, and is

reputed to enjoy some of the best feng shui in Hong Kong. It also has a nine-hole golf course managed by the Hong Kong Golf Club (open weekdays to the public). Further along the road is the exclusive Hong Kong Country Club. The long stretch of beach here offers a quiet place to soak in the sun or go for a swim.

REPULSE BAY

Repulse Bay (Cheen Soy Wan) ❺ is easily identified when you see the apartment block with a square hole in the middle. The bay was named after the battleship HMS *Repulse*, which took an active part in thwarting pirates who plundered here in the mid-19th century. Now widened to several times its original size and developed into a playground for tourists as well as urban Hong Kongers, Repulse Bay Beach has everything except peace and quiet.

The hills that rise steeply from the shoreline have a sombre history. It was here that invading Japanese troops came pouring down at the end of 1941 during World War II. The Repulse Bay Hotel, once one of the finest hotels in the East, was a military target because British and Canadian troops used it as a base to keep open the road between Stanley and Aberdeen. After three days of fighting, the hotel was taken, and Commonwealth prisoners were marched to Eucliffe Mansion (this

folly has also been demolished and replaced by villas), about half a kilometre (⅓ mile) from the hotel. Most of the prisoners were executed, and survivors were incarcerated at the Stanley Internment Camp.

The hotel was also demolished in the 1980s, and on the site today is The Repulse Bay, a luxury apartment complex; it has captured some of the old-world style in its renowned restaurants with verandas overlooking the lawn and beach. The complex includes the famous blue apartment building with the hole in its midst (*see margin, right*).

STANLEY

Fifteen minutes' drive further southeast is **Stanley** (Chek Chu) ❻, popular with Hong Kong residents for its restaurants and seaside ambience. Named after Lord Stanley, a 19th-century Secretary of State for the Colonies, Stanley was the largest indigenous settlement in Hong Kong when the British first set foot here in 1841. In fact, the local Tin Hau Temple documents that the town was founded in 1770 by the pirate

TIP

The large blue apartment building with the big square hole in the middle is the best-known sight in Repulse Bay. Some say the hole is a passageway for the heavenly dragon to come down from the mountains; others say it was put there to generate good feng shui; still others say it was just the architect's attempt at being funky. A replica of the old Repulse Bay Hotel stands in front of the apartment block, preserving a soupçon of grace from days gone by.

ABOVE LEFT: the famous hole at Repulse Bay. **BELOW:** the Maritime Museum at Murray House, Stanley.

Cheung Po Tsai, who had taken control of the island.

What to see in Stanley

Stanley Market (daily 10am–7pm), the principal attraction on Stanley peninsula, draws thousands of visitors at weekends – locals in search of a bargain as well as tourists looking for souvenirs to take home. A few steps from New Street, where the buses stop, is an extensive covered market packed with shops and stalls selling clothes (factory over-runs or seconds), rattan, fresh food, ceramics, budget art, hardware, brass objects, Chinese crafts – in fact, almost anything.

At the end of the open-fronted restaurants and bars along Main

Street, which skirts Stanley Main Beach, there is a modern shopping mall, directly opposite one of the SAR's most impressive architectural projects. **Murray House**, a former British Army barracks dating from 1848, was moved stone by stone from Central (it was located on the site now occupied by the Bank of China tower) and rebuilt on the waterfront.

The ground floor is currently home to the **Hong Kong Maritime Museum** (Tue–Sun 10am–6pm; charge), which traces Hong Kong's long connection with the sea and trade with China. The museum is divided into two sections. The ancient gallery looks at China's own shipping traditions, spice trade sea routes and the beginnings of

ABOVE RIGHT: Murray House. **BELOW AND BELOW RIGHT:** the south side of Hong Kong Island has several good beaches.

South Coast Beaches

If the weather's good and the water's clear, Hong Kong's beaches are great places to hang out. A total of 40 of them are gazetted (10 on the south coast of Hong Kong Island), which means there are facilities including toilets, showers, changing rooms, barbecue pits – and lifeguards from March to November. The sands are kept clean, but water quality varies dramatically – ratings are posted at lifeguard stations (along with a long list of things you are not allowed to do).

The nearest beach to Central is at Deep Water Bay, while along the coast is the larger, but more crowded, Repulse Bay beach. South Bay (Nam Wan), just below Repulse Bay, has a relaxed beach scene and the best view of the sunset. At weekends DJs at the open-air South Bay Beach Club provide a soundtrack. St Stephen's is the nicer of Stanley's two beaches and has a watersports hire centre. The east side of Cape D'Aguilar has the best surf: Big Wave Bay is the place for surfers and has a surf hire shop, while Shek O attracts a mixed group – beach-goers and surfers jostle with boogie boarders, swimmers and inflatables.

Recommended Restaurants, Bars, Pubs & Cafés on page 149

trade with the West. In the modern gallery there are exhibitions of steamships and a modern tanker, while a simulator lets you have a go at driving a container ship. Upstairs you'll find some airy restaurants. The museum is set to move to Pier 8 in Central at some point in the next few years.

The Old Police Station

East of the bus terminus is the **Old Stanley Police Station**, one of 94 declared monuments in Hong Kong. The early British settlers regarded a posting to Stanley Police Station (built in 1859) as highly dangerous. Only a dirt track connected the town to the city of Victoria (now Central), and

pirates frequently attacked and robbed the garrison. Stanley was all but abandoned in the 1850s, until the original police station was replaced by the building which stands today. The station is also thought to have been the last point of resistance to the advancing Japanese forces in the Battle of Hong Kong during World War II. On Christmas Day 1941, the town's commanding officer refused to believe the British had surrendered, and so the town fought on for a day after troops elsewhere had laid down their arms. That this historic building is currently occupied by a supermarket says a great deal about the parlous state of Hong Kong's heritage.

Other sights

Down the road is **Stanley Prison**, which is still in use, while the two-storey building topped with a mock guard tower next to its parade ground houses the quirky **Correctional Services Museum** (Tue–Sun 10am–5pm; free). Its nine galleries chart the history of Hong Kong's penal system, with creepy exhibits like a mock gallows and fake cells. It

TIP

If you are travelling direct to Stanley from Central, take the No. 6 bus from Exchange Square, which bypasses the Aberdeen Tunnel. You'll have the best views from the top deck going over the top along Wong Nai Chung Gap Road. Pass spindly skyscrapers appearing precariously balanced on the hillside, and enjoy the inexpensive white-knuckle ride down to Repulse Bay and Stanley.

ABOVE LEFT: shopping for bargains at Stanley Market. **BELOW:** the art of calligraphy.

Shek O main beach is one of the most pleasant on Hong Kong Island. Together with the aptly named Big Wave Bay to the north, it is also good for surfing.

ABOVE RIGHT: large, prominently displayed fish tanks at local seafood restaurants advertise the freshness of what's on the menu.
BELOW: looking down to Shek O from the Dragon's Back.

was also in Stanley Prison and at nearby St Stephen's College that the Japanese interned 2,800 non-Chinese civilian men, women and children.

To the right of the prison is the **Stanley Military Cemetery**, where tombstones commemorate early colonial military families, as well as those who died during World War II at the Battle of Hong Kong or at Stanley Internment Camp. Near the cemetery is **St Stephen's Beach**, with a watersports centre (www.lcsd.gov.hk/watersport/) that hires out sailing dinghies, windsurfing boards and kayaks if you can produce the appropriate certificate.

Beyond Stanley

From Stanley you can access two country parks with access to more remote beaches, or take on a stage or two of the Wilson, Hong Kong or Tai Tam trails and hike to some of the least visited spots on the island.

To reach **Tai Tam Country Park**, head north along Tai Tam Road towards the **Tai Tam Reservoirs** ❼, which feature Victorian aqueducts and dams. Made up of four reservoirs, Tai Tam can only meet Hong Kong's needs for three days (most of Hong Kong's water supply is piped in from China). The Park covers fully one-fifth of Hong Kong Island, and the reservoirs are a popular picnic spot. The well-marked walk up along the Hong Kong Trail to the north leads past pretty woodland and waterfalls; during the week it's most likely to be deserted. At the top, a newly developed trail around Wong Nai Chung Gap traces the events of the Battle of Hong Kong in 1941.

Big Wave Bay and Shek O

Following Tai Tam Road, then Shek O Road, around Tai Tam Bay will take you to the east coast of Hong Kong Island, where **Big Wave Bay**'s consistent surf and easily accessible location is a big draw for the Hong Kong surfing community. Boards and suits can be rented from the Surf 360 shop, just off the beach.

Just to the south, **Shek O** ❽ is a pleasant village whose market place has a collection of shops selling beach paraphernalia. There are also some laid-back restaurants well known for both Chinese and Thai cuisine. Stroll out to Shek O Headland, facing the islands of Tai Tau Chau and Ng Fan Chau, and to the right is the most easterly point of the island, Cape D'Aguilar.

Alternatively, take it all in by walking along the **Dragon's Back** from the trail marker above To Tei Wan to Shek O (stage 8 of the Hong Kong Trail), which takes hikers along ridges around these peaks for two or three hours before dropping down to Big Wave Bay. ❑

BEST RESTAURANTS, BARS, PUBS AND CAFÉS

Restaurants

Prices for a three-course dinner per person with one beer or glass of house wine:

$ = under HK$150
$$ = HK$150–300
$$$ = HK$300–500
$$$$ = over HK$500

Numerous restaurants and bars that embrace alfresco dining have opened in the South Side beach resorts in recent years. Stanley's renovated promenade and Murray House also have great dining and drinking venues.

Cantonese

Jumbo Floating Restaurant

Jumbo Kingdom, Sham Wan Pier Drive, Aberdeen
2553 9111 L & D daily. $$$
This iconic gaudy restaurant is almost obligatory for group tours, but is popular with locals, too. Take a free shuttle and expect to queue for the comparatively expensive Cantonese cuisine. Standards have improved.

Shek O Chinese and Thai Seafood Restaurant

303 Shek O Village 2809 4426 L & D daily. $
Popular, unpretentious open-air place serving Cantonese and Thai dishes on the crossroads in the centre of sleepy Shek O. Friendly staff serve steamed fish, tom yum soup and fishcakes.

Shu Zhai

80 Stanley Main St, Stanley
2813 0123 L & D Tue–Sun. $$
Local designer Calvin Yeung's stylish take on a traditional teahouse, set over two floors with a small courtyard. Enjoy dim sum and modern Chinese cuisine all day. Last order 10pm.

International

Black Sheep

350 Shek O Village 2809 2021 L & D daily. $$
International fare with a leaning towards the Med at this Shek O bistro. Plants and tropical decor add to its appeal.

Cococabana

U/G, Beach Building, Island Rd, Deep Water Bay 2812 2226 L & D Wed–Sun, D only Mon & Tue. $$$
Authentic Mediterranean cuisine from French chefs at this beachside restaurant. Table d'hôte dinner menu. Open all day weekends for drinks and food.

El Greco

5 Wai Fung St, Ap Lei Chau
2328 2138 L & D Closed Mon. $$
If you are heading out to Horizon Plaza in search of furniture, wine or designer bargains, the Greek homestyle cooking makes El Greco the ideal place to stop for lunch. Eat outside and take in the sea views.

Top Deck at the Jumbo

Jumbo Kingdom, Sham Wan Pier Drive, Aberdeen
2552 3331 L & D Tue–Sun. $$–$$$
Alfresco dining, Asian and Western dishes and fine seafood, in an elegant venue. Bookings essential for Sunday brunch with unlimited bubbly.

The Verandah

Repulse Bay Hotel 2812 2722 L & D daily. $$$$
Follow the sweeping drive through tropical gardens and enter the Art Deco dining room, with views across the South China Sea and European fine dining. It's expensive, but curious travellers could drop in for tea or drinks on the way to Stanley.

Wildfire

2/F, Murray House, Stanley
2813 6161 L & D daily. $$
Platters of pizzas plus steaks, salads and seafood on the top floor of beautiful Murray House. Roomy restaurant with balcony and bay views.

Bars, Pubs and Cafés

King Ludwig's Beer Hall, 2/F, Murray House, Stanley. Tel: 2899 0122. Impressive range of German bottled and draught beers and Schnapps in this colonial gem right on the waterfront.

Shek O Sailing, 273 Shek O Village. Tel: 2809 2268
Tiny little bar tucked away on Shek O's back beach, just the place for a sundowner. Decent beers, wine by the glass or bottle.

Smugglers Inn, 90A Stanley Main St, Stanley. Tel: 2813 8852. Jolly pub on Stanley's promenade serving cold pints and pub grub.

South Bay Beach Club, South Bay Beach. Tel: 2812 6015. The perfect place to chill out on Sunday afternoons with live DJs and cocktails.

Uno Beach Café, G/F, West Block, Deep Water Bay Beach. Tel: 2812 1826. Open daily, Uno serves drinks and snacks in a laid-back Latin-style café-bar right by the beach.

Recommended Restaurants, Bars, Pubs and Clubs on pages 164–7

KOWLOON

Always regarded as playing second fiddle to Hong Kong Island, the districts of Tsim Sha Tsui, Yau Ma Tei and Mong Kok in Kowloon nevertheless define the chaos and bustle of the SAR

Named after the nine dragons *(gau lung)* of legend that live in the hills that mark its northern edge, the Kowloon peninsula is one of the world's most crowded areas, with more than 2 million people squeezed into its 47 sq km (18 sq miles).

At the southern end is Tsim Sha Tsui (pronounced "chim-sa-choi"), once a sharp, sandy point but now an irrepressible shopping district. Further north are the more traditional areas of Yau Ma Tei and Mong Kok, where, despite the addition of a few new malls and high-rises, life is still very much lived on the streets and in the many street markets.

Kowloon is quite different from the glittering island across the harbour – it's a little rougher round the edges, and on the go later into the night. Away from the main tourist areas along and beside Nathan Road, where the broadest mix of nationalities and cultures can be seen any time of the day or night, Kowloon is "more Chinese", or perhaps some might say, more Hong Kong.

By day, save for the views from the waterfront and a few idiosyncratic sights, it is not an especially attractive place. Instead, it's all about atmosphere, and few can deny the electricity that charges life here, especially at night. Darkness also casts a forgiving light over its mishmash of urban design, and allows its thousands of neon lights to dazzle.

Yet it is changing, the transformation kick-started in part by the closure of Kai Tak Airport in 1998, after which buildings were allowed to soar beyond the former flight-path limits. Property developers dashed in to begin creating a new

Main attractions
HARBOUR VIEWS
TSIM SHA TSUI NEON-LIT STREETS
HONG KONG SPACE MUSEUM
HONG KONG MUSEUM OF ART
KOWLOON PARK
HONG KONG SCIENCE MUSEUM
HONG KONG MUSEUM
OF HISTORY
TEMPLE STREET NIGHT MARKET

LEFT: the neon-drenched Golden Mile of Nathan Road, Tsim Sha Tsui.
RIGHT: Bruce Lee on the Kowloon waterfront.

skyline for Hong Kong Island to look at, and look up to.

These days Kowloon has the tallest building in Hong Kong, and the fourth-tallest in the world, following the 2010 completion of the 484-metre (1,588-ft) **International Commerce Centre** (ICC). Located on top of the Kowloon MTR station and surrounded by luxury high-rise apartment towers, the 118-storey ICC has a viewing platform on the 100th floor and will boast the world's highest hotel when the Ritz Carlton moves into the top 15 storeys in 2011 *(see page 162)*.

AROUND THE STAR FERRY PIER

The obvious place to start exploring Tsim Sha Tsui is at the **Star Ferry Pier ❶**, where the ferries land from Central and Wan Chai. The functional concourse is the location of Hong Kong's most accessible **tourist information office** (run by the HKTB and open 8am–8pm daily), on the immediate right of the disembarkation point.

Just east of the Star Ferry Terminal is Tsim Sha Tsui's most obvious landmark, the former Kowloon–Canton Railway **Clock Tower**. Dating from 1921, the tower is the final vestige of the historic Kowloon–Canton Railway (KCR) Station, once the Asian terminus of a system that ran all the way (with a few changes en route) back to Europe. In the mid-1970s it was replaced by a new station to the east, at Hung Hom.

Immediately behind the tower is the unmistakable form of the **Hong**

ABOVE RIGHT: the venerable Clock Tower. **BELOW:** morning exercises. **BELOW RIGHT:** the Avenue of Stars.

Recommended Restaurants, Bars, Pubs and Clubs on pages 164–7

Kong Cultural Centre ❷, a minimalist structure with a sweeping concave roof covered in ugly tiles. When it was built in 1984, people were baffled by its absence of windows – an inexplicable decision to block out one of the world's most dramatic views. Nonetheless, the lack of view focuses attention on what's going on inside, and the place is extensively used. It is the home of the Hong Kong Philharmonic Orchestra and stages local and international opera, classical music, theatre and dance throughout the year. It is also a reliable source of information about arts and cultural events throughout the city.

Along the promenade

From the Star Ferry Pier eastward along the harbour, a **waterfront promenade** extends past the Cultural Centre and InterContinental Hotel towards **Tsim Sha Tsui East** and **Hung Hom Bay**, a stretch of reclaimed land packed with hotels, offices and shops. This provides a great vantage point for viewing the north shore of Hong Kong Island, one of the most spectacular cityscapes in the world. At 8pm each night, anywhere along the promenade is good for watching the Symphony of Lights, the world's largest sound and light show that illuminates the glittering skyline more than ever.

Beyond the Cultural Centre the promenade skirts the InterContinental Hotel and the New World Centre and becomes the **Avenue of Stars** ❸ – decorated with tributes to the famous and less so of Hong Kong and Chinese cinema, with Hollywood-style stars set in the pavement. Some of the monikers – Fung Bo Bo, Ivy Ling Po, Tso Tat Wah – will be familiar only to film buffs, but many other characters are honoured here, including San Francisco-born Bruce Lee, John Woo from Guangzhou, Beijing native Jet Li and the first Asian 007 girl – Michelle Yeoh.

Hong Kong Space Museum ❹

✉ 10 Salisbury Road ☎ 2721 0226; http://hk.space.museum 🕒 Mon, Wed–Fri 1–9pm, Sat–Sun & public holidays 10am–9pm, closed Tue 💲 charge, but free on Wed 🚇 MTR Tsim Sha Tsui

Just behind the Cultural Centre, the igloo-like **Hong Kong Space Museum** is a favourite with kids. The stars, planets and Chinese astronomical inventions are explored in two interactive exhibition halls. There are also daily IMAX movies on the hemispherical screen inside the Space Museum's dome. Films cover anything from dinosaurs to underwater exploration and, of course, space. The museum also produces two new multimedia planetarium shows each year.

Hong Kong Museum of Art ❺

✉ 10 Salisbury Road ☎ 2721 0116; http://hk.art.museum 🕒 Mon–Wed, Fri & Sun 10am–6pm, Sat 10am–8pm, closed Thur 💲 charge, but free on Wed 🚇 MTR Tsim Sha Tsui

The Cultural Centre – a bold architectural statement from the 1980s.

BELOW: exhibit at the Hong Kong Science Museum.

MONG KOK

Flower Market, **25**
Bird Market

24 Ladies Market

Soy Street
Reclamation Street
Portland Street
Shanghai Street
Canton Road
Ferry Street
Fife Street
Cho Fuk Street
Soy Street
Fa Yuen Street
Yin Chong Street
Kwong Wa St
Ho Man Tin St

Dundas Street
Hamilton St
Pitt Street

YAU MA TEI

KING'S PARK

HO MAN TIN

Fat Kwong St
Chung Hau St
Fat Kwong St

Waterloo Road
Wylie Road
Hau Man Tin Hill Road

Lai Cheung Rd
Ngo Cheung Rd

Waterloo Road
Shek Lung Street
Arthur Street
Yau Ma Tei

Chun Yi Ln

Man Street

Chi Man Street

22 Temple Street
Night Market

23 Tin Hau Temple

Broadway
Cinematheque **21**

21 Jade Market

Tung Prosperous Gardens
Kun Street
Temple Street
Public Sq. St

Park Rise

King's Park Rise

Queen Elizabeth Hospital

Baker St
Winslow St
Ho Lung Hang Rd

Kansu St
Man Cheong St
Man Ying St
Saigon Street
Pak Hoi Street
Ning Po Street
Battery Street
Reclamation St
Nanking Street

India Club

Gascoigne Road

Wylie Path
Wylie Road

Chatham Road

HUNG HOM

Yan Cheung Rd

ICC Elements, Kowloon MTR

Jordan Road

Cheong Lok St

Jordan

Cox's Path
Jordan Path

Gun Club Barracks

Min St
Bowring St
Temple St
Pilkem St
Parkes Street

Tak Hing St

South Chatham Road
Yuk Choi Rd
Cheong Wan Rd

Austin

Universal Theatre

Austin Rd West

Austin Road

Austin Road

Hillwood Road

Rosary Church **18**

HK Museum of History **17**

Cheong Wan Road

19

Hung Hom

West Kowloon Cultural District (WKCD) (proposed development)

KOWLOON PARK

St Andrew's

HK Observatory

Observatory Road
Knutsford Terr.

Chatham Court

HK Science Museum **16**

20 HK Coliseum

Science Mus.
Science Museum Pl.
Science Museum Rd
Science Museum Road Square

International Mail Centre

China HK City

HK Heritage Discovery Centre

Chinese Garden

Miramar Shopping Centre

14

Kimberley Road
Kimberley Road
Carnarvon Road
Granville Road
Granville Road

Energy Plz.

Hilton Towers

CENTENARY GARDEN

China Ferry Terminal

Sculpture Garden

12

11

13 Kowloon Mosque

Cameron Road
Prat Ave.

Mody St
Mody Lane
Mody Road

Hung Hom Bypass

TSIM SHA TSUI

TSIM SHA TSUI EAST

Harbour City **10**

Haiphong Road

Humphreys Ave.
Hart Ave.
Hanoi Rd

Carnarvon Road

Tsim Sha Tsui East Ferry Pier

Ocean Centre

Ocean Terminal

Former Marine Police HQ **6**

YMCA **7**

Peninsula Hotel

Star House

9

Peking Road
Middle Road
Hankow Road
Lock Rd
Ashley Rd
Kowloon Park Dr.
Canton Road

Tsim Sha Tsui
Mody Road

15

Minden Ave.

8 Blackhead Signal Tower

Chungking Mansions

SIGNAL HILL GARDEN

East Tsim Sha Tsui

Salisbury Road

Cross - Harbour Tunnel

1 Star Ferry Pier

Clock Tower

HK Cultural Centre **2**

HK Space Museum **4**

5 HK Museum of Art

InterContinental Hotel

3 Avenue of Stars

Central
Wan Chai

Victoria Harbour

0 ___ 400 m
0 ___ 400 yds

N

Hong Kong's largest public art gallery is the main venue for major visiting art exhibitions. The Museum of Art also displays traditional and contemporary calligraphy and painting, along with historic photographs, prints and artefacts of Hong Kong, Macau and Guangzhou. Other galleries exhibit Chinese antiquities and modern Chinese art.

Salisbury Road

Across the road from this swathe of unattractive architecture, various stretches of Salisbury Road have been under renovation since the 1990s, and are most easily accessed by subway via the underground Sogo department store.

Across the road from the Cultural Centre is a petite white 19th-century building that functioned as the **Marine Police Headquarters** ❻ until 1996. Now restored and re-opened as **Hullett House** (www.hullett house.com), a 10-suite boutique hotel with bars and restaurants in restored stables and holding cells. The small hill below Hullett House that gave marine policemen their

vantage point has been converted into a new faux-Victorian mall called 1881 Heritage. Typhoon signals were hoisted in the lighthouse that once sat at the tip of Kowloon.

On the right side of YMCA is the magnificent **Peninsula Hotel** ❼ *(see panel, below)*, which celebrated its 80th birthday in 2008. Overlooking the always-changing waterfront is Signal Hill Garden, which houses **Blackhead Signal Tower** ❽ (daily 9–11am, 4–6pm; free). The tower was built in 1907 to house the time-ball by which ships in the harbour adjusted their chronometers.

Maritime gateway

Immediately north of the Star Ferry Pier is **Star House** ❾, where *cheongsams*, porcelain, and almost every kind of Chinese handicraft, are on sale at the Chinese Arts and Crafts store.

Adjoining Star House on Canton Road is the mammoth **Harbour City** complex ❿, encompassing **Ocean Terminal, Ocean Centre** and Gateway Arcade. Inside there are over 700 stores and boutiques, plus three

The Hong Kong Museum of Art comprises six galleries, one of which is dedicated to changing exhibitions, mainly from China. The museum shop is the best place to look for art books and prints in Hong Kong.

BELOW AND BELOW LEFT: the Peninsula Hotel is the height of luxury.

The Pen

Back in the early 1920s, the newly formed Hong Kong and Shanghai Hotels Company commissioned architects to design "the finest hotel east of Suez". The Peninsula, as the property was named, opened in 1928 and almost immediately took centre stage of the then sleepy Kowloon's social life. In those early days of long-haul travel, guests arrived at the Kowloon Canton Railway terminus on Tsim Sha Tsui promenade after a first-class train journey from Europe via Moscow, Beijing and Shanghai, or disembarked from luxury liners moored on what is now Canton Road. Early guests included George Bernard Shaw, Noël Coward and philanthropist Cornelius Vanderbilt Jr.

Traditions have been assiduously maintained, and one can still enjoy an afternoon tea in the sumptuous gilt-corniced lobby accompanied by a string quartet on the balcony. A new tower added more rooms in the 1990s, and the Pen's fleet of Rolls-Royce limousines, its swish restaurants, spa and bars, ensure that it remains the ultimate Hong Kong hotel.

WHERE

Nathan Road is the
central trunk of Kowloon
running north from Tsim
Sha Tsui through Yau
Ma Tei to Mong Kok's
Boundary Street, which
marks the line drawn in
1856 when the land to
the south was ceded to
the British "in perpetu-
ity". In 1898 the
districts immediately
surrounding colonial
Kowloon were, along
with the New Territories,
leased to the British
until 1997.

ABOVE RIGHT:
Nathan Road neon.
BELOW: electronics
shops on Peking Road
in the heart of Tsim
Sha Tsui.

Marco Polo hotels and dozens of restaurants. More than 20 luxury cruise lines include Hong Kong as a port of call and regularly moor at the two berths here, although ships as large as the *Queen Mary II* are forced to moor at the deeper, but semi-industrial, Kwai Chung Container Terminal rather than disgorging their passengers directly into the malls and other entertainments of downtown Tsim Sha Tsui.

Running parallel with today's cruise-ship and ferry terminals is **Canton Road**, which marked the waterfront until the 1950s. Today it is the "front door" of Harbour City and home to an increasing number of designer-brand megastores. It also borders the western edge of Kowloon Park *(see opposite)*.

The heart of Tsim Sha Tsui

The "Golden Mile" was a nickname given to **Nathan Road** ⑪ in the 1960s after it had been transformed from a sleepy, tree-lined residential boulevard into a gaudy, neon-lit street lined with electronics shops, tailors, boutiques and other stores targeting tourists more than locals. Shops have changed, signs have multiplied, but Nathan Road still remains the core of the Tsim Sha Tsui shopping and entertainment district. This has now spread out along the

various cross streets, where run-down mansion blocks packed with shabby guesthouses and trading offices are oddly wedged between the shops, luxury hotels and the occasional skyscraper.

From the west side of Nathan Road, Peking and Haiphong roads connect with increasingly upmarket Canton Road. To the east there's plenty of shopping along Carnarvon, Cameron and Granville roads: here you will find factory outlets, inexpensive accessory shops, fashion boutiques and numerous bargains.

Nathan Road itself now boasts the very upmarket Lane Crawford department store, as well as larger mid-priced fashion stores, cut-price cosmetics stores and plenty of jewellery and electronic stores, where "buyer beware" is the order of the day. There are also the less salubrious looking arcades that overflow with a fascinating mix of booths and stores, including the ground floor of Chungking Mansions (*see panel, below*).

Kowloon Park ⑫

✉ Haiphong Road ☎ www.lcsd.gov.hk
🕒 5am–midnight 🎫 free Ⓜ MTR Tsim Sha Tsui

The shady old banyan trees of **Kowloon Park** date back to when the British Army's Whitfield barracks were established here in the 1890s. The 13.5-hectare (34-acre) park includes a Chinese garden with lotus ponds, children's playground, maze and an aviary park (access often restricted due to avian flu concerns). A **Sculpture Walk** displays work by local artists and is the venue for kung fu demonstrations every Sunday afternoon (2.30–4.30pm). At the northern end there's a large sports complex and indoor and outdoor swimming pool (daily 6.30am–noon, 1–5pm and 6–10pm). Two blocks of former Whitfield Barracks, which was built in 1910 to house

British and Indian troops, have been cleverly restored to create the **Hong Kong Heritage Discovery Centre** (Mon–Wed, Fri 10am–6pm, Sun 10am–7pm, charge). Galleries host temporary exhibitions and a permanent display that attempts to define Hong Kong's cultural heritage.

East of the park

At the southeastern corner of the park, on Nathan Road, is the **Kowloon Mosque ⑬**, with its four

The functional 17-storey Chungking Mansions block houses the majority of Hong Kong's budget guesthouses. Between 4,000 and 20,000 people are said to live and work in the building.

Chungking Mansions

Step inside Chungking Mansions at 36–44 Nathan Road, past the over-eager touts promoting guesthouses and Indian restaurants, and there, amid a heady aroma of spices, lies Hong Kong's own parallel non-Chinese non-Western world. Built in 1961, Chungking Mansions is home to the frugal backpackers and new arrivals from developing countries. Among the money-changers and wholesalers on the ground floor is a mix of stalls where you can buy anything from Bollywood DVDs, saris or samosas to electronics and alarm clocks. Head up to the mezzanine floor and tuck into some Nepali snack food and take in the scene. Many more restaurants along with guesthouses are upstairs, located in five blocks labelled A to E, accessed by small, overcrowded, unreliable lifts and dark stairwells that invariably prompt comparisons with Ridley Scott's *Blade Runner*. For the Chinese movie fan it's a chance to experience the twilight world portrayed in Wong Kar Wai's *Chungking Express*.

The Kowloon Park flamingos add a splash of colour to the surroundings.

ABOVE RIGHT:
Kowloon Mosque.
BELOW: Haiphong
Road marks the south-
ern limit of Kowloon
Park. **BELOW RIGHT:**
one of several lakes in
Kowloon Park.

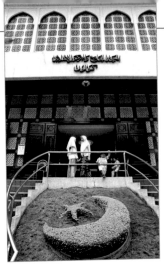

minarets and large, white-marble dome gracefully standing out from the clutter of shops and restaurants opposite. Built in 1984, it serves the territory's 80,000 Muslim residents, of whom about half are Chinese. The original mosque building, built in 1894, served the British Army's Muslim Indian troops.

Across the road are three colonial buildings, each over 100 years old, fronted by equally gracious banyan trees. At No. 138 the Victorian Gothic-style **St Andrew's Church** (1904) is the oldest Anglican church in Kowloon. Next door, set back from the road is the former Kowloon-British School, which opened in 1902 and now houses the **Antiquities and Monuments Office** (not open to the public). Up the hill behind Nathan Road, the **Hong Kong Observatory** has been moni-toring the weather here since 1883.

Alongside the entrance to the Observatory is the renovated Mira-mar Shopping Centre, with over 100 shops and access to Tsim Sha Tsui's trendy restaurant and entertainment area, **Knutsford Steps, Knutsford Ter-**race and **Kimberley Road** ⓮. This area also has a remarkable number of bridal shops, where young couples flock to hire or buy all manner of bridalware and to sit for pre-wedding photographs of the happy couple in full wedding gear that will be on dis-play at their wedding celebration.

Mody Road

Linking Nathan Road to Chatham Road is **Mody Road** ⓯ which,

Recommended Restaurants, Bars, Pubs and Clubs on pages 164–7

together with neighbouring Hanoi Road, is reinventing itself and going from grubby to groovy in one fell swoop. It is undergoing the first of what will no doubt be many makeovers in this slightly run-down but lively area, following the completion of K-11 a 64-floor skyscraper in 2007. The tower has brought upmarket office space, what it claims is Hong Kong's first 'art mall', and the Hyatt Regency Tsim Sha Tsui. As the district is 'renewed' it remains to be seen whether its appealing edginess will be lost in the process.

TSIM SHA TSUI EAST

Chatham Road runs parallel to Nathan Road and is home to two good museums and Hong Kong's largest university.

Hong Kong Science Museum ⑯

✉ 2 Science Museum Road ☎ 2732 3232; www.hk.science.museum ⏰ Mon–Wed, Fri 1–9pm, Sat–Sun & public holidays 10am–9pm, closed Thur ⓢ charge but free on Wed ⓧ MTR Tsim Sha Tsui East

The Science Museum has over 500 exhibits on permanent display in 18 galleries covering topics from telecommunications to food science. Highlights include the flight simulator and a 22-metre (72-ft) twin-tower energy machine, which is the largest of its kind in the world. The majority of exhibits are interactive and aimed at making the wide range of technology and science topics accessible for its primary audience of school students and young children.

Hong Kong Museum of History ⑰

✉ 100 Chatham Road South ☎ 2724 9042; www.hk.history. museum ⏰ Mon, Wed–Sat 10am–6pm, Sun & public holidays 10am–7pm, closed Tue ⓢ charge but free on Wed ⓧ MTR Tsim Sha Tsui East

Just opposite the Science Museum, the **Hong Kong Museum of History** documents the 6,000-year story of Hong

In common with other large museums in Hong Kong, the Museum of History has free admission every Wednesday.

BELOW: the ground-floor arcade at Chungking Mansions is as close as Hong Kong gets to a "Little India".

WHERE

The lurid gold building on Kowloon's western waterfront is the China Ferry Terminal, boarding point for ports throughout the Pearl River Delta. To the south is Ocean Terminal, the current dock for oceangoing cruise ships. With the advent of larger ships and the increasing popularity of cruising in Asia, Hong Kong plans to build a new cruise terminal by the former airport site at Kai Tak.

ABOVE RIGHT: colonial relic. **BELOW:** silk outfits for children.

Kong from neolithic times right up to the 1997 handover. The Hong Kong Story is the core exhibition, taking in developments from the Devonian period 400 million years ago to the 1997 handover. Most exhibits focus on more recent history, with imaginative displays and mock-ups of old-style teahouses, cinemas and a Cantonese opera stage, and many interesting old photographs.

Across Chatham Road, the **Rosary Church** was completed in 1905 to meet the needs of the growing Catholic community, as a result of a donation from a Portuguese expatriate, Dr Anthony Gomes.

From the Tsim Sha Tsui East area it is easy to return to the bright lights and shops of Tsim Sha Tsui. A network of underground walkways links the new Tsim Sha Tsui East station with various points around Tsim Sha Tsui and the MTR.

Hung Hom

Further east beyond the History Museum is Hung Hom Railway Station ⑲, built in 1975 to replace the old Kowloon station (by the Tsim Sha Tsui Clock Tower) as the terminus for trains from China. There are deartures every two or three days to Beijing and Shanghai, and several daily to Guangzhou. Ten minutes' walk away is Hung Hom Ferry Pier, with services to Central, Wan Chai and North Point.

The unusual-looking inverted pyramid situated on the harbour side of the station is the 12,000-seat **Hong Kong Coliseum** ⑳, one of the SAR's largest music venues. The indoor

Recommended Restaurants, Bars, Pubs and Clubs on pages 164–7

stadium hosts sell-out shows by Can-topop idols and international stars.

YAU MA TEI

Jordan MTR station at the northeast corner of Kowloon Park marks the transition from Tsim Sha Tsui to the more traditional Yau Ma Tei.

At the junction of Jordan and Canton roads there are several jade and ivory shops selling mah-jong sets. Shanghai Street still has shops selling red Chinese wedding dresses, embroidered pillowcases and other items for a Chinese bride's trousseau, as well as fascinating shops making pots and pans to order.

Ning Po Street and Reclamation Street are well known for their shops selling paper models of houses, cars and notes from "Hell Bank" that are burnt at funerals, which assure that the deceased will be well-off in the afterlife. At the junction of Kansu and Battery streets the **Jade Market** ㉑ (daily 9am–6pm) is packed with stalls. Dealers offer jade in every sculptable form, from large blocks of the raw material to tiny, ornately carved chips *(see panel, page 163).*

Temple Street Night Market

Shanghai Street continues north to Public Square Street, where you'll find an area once famous for its temples, but now renowned for the **Temple Street Night Market** ㉒ (daily 4pm–10pm). Running parallel to Shanghai Street, stalls start setting up in the late afternoon, but the market comes to life after after dusk. Best-known for its fake designer goods, this is the perfect place to hunt down that tacky memento, with stalls selling souvenir T-shirts, lighters, watches, bags, jeans, old coins, crafts, small electrical gadgets, mobile phones and toys. It's also good for bargain-price clothes. Palmists and physiognomists vie to reveal your destiny, and there are numerous *dai pai dongs* – basic Hong Kong-style diners serving up tasty seafood and hotpots to eat at functional fold-up tables and stools perched on the edges of the street.

One of the temples that gave the market its name is the **Tin Hau Temple** ㉓ (complex open daily 7am–5.30pm) on Public Square Street, which was originally built

Temple Street Night Market gets into full swing in the early evening. Prepare to bargain hard.

BELOW LEFT: Cantonese food is prepared as fresh as possible. **BELOW:** that cheap Rolex is a fake...

The Langham Place Hotel in Mong Kok has raised standards in the area.

closer to the harbour, and locals still visit it regularly to worship Tin Hau, the protector of fisherfolk, whose image is draped in intricately embroidered scarlet robes. To the right of the altar are 60 identical deities that represent every year of the 60-year lunar calendar. Worshippers place "Hell Bank" notes under the god dedicated to the years of their birth.

Hong Kong's only arts cinema, **Broadway Cinematheque**, is two blocks along from Temple Street, past Reclamation Street, opposite the elegant 1920s former Yau Ma Tei Police Station on Public Square Street. As well as four screens showing a broad mix of films, there is the laid-back Kubrick Bookshop Café to relax in and mull over your movie options.

West Kowloon reclamation

Further west past Reclamation Street, a 40-hectare (100-acre) parcel of the land reclaimed as part of the airport project has been earmarked to be the site of a huge **"cultural district"** comprising museums and performance space, as well as commercial and residential space. A public consultation process in 2003 resulted in the government taking the project back to the drawing board, and whatever is built is not likely to be completed before 2018. However, the new **Union Square** development nearby already includes Hong Kong's tallest residential block at 75 storeys, the Elements shopping mall and the city's tallest building – the **International Commerce Centre** (ICC; *see page 152*), towering above Kowloon MTR station at 484 metres (1,588ft). The Sky 100 (www.sky100.com.hk) observation deck on the 100th floor gives exceptional 360° views of the city (opening late 2010), while the floors above are home to the new Ritz Carlton Hong Kong. Indecision regarding the cultural complex means that the completed West Kowloon Promenade (accessible from Kowloon Station) is a brand-new, little-visited viewpoint that is ideal for viewing the harbour and the Hong Kong skyline.

MONG KOK

Mong Kok (properly Wong Kok in Cantonese: a long-dead sign writer got his letters mixed up) was for many years associated with sleaze. The area got a shock in 2004, when Langham Place, a glitzy combined office block, shopping mall and five-star hotel, opened next to the MTR station right in the heart of what used to be the seediest part of town. The shoddy bars and one-room bordellos continue to operate in nearby side streets, but the writing is on the wall. **Langham Place** – whose developer spent a dozen years buying up the tenements from different owners – is the future, soaring 255 metres (840ft) to the heavens.

A glimpse of an older Mong Kok can be seen at Lui Seng Chun, 119 Lai Chi Kok Road. A typical mid-20th-century *tong lau* (shophouse), its ground floor was occupied by a bone-setting medicine shop, while an extended family lived upstairs.

Many well-known Mong Kok streets, like Fa Yuen Street, known locally as "Sneaker Street" because of the preponderance of sports shops, are likely to be demolished in the near future as part of an urban regeneration scheme.

On the east side of Nathan Road, on Tung Choi Street, the so-called **Ladies' Market ㉔** (daily noon–10.30pm) sells everything from fake designer accessories and clothing to cheap cosmetics and toys. It is also a popular area for late-night shopping and dining. At the northern end of Tung Choi Street, **Goldfish Market** is a group of shops specialising in tropical fish and unusual goldfish.

Ten minutes walk to the north, approaching Boundary Street, the colourful **Flower Market ㉕** (7am–dusk) has a fascinating selection of cut flowers, house plants and feng shui flora. However, ongoing concerns about avian flu mean that the photogenic **Yuen Po Street Bird Market** (daily 10am–6pm) is often closed without notice. ❏

ABOVE: faces at the Bird Market.
BELOW LEFT: items for sale at the Yau Ma Tei's Jade Market.

China's Favourite Stone

Jade was formerly the preserve of China's elite. Belief in its powerful essence is nearly as old as Chinese civilisation itself, and its prominence in Chinese art and literature attests to its long-standing value. Jade was prized for the aesthetic beauty of the stone, the skill needed to carve it and the magical properties it was believed to possess.

Most jewellery was made from jade, favoured over gems and precious metals, and some people held that the stone glowed with the vitality of the owner or became tarnished if the wearer fell ill. The Chinese have long believed that wearing jade ornaments imparts good health, good luck and protection from evil spirits.

There are two types of jade: jadeite and nephrite. Early jade objects were carved from nephrite, a softer form of the stone that can be worked with primitive tools.

The best-known single piece of jade is Jade Mountain of the Great Yu Taming the Flood. According to records, the uncut stone was discovered in Xinjiang province and weighed more than 5 tonnes, requiring more than three years to transport to Beijing and six years for a team of artisans to carve.

BEST RESTAURANTS, BARS, PUBS AND CLUBS

Restaurants

Prices for a three-course dinner per person with one beer or glass of house wine:

$ = under HK$150
$$ = HK$150–300
$$$ = HK$300–500
$$$$ = over HK$500

It's hard not to find a restaurant in Kowloon. Try Knutsford Terrace for a choice of small restaurants and bars with a cross-section of cuisine, Chungking Mansions for Indian food or Harbour City for new waterfront dining options.

Cantonese

Hoi King Heen

B2, Grand Stanford Inter-Continental Hotel, 70 Mody Rd, Tsim Sha Tsui East
☎ 2731 2883 ⊚ L Mon–Sat, D daily. **$$$** [p305, D3]
Hoi King Heen offers endlessly creative Cantonese fine dining for those in the know. Chef Leung is famous for his ability to adapt novel ingredients into classic Cantonese cooking. A quality operation.

Royal Garden Chinese Restaurant

B2, The Royal Garden Hong Kong, 69 Mody Rd, Tsim Sha Tsui ☎ 2724 2666 ⊚ L & D daily. **$$** [p305, D3]
A visit to this ornate hotel restaurant takes in fish ponds, an arched wooden bridge and tiled canopies. The kitchen serves top dim sum and ocean-fresh seafood.

Super Star Seafood Restaurant

1/F, TST Mansion, 83–97 Nathan Rd, Tsim Sha Tsui ☎ 2628 0339 ⊚ L & D daily. **$$** [p304, C3]
An authentic Cantonese experience that is loud and lavish. The dish in demand is the steamed grouper picked from the fish tanks, but anything on the menu will be good.

T'ang Court

1/F, Langham Hotel, 8 Peking Rd, Tsim Sha Tsui ☎ 2375 1333 ⊚ L & D daily. **$$$** [p304, B4]
Among the most stylish Cantonese hotel restaurants in town. The lush interior brims with sumptuous opulence, but don't let that distract you from a menu that dotes on bird's nest and abalone.

Other Chinese

Heaven on Earth

G/F and 1/F, 1 Knutsford Terrace, Tsim Sha Tsui ☎ 2367 8428 ⊚ D only Mon–Sat. **$$** [p304, C2/3]
Brightly coloured Heaven on Earth stands out among the bars and restaurants of lively Knutsford Terrace. The menu crosses China from Sichuan to Shanghai with a few light, modern touches.

Hutong

28/F, 1 Peking Rd, Tsim Sha Tsui ☎ 3428 8342 ⊚ L & D daily. **$$$** [p304, B4]
Some serious Sino-chic featuring an intoxicating mixture of the antique and the up-to-date. The menu offers classic northern Chinese cuisine with a fresh contemporary twist.

M Garden (Vegetarian)

6D Grand Tower, 639 Nathan Rd, Mong Kok ☎ 2787 3128 ☯ L & D daily. $-$$ [p302, B2]

Popular vegetarian restaurant, offering Chinese-style vegetarian and interesting "meat-like" dishes.

Peking Restaurant

1/F, 227 Nathan Rd, Jordan ☎ 2730 1315 ☯ L & D daily. $ [p304, C2]

The Peking is a nostalgic blast from the past, manned by white-gloved geriatrics with limited attention spans. The menu features good-quality roast duck and traditional accompaniments.

Spring Deer

1/F, 42 Mody Rd, Tsim Sha Tsui ☎ 2366 4012 ☯ L & D daily. $$ [p305, C3]

Always busy, so reserve ahead at this classic restaurant. Peking Duck with pancakes, and shredded beef are highlights. Menu, decor and efficient staff have stayed the same for 30 years, adding to its retro charm.

French
Gaddi's

The Peninsula, Salisbury Rd, Tsim Sha Tsui ☎ 2315 3171 ☯ L & D daily. $$$$ [p304, C4]

The historic Peninsula Hotel's French haute cuisine legend is a high-

society magnet, serving flawless food in some splendid surroundings. Jacket and tie required. The chandeliered dining room exudes genuine antique opulence.

Spoon

InterContinental Hotel, 18 Salisbury Rd, Tsim Sha Tsui ☎ 2313 2256 ☯ L & D daily. $$$$ [p304, C4]

Spoon is smack on the waterfront in the upmarket InterContinental hotel. French quality with a contemporary menu. Diners can get creative by choosing ingredients from which the chef will conjure some magic.

Indian
Branto

1/F, 9 Lock Rd, Tsim Sha Tsui ☎ 2366 8171 ☯ L & D daily. $ [p304, B3]

A lively Indian vegetarian retreat with thalis, idlis and dosas offering great value for money.

Delhi Club Mess

Block C, 3/F, Chungking Mansions, 36–44 Nathan Rd ☎ 2368 1682 ☯ L & D daily. $ [p304, C4]

A long-standing favourite for inexpensive Indian cuisine, Delhi Club is an easy introduction to Chungking and serves a good choice of dishes.

International
Cucina

6/F, The Marco Polo Hong Kong, 3 Canton Rd ☎ 2113

0808 ☯ L & D daily. $$$ [p304, B4]

The menu roams from Asia to Italy, and chefs in the open kitchen work hard to compete with the harbour views and outdoor terrace. Tapas are served early evening, and as late-night bar snacks.

Misocool

B231-B233, K11, 18 Hanoi Rd, Tsim Sha Tsui ☎ 3122 4477 ☯ L & D daily. $ [p304, C3]

Misocool is a trendy setting for noodles and bento boxes and overcomes its basement location with style. Reminiscent of the Wagamama chain of Asian restaurants in the UK.

Oyster and Wine Bar

18/F, Sheraton Hotel, 20 Nathan Rd, Tsim Sha Tsui ☎ 2369 1111 ☯ L & D daily. $$$ [p304, C4]

This seafood emporium offers wide-angle views across the harbour and serves a cosmopolitan and ever-changing collection of jet-fresh oysters. The wine list is well chosen, and the staff know their Kuamamotos from their Sydney Rocks.

The Parlour

G/F Hullett House, 2a Canton Rd, Tsim Sha Tsui ☎ 3988 0101 ☯ L & D daily. $$-$$$ [p304, C4]

The latest location for a classy brunch, afternoon tea or cocktails. Desserts are a speciality

of the house. Fans whir over The Parlour's palm-lined colonial verandah and inside there's a funky mix of chinoiserie to enjoy when the view of the Cultural Centre becomes too much.

The Place

Langham Place Hotel, 555 Shanghai St, Mongkok ☎ 3552 3388 ☯ L & D daily. $$ [p302, B2]

Hong Kongers love generous buffets because they allow them to try as much as they want from a wide choice of food presented fresh and ready to eat. The terrace is a wonderful opportunity to observe the contrast between the disappearing old Hong Kong and high-tech, big-money new.

Salisbury Dining Room

4/F, South Tower, The Salisbury YMCA, 41 Salisbury Rd, Tsim Sha Tsui ☎ 2268 7818 ☯ L & D daily. $ [p304, B4]

Pleasing prices and excellent-value views of the harbour. Choose from international buffets, afternoon tea-set and an à la carte menu. Book ahead for window table for 8pm fireworks.

Italian
Tutto Bene

7 Knutsford Terrace, Tsim Sha Tsui ☎ 2316 2116 ☯ L & D daily. $$$ [p304, C2/3]

Alfresco dining on a small terrace or garden, romantic Tutto Bene is a

LEFT: Cantonese restaurants outnumber all others.

Prices for a three-course
dinner per person with
one beer or glass of
house wine:

$ = under HK$150
$$ = HK$150–300
$$$ = HK$300–500
$$$$ = over HK$500

little piece of Italy in the
heart of Kowloon.

Japanese
Aqua

29/F, 1 Peking Rd, Tsim Sha
Tsui ☎ 3427 2288 ☺ L &
D daily. **$$$** [p304, B4]
Aqua's vista from the
pinnacle of a Kowloon
skyscraper is integral to
its glamorous interior,
and it benefits from
pyrotechnic displays over
the harbour. Japanese
(Aqua Tokyo) and Italian
(Aqua Roma) menus.

Hibiki

15 Knutsford Terrace, Tsim
Sha Tsui ☎ 2316 2884
☺ L & D daily. **$$** [p305, C2]

Neo-Japanese temple to
tempura, sushi, sashimi
and Kobe beef. Dark
wooden textures and
subdued lighting pro-
mote a cosy and com-
fortable ambience,
complemented by a com-
prehensive sake list.

Nadaman

LL2, Kowloon Shangri-La
Hotel, 64 Mody Rd, Tsim
Tsui ☎ 2733 8751 ☺ L &
D daily. **$$$** [p305, D3]
This exceptionally stylish
Japanese hot spot is a
satellite of a Tokyo chain
with a solid reputation,
and is a showcase of
authentic Japanese cuis-
ine. Nadaman is where
Hong Kong's discriminat-
ing Japanese community
chooses to eat.

Robatayaki

Harbour Plaza Hotel,
20 Tak Fung St, Hung Hom,
Kowloon ☎ 2996 8438

☺ L & D daily. **$$$$**
[off p305, E2]
Informal Japanese
barbecue where guests
sit around the chef, who
grills to order. There's
an excellent choice of
high-quality meat and
seafood on the menu.

Korean
Arirang

G07 Ocean Terminal, Tsim
Sha Tsui ☎ 2956 3288
☺ L & D daily. **$$** [p304, B4]
This Korean stalwart,
with its pale-wood and
marble interior, is great
for social occasions as
diners grill slices of meat
or fish on a barbecue
brazier set into each
table, with kimchee and
pickled garnishes.

Middle Eastern
Olive

R008, 3/F, Elements, 1
Austin Rd West, West
Kowloon ☎ 2810 8585
☺ L & D daily. **$$$–$$$$**
[p304, A2]
Melbourne chef Greg
Malouf describes his
restaurant's cuisine as
modern Middle Eastern.
It's worth the time to
track down the roof
garden at Elements mall,
to enjoy the Arabesque
Mezze or mixed grill.

Mongolian
Nomads

55 Kimberley Rd, Tsim Sha
Tsui ☎ 2722 0733 ☺ L &
D daily. **$–$$** [p305, C2/3]
The crowd-pleasing all-
you-can-eat Mongolian

barbecue allows you to
choose exactly what you
want to eat: chefs then
cook it all up with
delicious sauces.

Southeast Asian
Good Satay

Shop 148, 1/F, Houston
Centre, 63 Mody Rd, Tsim
Sha Tsui. ☎ 2739 9808
☺ L & D daily. **$** [p305, D3]
Tasty Indonesian,
Malaysian and Singa-
porean food including
Hainan chicken rice and
satay specialities.

Spanish
El Pomposo

R009 Roof Garden, Elements
1 Austin Rd West, West
Kowloon
☎ 2196 8123 ☺ L & D
daily. **$$** [p304, A2]
Tasty tapas at the foot
of Hong Kong's tallest
building. with a full
menu of Spanish
cuisine and excellent
platters. Sit back with a
Sangria and enjoy the
ambience. Occasional
Latin music nights, with
dancing under the stars.

Swiss
The Swiss Chalet

12–14 Hart Ave, Tsim Sha
Tsui ☎ 2191 9197 ☺ L & D
daily. **$** [p305, C3]
Authentic Swiss cuisine
in a cosy restaurant that
comes with cowbells
and an Alpenhorn on the
walls. Traditional fare
includes speciality meat
fondue, *raclette* and
chocolate fondues.

LEFT: a fast-food joint. **ABOVE RIGHT:** there is no
shortage of modish bars in Tsim Sha Tsui.

Bars, Pubs and Clubs

Aqua Spirit, 1 Peking Rd. Tel: 3427 2288. Amazing views of the skyline in this trendy bar, but the price of the drinks will bring a tear to your eye.

The Backyard, Langham Place Hotel, 555 Shanghai St, Mong Kok. Tel: 3552 3250. Mong Kok's most stylish option for drinks with a view. Kick back on the loungers and beanbags and take in the urban view. Cocktails by the glass or jug.

Bahama Mama's, 4–5 Knutsford Terrace. Tel: 2368 2121. Caribbean-themed bar spilling onto the street.

Balalaika, 2/F, 10 Knutsford Terrace. Tel: 2312 6222. Russian restaurant with vodka bar. Don fur hat and coat and down shooters in the walk-in fridge.

Biergarten German Pub and Restaurant, G/F, 8 Hanoi Rd, Tsim Sha Tsui. Tel: 2721 2302. Favourite with all lovers of German food and beers.

Black Stump, G/F 1 Knutsford Terrace, Tsim Sha Tsui. Tel: 2721 0202. First stop on Knutsford Terrance is this modern Australian-style bar. There's outdoor dining and – innovatively – your own beer pump on the table.

Bulldog's Bar and Grill, G/F, Tsim Sha Tsui Centre, Mody Rd, Tsim Sha Tsui East. British-style sports pub located close to a good selection of restaurants.

Club PP, UG2/F, Chinachem Golden Plaza, 77 Mody Rd, Tsim Sha Tsui East. Tel: 2739 1084. New mega club.

Fatt's Place, 2 Hart Ave, Tsim Sha Tsui. Tel: 3421 1144. Good selection of beer, and 11 burgers named after famous "Fatts".

Felix, The Peninsula, Salisbury Rd, Tsim Sha Tsui. Tel: 2315 3188. A sublime Philippe Starck-designed bar perched on top of the legendary Peninsula Hotel. Check out the celebrated urinals.

Mariners' Rest, 2a Canton Rd, Tsim Sha Tsui. Tel: 3988 0103. Take a tot of rum or a glass of beer and enjoy the authentic old-world ambience in this cosy little bar. The former police holding cells must have seen their fair share of drunken sailors. Gastro pub fare available. 11am–11pm.

Mes Amis, G/F, 15 Ashley Rd, Tsim Sha Tsui. Tel: 2730 3038. Lively wine bar, ideally located for a drink

before or after dinner in Tsim Sha Tsui.

Morton's of Chicago, 4/F, Sheraton Hong Kong Hotel, 20 Nathan Rd, Tsim Sha Tsui. Tel: 2732 2343. During happy hour (5–7pm), Morton's serves free mini steak sandwiches with its classic Mortinis.

Ned Kelly's Last Stand, 11A Ashley Rd, Tsim Sha Tsui. Tel: 2376 0562. A HK institution, with live Dixieland jazz every night.

PJ Murphy's, Basement, Imperial Hotel, 32 Nathan Rd, Tsim Sha Tsui. Tel: 2782 3383. Vast Irish-style pub, with Guinness and Celtic music offering a haven from the neon. Open

7am–2.30am; daily happy hours 5–8pm.

Rick's Café, 53–9 Kimberley Rd. Tel: 2311 2255. Loud basement bar/club, which is usually packed.

Santa Lucia, 38/F, Hotel Panorama, 8A Hart Avenue, Tsim Sha Tsui. Tel: 3550 0262. Towering above TST, a quiet nook for a drink with a breathtaking panoramic view.

Spasso Ristorante and Bar, Level 4, Ocean Centre, Harbour City, Tsim Sha Tsui. Tel: 2730 8027. Watch the sunset from the terrace and choose from 50 wines by the glass. "Aperitif Moment" 5.30–7.30pm.

SHOPPING

Trading, buying and selling, shopping – it's why Hong Kong was founded and what it still does best

Hong Kong prides itself on being a shopper's paradise, and most locals are insatiable shoppers. If you love to shop, you will love Hong Kong. Whether it's in a mall – Hong Kong has some of the largest and most glamorous in the world, packed with designer names – or down on street level in one of the lively street markets or dusty "antique" stores, there is no shortage of finds.

These days, Hong Kong may not be the bargain basement it once was, but there is no sales, value-added- or luxury tax, which gives it the edge over some other Asian destinations. Best of all, Hong Kong's compact size means that it's easy to cover a lot of shopping ground in a remarkably short time.

ABOVE: it is easy to find clothing in all price brackets. Home-grown mid-priced brands include Giordano, Bossini and Esprit. For funkier finds and factory outlets, head to Causeway Bay and explore the side streets of Kowloon.

ABOVE: Hong Kong is well known for its electronics shops, although prices are less keen than they were.

RIGHT: gold jewellery is always a popular gift. If the shop describes it as *chuk kam*, it is at least 99 percent pure.

LEFT: Shanghai Tang's Pedder Street store (Central) evokes old Hong Kong and sells clothes and gifts that are distinctively "modern Chinese chic".

ABOVE: the SOGO shopping centre in Tsim Sha Tsui.

BELOW: Causeway Bay, packed with shoppers on a Saturday afternoon. In 2010, US fashion chain Forever 21 assigned to pay HK$11m a month for a six-storey retail space in the area.

Hong Kong's smart shopping malls compete for customers with opulent architecture, famous name shops, live entertainment, cinemas and restaurants.

Traditional Chinese clothes for little emperors and princesses are available at street markets like The Lanes in Central or at Stanley Market. Bargaining is expected.

Expert tailors whip up custom-made shirts and suits in less than a week. Choose from fine fabrics imported from all over the world.

Alarm clocks, posters, ornaments and musical lighters inspired by retro-Chinese propaganda art are found at Temple Street Night Market and Cat Street Bazaar.

Hollywood Road is lined with galleries and stores selling antiques and decorative items – everything from faux terracotta warriors to genuine Tibetan relics.

Known in China as the royal gem, most natural jade is a greenish-white. Various methods are used to stain it pink, violet, red and other colours.

HONG KONG'S MARKETS

There's plenty of fun to be had at Hong Kong's street markets. Ladies' Market and Temple Street Night Market in Kowloon are overflowing with a mix of tacky souvenirs, cheap clothes and the odd "real find", with a unique urban Kowloon backdrop. By day the Flower Market near Prince Edward MTR is packed with unusual flowers and plants. To see, and smell, an authentic Hong Kong wet market, visit Wan Chai Market off Spring Garden Lane or Graham Street in Central. Also in Central, The Lanes sell souvenirs, sportswear, pashminas, linen, knitwear and chinoiserie. Stanley Market sells similar goods plus factory overruns, but its popularity is due to the number of stalls, and the chance to relax in a seaside café-bar to recharge your batteries.

LEFT: Hong Kong merchants have traditionally grouped together according to what they sell. Antique-lovers, collectors and art fans will find a whole street of stores selling antiques and bric-a-brac along Hollywood Road and neighbouring Cat Street. The Jade Market on the corner of Kansu and Battery Street has 450 stalls selling jade items.

TOP LEFT: attractively decorated chops (Chinese name stamps) make a good souvenir purchase. Man Wa Lane in Western District is the best place.

ABOVE: jade necklaces at Kowloon's Jade Market.

LEFT: Mao memorabilia for sale on Cat Street.

BELOW: every character has a special meaning, and a calligrapher can transform a simple phrase into a work of art.

SHOPPING IN SHENZHEN

Shenzhen appeals to anyone with an eye for a bargain, but be warned that a shopping trip up here can require stamina. Most shoppers from Hong Kong see no need to venture beyond Lo Wu Commercial City, right on the border. This vast shopping arcade sells cheap clothes and shoes, factory over-runs, outrageous fake-designer goods, pens, cufflinks, toys and all manner of home furnishings, electronics, and a phenomenal number of handbags, wallets and purses.

There are over 2,000 booths spread over five floors. Clothes can be tailor-made, or they will copy a favourite garment for a fraction of the price in Europe or North America. The whole of the fifth floor is devoted to a fabric market surrounded by tailors. Jewellery rules on the second floor, with plenty of pearls, semi-precious stones and costume jewellery. Take a break to have a foot massage and pedicure for less than HK$50, while you plan your next purchase.

ABOVE: Hong Kong's street markets are as much about the atmosphere as the shopping. Check every item thoroughly, and don't be afraid to bargain via the stallholder's calculator. "Ho gwai" – very expensive! – is the only phrase you need to know.

RIGHT: Stanley Market is the closest Hong Kong gets to a Western-style flea market. It is best-known for its clothing (mostly casual wear), including silk and leather items, but there is a lot more for sale besides – everything from surfwear and designer kids clothes to art and antiques.

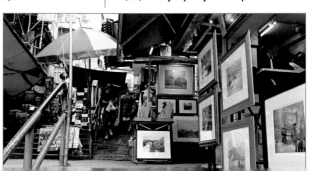

NEW KOWLOON

In addition to being home to Hong Kong's most famous temple and the region's largest Buddhist nunnery, these urban districts at the upper end of Kowloon peninsula merit exploration for those interested in the grittier side of the SAR

BELOW: a typical street in the area. **ABOVE RIGHT:** the Chinese Christian Cemetery. **FAR RIGHT:** Kowloon Walled City Park.

Kowloon proper ends at Boundary Street in Mong Kok, which between 1860 and 1898 defined the frontier between Hong Kong and China. Although officially part of the New Territories, the districts immediately north of this street are more commonly known as New Kowloon. The densely populated neighbourhoods of Kwun Tong, Kowloon City, Wong Tai Sin and Sham Shui Po, wedged up against the mountains to the north, are occupied by housing estates, shopping malls and decaying factories and warehouses – this was the location of most of Hong Kong's light industry until it shifted over the border to China in the 1980s. Many of the older buildings are being torn down to be replaced with more upmarket residential towers and mega malls.

Passengers flying into Hong Kong used to have a close-up view of life in New Kowloon as they flew into the old airport at Kai Tak. By 2013, when the new cruise terminal is scheduled to open, it is likely passengers disembarking will find an area that has been transformed yet again.

Kowloon City

Kowloon City ❶ is best seen on foot, starting at Lok Fu MTR Station. Walk up Wang Tau Hom East Road as far as Junction Road, then turn left and continue west. Along Junction Road, the **Chinese Christian Cemetery** on the left is a stark reminder of the lack of space in Hong Kong, with graves stacked up like sardines on concrete terraces.

Next door to the cemetery is the tiny **Hau Wong Temple**, with traditional roof tiles and incense spirals hanging from the rafters. Built in 1730, the temple is dedicated to Yang Liang Jie, a loyal and courageous

general of the exiled Song dynasty's boy-emperor Ping. The general's birthday is celebrated on the 16th day of the sixth month on the lunar calendar. The temple-keeper acts as a medium interpreting the advice of Hau Wong by means of *kay fook* – praying for the god's blessing.

Remembering the Walled City

Continue past the temple for 10 minutes until the junction with Carpenter Road, then turn left and head past Kowloon City Plaza on the left to reach **Kowloon Walled City Park ❷** (daily 6.30am–11pm; MTR Lok Fu). The park marks the area where the notorious Walled City stood until it was finally demolished in 1992 *(see panel, following page)*. Opened in 1995 by then Governor Chris Patten, it is an attractive space in the middle of dowdy swathes of grey urban decline. Modelled on the Jiangnan garden style of the early Qing dynasty, it

EAT

The area is known for the scores of Thai and other Asian restaurants in the streets just south of the Walled City Park and off Nga Tsin Wai Rd. Nothing fancy, just small cafés and modest restaurants serving good authentic Asian cuisine.

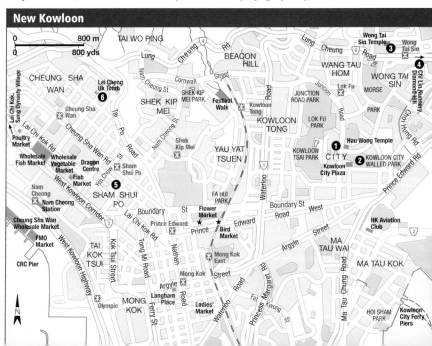

New Kowloon

TIP

The Chinese are generally relaxed about tourists visiting temples, but it's polite to bear in mind some rules of etiquette regarding photography. There is usually a sign to indicate if taking photographs of the interior is banned, but, nonetheless, it is considered disrespectful to take pictures of people worshipping unless you have their permission.

ABOVE RIGHT AND BELOW RIGHT: the Walled City shortly before it was demolished in the early 1990s.

features a chess garden as well as the Mountain View Pavilion, from which Lion Rock looms large to the north. The southern gate of the old Walled City has been preserved, along with two old cannons, while an information centre contains a photographic exhibition detailing the peculiar history of the city, its demise and the subsequent construction of the park, as well as displaying relics found within the walls.

Wong Tai Sin Temple ❸

✉ 2 Chuk Yuen Village, Wong Tai Sin
📞 2327 8141 🕐 daily 7am–5.30pm (all night on Lunar New Year's Eve)
💲 free 🚇 MTR Wong Tai Sin

Probably the liveliest and most colourful place of worship in Hong Kong, and the most rewarding for outsiders to visit, is **Wong Tai Sin Temple**, which sits opposite the eponymous MTR station.

The Walled City

In pre-colonial times, the site that was to become the notorious Walled City was occupied by a fortress. It continued to be used by the Chinese after 1841 (partly to monitor British activities), and when Britain leased the New Territories (which included this part of Kowloon) in 1898, the site was excluded. At first, the Qing-dynasty officials remained, but British troops were soon dispatched, and they were expelled.

Yet British law was never fully implemented within the walled compound, and it soon deteriorated into a semi-lawless enclave which was left to its own devices. After World War II, illegal low-rise blocks began to appear, resulting in a multi-storey squatter area with unauthorised electricity and water supplies. By the 1950s, the dank alleyways had become a real-life vice city – a squalid haven for drug addicts, triad gangs, illegal immigrants and brothels, as well as unlicensed doctors and dentists.

In true imperial style, the British simply turned a blind eye, but through the 1970s pressure mounted for them to act. Beijing vehemently opposed demolition plans, regarding it as Chinese territory, but eventually 35,000 residents were resettled in housing estates, and the entire block was razed to the ground, a process completed in 1992.

Recommended Restaurants on page 177

Wong Tai Sin, the Daoist god of healing, is said to have discovered the secret of transforming cinnabar (vermilion, a red mercuric sulphide) into an elixir for immortality. A painting of the god was brought to Hong Kong from China in 1915, and was first placed in a small temple in Wan Chai, before being moved to Wong Tai Sin to benefit, it was said, from the feng shui between formidable Lion Rock and the sea. Since Wong Tai Sin is also the god of good fortune, the Chinese, who are too cautious to rely solely on luck, flock to the temple to ask him for advice on all matters, including such worldly concerns as horse-racing and stock-market tips. The sound of rattling *chim* – a container holding dozens of fortune sticks *(see margin, right)* – resounds all day long. English-speaking fortune-tellers will also provide chapter and verse on the future using a number of other methods. They are especially good (from a parental point of view) with children.

The optimum times to visit are during Chinese New Year or at Wong Tai Sin's birthday on the 23rd day of the eighth lunar month (between mid-September and mid-October), when thousands of worshippers crowd into the temple to light incense, burn paper money and rattle *chim* sticks.

Chi Lin Nunnery ❹

✉ 5 Chi Lin Drive, Diamond Hill
☎ 2354 1730 🕒 daily 9am–4.30pm, garden 7am–7pm 💲 free 🚇 MTR Diamond Hill

One MTR stop to the east of Wong Tai Sin, the **Chi Lin Nunnery** is the largest Buddhist nunnery in East Asia. Nuns have lived here since 1937, but today's structure dates only from 1998, having been rebuilt in wood without the use of a single metal nail. The complex comprises a number of Buddhist halls and a tranquil garden with lotus ponds in front of the main entrance.

The Hall of Celestial Kings houses a statue of the Maitreya Buddha (Milefo), the Buddha of the Future and a heavenly being who will descend to Earth to save humanity. Guardians of the Four Directions

Bamboo chim sticks at Wong Tai Sin Temple are used for fortune-telling. People shake the container until a single chim falls out. Each has a number that is later interpreted, for a fee, by a fortune-teller at one of the rented stalls.

BELOW: Wong Tai Sin Temple.

The Chi Lin Nunnery is reputedly the largest building in the world to have been constructed without the use of a single nail.

surround him. On the left is a hall commemorating the goddess of mercy, Guanyin, who sits inside a grotto. On the right is Baishiyaja Guru (Medicine Master), accompanied by the Sun and Moon Bodhisattvas, Buddhist redemption deities. The most impressive statue is the golden Sakyamuni Buddha, resting on a lotus altar in the Main Hall. Across the road, the **Nian Lin Garden** (7am–9pm, daily, free) is one of the most beautiful Chinese gardens in Hong Kong. Also following Tang aesthetics, the garden features ornamental rocks, pavilions, water features and beautifully-shaped rare trees. A Buddhist vegetarian restaurant is hidden behind a waterfall.

Below Lion Rock

The relentless sea of high-rises starts thinning to the north of New Kowloon, around Kowloon Tong MTR station. This area, wedged between Kowloon City and Sham Shui Po, is the wealthiest in Kowloon and is full of luxury low-rise housing, plus the highest concentration of kindergartens, schools and universities in the city – amounting to over 200 institutions. In a typically odd Hong Kong style, the area is also famous for its "love hotels", discreetly situated behind high walls, with gates manned by security guards. Rooms at 41 Cumberland Avenue, Bruce Lee's former home were until recently, also rented by the hour. Now it is being restored and will be open to the public as a tribute to the kung fu star.

For visitors there's more of interest at **Festival Walk**, located above Kowloon Tong MTR station, with upmarket shops, restaurants, an 11-screen cinema and an ice rink.

Sham Shui Po

Sham Shui Po ❺ is situated to the west of Kowloon Tong, well off the tourist trail but nonetheless easily accessed by MTR. The area is as good a place as any to get an idea of the development of Hong Kong's architecture, from grim H-block resettlement estates hastily constructed in the 1950s to clean, modern apartment blocks erected in the 1980s. Sham Shui Po Police Station, at Lai Chi Kok Road and Yen Chow Street, is one of Kowloon's remaining colonial pre-war buildings. During World War II, the station was occupied and used by the Japanese to interrogate prisoners of war, and nowadays residents report a ghostly British soldier wandering around at night.

If you know your way around electronic devices and computers, Sham Shui Po is high-tech heaven – even though much of it looks like a flea market. Arcades and stalls selling computers and related merchandise can be found on Yen Chow Street and Ap Liu Street, where there are also street stalls selling cheap goods – from old stereos and vinyl records to

Lei Cheng Uk Tomb ❻

✉ 41 Tonkin Street, Sham Shui Po
☎ 2386 2863 ⓒ Mon–Wed, Fri & Sat
10am–6pm, Sun 1–6pm ⓢ free
🚌 no.2 from Kowloon Star Ferry Pier
🚇 MTR Cheung Sha Wan

The Lei Cheng Uk Housing Estate is home to one of Hong Kong's archaeological treasures, discoveries made in 1955 by workers excavating the hillside. The tomb here is a Han-dynasty burial vault dating back to between AD 100 and 200, when Kowloon was under the administrative control of the Wu Empire, which took control of southern China in the period following the collapse of the Han Empire. Four barrel-vaulted chambers form a cross under a domed vault, and there are a few funerary exhibits on show. A 3-D animation helps you to visualise the tomb. ❏

EAT

Chi Lin Nunnery's dining hall serves Buddhist-style vegetarian food on Sundays only between 11am to 3pm.

broken computers, TVs and household appliances. Many of the latest gismos, from game consoles to DVD players, are parallel imports – *sui foh* – goods imported directly from other countries available at lower prices, but without guarantees or instructions. Rip-offs do occur, and it's advisable to check items before buying. The Dragon Centre on Yen Chow Street is a 10-storey mall with ice rink on the eighth floor, and a children's entertainment arcade.

ABOVE LEFT: street art, Sham Shui Po.

RESTAURANTS

Kowloon City is known for its unusual density of Thai and ethnic Chinese restaurants. No fancy dining here – you will probably share a table – but fearless foodies will enjoy exploring these places well off the tourist trail. Festival Walk in Kowloon Tong has a good selection of restaurants and cafés to suit all budgets.

Cantonese
Jasmine
G/F Festival Walk, Kowloon Tong ☎ 2333 0222 ⓒ L & D daily. $$
A light, modern approach to Chinese food, with the emphasis on plenty of

vegetables and tofu, and a good selection of desserts and teas.

Tso Choi Koon
17–19A Nga Tsin Wai Rd, Kowloon City ☎ 2383 7170 ⓒ L & D daily. $
A true home-style Cantonese restaurant. Opt for glutinous congee, fried chicken or fish. No English spoken. Definitely for the adventurous.

Chinese Muslim
Muslim Restaurant
1 Lung Kong Rd, Kowloon City ☎ 2382 2822 ⓒ L & D daily. $
Straightforward eatery catering to Chinese Muslims, with halal

dishes typical of Xinjiang province. Specialities include mutton with scallions, a range of grilled kebabs and some very filling stuffed breads.

American
Dan Ryan's Chicago Grill
LG228, Festival Walk, Kowloon Tong ☎ 2265 8811 ⓒ L & D daily. $$$
If you're hungry, there's a menu of huge portions of consistently good food. If you just want a glass of Miller beer or a coffee, that's fine.

Thai
Golden Orchid
12 Lung Kong Rd, Kowloon City ☎ 2383 3076 ⓒ L & D daily. $
The area south of the

Walled City Park is home to a large Thai community, with many excellent restaurants.

Wong Chun Chun
23 Tak Ku Ling Rd, Kowloon City ☎ 2716 6269 ⓒ L & D daily. $$
Identified by a purple-and-gold exterior, this three-storey palace of Thai food is located on the corner of Tak Ku Ling and Nga Tsin Wai roads. Enjoy a royal feast at reasonable prices.

Prices for a three-course dinner per person with one beer or glass of house wine:
$ = under HK$150
$$ = HK$150–300
$$$ = HK$300–500
$$$$ = over HK$500

HONG KONG'S FESTIVALS

The city is at its most colourful during one of the traditional Chinese festivals

Despite the brash modernity, Hong Kong is a city whose population remains close to its roots, where temple deities and ancestors are honoured with equal fervour. These traditions are at their most vibrant and visible during the colourful Chinese festivals. **Lunar New Year**, in January or February, is the major annual event, a time for being with family, when most businesses shut down for at least a week. Children and the unmarried receive *lai see*, lucky red packets containing newly minted money. Employees get a bonus. Shops are decorated in fine style, and there are noisy dragon dances and processions. On the 15th day of the Lunar New Year the **Spring Lantern Festival** involves the hanging of colourful traditional lanterns in homes, restaurants and temples. Fishermen decorate their boats in bright colours and flock to Tin Hau temples around the territory on the **Birthday of Tin Hau**, the goddess of the sea, in April or May. Various Tin Hau temples – notably at Sai Kung in the New Territories – there are parades with lion dances and floats. The **Cheung Chau Bun Festival** *(see page 207)* in May is one of the most exciting local festivals; figures in historical costumes parade on stilts or ride on floats across the island. During the **Dragon Boat Festival** in June, elaborately decorated dragon boats race to the beat of loud drums. Many people's favourite is the **Mid-Autumn Festival** (Moon Festival) in September: paper lanterns of all shapes and sizes are illuminated and taken out to public parks – notably Victoria Park in Causeway Bay. People also eat special sweet cakes known as mooncakes.

ABOVE AND BELOW: lion dances are performed to bring good luck and usher in the Lunar New Year, accompanied by firecrackers to scare off evil spirits. Sometimes there will be a dragon dance as well: this involves a larger group who hold the dragon aloft, whereas the lion dance is performed by just two people.

ABOVE LEFT: the Cheung Chau Bun Festival originated as a peace offering to the ghosts of pirates *(see page 207)*.

ABOVE: Hong Kong's Dragon Boat Festival (June) owes its existence to an event around 200 BC. Chu Yuan, a poet who had fallen out of political favour with the king, jumped into a river in protest and drowned. The frantic paddlers of today recreate the desperate actions of Yuan's friends as they tried to save him.

BELOW: the climax of the Chinese New Year celebrations is the awesome fireworks display over the harbour. Most of the city's skyscrapers are lit up with stunning displays throughout the festive period.

THE CHINESE ZODIAC

Chinese festivals operate using the lunar calendar. Beginning with Chinese New Year in late January or early to mid-February, the year is divided into 12 months of 29 days, with an extra month added every two and a half years.

The calendar operates in 60-year cycles, divided up into five smaller cycles of 12 years. Each year is represented by an animal, and each of the five cycles by an element (wood, water, metal, earth and fire). As with Western astrology, the year of a person's birth is thought to provide clues into his or her character. The 12 animals are:

Rat: (1948, 1960, 1972, 1984, 1996, 2008) charming, imaginative but quick-tempered.

Ox: (1949, 1961, 1973, 1985, 1997, 2009) a leader, conservative and patient.

Tiger: (1950, 1962, 1974, 1986, 1998, 2010) sensitive, emotional, stubborn.

Rabbit: (1951, 1963, 1975, 1987, 1999, 2011) popular, sentimental, cautious.

Dragon: (1952, 1964, 1976, 1988, 2000, 2012) charismatic, clever, prone to indiscretion.

Snake: (1953, 1965, 1977, 1989, 2001, 2013) wise, thoughtful, charming, intuitive.

Horse: (1954, 1966, 1978, 1990, 2002) hard-working, intelligent but egotistical.

Ram: (1955, 1967, 1979, 1991, 2003) artistic, pessimistic, generous.

Monkey: (1956, 1968, 1980, 1992, 2004) intelligent, witty, popular but distrustful.

Rooster: (1957, 1969, 1981, 1993, 2005) extravagant, brave, hard-working.

Dog: (1958, 1970, 1982, 1994, 2006) honest, faithful, dependable but a worrier.

Pig: (1959, 1971, 1983, 1995, 2007) clever, sincere, honest but prone to set difficult goals.

Recommended Restaurants, Bars & Pubs on page 199

THE NEW TERRITORIES

Hong Kong's northern hinterland is well off the tourist trail, which is surprising given its magnificent scenery. Some splendid beaches and ancient walled villages add to the appeal

CHINA

Hong Kong

The buffer between the dense urban area of Kowloon and the boundary with mainland China, the New Territories are an odd mixture. Nobody is ploughing with water buffalo any longer, but there are corners where time seems to have not so much stood still as gone into reverse. Conversely, other areas are as modern as anywhere else in the SAR, notably the New Towns such as Sha Tin and Yuen Long – and this is where more than half of Hong Kong's population live. Transport links are good, with the MTR's East Rail running straight up the middle to the border with mainland China, supplemented by the MTR West Rail and Ma On Shan lines and the Light Rail. Away from the electrified rails, there are calm beaches to seek out, remote villages and lofty mountains to hike – after all, some two-fifths of the SAR is designated as country park.

SHA TIN AND SURROUNDINGS

Sha Tin ❶ is one of Hong Kong's largest New Towns, but it also offers plenty of recreation. Massive housing projects occupy what were once lush rice paddies whose produce was reserved for the emperor, while the New Town Plaza, an extensive shopping and entertainment complex, offers cinemas, designer boutiques and a musical fountain that never fails to draw appreciative crowds.

Ten Thousand Buddhas Monastery

✉ Sha Tin 📞 2691 1067; www.10kbuddhas.org 🕐 daily 9am–5pm 💲 free 🚌 Citybus 170 (from Aberdeen) 🚇 MTR Sha Tin

Main attractions

TEN THOUSAND BUDDHAS
  MONASTERY
HONG KONG HERITAGE MUSEUM
TAI PO KAU NATURE RESERVE
SAI KUNG
HIKING IN SAI KUNG COUNTRY PARK
HONG KONG WETLAND PARK
KAM TIN WALLED VILLAGES
KADOORIE FARM AND
  BOTANIC GARDEN

PRECEDING PAGES: farm workers in the New Territories. **LEFT:** Plover Cover Country Park in the far northeast. **RIGHT:** statues at the Ten Thousand Buddhas Monastery.

The walk up to the Ten Thousand Buddhas Monastery.

The Sha Tin Valley has several places of worship including the remarkable **Ten Thousand Buddhas Monastery** . Follow the signposts from Grand Central Plaza and IKEA, then climb the 431 steps flanked by gold-painted effigies of enlightened beings up the hillside above Sha Tin station. Founded in 1949, the monastery has five temples. The name is, in fact, over-modest – the main altar room alone accommodates close to 13,000 Buddha statues along its walls. The temple is guarded by huge, fierce-looking statues of various gods, and by similarly ferocious watchdogs that are chained up in the daytime. The complex also contains an impressive nine-storey pagoda of Indian architectural design, commemorating a Buddha who was believed to be the ninth reincarnation of Prince Vishnu.

A further 69 steps up the hill is the **Temple of Man Fat**, containing the preserved remains of the man who created this temple-and-pagoda complex: Yuet Kai, a monk who spent a lifetime studying Buddhism

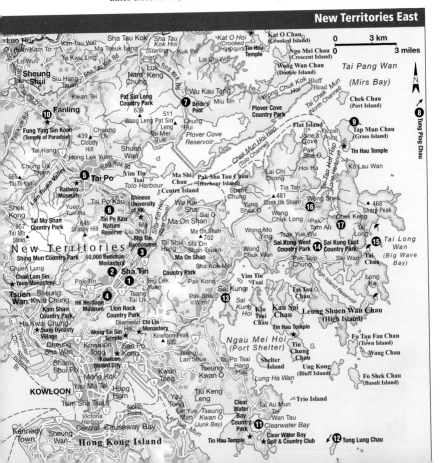

New Territories East

Monastery you can look across the valley at **Amah Rock**, which looks like an *aa maa*, or mother, with a baby on her back. Legend has it that a local fisherman went to sea and did not return. His wife waited patiently for his return but he did not appear.

After a year the gods took pity on her and turned her into stone. Today the rock is a place of worship for Chinese women, and stands as a symbol of women's loyalty and fidelity.

Romer's tree frog, an endangered species found in the New Territories.

and living a meditative life. His greatest concern was to achieve immortality – an objective which seemed to have failed when he died and was buried. Yet when his body was exhumed (to be moved to its final resting place, according to Chinese custom), it was perfectly preserved and radiated a ghostly yellow glow. Since there was obviously something supernatural about Yuet Kai, it was decided to preserve his body in gold leaf for posterity.

From the Ten Thousand Buddhas

A major destination in the valley is the Hong Kong Jockey Club's **Sha Tin Racecourse** ❸, which has its own MTR station. Around 30,000 punters flock here for the weekend race days, but the crowd can triple on cup days such as the Hong Kong Derby, the Queen Elizabeth II Cup and the Hong Kong International Races. Tourists can buy special tourist badges at the track or at off-site betting offices, which grant them access to the members' enclosure and a front seat on Hong Kong's racing world. *For more on horse-racing, see pages 136–7.*

ABOVE LEFT AND BELOW: natural shades at Tai Po Kau.

The Hong Kong Heritage Museum is one of the New Territories' main attractions.

Hong Kong Heritage Museum

✉ 1 Man Lam Road, Sha Tin
📞 2180 8188; www.heritage museum.gov.hk ⏰ Mon, Wed–Sat 10am–6pm, Sun 10am–7pm, closed Tue
💲 charge, but free on Wed
🚌 KMB routes 72A, 80M, 86, 89, 282 🚇 MTR Che Kung Temple

ABOVE RIGHT: sub-tropical foliage.
BELOW RIGHT: a small population of pangolins survive in the forest at Tai Po Kau.

If you are in Sha Tin already, it is easy to take a five-minute taxi ride from the main station to the superb and spacious **Hong Kong Heritage Museum ❹**, which opened in 2000. This is Hong Kong's largest museum, with 12 exhibition halls including the T.T. Tsui Gallery of Chinese Art, an exhibition devoted to the development of the New Territories, one on the history of Cantonese opera and another detailing the evolution of local toys. The displays are comprehensive and imaginative.

Two stops along from Sha Tin is the Chinese University of Hong Kong, with its highly respected **Art Museum** (Mon–Sun 10am–5pm; free;

tel: 2609 7416; www.cuhk.edu.hk) showcasing a collection of over 7,000 pieces from its extensive collections of Chinese art from ancient to pre-modern times.

TAI PO AND THE NORTHEAST

Further north (back on the main MTR East Rail line) is the market town of **Tai Po ❺**, which means "buying place". The old town is at the northeastern end of Tolo Harbour, where the highway crosses the Lower Lam Tsuen River. The **Hong Kong Railway Museum** (Wed–Mon 9am–5pm; tel: 2653 3455; free), complete with vintage train carriages, is housed in the former train station between

Tai Po Kau Nature Reserve

A short taxi ride from Tai Po Market MTR station, or a 20-minute walk from the car park near the 14-milestone on Tai Po Road, Tai Po Kau is the oldest of Hong Kong's reserves. Planting began here in 1926 as part of the government's attempt to reforest the New Territories (much of the original forest cover had long since disappeared, and what was left was destroyed during the Japanese Occupation).

Today, the 460 hectares (1,136 acres) of forest shelter a good proportion of Hong Kong's flora and fauna. Native tree species include litsea, giant bean, sweet gum, camphor, acacia, paperbark and the joss-stick tree (*Aquilania sinensis*) – used for making fans and joss sticks. A colourful variety of birds – including such exotica as rufous-capped babblers, scarlet-backed flowerpeckers and greater necklaced laughing thrushes, amongst an assortment of bulbuls and minivets – make the reserve their home. March, April and September are the best "birding" months. Mammals are also well represented, although mostly difficult to observe – the exception being the rhesus macaque monkeys, which can be quite aggressive, particularly if there is food around (avoid feeding them). Barking deer, civet cat, pangolin and porcupine are far more elusive.

today's Tai Wo and Tai Po Market MTR stations – a 10-minute walk: follow the map and signs in MTR stations. Alternatively, take a taxi.

Catch bus 64K or hop in a taxi from Tai Wo station to visit the **Wishing Trees**, a pair of banyans which have become popular with locals for their alleged properties. The idea is to make a wish, write it down on the streamer provided and then hurl this into the tree. Unfortunately, the two elderly banyans started collapsing under the strain, and for now wishes are placed nearby on a wooden rack.

One of the best places to escape from urban Hong Kong is the **Tai Po Kau Nature Reserve** ❻ *(see panel, opposite)*.

Tolo Harbour

To the northeast, the coast around **Tolo Harbour** has become more built up in recent years, but once past Shuen Wan, Ting Kok Road must rank among the most picturesque routes in Hong Kong, leading round to the Plover Cove Reservoir, Bride's Pool and Starling

Inlet. A ride on KMB bus 75K from Tai Po Market to Tai Mei Tuk lets you enjoy the panoramas. At weekends and on public holidays, the roadside barbecue areas teem with noisy groups, but even then, a five-minute walk into the hills brings peace and solitude. The area around **Bride's Pool** ❼, with waterfalls and woodland glades, is especially beautiful, while the village of Luk Keng to the north still has several fine old inhabited houses. Like many semi-abandoned villages Luk Keng was once home to a few thousand people. Its decline began in the 1950s and 60s, when rice farming became unprofitable. The nearby village of Nam Chung marks the northern end of the **Wilson Trail**, a 78-km (49-mile) walking route that runs from Stanley on Hong Kong Island to the northern end of the New Territories.

Mirs Bay Islands

Out at Mirs Bay (Tai Pang Wan) in the far northeast of the SAR, **Tung Ping Chau** ❽ (not to be confused with Peng Chau near Lantau) is one of Hong Kong's remotest islands, just

Punters at the Hong Kong Jockey Club's Sha Tin Racecourse check the racing statistics and watch the thoroughbreds going through their paces on the world's longest television screen. Measuring 70.4 metres (231ft), the LED screen is as long as a Boeing 747. An average of 40,000 people bet on every race, giving the Jockey Club a race-day turnover in excess of HK$1 billion.

BELOW: junks moored near Sai Kung.

Hiking in the Hills

One of Hong Kong's greatest assets is its mountainous countryside, and the open grassy hills of the New Territories offer superb hiking opportunities

In a rocky gully the air is dank. Far above, hidden by a wall of trees, are the upper slopes of Tai Mo Shan (957 metres/ 3,140ft), the great massif that encompasses the central New Territories, and Hong Kong's highest point. Cutting down through the mountain, water cascades beyond rocks green with slime. Lower down, gurgling amidst bamboo thickets, the stream descends into the sprawling bowl of the Shing Mun Valley.

Further to the east, on the beautiful Sai Kung peninsula, the steep grassy slopes of Sharp Peak (468 metres/1,535ft) plunge down to Tai Long Wan – a bay ringed by crescent beaches. Ranges stretch into the distance, looming above seldom-visited valleys.

In the far northeast is Pat Sin Leng (639 metres/2,096ft) – grand, challenging and the northern limit of the Hong Kong uplands. Jagged ridges rise up above sheer escarpments. Valleys with rich biodiversity occupy land where, just 40 years ago, rice farmers tilled the land. Old homes, empty and forlorn, stand amidst the fields.

The New Territories' countryside remains largely empty. With its steep peaks, deep valleys and ocean views, it epitomises the Chinese term for "landscape" – *shan shui*, literally "mountains and water". The landscape is criss-crossed with numerous hiking trails, varying from family walks to signposted nature trails to rugged upland and coastal hikes leading into areas where one rarely sees another soul. Excellent public transport makes access quite easy.

From the Shing Mun Valley, a 14-km (9-mile) hike takes you up and across impressive boulder slopes, past the massive summit of Tai Mo Shan, and down through the lush and beautiful Pak Nga Shan Valley – site of Kadoorie Farm and Botanic Garden (*see page 198*).

The ideal hike on the Sai Kung peninsula is the route that connects Sharp Peak with Tai Long Wan, a circular route of about 15 km (9½ miles). Noodle shops in a few places offer welcome refreshment, and the clean beaches are great for swimming.

The hike up and over the Pat Sin Leng range is only about 10km (6 miles), but the distance can be misleading. Here a series of sharp up-and-down peaks mark a dramatic, airy ridgeline, with the views sweeping south towards Hong Kong and north into China proper.

For the ambitious, the MacLehose Trail (*see page 193*) crosses the entire width of the New Territories, extending for some 100km (62 miles) from Sai Kung to Tuen Mun, while the Wilson Trail (70km/44 miles) runs north from Stanley on Hong Kong Island to the Pat Sin Leng range. ❑

For more on hiking, see page 280.

LEFT: in the wilds of the New Territories above the Shing Mun Valley. **ABOVE:** on the trail: autumn and winter are the best seasons for hiking.

TIP

The Tsui Wah Ferry Service (tel: 2272 2022; www.traway.com.hk) operates ferries to some of Hong Kong's remote islands. Ferries for Tung Ping Shan depart at 9am from Ma Liu Shui pier near University MTR station at weekends, and the journey takes approximately 90 minutes. Ferries to Tap Mun also depart from Ma Liu Shui, but the best option is to take a scenic 60-minute ride on the 94 bus from Sai Kung to Wong Shek Pier, where boats run every two hours daily; journey time is 30 minutes.

ticularly from the top of the hills next to the 100-year-old **Tin Hau Temple**. While there are dozens of Tin Hau temples all over Hong Kong, this one is special because it is the last before the open sea. When the east winds roar, their sounds can be heard in a crevice under the altar – this eerie howling is seen as a warning of storms to come. Former island residents who may have emigrated to all parts of the globe will make a special effort to come back to the temple for major festivals.

Parts of Tap Mun are covered with thick, impenetrable scrub, but in the upper reaches much of it is abandoned agricultural land, and the cows that once pulled ploughs are now feral and roam freely.

3km (2 miles) off the Guangdong coast. From its hilltops, you can get a panoramic view of the mainland's Bao An area. Once supporting a population of close to 3,000, it is practically deserted today, with all but a handful of locals having either emigrated or moved to Hong Kong's urban areas. Ping Chau has a fascinating landscape, made up of what are known as 'thousand layer rocks' – colourful and unusually shaped sedimentary rock. The island is now one of the eight areas making up the Hong Kong Geopark (www.geopark. gov.hk).

At the northwestern end of Mirs Bay close to the Sai Kung peninsula is **Tap Mun Chau ❾** (also called Grass Island), a 30-minute boat ride from Wong Shek Pier *(see margin tip, right)*. A dramatic decline in fish stocks has caused a collapse of the fishing industry, and of communities like Tap Mun: today many of the houses stand empty, although the village retains a single seafood restaurant, Loi Lam's, that makes the journey worthwhile (and is packed out at weekends). A path winds through the village, up past the fortress-like police station, and onto a grassy plateau whose brisk winds make it extremely popular with local kite-flyers.

There are terrific views from the northern point of the island, par-

Fanling

Fanling ❿ and its neighbour Sheung Shui are New Towns with over a quarter of a million residents. Fanling

ABOVE LEFT: on the Lung Yeuk Tau Heritage Trail. **BELOW:** burning spirit money.

is also home to the largest Taoist institute in Hong Kong – **Fung Ying Sin Koon** (Temple of Paradise; daily 9am–5pm), close to Fanling MTR station. There is an intricate system of pathways around this newly rebuilt temple, and plenty of shady benches suitable for meditation.

From Fanling station, it's a short ride on the 64K minibus to the **Leung Yuk Tau Heritage Trail**, starting at **Shung Him Tong** – a village founded in 1901 by Hakka Lutherans fleeing persecution across the border. The trail wends its way around several walled villages before reaching the venerable **Tang Chung Ling Ancestral Hall** (Wed–Mon 9am–1pm, 2–5pm; free). Originally built in 1570, the hall remains a focal point of the Tang clan (*see margin page 197*).

On a more earthly level, the well-know **Hong Kong Golf Club** (www.hkgolfclub.org) just outside Fanling has three exceptionally good 18-holers, known as the Old, the New and the Eden. It is the site of the Hong Kong Open Tournament every February, and is open to non-members on weekdays.

Hakka women shield their faces with the black curtains around the brims of their wide hats. Theirs is a matriarchal society, and women think nothing of labouring alongside men at heavy manual jobs.

BELOW: a still from a Shaw Brothers martial arts movie.

CLEARWATER BAY TO SAI KUNG

These eastern areas of the New Territories are some of the most attractive parts of Hong Kong. The Sai Kung peninsula is the most scenic area, with rolling hills, mountains, reservoirs, craggy coves and over 70 islands. It is at its most rewarding if you can hike into the hills or take to the water on a ferry, speedboat or junk.

Clearwater Bay

The **Clearwater Bay peninsula** ⑪ is a sought-after residential area that is blessed with some great beaches and

Shaw Brothers Movies

Clearwater Bay Road runs past the former Shaw Brothers Movie Studio, once a cornerstone of the local film industry. Founded by six brothers from Shanghai in 1958, for three decades, the Shaw Brothers often churned out over 30 films a year. They are best known for their martial arts movies, but romance, opera and dramas were also produced, and many of their library of over 1,000 films are now considered classic Hong Kong movies. Shaw Brothers has built one of the world's most advanced film production and digital post production facilities in a new US$180 million building on the hill above Tseung Kwan O. The patriarch of the empire, Sir Run Run Shaw, turned 100 in 2007.

Recommended Restaurants, Bars & Pubs on page 199

possibly the freshest air in Hong Kong. The single access road leads past the former **Shaw Brothers Movie Studio** *(see panel, opposite)* to reach the exclusive **Clearwater Bay Golf & Country Club**, easily recognised by its landmark pyramid-shaped clubhouse. Non-members can play here, but green fees are high.

An indentation in the shoreline forms **Joss House Bay**, which comes to life once a year on the birthday of the sea goddess Tin Hau. Hundreds of fishing junks and sampans head for the **Tin Hau Temple** here to pay their respects to the Queen of Heaven and Goddess of the Sea. This temple was built by two brothers allegedly saved by Tin Hau after their junk was destroyed by a typhoon in the 11th century. To cope with up to 10,000 visitors during the annual Tin Hau festival *(see panel, below)*, ferries run for one day only from North Point on Hong Kong Island.

Tung Lung Chau

Also known as Nam Tong Island, **Tung Lung Chau** ⑫ is located off the southern tip of the Clearwater Bay peninsula. The island's biggest attraction is **Tung Lung Fort** (Information Centre daily 9am–4pm; open access to the fort) built about 300 years ago and renovated in recent years. To find the fort, follow the path from the hamlet at the ferry pier over the rolling, open landscape of northern Tung Lung. The fort is perched on a low headland in the northeast. It was abandoned in 1810, but its interior is reasonably well preserved, with the bases of the partitions between the rooms visible.

On the north shore of Tung Lung

TIP

There are some good beaches around Clearwater Bay, and compared with the wilder stretches of sand further north in Sai Kung, they are easily accessible on the no. 91 bus from Diamond Hill MTR station.

ABOVE LEFT: Clearwater Bay Golf and Country Club. **BELOW LEFT:** Tin Hau Temple statue. **BELOW:** the Tin Hau Temple at Joss House Bay.

The Tin Hau Festival

Tin Hau, the Taoist goddess of the sea, is revered by fishermen all along the China coast. To the people of Fujian and Taiwan, she is Matsu, while the Macanese call her A-Ma, and her deification is based on the legend of Lin Moniang, a Fujianese girl who lived in the 10th century. Asleep during a storm, she dreamt that her two fisherman brothers were drowning, and that she managed to save them. When the brothers miraculously survived the real storm, the story spread, and Lin became the object of fishermen's prayers for protection from the dangers of the sea.

The festival of her birth, taking place on the 23rd day of the third lunar month (between mid-April and mid-May), is a noisy celebration at its liveliest around the Tin Hau Temple in Joss House Bay *(see above)*, an occasion of brightly coloured boats, dragon dances, drums and a great deal of noise.

TIP

The MTR (formerly KCR) East Rail, West Rail, Tsuen Wan Line, Tung Chung Line, Ma On Shan Line and Kwun Tong Line – together with the Light Rail – make getting around much of the New Territories quick and straightforward. Trains start running at 6am in the morning, and all lines cease operating by midnight.

ABOVE RIGHT:
boats at Sai Kung.
BELOW RIGHT:
traditional transport remains important in parts of the New Territories.

Chau are some rock carvings on the cliffs depicting the daily lives of people who lived in this area several hundred years ago. It is a perfect place to enjoy the beautiful sea view, with waves rushing to the shore and hiking trails lead along the cliffs and hills. As with most of the outlying islands, there is no regular ferry to Tung Lung, but *kaido* boats from Sai Wan Ho on Hong Kong Island operate on most weekends (tel: 2513 1103).

Sai Kung

Hiram's Highway branches off Clearwater Bay Road just before the University of Science and Technology, and leads down to the town of **Sai Kung** ⓭. The road is named after a brand of sausage made by Hiram K. Potts that the highway's builder, John Wynne-Potts, devoured by the tin. While the fringes of Sai Kung have fallen prey to development, this town and its neighbouring villages retain a strong seaside flavour. Along the seafront, sea creatures in tanks are a sure sign that seafood is on the quayside restaurants' menus, and Sai Kung Town also has good pubs and alfresco international restaurants. Further east along the seafront you can catch the ferry to Kau Sai Chau golf course, the only public links in Hong Kong.

The road from town runs out to **Sai Kung Country Park** ⓮, the start-

Island-hopping from Sai Kung

Some of the most easily accessible outlying islands sit in the Inner Port Shelter (Ngau Mei Hoi) offshore from Sai Kung village, which at one time was a British military firing range. It's all peace and quiet nowadays, though, and the harbour, home to more gin palaces than junks, makes a very photogenic start to the trip. Sampan owners will either make a one-hour tour for about HK$100 (bargain hard!), dropping you off for a short stroll at whichever island you desire, or charge around HK$300 to take you to your destination and then pick you up later. One of the nicest beaches is at Hap Mun Bay on Kiu Tsui Chau (Sharp Island), with fine sand and water that is usually clear. You can also camp overnight here, and there are barbecue pits for a cook-out. If recent visitors or perhaps a recent storm have left the beach in a mess, don't hesitate to move on round the harbour: there are other strands on Pak Sha Chau (White Sand Island) and tiny Cham Tau Chau (Pillow Island). Yim Tin Tsai (Little Salt Field) Island is remarkable for its Catholic chapel, which sees little use now, as many of the islanders have moved away. Remember that whichever island you pick, you should take enough food and drink to keep you going, and sunscreen and mosquito repellent are also advisable.

Recommended Restaurants, Bars & Pubs on page 199

ing point of the **MacLehose Trail**. The trail stretches for 100km (60 miles) through mostly open country, from one side of the New Territories to the other, across the high grassy hills as far as Tuen Mun. The trail is well marked, and there are places to camp along the way. Some parts are extremely steep and hard-going, but anyone who is used to hiking should have no problems tackling the shorter sections or any of the other walks in this area. At the very end of the road into the country park, **Hoi Ha** provides a small stretch of sand on the edge of the eponymous marine reserve.

The jewel in Sai Kung's crown is **Tai Long Wan** (Big Wave Bay) Beach ⑮. The usual way of getting there involves a two-hour trek, either around the High Island Reservoir or by cutting across the hills along the MacLehose Trail Stage 2 from the road at Pak Tam Au. Others opt to take a bus or taxi to Wong Shek *(see below)* and hop on a speedboat (HK$20 per person) for a thrilling 15-minute ride round to Chek Keng, then join the MacLehose Trail and hike for

an hour over the ridge to the bay. Whichever way you arrive, the effort is more than worth it. There are two long swathes of very pale and powdery sand, and usually enough surf to make it worth lugging a surfboard over the hill. There is also a café-cum-shop selling cold beer and hot noodles, and enough open space to romp far and wide. The one downside of Tai Long Wan is that there is a strong undertow, so don't swim out too far. A day of rest and relaxation here makes it difficult to believe that this is part of Hong Kong.

Beyond the crest at Pak Tam Au, the road swoops down through woods and little villages to Wong Shek pier, but from just below the top it's worth pausing to admire the pristine views.

At **Wong Shek** ⑯ (Bus 94 from Sai Kung) the Jockey Club watersports centre hires out dinghies and wind-surfing boards (tel. 2328 2311; closed Tue). This is also a popular picnic and barbecue site – perhaps because it's seen as the "end of the line", just about as far away from the city as it's possible to get by road.

Prevailing easterly or northeasterly winds for much of the year make the waters off Sai Kung and Clearwater Bay favoured spots for surfing and wind-surfing.

BELOW: the fabulous white sands at Tai Long Wan.

Kwai Chung container terminal is the world's third-busiest.

the harbour to the shore of the western New Territories is dominated by container ships, cranes and a network of bridges crossing from Lantau to Tsing Yi Island and on to Kowloon. Kwai Chung container port is one of the three busiest ports in the world, transporting goods from factories in Guangdong to ports worldwide.

Chek Keng ⑰ is nearly deserted nowadays, but it's fascinating to wander round the old buildings and paddy fields and imagine the time when the New Territories were a land apart, with people living on what they could earn from soil and sea. This remains a gloriously empty part of Hong Kong that even locals know little about.

THE WESTERN NEW TERRITORIES

BELOW: the Tsing Ma Bridge, "Hong Kong's Golden Gate".

Looking to the northwest from Hong Kong Island, the view across

The busy port and the need for road and rail links to the airport on Lantau prompted the investment of public funds into huge infrastructure projects, including some dramatic new bridges. Opened in 1997, the **Tsing Ma Bridge ⑱** is some 2.2km (1½ miles) long, with majestic 200-metre (650-ft) twin towers. The world's longest road and rail suspension bridge, it links Lantau (and the airport) with Tsing Yi Island. The entrance to the Rambler Channel between Container Terminal 9 on Tsing Yi and the eight other container terminals at Kwai Chung is spanned by **Stonecutters' Bridge**, 1.6km (1 mile) long, with cables radiating from its 295-metre (970ft) towers.

Tsuen Wan

Behind the industrial area at Kwai Chung is the urban sprawl of **Tsuen Wan** ⑲, one of the largest New Towns with a population of over 1 million. The Chinese presence here seems to have begun about the 2nd century AD. In the 13th century, the Chinese Empire extended to this area because the emperor was being driven south by invading Mongols. In 1277, the emperor and his entourage arrived in Tsuen Wan. Later, in the mid-17th century, when the Formosan pirate Koxinga was building his empire, the Manchu government ordered a mass evacuation of coastal areas to save the populace from the marauding buccaneer. Koxinga's forces demolished the vacated settlement of Tsuen Wan, and it was not repopulated until the end of the 17th century.

The main reason to make the long MTR journey out here is to poke around the **Sam Tung Uk Museum** (Wed–Mon 9am–5pm; free), a beautifully restored Hakka walled village. The narrow alleyways trace a path past a central ancestral hall, an exhibition room and rows of tiny cubicles stocked with period furniture and farming tools.

Tsuen Wan's most modern building is also the sixth tallest in Hong Kong. The top 40 storeys of the 319-metre (1,046-ft) Nina Tower is L'Hotel Nina, named like the tower after the late Nina Wang, who was Hong Kong's richest woman when she died in 2007, leaving her fortune to her feng shui master.

TIP

The Yuen Yuen Institute (daily 9am–5pm; free) near Tsuen Wan is popular on organised tourist itineraries. It was set up in 1950 and is the only temple in Hong Kong dedicated to all three major Chinese religions: Taoism, Buddhism and Confucianism, and actively promotes the integration of the three religions' philosophies. There is a good vegetarian restaurant on site.

ABOVE LEFT: aged resident of the New Territories.

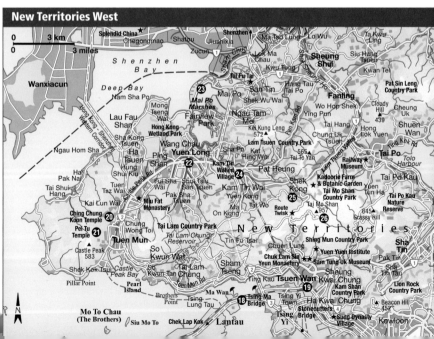

New Territories West

Public housing in New Towns such as Yuen Long accommodates a large proportion of the population.

BELOW: agriculture has diminished in the New Territories over the past 50 years.

Beyond Tsuen Wan

West of Tsuen Wan, the Tuen Mun Highway passes another impressive airport-related bridge – **Tsing Long** – before reaching the sprawling New Town of **Tuen Mun**.

Near **Castle Peak**, the large mountain west of Tuen Mun that is mostly occupied by army firing ranges, and adjacent to the Ching Chung Light Rail Transit (LRT) station, is the huge temple of **Ching Chung Koon** ⓴ (daily 9am–5.30pm). Dedicated to Lui Bun, one of the so-called Daoist immortals, the temple houses numerous valuable Chinese art treasures (not on show). Despite a starring role in the opening scene of Bruce Lee's *Enter the Dragon*, in Hong Kong it is best known as a columbarium, where the ashes of the deceased are stored. Niches containing ashes, often featuring photographs of the deceased, are looked after by temple attendants. Ching Chung Koon is also home to a few elderly residents, for whom it provides medical services. There is a vegetarian canteen selling basic, filling fare for visitors.

With land always at a premium in Hong Kong, the issue of the 7 million population's final resting places occasionally comes to the fore. With niches in well-known temples and columbaria commanding such high prices, a number of illegal facilities were discovered in 2010 on remote islands and areas in the New Territories – and, in a few cases, inside apartments within residential housing blocks.

On the slopes of Castle Peak stands a temple that is smaller but no less intriguing for that – **Pei Tu Temple** ㉑, dedicated to the eponymous monk, a famous figure in Chinese mythology.

Yuen Long

In 1898, when the British took a census of their newly leased New Territories, **Yuen Long** ㉒ was a traditional market town set among 50 or so villages in the middle of the largest flood plain in the New Territories. The census logged 23,000 people in the Yuen Long district. Now the population is over 540,000, most of whom live in the high-rise blocks of Tin Shui Wai and Yuen Long New Towns. A few remarkable remnants of the past remain, however, and the area can be explored via the overland Light Rail, buses and the MTR. It is also the starting point for exploring the mangroves and mudflats of Hong Kong's wetlands.

From Tin Shui Wai MTR it's a short walk to the **Ping Shan Heritage Trail**, a short 1-km (⅔-mile) stroll through more half a dozen historical Chinese buildings of which the highlight is the only surviving intact pagoda in Hong Kong – the **Tsui Sing Lau** (Pagoda of Gathering Stars), built in 1486 to improve the village's feng shui.

Hong Kong Wetland Park

✉ Wetland Park Road, Tin Shui Wai
☎ 2708 8885; www.wetlandpark.com
🕐 Wed–Mon 10am–5pm, Sun 10am–
7pm, closed Tue 💲 charge 🚌 KMB &
Long Win buses 69M, 69X, 264M,
269B, 269C, 269D, 276A, E34
🚇 LRT Wetland Park

The Hong Kong Wetland Park
allows visitors to explore the diversity of Hong Kong's wetland ecosystem by following wooden decking
paths that meander through an area
of coastal marshland.

Within the 61-hectare (151-acre)
area there are several hides with
good-quality telescopes for bird-
watching. So far 129 bird species
have been recorded here, including
numerous varieties of egrets and
herons, and the rare black-faced
spoonbill. An indoor visitor centre
houses educational interactive exhibitions on conservation issues.

The Mai Po Marshes

For the dedicated birdwatcher or
naturalist, a visit to the **Mai Po
Marshes** ㉓ is a must. Managed by
the World Wide Fund for Nature
(WWF), this expanse of mangroves
and mudflats is a stopping point on
the migratory routes of more than
400 different species of birds. The

WWF runs scheduled tours, but
visits must always be booked in
advance (tel: 2526 4473; www.
wwf.org.hk; charge).

Kam Tin Walled Villages

East of Yuen Long, the walled villages of **Kam Tin** ㉔ can be reached
easily by MTR (Kam Sheung Road
station) or the 64K bus. The most
popular for visitors is the Kat Hing
Wai village, which stands incon-
gruously surrounded by modern
housing as heavy vehicle traffic
trundles past (to get there, take the
MTR West Rail to Kam Sheung
Road Station). Some 400 people
live there, and most of them still
share the same surname, Tang.

Built in the 1600s, the fortified village shelters behind walls 6 metres (20
ft) thick, with guard-houses at each
corner, arrow slits for fighting off
attackers and a moat, although the
authenticity may seem compromised
by some modern buildings inside. Visitors can enter for a nominal charge,
although the ladies in traditional
Hakka dress are experienced models
and will expect a fee.

*The five Great
Clans in the New
Territories first
moved into Guang-
dong during the Han
dynasty, then to
Hong Kong during
the Song and Yuan
dynasties. The five
clans were the Tang,
Hau, Pang, Liu and
Man. The Tangs
settled in the Yuen
Long area and were
the architects of the
buildings along the
Lung Yeuk Tau and
Ping Shan Heritage
Trails (see pages
190, 196), and the
Kam Tin walled
villages (see left).*

**ABOVE LEFT AND
BELOW:** the Mai Po
Marshes, haven for
birdlife.

KIDS

Kadoorie Farm is a great place to take children. As well as the chance to experience the local flora up close, there's an amphibian and reptile house, insect house and various farm animals to see. Injured birds of prey are treated and released back into the wild from the Raptor Sanctuary, and there is also a wildlife rescue centre. You must phone (tel: 2483 7200) before you visit.

ABOVE RIGHT: Kat Hing Wai walled village.
BELOW: the view from Ma On Shan.

Across the central mountains

From Kam Tin it is possible to take a scenic route via **Shek Kong** ㉕, once the British military garrison and airfield but now home to a skeleton force of the Chinese People's Liberation Army. The far end of the village marks the start of **Route Twisk** (an acronym for Tsuen Wan/Shek Kong), one of the most panoramic drives in Hong Kong.

An alternative route is to take the 64K bus that crosses the HKSAR from Yuen Long to Tai Po, and for just a few dollars enjoy the sights along the Lam Kan Road as it winds along through the contrasts of the 21st-century New Territories – scrap metal yards, abandoned cars, containers and creeper-covered heavy machinery among sprawling villages of Spanish villas, surrounded by majestic mountains and lush forests, with glimpses of the spires of Hong Kong and Shenzhen on either side.

From the top of Route Twisk near Hong Kong's highest peak, **Tai Mo Shan** ㉖ (957 metres/3,140ft), one can look over to China and down to

Hong Kong Island. Continue on Lam Kam Road to Pak Ngau Shek in the Lam Tsuen valley to reach Kadoorie Farm.

Kadoorie Farm and Botanic Garden

✉ Lam Kam Road, Tai Po district
☎ 2483 7200; www.kfbg.org.hk
🕐 daily 9am–5pm ⑤ free 🚇 MTR
Kam Sheung Road, then 64K to Tai Po

Located at the foot of Tai Mo Shan in grounds of 1.5 sq km (½ sq mile), **Kadoorie Farm** is about as far from urban Hong Kong as it is possible to get. Set up in the 1950s, when it provided pigs and chickens to help newly-arrived refugees become self-sufficient, Kadoorie has since evolved into a conservation centre and wild animal sanctuary *(see margin, left)* and is a pioneer of organic farming in Hong Kong.

It's a fairly steep walk up the landscaped hillside to the peak, Kwun Yum Shan 552m (1,811ft), but the magnificent views across the New Territories to Shenzhen bring a fitting reward. Alternatively, you can call ahead to coordinate your visit with the twice-daily shuttle bus that runs from the farm to the peak. ❑

BEST RESTAURANTS, BARS AND PUBS

Restaurants

Prices for a three-course dinner per person with one beer or glass of house wine:
$ = under HK$150
$$ = HK$150–300
$$$ = HK$300–500
$$$$ = over HK$500

There are relatively few good restaurants in the New Territories, but there are plenty of inexpensive local cafés and chain restaurants in malls, which are usually close to transport hubs. Sai Kung is a good place to end a day's sightseeing or hiking with a large range of establishments to choose from close to the waterfront.

Cantonese

Chun Kee Seafood Restaurant

53 Hoi Pong St, Sai Kung. 🛈 3286 1779 🍽 B, L & D daily. **$$$**
Alfresco dining on the Sai Kung waterfront featuring a range of Cantonese dishes with shrimps, scallops and lobster galore. Open for dim sum, too.

Nang Kee Goose Restaurant

Sham Tseng San Tsuen, Sham Tseng 🛈 2491 0392 🍽 L & D daily. **$$**
Roasting goose is a serious business in Hong Kong, and wide consensus states that the Nang Kee has the best goose, despite its off-the-beaten-track location and a large number of similar restaurants nearby. Fork out for a taxi from Tsing Yi or Tsuen Wan MTR stations.

Indian

Asra

1/F, Sha Tin Galleria, Shop 15, 18–24 Shan Mei St, Fo Tan, Sha Tin 🛈 3188 0852 🍽 L & D daily. **$$**
Catch a taxi from Sha Tin MTR to get to this Indian restaurant that prides itself on sharing the diversity of Indian cuisine with its broad range of customers. Plenty of vegetarian choices, meat kebabs and curries, and a surprisingly green view.

Shahjahan Restaurant

90 Sung Mun San Tsuen, Kam Tin, Yuen Long 🛈 2475 7422 🍽 L & D daily. **$**
Delicious Indian, Pakistani and Nepalese snacks and meals are available in this no-frills roadside restaurant incongruously located in the middle of the Hakka stronghold of Kam Tin.

International

Jaspa's

13 Sha Tsui Path, Sai Kung 🛈 2792 6388 🍽 L & D daily. **$$$**
Jaspa's has an Australian approach to food. Big portions, lots of grilled meats, salads, a few Asian flavours and alfresco dining. Always busy for weekend brunch.

Olive Café & Bar

G/F Grand City Plaza, 1–17 Sai Lau Kok Rd, Tsuen Wan 🛈 2412 3836 🍽 B, L & D daily. **$$**
A short walk from the Sam Tung Uk Museum through the MTR station and Grand City Plaza takes you to Olive for good value, tasty European cuisine with a leaning towards Italy. Homemade desserts include tiramasu and serradura pudding.

One-thirtyone

131 Tseng Tau Village, Sai Kung. 🛈 2791 2684 🍽 D only during week, L & D Sat & Sun. By reservation only. **$$$$**
Located in a remote house surrounded by beautiful scenery, this unique restaurant is the place to go for a celebration or a romantic meal. Chef Gary Cheuk serves a fine fixed-price menu for dinner (HK$900 without wine) or lunch (HK$500) at weekends.

Steamers

G/F, 66 Yi Chun St, Sai Kung 🛈 2792 6991 🍽 B, L & D daily. **$$**
Open from 9am for its traditional breakfasts, and with a good choice of food throughout the day. There is a lovely outdoor terrace garden and a popular bar.

Bars and Pubs

After 5 Wine Bar, 5 Mei Sun Lane, Tai Po. Tel: 2663 3551. A congenial place, 10 minutes' walk from Tai Wai Station. The bar serves American food; its speciality is fresh seasonal oysters.

The Boozer, 57 Yi Chun St, Sai Kung. Tel: 2792 9311. Lively bar with sports screens, a video jukebox and a pole for dancing around – on the bar.

Duke of York, G/F, 42–56 Fuk Man Rd, Sai Kung. Tel: 2792 8435. Old-style British pub, with food and draught beers.

Li Bai Bar, Harbour Plaza Resort City, 18 Tin Yan Rd, Tin Shui Wai. Tel 2180 6688. A rare watering hole in Tin Shui Wai. Pause for a drink and a game of darts or pool if you are in the neighbourhood.

Poets, 55 Yi Chun St, Sai Kung. Tel: 2791 7993. Plenty of banter about all topics at this cosy Sai Kung bar.

HONG KONG'S WILD SIDE

A series of country parks occupy over 40 percent of the SAR's land area, and offer easily accessible respite from this most stressful of cities

One of the many unusual aspects of Hong Kong is the contrast between some of the world's most densely populated urban areas and the utterly empty countryside that surrounds them. In parts of the New Territories and Outlying Islands it is possible to walk for mile after mile in dramatic mountain scenery, enjoy superb natural views, and see no-one for hours on end.

For its modest size, Hong Kong has some impressive mountains – at 957 metres (3,140ft) Tai Mo Shan is on a par with the highest mountain in England, and several others in the New Territories and Lantau are not far behind. A well-signposted network of hiking trails extends across all 22 country parks, with some longer distance routes such as the MacLehose, Wilson and Hong Kong Island trails.

Areas of woodland occur at lower and middle levels, sometimes as a result of reforestation, but most upland areas were deforested long ago by the agricultural needs of villagers. The higher areas are almost all grassland and shrubland, bright green in summer, brown in the dry winters.

ABOVE: this peaceful mountain stream, fed by run-off from Mount Kellett, is just a few hundred yards from the tower blocks and traffic of Aberdeen.

ABOVE: the convoluted coastline of the New Territories has some fine stretches of beach – nowhere more so than at Tai Long Wan on the eastern edge of Sai Kung Country Park.

LEFT: grass fires are common in Hong Kong when the humidity drops during the dry months from October to January, sometimes ravaging entire hillsides. Warnings are displayed at country parks when the risk is high.

HONG KONG'S FAUNA AND FLORA: WHERE TROPICAL MEETS TEMPERATE

Located on the eastern edge of the Eurasian land-mass, Hong Kong lies in a transition zone between the cooler lands to the north and the tropical south. The cool winters brought by the northeast monsoon winds mean that the natural vegetation cover is not tropical "jungle", but rather broad-leaved forest with temperate oaks and laurels as well as tropical species such as lianas, banyans and fan palms. The original forest cover disappeared centuries ago to be replaced either by agriculture or grassland (on the hills), but some areas are now successfully reforested.

A wide variety of wildlife survives in Hong Kong. The Tai Po Kau Nature Reserve shelters rhesus macaques, pangolins, civet cats and barking deer as well as a large diversity of birds, amphibians and reptiles. The Mai Po Marshes are an important resting point for migratory birds. Marine life has been badly hit by pollution, but Chinese river dolphins can still be seen off the coast of Lantau.

RIGHT: a rhesus macaque at Tai Po Kau Nature Reserve. Although this species, and the closely related long-tailed macaque, are indigenous to the region around Hong Kong, the present population of rhesus macaques are descendants of individuals released into the area in 1913.

TOP: the odd-looking litchi lantern bug.

LEFT: a fiddler crab at Hong Kong Wetland Park.

RIGHT: the largest of Hong Kong's indigenous snakes, the Burmese python continues to grow throughout its life and can reach over 9 metres (30 ft) in length.

THE OUTLYING ISLANDS

Each of the three principal outlying islands, Lantau, Cheung Chau and Lamma, makes a rewarding day trip from the city. Attractions include sandy beaches, seafood restaurants, appealing villages, beautiful scenery and – on a different note – Lantau's Disneyland theme park

Main attractions

PO LIN MONASTERY
BIG BUDDHA
NGONG PING CABLE CAR
TUNG CHUNG FORT
TAI O
CHEUNG SHA BEACH
DISNEYLAND
CHEUNG CHAU VILLAGE
PAK TAI TEMPLE
LAMMA ISLAND
   SEAFOOD RESTAURANTS
YUNG SHUE WAN TO SOK
   KWU WAN WALK

BELOW: rural islander.

A substantial majority of Hong Kong's visitors arrive at the state-of-the-art international airport on what used to be an "outlying island", but one which is now joined by road-and-rail suspension bridge to Kowloon. Within a short space of time they are being whisked into the city aboard the smooth Airport Express train, passing not towering skyscrapers but lofty mountains which are part of Lantau's country parks. Such are the contrasts on Hong Kong's islands.

Lantau's peaceful countryside has suffered from the dual onslaught of the airport and the construction of the Disneyland theme park, but Hong Kong's other large outlying islands, Lamma and Cheung Chau, are far less developed. Here there are no proper roads (just narrow concrete paths), and few structures are higher than three storeys. The remainder of the islands – more than 230 of them – are either uninhabited or support small rural communities.

This scattered archipelago provides a glimpse of Hong Kong through the looking-glass, a portion of the South China coast that reflects both rapid change and timeless cohesion. Naturally, many young islanders have moved away into the city and left their homes to ageing parents. Until recently, fishing was the main source of income for the remaining islanders, but times have changed, and the most profitable businesses are now property, restaurants and tourism.

LANTAU

Lantau ("broken head" in Cantonese) is by far the largest of Hong Kong's islands. Its north and east are dominated by the new airport, a four-lane highway, and double railway lines which thunder along the shore to the apartment blocks of

Recommended Restaurants, Bars & Pubs on page 211

Tung Chung, Tsing Ma Bridge and the Disneyland theme park. The rest of the island is predominantly rural. In the south are long beaches and small townships such as Mui Wo (Silvermine Bay), linked by ferries and packet boats *(kaido)* to Peng Chau (pleasant, though hardly a must-see) and Cheung Chau. In the far west of Lantau, Tai O and Fan Lau are favourite destinations for day-trippers, and there are good coastal and hill walks.

The centre of Lantau is dominated by lofty mountains, notably Lantau Peak (934 metres/3,064 ft) and Sunset Peak (869 metres/2,851 ft), criss-crossed with wandering pathways and dusty trails linking a number of Buddhist monasteries. The 70-km (43-mile) Lantau Trail and other intersecting side routes are good for a short stroll, a day trip or overnight trek. A particularly good hike circles the 20,900-million-litre (5,500-million-gallon) **Shek Pik Reservoir**, on the western slopes of Lantau Peak. Alternatively, a coastal path runs from Shek Pik round to Tai O.

Po Lin Monastery ❶

✉ Ngong Ping, Lantau ☎ 2985 5248; www.plm.org.hk 🅒 daily 10am–6pm 🅢 free 🚌 No.2 bus from Mui Wo Ferry Pier, No. 21 from Tung Chung (or by taxi or cable car) 🚇 MTR Tung Chung, then taxi or cable car

Up on the mountainous central spine is one of Hong Kong's best-known attractions, the red, orange and gold **Po Lin Monastery** (Precious Lotus Monastery). The large complex, which dates back to the 1920s, is busier and noisier than the average Buddhist retreat. Its canteen serves good vegetarian meals between 11.30am and 4.30pm. The real crowd-puller, however, is the **Big Buddha**, at 24 metres (79 ft) the

TIP

Ferries operate from Pier No.6 in the Outlying Islands Ferry Piers in Central to Mui Wo (Silvermine Bay) on Lantau approximately every 30–50 minutes throughout the day on weekdays, and every 40–60 minutes at weekends. Journey time is either 30 minutes on a "fast ferry" or 50 minutes on an "ordinary ferry". For information, tel: 2131 8181. It is a very scenic 45-minute bus ride from Mui Wo to either Ngong Ping or Tai O.

ABOVE LEFT: the larger outlying islands have good ferry links with Central. **BELOW:** dragon boat on Cheung Sha Beach, Lantau.

TIP

Much of the central part of Lantau is dotted with small Buddhist monasteries. West of Po Lin, in the direction of Tai O on Lantau's northern coast, is an excellent walking path that traverses mountain ridges, canyons and streams en route to Lantau's Ying Hing Monastery, a haven rich with traditional Buddhist paintings and statues. The monastery sits on a slope and commands a fine view of the surrounding mountains, farmland and the South China Sea.

ABOVE: Po Lin monk. **ABOVE RIGHT:** one of the smaller Lantau monasteries. **BELOW:** the Big Buddha overlooking Po Lin.

world's largest outdoor bronze statue of a seated Buddha, completed here in 1990. A long flight of steps leads up to the statue, with fantastic views from the top when the weather is clear, while an exhibition in the base of the statue explains how it was built.

The monastery has managed to retain a semblance of serenity despite the proximity of the airport and the number of tourists who come here to see the Big Buddha – their access eased by the Ngong Ping 360 cable car *(see following page)*.

Ngong Ping Village

A recent arrival on the Po Lin tourist trail, the **Ngong Ping Village** is a slightly tacky Buddhist-themed attraction (Mon–Fri 10am–6pm, Sat 10am–6.30pm; free) complete with gardens, teahouses and theatre shows about Buddhism for adults and

Recommended Restaurants, Bars & Pubs on page 211

children – rather quixotically offering a "Journey of Enlightenment".

An alternative way to reach the central Lantau heights is by taking the **Ngong Ping 360 Cable Car** (Mon–Fri 10am–6pm; Sat–Sun 9am–6.30pm; www.np360.com.hk; charge) from Tung Chung (a short walk from the MTR station), which gives views across Lantau and the airport – although haze can spoil this. Glass-floored Crystal Cabins add extra excitement to the journey. Once at the top, stroll through Ngong Ping's gardens to the Big Buddha.

Tung Chung Fort

Best accessed by hiking from Ngong Ping or Lantau Peak, **Tung Chung Fort** overlooks the eponymous new town. A fort has existed on the site since the 12th century, protecting the area from pirates and other "outer barbarians". The thick ramparts, including six old cannons, date back to the 19th century, when the Qing Army established a garrison here; this remained until the New Territories (of which the Outlying Islands form a part) was leased to Britain in 1898.

Tai O

One of Lantau's older communities, remote **Tai O ❷** is located on the northwest coast, closer – as the crow flies – to Macau than to Central. Here, the Tanka "boat people", who traditionally lived on their boats near shore, have become semi-land dwellers. Along **Tai O Creek**, they have also built rickety homes on stilts over parts of the creek.

The Birthday of the Lord Buddha is celebrated at Po Lin on the eighth day of the fourth lunar month (almost always in May).

ABOVE LEFT: the Ngong Ping 360 Cable Car.

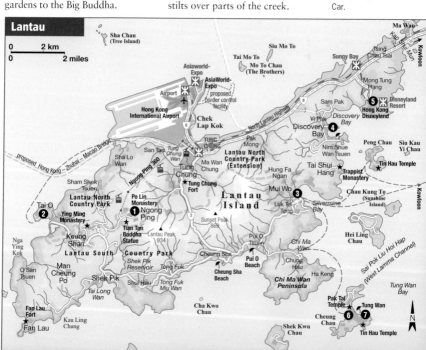

From the 7th century until the 1960s, Tai O was a centre of the salt industry. These days, however, the dried salted fish sold to tourists in the narrow village streets is largely imported from the Philippines.

ABOVE RIGHT: brown winter landscape on Lantau. **BELOW:** Ngong Ping Garden.

The old rope-ferry that was once a feature of Tai O has been replaced by a bridge. Beneath its arch, boatmen offer trips out to see Hong Kong's pink dolphins, who somehow manage to exist in the polluted waters offshore; it is better not to harrass the dolphins and to take a trip with the environmentally sensitive **Hong Kong Dolphinwatch** *(see page 281)*.

Mui Wo and the southern beaches

Lantau is famed for the long, smooth and often empty beaches that line much of its southern coastline. The most popular and crowded beach is at **Mui Wo** (Silvermine Bay) **❸**. A clutch of bars and restaurants has opened in the village, roistering affairs that become very busy at weekends.

A 15-minute bus ride will take you to the stunning, sweeping bay that is **Cheung Sha Beach**. Stretching for 3.2km (2 miles), it is one of Hong Kong's longest beaches and has watersports and other activities. Kite-surfing, skim-boarding, al fresco dining and a small village of teepee-style accommodation make the stretch of Cheung Sha known as **Palm Beach** a real getaway.

Largely cut off from the rest of the island is a major real-estate development called **Discovery Bay ❹**, a well-planned but rather soulless complex that includes a golf course. "DB" is a magnet for expats with a hankering for suburbia, and has excited comparison with the *The Truman Show*.

Hong Kong Disneyland ❺

✉ Sunny Bay, Lantau 📞 1 830 830; www.park.hongkongdisneyland.com 🕙 daily 10am–7pm, 8pm or 9pm, check website for details 💲 charge 🚌 R11, R21, R22, R32, R44 🚇 MTR Disneyland

Hong Kong's long-awaited new theme park opened its doors to the public in 2005, complete with its own MTR station, two hotels, shops, restaurants and the sort of amusements that thrill at more-or-less similar (if larger) venues in Paris, Tokyo and the US. There are four themed areas. *For more details see pages 212–213.*

Recommended Restaurants, Bars & Pubs on page 211

CHEUNG CHAU

Cheung Chau ("long island" in Cantonese) is the most densely populated of the outlying islands. The curving waterfront promenade, the *praya*, is one of the most pleasant places in Hong Kong, especially after sunset when its alfresco restaurants burst into life only yards from the fishing vessels bobbing at anchor. Home to Hong Kong's first and so far only Olympic gold medallist (from Atlanta 1996), Lee Lai-shan, Cheung Chau has a strong windsurfing tradition, centred on Afternoon Beach (Kwun Yan Wan).

Cheung Chau village ❻

The village of **Cheung Chau**, near the ferry dock, is a tangle of alleyways. There are no vehicles on the island apart from small motorised carts and an amusing bonsai-sized police car, fire engine and ambulance, a phenomenon that grants an automatic serenity. Head off in any direction from the ferry terminal and you will pass a variety of modern and traditional shops and numerous seafood restaurants.

A short distance to the left of the ferry dock, up the main road, is **Pak Tai Temple**, built in 1783 and dedicated to the god Pak Tai, protector of fishermen and the island's saviour from plague during the late 1700s. Inside, in front of the altar, are statues of two generals, Thousand-Li Eye and Favourable Wind Ear, who were said to be able to see or hear anything at any distance.

The Bun Festival

Each year the island hosts the four-day **Bun Festival**, usually in May. Known as *Ching Chiu* in Cantonese, it originated many years ago after the

TIP

Hong Kong's most eccentric accommodation can be found at Lantau Mountain Camp, located 770 metres (2,526 ft) up Sunset Peak. The camp consists of 20 small stone huts, built before World War II as a rest haven for Christian missionaries taking time off from their work in China. The huts can also be rented by laymen who book in advance.

ABOVE LEFT: the Sleeping Beauty Castle at Fantasyland, part of the Disneyland complex. **BELOW:** alfresco seafood restaurants are easy to find on the outlying islands.

TIP

Ferries operate from the Outlying Islands Ferry Piers in Central to Cheung Chau every 30 minutes daily. For information call First Ferry, tel: 2131 8181. Lamma ferries are run by Hong Kong and Kowloon Ferry Ltd (HKKF), tel: 2815 6063. Services run at 20–60-minute intervals to Yung Shue Wan, less frequently to Sok Kwu Wan.

ABOVE RIGHT: the tradition of Bun Festival buns is of obscure origin. **BELOW:** Pak Tai Temple.

discovery of a nest of skeletons, believed to be the remains of people killed by pirates. The island was subsequently plagued by a series of misfortunes; to placate the restless spirits of the victims, offerings were made once a year. How pastry buns came into this story is anybody's guess.

During the festivities, giant bamboo towers covered with edible buns are erected in the courtyard of Pak Tai Temple. In the past, the local men would climb up the towers to pluck their lucky buns – the higher the bun was, the more luck it would bring. After one of the towers collapsed in 1978, bringing broken bones and bruises rather than luck, the free-for-all was stopped. The ritual was revived in 2005 in a more controlled environment; now only pre-qualified competitors can risk their necks.

Another attraction during the festival are the colourfully-clad "floating children", who are hoisted up on stilts and paraded through the crowds. Other festive events include performances of Chinese opera and dramatic lion dances.

Around Cheung Chau

Scattered about the island are several temples dedicated to Tin Hau, goddess of the sea. Cheung Chau was once the haunt of pirates, including the notorious Cheung Po Tsai. As on the other outlying islands, "Family Trail" walks are well-marked and lead to **Cheung Po Tsai Cave** as well as other scenic spots.

There are also some excellent beaches. The main strand is **Tung Wan ❼**, on the other, eastern, side of the narrow isthmus from the harbour. Below the Warwick Hotel at the southern end of the sands is a 3,000-year-old Bronze Age rock carving. Other good beaches are

Afternoon Beach (Kwun Yam Wan), just past the rock carving, and Pak Tso at the island's southwestern tip.

LAMMA

The second-largest of the outlying islands is **Lamma**. Rich in grassy hills and picturesque bays, the rugged terrain means that there is only a very small area of farmland. Archaeologists have associated Lamma with some of the earliest settlements in the region.

Lamma has a population of around 6,000, mostly concentrated in and around the village of Yung Shue Wan. Among them are a sizeable number of expatriates (over 60

nationalities live here), who value the green surroundings, peace and quiet (and the low rents). Despite the frequent ferry service to Central, only 30 minutes away, this roadless island remains distinctly slow-paced – although it can get crowded with day-trippers at weekends.

Yung Shue Wan

Yung Shue Wan (Banyan Bay), at the northern end of Lamma, is one of two ferry gateways to the island. The village has a good supply of restaurants serving Japanese, Thai, Mediterranean and Indian cuisine, as well as several Chinese seafood establishments on the waterfront.

Lamma Island has a large population of expats keen to escape from the noise and pollution of the city. Its reputation as something of a bohemian/arty/hippy colony – at its tie-dyed peak in the late 1980s and early 1990s – has faded, but not entirely disappeared.

BELOW: the power station on Lamma.

Lamma Power

One easy way of identifying Lamma from a distance is by the three chimney stacks of the power station, close to the island's northwest tip. This coal-burning power station provides all the electricity for Hong Kong Island.

In a recent nod to environmental concerns, Hong Kong Electric has built one 46-metre (151-ft) wind turbine on the hillside above Yung Shue Wan. Given its breezy open location, Lamma Winds – as it is officially called – is a pleasant spot to stroll up to and take in the views, particularly if you don't have time to do the Sok Kwu Wan hike. From Yung Shue Wan, walk towards Hung Shing Ye for five minutes until you reach a crossing with a wider "road". Turn left and follow this uphill for 15 minutes.

Lamma is famous for its seafood restaurants, and at weekends stalls appear on Yung Shue Wan's main street selling fishy delicacies such as the skewered squid pictured here. Restaurant favourites include deep-fried squid, broccoli with scallops and garlic prawns.

ABOVE RIGHT: Hung Shing Ye Beach.
BELOW: the harbour at Yung Shue Wan.

On a side street just past the town's main intersection is Yung Shue Wan's 100-year old **Tin Hau Temple**, guarded by a pair of stone lions. Inside, behind a red spirit stand (to deflect evil spirits), is the main shrine with images of the beaded and veiled Tin Hau.

The walk to Sok Kwu Wan

It is only a short stroll from Yung Shue Wan out into the countryside. The main path, signposted to **Hung Shing Ye Beach**, passes neat vegetable plots and three-storey buildings (nothing higher is permitted, with the exception of the power station chimeys that loom behind the hill to the right). The beach itself is a pleasantly clean stretch of sand.

The path then rises steeply into the hills as it heads south to Sok Kwu Wan, Lamma's other main village. This popular walk, which can be completed in an unhurried hour and a half, treats hikers to views out across the sea, while on the other (left) side the vista extends across the Lamma Channel to the scattered tower blocks of Hong Kong Island's southern shore.

Sok Kwu Wan lies on the eastern shore of a long fjord-like inlet known as Picnic Bay, and is a popular weekend pleasure-junk mooring. The bay brims with floating fish farms, all tended by a fleet of boats of various shapes and sizes, and is one of the main suppliers of Hong Kong's seafood restaurants. Not surprisingly, the village has a long string of seafood restaurants, beguiling in the evening with bright lighting displays and marvellous aromas. Entrepreneurial villagers have set up the **Lamma Fisherfolk's Village** (daily 10am–7pm; charge includes shuttle) in a red-sailed junk in the bay, to teach visitors about traditional fishing communities and their crafts.

Po Toi

Po Toi is a group of islands located in the southernmost area of the SAR, southeast of Stanley, and inhabited by only a handful of people. Reached by *kaido* from Aberdeen or Stanley, the main island, Po Toi, is home to a large rock resembling a snail. Under the rock is a cave with carvings shaped by wind and rain. The open-air restaurants near the pier in the south serve excellent seafood. *For details on the islands in Mirs Bay and the eastern New Territories, see pages 187, 191.*

BEST RESTAURANTS, BARS AND PUBS

Restaurants

Prices for a three-course dinner per person with one beer or glass of house wine:

$ = under HK$150
$$ = HK$150–300
$$$ = HK$300–500
$$$$ = over HK$500

For many locals and expats, alfresco dining at any of the seafood restaurants on the outlying islands is a highlight of Hong Kong. You'll also find a good choice of small international restaurants and bars, many close to the waterfront.

Cheung Chau

Cantonese

East Lake Restaurant
85 Tung Wan Road ☎ 2981 3869 ◎ B, L & D daily. **$$**
Just the place for an inexpensive Cantonese meal while exploring Cheung Chau.

Lamma

Cantonese

Han Lok Yuen (The Pigeon Restaurant)
16–17 Hung Shing Yeh ☎ 2982 0680 ◎ L & D daily. **$$**
Overlooking the beach at Hung Shing Yeh, a 20-minute walk from Yung Shue Wan. The shaded terrace is scattered with round tables groaning with plump pigeons roasted a tempting golden brown.

Lamcombe
47 Main St, Yung Shue Wan ☎ 2982 0680 ◎ L & D daily. **$**
Halfway along the main street. Walk through the busy kitchen to reach the seaview terrace, then try the crispy deep-fried squid and other favourites.

Peach Garden Seafood Restaurant
8 First St, Sok Kwu Wan ☎ 2982 8581 ◎ L & D daily. **$**
Friendly family-run restaurant five minutes walk beyond more group-orientated venues. Enjoy outdoor seating, tasty Cantonese cuisine and seafood cooked to order.

Rainbow Seafood Restaurant
16–20 First St, Sok Kwu Wan ☎ 2982 8100 ◎ L & D daily. **$$**
Rainbow runs a free shuttle from Central Pier 9. Garlic prawns and lobster in 10 kinds of butter are signature dishes.

Sampan Seafood Restaurant
16 Main St, Yung Shue Wan, Lamma ☎ 2982 2388 ◎ B, L & D daily. **$$**
Open from 7am, dim sum is served alfresco until around 11am. Go up to the counter and check out the baskets. A la carte menu for lunch and dinner.

International

The Waterfront
58 Main St, Yung Shue Wan, Lamma ☎ 2982 1168 ◎ B,L & D daily. **$–$$**
Five minutes from the ferry pier, the Waterfront offers tasty fare from around the globe and has a kids' menu – rare in these parts. Great sunset views.

Vegetarian

Bookworm Café
79 Main St, Yung Shue Wan, Lamma ☎ 2982 4838 ◎ B, L & D daily. **$–$$**
Choose from a long menu of veggie and vegan staples, and home-made cakes. Consistently good.

Lantau

International

N.E.W.S Bistro
40 Cheung Sha Lower Village, Lantau ☎ 2984 0113 ◎ L & D Wed–Mon. **$**
Twenty minutes by cab from the ferry terminal at Mui Wo on Lantau, with an eclectic menu of Asian and Western favourites on the beachfront.

South African

The Stoep
32 Lower Cheung Sha Village, Lantau ☎ 2980 2699 ◎ L & D daily. **$$–$$$**
Relaxed outdoor dining South African-style on the beach. Feast on home-made bread and dips, *bobotie* and, best of all, there's a *braai* for great barbecue meat.

Bars and Pubs

B & B, 22 Main St, Yung Shue Wan, Lamma. Tel: 2982 4388. Beer and babble inspired the name. Sit out back on the waterfront.

China Beach Club, 18 Tung Wan Tau Rd, Mui Wo, Lantau. Tel: 2983 8931. Cool bar/restaurant with views across the bay.

Deli Lamma, 36 Main St Yung Shue Wan, Lamma. Tel: 2982 1583. Quirky bar/restaurant with an eclectic menu, 'The Deli' is the place to sit back and watch your afternoon drinks turn into sundowners.

Seaside Café, 1 Hak Pai Road, Cheung Chau. Tel: 2981 2772. Bar café with terrace overlooking bay.

Starz Wine Bar, G/F, UA Cinema, Citygate, Tung Chung, Lantau. Tel: 2109 0612. Neat little bar, with light meals.

THEME PARKS

Hong Kong's new Disneyland and long-running local competitor Ocean Park make the SAR a good bet for a family holiday

When Hong Kong Disneyland opened in 2005, it seemed that the writing was on the wall for its local counterpart, Ocean Park. A major renovation and expansion soon put paid to that idea, and now both parks attract a similar number of thrill-seeking locals and tourists. In fact, each offers a quite different day out – as the name suggests, an aquarium forms a big part of Ocean Park's draw, while Disneyland has its own unique appeal for small children. Both have rollercoasters and other rides for thrill-seekers – although Ocean Park has more for older kids.

Disneyland *(see page 206 for opening times and other details)* is divided into four themed areas (Main Street USA, Fantasyland, Adventureland, and Tomorrowland). Tickets give access to all. As with other Disneyland parks, be prepared to queue – it's best to avoid weekends and the hottest months: waiting in line with bored, over-heated children is no fun for anyone.

As well as its impressive aquariums, **Ocean Park** *(see page 144)*, on Hong Kong Island's south coast, has a mile-long cable car, various thrilling rides, dolphin shows and pandas.

ABOVE: the Autopia attraction at Tomorrowland. This part of the park focuses on space exploration, and features a rollercoaster, a Buzz Lightyear shoot-em-up game and other thrills.

BELOW: the Disneyland ticket booth at the Peak Tower.

TOP LEFT: Disneyland has its own MTR line complete with appropriately kitted-out trains.

LEFT: meeting the familiar Disney characters never fails to thrill the smaller children.

A Difficult Start

Complete with its own MTR line, two large resort hotels and projected annual visitor numbers of 10 million (later revised downwards to 5–6 million), Hong Kong Disneyland was intended as a major shot in the arm to the ailing local economy when the project was announced in 1999. Yet by the time it opened on 12 September 2005 (on one of the SAR's most polluted days ever), years of reclamation and construction work had racked up an estimated bill of US$1.8 billion. Critics argue that the whole thing is a heinous waste of government money, particularly as visitor numbers continue to fall short of predictions (in 2009 4.8m visited, down from 5.2m in 2006). Three new themed areas – Grizzly Trail, Mystic Point and Toy Story Land – are under construction and due to open in 2014, adding 5 hectares (12.3 acres) and more than 50 attractions.

ABOVE: There is a nightly fireworks display over Disneyland's Sleeping Beauty Castle, at the centre of Fantasyland, one of the park's four themed areas.

BELOW: The walk-through shark aquarium, one of three aquariums at Ocean Park. Other animals at the park include seals and sea-lions, exotic birds and four giant pandas.

ABOVE: the Mine Train rollercoaster at Ocean Park is one of the scarier rides on offer, although the Dragon rollercoaster is faster. If you want more thrills, try the (56-metre 185-ft) Abyss Turbo Drop, the Space Wheel and the Flying Swing. There are also more sedate helium balloon rides and a ferris wheel.

RIGHT: the Ocean Theatre entertains with sea lion and dolphin shows. It is even possible to apply for a swimming session with the dolphins (tel: 2552 0291).

Recommended Restaurants, Bars, Clubs & Cafés on pages 231–3

MACAU

Often perceived as existing in the shadow of its illustrious neighbour, Macau is in fact quite different to Hong Kong. A major tourism drive has brought flashy casinos and rapid change, but the unique Portuguese ambience still survives

I f ever the Pearl River Delta had "bling", it's now, and nowhere is this more obvious than in Macau. Established by the Portuguese in 1557 as the first European colony on China's shore, Macau was for much of recent history a sleepy outpost, playing second fiddle to its high-profile neighbour. Things have changed quickly since it returned to China in 1999 – becoming, like Hong Kong, a Special Administrative Region of the People's Republic.

These days Macau has a new lease of life as the "leisure capital of Asia". Cashing in on the new wealth in China, and the Chinese love of gambling, what was until recently a rather low-key casino scene has exploded into a brash, gaudy, full-scale celebration of greed to rival Las Vegas. A huge reclamation project has merged the islands of Coloane and Taipa to form a new entertainment area of spectacular themed casinos and luxury hotels. Nowadays more than 2 million visitors a month pour in by ferry from Hong Kong, or over the land border, to try their luck at the tables. Visitor arrivals are approximately 2 million per month.

PRECEDING PAGES: São Lourenço church. **LEFT:** the casino industry now accounts for over half of Macau's GDP. **RIGHT:** São Domingos church on Largo do Senado.

Yet amidst all the crowds and pizzazz, sizeable areas of old Macau survive – graceful old buildings redolent of southern Europe, overlooking cobbled streets shaded by ancient banyan trees. If it's a peaceful "Mediterranean in China" experience you are after, head over to the main square of either Taipa or Coloane village for lunch.

MACAU'S HISTORIC CENTRE

In the years leading up to the 1999 handover, the Portuguese (who in

Main attractions
LARGO DO SENADO SQUARE
RUINS OF SÃO PAULO
MONTE FORT
MACAU MUSEUM
CAMÕES GARDEN
SANTO AGOSTINHO CHURCH
A-MA TEMPLE
MACAU TOWER
NAPE
GUIA LIGHTHOUSE
TAIPA HOUSES MUSEUM
THE VENETIAN
COLOANE VILLAGE

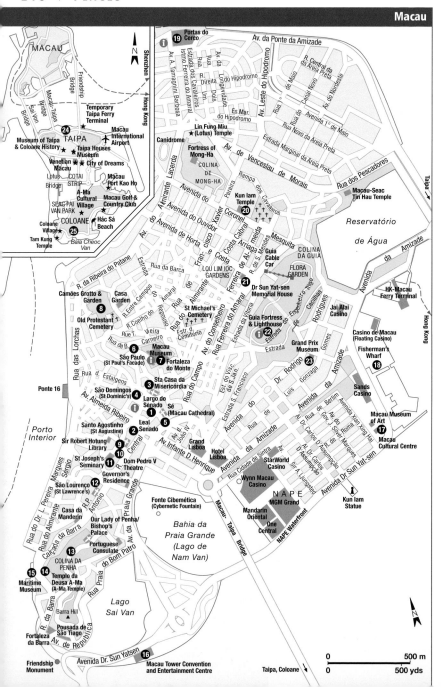

MACAU

Shenzhen

Hong Kong

Friendship Bridge

Macau-Taipa Bridge

Sai Von Bridge

Temporary Taipa Ferry Terminal

Macau International Airport

24 TAIPA

Museum of Taipa & Coloane History

Taipa Houses Museum

Venetian Macau ★★ City of Dreams

COTAI STRIP

Lotus Bridge

SEAC PAI VAN PARK

A-Ma Cultural Village

Macau Golf & Country Club

Macau Port Kao Ho

COLOANE

Coloane Village

Hác Sá Beach

25

Tam Kung Temple

Baía Cheoc Van

19 Portas do Cerco

Av. da Ponte da Amizade

Estrada dos Cavaleiros
Istmo Ferreira do Amaral

Av. A. Tamagnini Barbosa

Rua da Longevidade

R. Direita

Rua Dois

R. Central da da Areia Preta

Av. do Hipódromo

de Maio

Av. do Nordeste

Av. do Cabral Novo

Lin Fung Miu ★ (Lotus) Temple

Av. Leste do Hipódromo

Avenida 1° de Maio

Canidrome

Es. Mar. do Hipódromo

Rua Nova da Areia Preta

Fortress of Mong-Ha

COLINA DE MONG-HA

Av. de Venceslau de Morais

Estrada Marginal da Areia Preta

Rua dos Pescadores

Rampa dos Cavaleiros

Macau-Seac Tin Hau Temple

Kun Iam Temple **20**

Av. Amizade

Taipa

Hong Kong

Reservatório de Água

Pereira

Costa Cabral

Av. do Ouvidor

Costa Arriaga

Avenida do

Mesquita

COLINA DA GUIA

Guia Cable Car

FLORA GARDEN

Camões Grotto & Garden **8**

Casa Garden

LOU LIM IOC GARDENS

St Michael's Cemetery

21 Dr Sun Yat-sen Memorial House

HK-Macau Ferry Terminal

Old Protestant Cemetery

Rua E. Entre Campos

R. Coelho do

Amaral

São Paulo (St Paul's Facade) **6**

R. Repouso

Rue T. Vieira

Carneiro

Rua de B.

Macau Museum **7** Fortaleza do Monte

Guia Fortress & Lighthouse **22**

Jai Alai Casino

Casino de Macau (Floating Casino)

Grand Prix Museum **23**

Fisherman's Wharf **18**

Ponte 16

Rua dos Estalgens

São Domingos (St Dominic's) **3**

Sta Casa da Misericórdia **4**

Largo do Senado

Sé (Macau Cathedral) **5**

Sands Casino

Av. Almeida Ribeiro

São Domingos (St Dominic's)

Santo Agostinho (St Augustine) **2**

Leal Senado

Grand Lisboa

Hotel Lisboa

StarWorld Casino

Macau Museum of Art **17**

Macau Cultural Centre

Porto Interior

Sir Robert Hotung Library **9**

St Joseph's Seminary **10**

Dom Pedro V Theatre **11**

Governor's Residence

Wynn Macau Casino

N A P E

São Lourenço (St Lawrence's) **12**

Fonte Cibemética (Cybernetic Fountain)

Bahia da Praia Grande (Lago de Nam Van)

MGM Grand

Mandarin Oriental

One Central

Kun Iam Statue

NAPE Waterfront

Casa da Manderin

13

Our Lady of Penha/ Bishop's Palace

Portuguese Consulate

COLINA DA PENHA

15 Maritime Museum

14 Templo da Deusa A-Ma (A-Ma Temple)

Lago Sai Van

Barra Hill

R. da Barra

Pousada de São Tiago

Fortaleza da Barra

Av. de República

Friendship Monument

Avenida Dr. Sun Yatsen

16 Macau Tower Convention and Entertainment Centre

Taipa, Coloane

| 0 | | 500 m |
| 0 | | 500 yds |

Recommended Restaurants, Bars, Clubs & Cafés on pages 231–3

2010 still account for around 5 percent of the resident population) set about ensuring that Macau's cultural heritage – and their influence – would be preserved. Buildings were renovated, squares re-cobbled, and pastel paints once more brightened up the grey streets.

The 25 sites that now comprise the Historic Centre of Macau were added to Unesco's World Heritage list in 2005, acknowledging their importance as the oldest and most intact example of European architecture on Chinese soil and as a symbol of cultural exchange between East and West. Sites include Chinese temples, Portuguese churches, scenic squares and the first lighthouse in China. Best explored on foot, there are two well-signposted main routes, which are fairly shady, and there are enough buildings open to the public to provide respite on a humid day.

Largo do Senado Square ❶

The best place to start any foray into Old Macau is the **Largo do Senado** (Senate Square), the old city's main square, covering some 3,700 sq metres (4,425 sq yds), which has been repaved with a bold Portuguese wave-pattern mosaic. A handy **tourist information centre** is situated right on the square (daily 9am–6pm).

Across the main road (Almeida Ribeiro) is the **Leal Senado ❷** (Loyal Senate; daily 9am–9pm), regarded by most as the best example of Portuguese architecture in Macau. It now houses the Institute of Civil and Municipal Affairs. The Leal Senado was dedicated in 1784, and its façade completed in 1876. The title "Loyal" was bestowed on Macau's Senate in 1809 by Portuguese King John VI, who was Prince Regent at the time, as a reward for continuing to fly the Portuguese flag when the Spanish monarchy took over the Portuguese throne in the 17th century. An inscribed tablet here, dating from

1654, grants Macau its sacred title: "City of the Name of God, Macau, There is None More Loyal". Head up the staircase to the fine wrought-iron doors and beyond to a small courtyard with *azulejos* tiles. Up more stairs, the **library** (Mon–Fri 1–7pm) and council chamber show fine examples of Old World woodwork. Half the offices on the ground floor have been converted into a gallery which is used for special exhibitions (Tue–Sun 9am–9pm).

Ecclesiastical treasures

Back on Largo do Senado square, opposite the tourist office, is the white church of **Santa Casa da Misericórdia ❸** (Holy House of Mercy), with its small museum of religious artefacts (Mon–Sat 10am–1pm, 2.30– 5.30pm; charge). At the northern end of the square is the butter-coloured **São Domingos ❹** (St Dominic's), one of the oldest of Macau's churches. It dates from the 17th century, but the Spanish Dominicans built a chapel and con-

Southern European architecture, often with an unmistakable oriental element, gives much of old Macau a unique flavour. The central square, Largo do Senado, is lined with superb examples, both secular and ecclesiastical.

BELOW: the historic library at the Leal Senado.

The magnificent façade of São Paulo (St Paul's) is probably Macau's best-known landmark.

BELOW: the steps of São Paulo at Chinese New Year.

vent on this site as early as 1588. At the back is the **Museum of Sacred Art** (daily 10am–6pm).

Take a short walk up a *travessa* to the Sé ❺ (Macau Cathedral), mother church of the Macau diocese after 1850, which at the time included all of China, Japan and Korea. The stained-glass windows are the main attraction of this rather plain building.

São Paulo ❻

From São Domingos follow the pavement north along one of Macau's main shopping streets before turning uphill to the ruins of **São Paulo** (St Paul's; open access). Its towering façade and impressive grand staircase are the most striking of all Macau's churches. Unfortunately, the site must have bad feng shui. The first church on the site was destroyed by fire in 1601. It was rebuilt, but in 1835 another inferno swept through the church, destroying the adjacent college and a library reputed to be the best east of Istanbul. The classical façade – crafted by Japanese Christians who had fled

persecution in Nagasaki – survived. In 1904, efforts were made to rebuild the church, but little progress was achieved. Still, today the grand façade of São Paulo remains Macau's most enduring icon.

Fortaleza do Monte ❼

✉ Praceta do Museu de Macau
☎ (853) 2835 7911 ⏰ daily
7am–7pm ⓢ free

Overlooking the façade of São Paulo are the massive stone walls of the fort (usually called **Monte Fort**), built in the early 1600s. When Dutch ships attacked and invaded Macau in 1622, the half-completed fortress was defended by 150 clerics and African slaves. A lucky cannon shot by an Italian Jesuit, Geronimo Rhu, hit the powder magazine of the Dutch fleet's flagship and saved the city. Access is free, and there are great views over the city from the cannon-lined ramparts.

The **Macau Museum** (Tue–Sun 10am–6pm; charge, but free on 15th of every month) was opened on the site of the fortress in 1998. Three

Recommended Restaurants, Bars, Clubs & Cafés on pages 231–3

floors of lively and well-captioned exhibits chart the history of the enclave and its citizens, from its first settlement through to the handover to the Chinese.

Camões Grotto & Garden ❽

A 15-minute stroll to the west of the fort will take you to the picturesque **Camões Garden** (daily 6am–11.30pm), where Luís de Camões, the celebrated Portuguese soldier-poet, is said to have composed part of the national epic, *Os Lusiadas* (The Lusiads). A bronze bust of

Camões rests in the garden's grotto. Above the grotto is an observatory built by a French explorer, Count de La Pérouse. The garden features in many paintings by George Chinnery, the most famous 19th-century "China Coast" artist, who is buried in the nearby **Old Protestant Cemetery**, which is a fascinating historical snapshot of the early foreign community here.

Nearby **Casa Garden** (Mon–Fri 9.30am–6pm) is an 18th-century house and garden that was home to East India Company officials and is now a cultural institute.

South of Largo do Senado

Most of Macau's Unesco-listed sites lie to the south of Largo do Senado, across Avenida de Almeida Ribeiro, in a string all the way to the southern tip of the peninsula. The first of these is **Santo Agostinho ❾** (St Augustine), an attractive baroque-style church that is the largest in the region. Spanish Augustinians founded a church here in 1586, but the present structure dates from 1814, and its ornate façade from 1875.

TIP

Macau has several tourist information offices: the central office is at Largo do Senado, open daily 9am–6pm, tel: (853) 8397 1120. The office at the Macau Ferry Terminal is open daily 9am–10pm, tel: (853) 2872 6416. There are kiosks at Guia Lighthouse (daily 9am–1pm, 2.15–5.30pm), at the border gate (daily 9.15am–1pm, 2.30–6pm) and the airport (daily 9am–1.30pm, 2.15–7.30pm, 8.15–10pm).

ABOVE LEFT: 17th-century cannon at Monte Fort. **BELOW:** the walls of the fort.

SHOP

Within two minutes walk of the A-Ma Temple there are a handful of long-established Portuguese restaurants on Rua Almirante Sergio Porto Interior, including A Lorcha and Restaurant Littoral.

Across the square (Largo de Santo Agostinho) and also on the Unesco list is the **Sir Robert Hotung Library** (Mon–Sat 10am–7pm, Sun 11am–7pm), dating from 1894, and the beautifully restored **Dom Pedro V Theatre** ❿. Built in 1860, this was the first western-style theatre in China, and often opens for concerts and performances during Macau's many arts festivals.

Another venerable building on the square (but accessed from Rua do Seminario around the corner) is **St Joseph's Seminary** ⓫ (church open 10am–5pm), dedicated in 1728 when its sole purpose was to establish Jesuit missions in China – a task it performed with gusto. Today its vast halls, classrooms and living quarters have mostly disappeared, but its architecture and sculptures are worth viewing, and the beautiful chapel is open to the public. The statues within were salvaged from São Paulo in 1835.

A little further south, the imposing pale-yellow church of **São Lourenço** ⓬ (St Lawrence's) (Mon 10am–4pm, Sat 10am–1pm) is raised up above street level and surrounded by a small

garden. The church was originally built in the 1560s, and most families of Portuguese sailors used to gather on the front steps of the church to pray and wait for their return, so it was known in Cantonese as Feng Shun Tang (Hall of the Soothing Winds). The elegant church was most recently rebuilt in 1846. The grand double staircase leading up from the street, iron gates, towers and crystal chandeliers are European, but the roof is made of Chinese tiles.

The southern tip

Take a detour up **Colina da Penha** ⓭ (Penha Hill) for sweeping views and to visit the **Chapel of Our Lady of Penha**, dating back to 1622 but largely rebuilt in 1837. While not listed as a Unesco site, the chapel and **Bishop's Palace** next door were once the centres of Roman Catholic missionary work in the region.

Continuing on the Unesco World Heritage route, there are more examples of the influence of different cultures on architectural styles. The peaceful piazza of **Largo do Lilau** marks one of the earliest Portuguese

BELOW: Macau is a great place to buy characterful old furniture.

Recommended Restaurants, Bars, Clubs & Cafés on pages 231–3

relief stone carving here said to be a rendering of a Chinese junk that carried the goddess A-Ma from Fujian province through typhoon-ravaged seas to Macau, where she walked to the top of Barra Hill and ascended to heaven.

In front of the temple is the interesting **Maritime Museum** ⑮ (Wed–Mon 10am–5.30pm; charge, but free on Sun), with displays tracing the history of shipping in the South China Sea.

North of the A-Ma Temple, Macau's run-down **O Porto Interior** (Inner Harbour Area) is hoping to share in the boomtown success of elsewhere in Macau, with its own Vegas-style casino. Opened in 2008, the 2.3-hectare (5¾-acre) Ponte 16 casino and entertainment resort includes a Sofitel hotel. Facing Zhuhai, Ponte 16 boasts that it has "one river, two banks" scenery and European-Chinese architecture.

To the south, the impressive walls of the old **Fortaleza da Barra** (Fortress of Barra) rise far above the avenue guarding the entrance to the Inner Harbour.

There is disagreement over the correct spelling: Macau or Macao? The latter form is making something of a comeback, and the burgeoning casino industry seems to prefer it. Most official sources, as well as locals and westerners, continue to use "Macau", however. To add to the confusion, it is known as Aomen in pinyin Chinese.

residential areas. Nearby, the **Casa da Mandarin** (Mandarin's House) on Antonio de Silva Lane is a traditional Chinese courtyard-style residence, dating back to 1881. Further south, the **Moorish Barracks** (daily 9am–6pm) were built in 1874 to house policemen recruited from another Portuguese enclave, Goa.

A-Ma Temple and the Maritime Museum

The **A-Ma Temple** ⑭ (Templo da Deusa A-Ma; daily 7am–6pm) squats beneath Barra Hill, at the entrance to Macau's Inner Harbour. It is the oldest temple in the territory, said to date back 600 years to the Ming dynasty. It was certainly there in 1557, when Macau was ceded to Portugal. The original temple was believed to have been erected by fishermen from southeast China and dedicated to Tin Hau, the patron goddess of fishermen and called A-Ma in Macau. It was then called Ma Kok Miu (Ma Point Temple). The Chinese named the area A-Ma-Gao, or the Bay of A-Ma. The oldest surviving part of this temple is a lower pavilion to the right of its entrance. There is a coloured bas-

ABOVE LEFT: typical backstreets in the old town. **BELOW:** worship at the A-Ma Temple.

The bronze Kun Iam statue on the NAPE waterfront, designed and crafted by Portuguese artist Christina Reiria.

NEW MACAU

Much of the what can be termed New Macau has been built on reclaimed land to the south and east of the natural peninsula, an area known as the NAPE *(see below)*, which forms a grid of casino- and hotel-lined streets close to the Hong Kong Ferry Terminal. Further south, beyond Nam Van Lake and its colourful, if erratic, "cybernetic fountain", lies Macau's most prominent new tourist attraction – the 338-metre (1,110-ft) **Macau Tower** . Take the lift to the observation deck (daily 10am–9pm; charge) for 360-degree views of Macau, and look through its glass floors (not recommended for vertigo sufferers). Thrill-seekers can "skywalk" around the edge of the clear handrail-free platform, climb all the way to the top of the mast, or leap off in a controlled bungee jump.

From the tower it's easy to see Macau's changing shape and other new landmarks. The orange-and-white **Hotel Lisboa** that was once the main landmark now looks quaintly retro and is dwarfed by new developments, including the garish 44-storey **Grand Lisboa** hotel and casino that is modelled on a lotus root but also resembles a giant mirror-covered turnip.

The NAPE and Fisherman's Wharf

To the south of the Avenida da Amizade lies the **NAPE** (Novos Aterros do Porto Exterior), a rectangle of reclaimed land that is one of the most up-and-coming areas in Macau. The area is home to some typically opulent 21st-century Macau developments – the copper-coloured Wynn Macau, the gold-

five floors and host major international exhibitions. There is a permanent collection of over 3,000 works of Shiwan ceramics, calligraphy and art from Macau and China.

Towards the Hong Kong Ferry Terminal an artificial volcano marks the entrance of the über-kitsch **Fisherman's Wharf** entertainment area ⑱ (daily; 10am–10pm; free admission but charge for rides). Inside the volcano there's a roller-coaster, a water-ride and various other amusements. The mixed bag of architectural styles is arranged in three themed sections – Dynasty Wharf, East Meets West and Legend Wharf – and range from old Cape Town and Miami to the Tang dynasty. There are shops, a boutique hotel and dozens of restaurants dishing up food from all over the world.

NORTHERN MACAU

Between Barra and the border with Guangdong, the northern end of Macau is predominantly nondescript residential and semi-industrial blocks. As in Hong Kong, most of the once-flourishing garment and textile busi-

and-silver MGM Grand, the 34-storey StarWorld Casino and the golden Sands Macau, symbolising the new breed of Vegas-style gambling palaces for which Macau is becoming famous. There are also a large number of restaurants and bars in the immediate vicinity.

The state-of-the-art **Macau Cultural Centre** ⑰ is located at the junction of Avenida Man Sing Hai and Avenida Dr Sun Yat-sen, and has two auditoria that host a regular programme of performances and shows. Next door, the spacious galleries of the **Macau Museum of Art** (Tue–Sun 10am–5pm; charge) are spread over

ABOVE LEFT: Fisherman's Wharf. **BELOW:** the Macau Tower offers various activities for thrill-seekers.

Macau's Casinos

Macau's shiny new Vegas-style casinos not only pack in the punters, they also include vast hotels and state-of-the-art entertainment and business facilities

Macau's premier entertainment rumbles to the rattle of the roulette ball with the speed of a croupier shuffling a deck of cards. Gambling – or gaming, as the industry would have it – is Macau's prime revenue-earner, fleecing the pockets of millions of mainland Chinese and other nationalities every year, but equally sending a few on their way with riches beyond the dreams of avarice. At present, the 34 (and counting) casinos fall into two distinct groups. The first is epitomised by the original Lisboa, owned by gazillionaire Stanley Ho, who for many years grew (metaphorically) fat on a gaming monopoly. These older casinos are comparatively low-rent, with milling hordes crowding around the tables and snatching at the handles of the Hungry Tigers, as fruit machines are called.

The second group is very different. In 2002 it was finally agreed to open the industry up to other players from outside the region. Sheldson Adelson's Las Vegas Sands was the first to get started, with the Sands Macau a gilded edifice on the new Macau peninsula skyline. The Greek Mythology Casino gave a totally new face to the low-key island of Taipa, and American mogul Steve Wynn soon followed suit and opened his first Asian casino, Wynn Macau's, a stone's throw from Ho's new venture, the fantastically lurid Grand Lisboa, and daughter Patsy's joint venture with Vegas, the MGM Grand Macau.

To the south, meanwhile, development continues on reclaimed land that links the islands of Taipa and Coloane. Cotai, as it has been named, is already home to the spectacularly vast Venetian Macau casino, which opened in August 2007 *(see page 229)*. Across the road The City of Dreams is a joint-venture between Australia's gaming giant Crown and Ho's son Lawrence.

The Cotai Strip is trademarked by Las Vegas Sands, which owns The Venetian, Four Seasons Macau and is building more hotels with a total of at least 20,000 rooms. These will be managed by illustrious brands such as Shangri-La and Sheraton, and will feature even more retail space, convention facilities, sports and entertainment venues. The Strip is only part of Cotai; other mega developments under way include the US$3 billion Galaxy World Resort, which will have three hotels and a 1930s-Shanghai-themed casino.

Even the financial crisis didn't stop China's newly flush punters streaming in. Revenues have surged each year since 2005, and while Las Vegas had its worst year in 2009, Macau's revenues still grew by 10 percent. The entire state of Nevada (248 casinos) took US$847.1 million in 2009, but tiny Macau (34 casinos) earned US$1.42 billion in revenue and claimed the title of the world's No 1 gambling destination in 2009. ❑

LEFT: the Wynn Casino.
ABOVE: a croupier at The Venetian.

Recommended Restaurants, Bars, Clubs & Cafés on pages 231–3

nesses have moved over the border. By 2014, Macau's Light Rail network will loop around here, connecting the border gate with the downtown area, the airport and Cotai.

Border gates

At the modern border gate between the Special Administrative Region and Zhuhai over the road in mainland China, a park has been created around the former gateway, **Portas do Cerco ⑲**, which was built in 1870 and is inscribed with a quote from Portuguese poet Camões: "Honour your country, for your country is watching you". The crossing is open from 7am to midnight, and the casino shuttle buses line up to meet the punters arriving from the mainland by land.

Around 500 metres (550 yds) to the south is the **Fortress of Mong-Ha**, on the hill of Colina de Mong-Ha, constructed to provide a defence vantage to guard the Portas do Cerco. Built in 1849, the fort's barracks now hold the 24-room Pousada da Mong-Ha and Macau's Institute of Tourism Studies, whose students now staff the small hotel and restaurant.

Temples and Memorials

Near the southern foot of Colina de Mong-Ha sits **Kun Iam Temple ⑳**, dedicated to Guanyin, the Buddhist goddess of mercy, and dating back to 1627. The first Sino-American Treaty was signed here in 1844 by Ki Ying, China's viceroy in Guangzhou, and Caleb Cushing, who was the United States' "Commissioner and Envoy Extraordinary and Minister Plenipotentiary" to China.

Most organised tours make a quick visit to the **Dr Sun Yat-sen Memorial House ㉑** (Wed–Mon 10am–5pm; free). The memorial is close to the Kiang Vu Hospital where Sun practised medicine as one of the first Western-trained Chinese doctors in this area, before he became known as the father of modern China.

Nearby are the Suzhou-style **Lou Lim Ioc Gardens** (daily 6am–9pm), with lotus ponds, bridges and ornamental mountains, resembling a classical landscape painting.

Macau's highest point

The **Colina da Guia**, the highest point in Macau, rises to the east of the Sun Yat-sen House and is home to the **Guia Fortress and Lighthouse ㉒** (daily 9am–5pm; free), one of Macau's classic landmarks – albeit one that is becoming harder to spot amid all the new skyscrapers. Part of the Historic Centre of Macau, this 17th-century Western-style lighthouse

The Macau Grand Prix is the biggest event in Macau's sporting calendar. The race starts in front of the Lisboa Hotel and winds its way through 6km (4 miles) of city streets. The two-day event takes place on either the third or the final weekend in November.

ABOVE LEFT: jetfoils from Hong Kong take just one hour to reach Macau. **BELOW:** the 17th-century lighthouse on Guia Hill.

TIP

If you are heading straight to the Cotai strip casinos (or Coloane or Taipa) from Hong Kong, consider taking the Venetian's CotaiJet Service (www.cotaijet.com.mo) to avoid tedious immigration queues and traffic jams. They run on the hour from Hong Kong's Shun Tak Centre to the Taipa Ferry Terminal (near Macau airport), and back to Hong Kong on the half hour from Taipa. *For more information see page 260.*

ABOVE RIGHT & BELOW: The Venetian, vast in scale and ambition.

– the oldest on the Chinese coast – once guarded the coastal approaches. Besides the views, there is a small art gallery. A cable car links the hilltop with a small local park and aviary at **Flora Garden** below (7am–6pm).

Each November, the streets of Macau are taken over by the Macau Formula 3 Grand Prix and the Macau Motorcycle Grand Prix. Learn more about the "Guia Race" history of these exciting road races at the **Grand Prix Museum** ㉓ (Wed–Mon 10am–6pm; charge) at 431 Rua de Luis Gongazaga Gomes in the basement of the Tourism Activities Centre. Next door, the **Wine Museum** (Wed–Mon 10am–6pm; charge) tells the story of Portuguese wines.

TAIPA AND COLOANE

The "other" Macau is not on the peninsula that is generally regarded as Macau, but consists of the two outlying islands of Taipa and Coloane – which are now really one island, joined together by Cotai – 620 hectares (1,550 acres) of reclaimed land, home to The Venetian casino *(see opposite)*.

Taipa

Taipa ㉔ was once the centre for junk-building and firecracker manufacture, and in the early 1700s became the busy centre for Western trade with China when an imperial edict banned English and French ships from Guangzhou, insisting they moor at Taipa instead.

Today it has its share of new casinos. including the hilarious Greek Mythology Casino complete with Roman centurions, and the more sophisticated Altira Macau. Bets can be placed on horses at the Macau Jockey Club Racecourse, which has racing on Friday nights and Saturday afternoons except in August and September.

In **Taipa Village** local history and developments are explained in the three-storey mint-green **Museum of Taipa and Coloane History** (Tue–Sun 10am–6pm; charge). Head east along Rua Correia da Silva and explore the narrow streets around the village square, where you will find many good restaurants.

Overlooking the main square is **Our Lady of Carmel**, a neoclassical church built in 1885. Nearby, on the Avenida da Praia, is the **Taipa Houses Museum** (Tues–Sun 9.30am– 5pm; charge), five beautifully restored houses, each of which now functions as a museum: the Macanese House, House of the Islands, House of the Portugal Regions, Exhibition Gallery and House for Reception. From this olde-worlde location you can gaze across the water to the amazing City of Dreams and the vast **Venetian Macao-Resort-Hotel**: nowhere is the contrast between new and old Macau more striking.

Coloane

Coloane  is almost twice as big as Taipa, and what was once the last hiding place for pirates is now a green retreat from the SAR's bustle, casinos and construction with beaches, country parks and a charming village to explore.

Peaceful **Coloane Village** lies in the southwest of the island. The Chapel of St Francis Xavier, built in 1928, commemorates the successful recapture of a group of children kidnapped by pirates in 1910. The chapel looks onto Coloane's tiny Portuguese-style village square, which comes alive with restaurant tables and festivities at weekends and during holidays.

The Venetian Macao-Resort-Hotel opened in 2007. Within is the world's largest casino, equipped with almost 800 gaming tables and 6,000 slot machines. The 38-floor hotel contains 3,000 suites. Outside, there's an observation deck in the Campanile tower, and gondola rides along the moat.

With its fake sky, canals and gondolas, most children will enjoy exploring the Venetian, The circus company Cirque de Soleil performs its spectacular show most days in the 8,000-seat arena. Across the road, City of Dreams has special effects at the Bubble theatre and Franco Dragone's House of Dancing Water. There is also has an enormous indoor play area for the under-12s.

ABOVE RIGHT: The Venetian's "St Mark's Square", complete with fake sky. The surrounding "Grand Canal Shoppes" is a full-scale shopping mall.
BELOW: temple in Coloane Village.

From the square you can explore the narrow lanes that hide a few small furniture shops and cafés. It all makes Coloane an easy place to spend half a day exploring – and an even easier place to sit with some Portuguese wine and Macanese food and watch the world go by while others lose and win fortunes at the gaming tables a few miles away.

Further south, by the pretty bay at Cheoc Van, there's an open-air pool next to the white sandy beach. The Pousada da Coloane overlooks the bay, and from this pleasant family-run hotel and restaurant you can follow a well-signposted trail for 45-minutes up to the island's peak and the **A-Ma Cultural Village** (daily 8am–6pm; charge). On the last part of your climb, you will hear piped music coming from speakers hidden in the bushes shortly before being rewarded by the sight of a vast, newly-built Qing-dynasty-style complex complete with temples, a bell tower, drum tower, the Tian Hou Palace and a museum. The 170-metre (560-ft) peak is marked by an impressive 20-metre (65-ft) statue of the goddess A-Ma, which can be seen from the sea. Shuttle buses run between the complex and the Façade at Estrada de Seac Pai Van every 30 minutes.

Coloane's other hotel is the grander Westin Resort Macau, built into the hillside overlooking Hac Sa (black sands) Beach. The Macau Golf and Country Club's 18 holes begin on the hotel's "roof". Close to the beach is the ever-popular Fernando's restaurant where lunches rarely finish before dusk. ❏

BEST RESTAURANTS, BARS, PUBS, CLUBS AND CAFÉS

Restaurants

Prices for a three-course dinner per person with one beer or glass of wine (MOP$ = patacas):
$ = under MOP$150
$$ = MOP$150–300
$$$ = MOP$300–500
$$$$ = over MOP$500

Macau is a great place for eating out. It's cheap, and the local cuisine features elements from the far-flung Portuguese colonies of old, with African, Brazilian, Goan and Chinese influences combining with those from the European homeland.

Portuguese/ Macanese

Clube Militar de Macau
975 Avenida de Praia Grande 📞 2871 4009 🍴 L & D daily. $$$
This former officers' mess dating from 1870 makes a wonderfully attractive setting, and the Clube Militar still attracts the cream of the city's Portuguese and Macanese society. Truly Portuguese cuisine and an excellent wine list.

Fernando's
9 Praia Hac Sa, Coloane 📞 2888 2531 🍴 L & D daily. $$
At weekends, and on many weekdays, scores of diners queue for tables at this beachfront institution on the southern end of Coloane Island. Crispy African chicken, prawns in clam sauce and casseroled crab are all excellent, and even the salad is exceptional.

IFT-Educational Restaurant
Colina da Mong-Ha 📞 2856 1252 🍴 L & D Mon–Fri only. $$
Exploring the north of Macau is a good excuse to visit this old fort where culinary and hospitality students at Macau's Institute for Tourism Studies prepare international and Macanese favourites.

A Lorcha
289 Rua Almirante Sérgio 📞 2831 3193 🍴 L & D Wed–Mon. $$
One of the best of Macau's Portuguese restaurants, serving pork with clams, *feijoa* (pork-and-bean stew) and seafood rice.

O Manuel
90 Rua Fernão Mendes Pinto, Taipa 📞 2882 7571 🍴 L & D Thur–Tue. $$$
This unassuming but popular restaurant fully deserves its reputation. Portuguese treats include cod fishcakes, grilled sardines and *calde verde* (Portuguese vegetable soup).

Nga Tim Café
8 Rua Caetano, Coloane Village, Coloane 📞 2888 2086 🍴 L & D daily. $$
Eat alfresco in Coloane village square at Nga Tim, with a straightforward menu of Portuguese and Macanese classics, like African chicken and garlic prawns.

A Petisqueira
15A & B Rua São João, Taipa 📞 2882 5354 🍴 L & D Tue–Sun. $$
Fish and seafood are a must here: prawns, seafood salads, sea bass and Portuguese-style cod dishes.

O Porto Interior
259 Rua Almirante Sérgio 📞 2896 7770 🍴 L & D daily. $$–$$$
Enjoy fine Macanese classics in an attractive restaurant decorated with interesting prints and artefacts.

Pousada de Coloane
Praia de Cheoc Van, Coloane 📞 2882 2143 🍴 B, L & D daily. $$
The terrace alone at this family-run hotel is a reason to stop here. The bougainvillea-clad restaurant rustles up everything from grilled chorizo and African chicken to *acorda* (mashed bread with seafood).

RIGHT: lunchtime at Fernando's.

Prices for a three-course dinner per person with one beer or glass of wine (MOP$ = patacas):
$ = under MOP$150
$$ = MOP$150–300
$$$ = MOP$300–500
$$$$ = over MOP$500

O Santos
20 Rua da Cunha, Taipa
☎ 2882 5594 ◉ L & D
Wed–Mon. **$$–$$$**
Tuck into filling fare such as stuffed pork loin and curried crab, surrounded by football memorabilia.

Asian
Star Hub Café
3 Rua Francisco H. Fernandes, NAPE ☎ 2875 7733
◉ B,L & D daily. **$–$$**
This colourful, no-frills eatery delivers its promise of a "uniquely Singapore and Vietnam dining experience", with tasty and inexpensive dishes.

Wong Chi Kei Congee and Noodle
17 Largo do Senado
☎ 2833 1313 ◉ L & D
daily. **$**
Step off the main square to grab a bowl of wonton noodles and a seat in this traditional-style restaurant.

French
Aurora
10/F, Altira Macau, Taipa
☎ 2886 8868 ◉ L & D
daily. **$$$$**
Stylish Aurora mixes exquisite modern French cuisine with a relaxed Australian vibe. Lounge back on the sofas outside on the spacious terrace post-dinner and take in the bright lights of the Macau peninsula.

La Bonne Heure
12A & B Travessa de São Domingos ☎ 2833 1209.
◉ L & D Thur–Tue. **$$**

Cafés in Macau
The Macanese are fond of coffee, and unlike Hong Kong, where the habit has only really caught on in recent years, Macau has some great little traditional cafés serving good coffee (and tea) with delectable local snacks like *pastel de nata* (Portuguese egg tart), or savoury varieties such as pork chop buns. There are several of these cafés in the old town around Largo de Senado and São Paulo, and Lord Stow's Bakery in Coloane village can be singled out for special praise.

French cuisine prepared by chef who trained under Robuchon. Cosy bistro has art exhibitions and stays open for post-dinner drinks and music until 1am Friday nights.

La Comédie Chez Vous
Avenida Xian Xing Hai, Edificio Zhu Kuan (opp. Cultural Centre) ☎ 2875 2021
◉ B, L & D daily. **$–$$**
The ground-floor café, serving memorable crêpes, is popular for breakfast (8am–noon).

Lunch or dine in the upstairs restaurant.

Robuchon A Galera
3/F, Hotel Lisboa, 2 Avenida de Lisboa ☎ 2857 7666
◉ L & D daily. **$$$$**
Joel Robuchon, lauded by the Parisian media as "chef of the century", chose the Lisboa Hotel as the location for his first establishment outside France, now boasting three Michelin stars and regarded as one of the best restaurants in Asia. Fiendishly expensive for dinner; good value for lunch.

Italian
Antica Trattoria
40–42 & 46 Avenida Sir Anders Ljuungstedt, NAPE
☎ 2875 5103 ◉ L & D
daily, closed 2nd Tue each month. **$$**
One of three restaurants run by different members of the same

LEFT: Macanese food combines influences from the former Portuguese colonies – including Brazil, Mozambique and Goa – as well as the European homeland.

Macanese–Italian family, Antica Trattoria is a Macau institution, serving up great pasta, pizza and Italian snacks.

Caffé Toscana

11 Travessa de São Domingos ☎ 2837 0354 ☺ L & D daily. **$–$$**
Small café with a mezzanine dining area. Stop off for pizza or focaccia while exploring the Largo do Senado area.

Cozinha Pinocchio Taipa

195 Rua do Regedor, Taipa. ☎ 2882 7128 ☺ L & D noon–1am. **$-$$**
Established some 25 years ago, Pinocchio recently moved to a vast two-storey building close to Taipa's main square. Food is classic Portuguese, with plenty of grilled meats and fish. Specialities include curry crabs, codfishcakes and mussels.

Il Teatro

Wynn Macau, Rua Cidade de Sintra ☎ 2888 9966 ☺ D only. **$$$$**
Classy southern Italian restaurant overlooking the lake where the choreographed fountains perform nightly.

La Gondola

Estrada de Checo Van, Coloane ☎ 2888 0156 ☺ L & D daily. **$-$$**
Kick back by the beach in Coloane at this excellent Italian, hidden by the swimming pool. Pizzas, pastas, salads – it's all good and another wallet-friendly Macau bargain.

Pizzeria Toscana

Calcada da Barra, 2A Edificio Cheong Seng ☎ 2872 6637. ☺ L & D daily. **$$**
Located in the Barra area near Moorish barracks. Great value. The clam linguine is recommended.

Bars, Pubs and Clubs

Apart from the action around the 24-hour casinos, Macau's nightlife also offers loud and lively bars in the NAPE area, sophisticated hotel bars vying to outdo each other, and some relaxed sports bars and pubs.

38 Lounge

38/F, Altira Macau, Avenida de Kwong Tung, Taipa. Tel: 2886 8868. One of the most spectacular views in Macau from the top of hotel tower. Outdoor terrace, open 24 hours a day. DJs Wed–Sun 10am–2am.

Al's Diner

Block 1, New Orleans, Fisherman's Wharf. Tel: 2872 8206. Lively Hong Kong bar brings US beer, burgers and music across the Delta.

Bellini Bar

Venetian Macau Resort Hotel, Cotai. Tel: 6646 3838. Located in a corner of the Venetian's vast casino floor, the Bellini Bar has live music and is a neat nook to hang out in and watch the gaming action.

Blue Frog Bar and Grill

1037, Level 1, Grand Canal Shoppes, The Venetian Macau, Cotai. Tel: 2882 8281. Brings a contrasting touch of Shanghai "hip comfort" to The Venetian.

Casablanca

1369–1373 Avenida Dr Sun Yat-sen, NAPE. Tel: 2875 1281. One of the many open-fronted bars in NAPE, a good place to bar-hop.

Guia Circuit Pub

G & 1/F, Building Zhu Kuong, Rua de Londres, NAPE, Macau. Tel: 2875 2199. Grand Prix themed bar, with memorabilia all over the walls and screens playing racing videos so you can enjoy Macau's famous race every day of the year.

Macau Soul

31 Travessa de Paixão. Tel: 2836 5182. Superb little bar, 10 minutes walk from Leal Senado. Regular exhibitions and live music, with over 320 Portuguese wines by the glass, plus tapas and light snacks. Mon, Tues, Thurs, 12:30–10pm, Fri–Sun 12.30pm–12am.

MP3

1333 Avenida Dr Sun Yat-sen, NAPE. Tel: 2875 1306. With dancing girls, DJs and an all-you-can-drink happy hour (6–9pm), MP3 is one of the loudest bars in NAPE.

Old Taipa Tavern

21 Rua dos Negociantes, Taipa Village. Tel: 2882 5221. Pleasant pub in Portuguese-style building. Live music and sports screens.

Rascals

Rua do Regedor, Edificio Chun Fok San Chun, Bloco II. Tel: 2882 7051. Lively sports bar in Taipa village showing sports from across the globe.

Vasco

1/F, Grand Lapa Macau. Tel: 793 3831. Sip away on a themed cocktail in sophisticated hotel lounge bar. Piano music in evening.

Veuve Cliquot Lounge

MGM Grand Macau, NAPE, Macau. Tel: 8802 8888. As this is the first dedicated Veuve lounge in the world, the yellow-labelled bubbly is the best seller here.

Whisky Bar

16/F, Star-World Hotel, Avenida da Amizade, Macau. Tel: 2838 3838. Almost 100 different whiskies, including 60-year-old malts, on offer at this sophisticated cigar lounge. Open until 2am.

Pearl River Delta

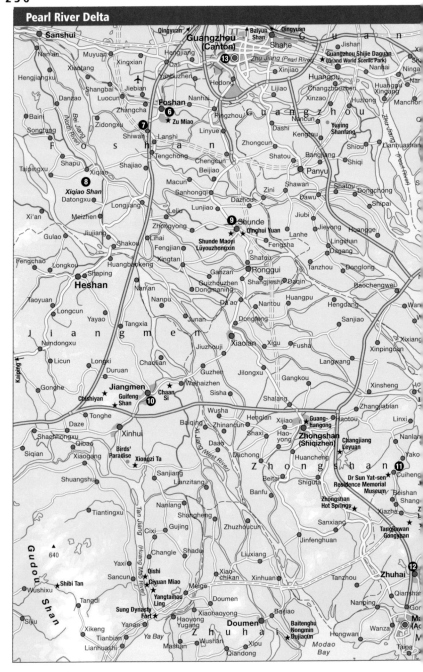

Sanshui

Nan'an
Muyuan
Xiaotang
Xingxian
Hengjiangxu
Danzao
Shangbai
Luocun
Zhangcha
Zidongxu
Shiwan
Lanshi
Taipingxu
Shapu
Xiqiao
Datongxu
Xi'an
Meizhen
Gulao
Jiujiang
Fengchao
Longkou
Shaping
Heshan
Taoyuan
Longcun
Yayao
Nandongxu
Licun
Longki
Duruan
Gonghe
Chishiyan
Jiangmen
Guifeng Shan
Tonghe
Daze
Shachhongxu
Xinhui
Qibao
Siqian
Xiaogang
Shuangshu
Tiantingxu
Gudou Shan
640
Wushixu
Shibi Tan
Tangdi
Siju
Xikeng
Tianbian
Lianhuashi

Qingyuan
Guangzhou (Canton)
Baiyun Shan
Qingyuan
Shahe
Hengjiang
Dali
Yanbuzhen
Nanhai
Foshan
Zu Miao
Ringzhou
Jiebian
Nanhai
Hedong
Zhu Jiang (Pearl River)
Guangzhou Shijie Daguan (Grand World Scenic Park)
Jishan
Nanhai
Ninga
Huangpu
Changzbouzhen
Xinzao
Manchor
Huangpu
Xingang
Huzlong
Lijiao
Nancun
Yuying Shanfang
Lianhuashan
Dashi
Kengtou
Zhongcun
Shatou
Banghang
Shiou
Xinjiao
Xiqiao Shan
Tengchong
Chengcun
Beijiao
Macun
Sanhongqi
Zhongyong
Lihai
Fengjian
Xingtan
Huangbaokeng
Nan'an
Nanpu
Tangxia
Junan
Jiuzhouji
Chaolian
Guzhen
Waihaizhen
Chaan Si
Jiangmen
Jilongxu
Gangkou
Wusha
Henglan
Xijiao
Baiqing
Zhinangun
Shaxi
Haoyong
Daao
Dachong
Beitai
Shiguta
Banfu
Nanlang
Shangheng
Gujing
Zhuzhoucun
Cixi
Changle
Shadu
Yaxi
Sancun
Qishi
Ciyuan Miao
Yangtaihou Ling
Sung Dynasty Fort
Haoyong
Yanan
Yugang
Xiaohaoyong
Doumen
Baijiao
Wushan
Ya Bay
Mashan
Qiandong
Xipu

Lunjiao
Shunde
Qinghui Yuan
Shunde Maoyi Lüyouzhongxin
Fengsha
Shatou
Ronggui
Ganzan
Guizhouzhen
Dongmaning
Shangjieshi
Daqin
Da'ao
Nantou
Huangpu
Dongfeng
Xiaolan
Xigu
Fusha
Langwang
Sisha
Shalang
Guang-hangong
Haotou
Zhongshan (Shiqizhen)
Changjiang Leyuan
Huancheng
Zhongshan Hot Springs
Sanxiang
Jinfenghuan
Liuxiang
Xiao chikan
Xinhuan
Tanzhou
Nanping
Baitenghu
Nongmin
Dujiacun
Hongwan
Wanza
Modao Bay

Zini
Dazhou
Shawan
Dawu
Panyu
Jiubi
Jieyong
Lanhe
Shatou
Lingshan
Dagang
Tanzhou
Donglong
Hengdang
Sanjiao
Zhangliabian
Linxi
Nanlan
Yako
Cuiheng
Dr Sun Yat-sen Residence Memorial Museum
Beishan
Shang
Xiazha
Tangjiawan Gongyhan
Zhuhai
Qiansharu
Taipa

Shatou
Dongchong
Shipai
Huangge
Baochengwei
Wan
Xixiang
Xinpingcun
Xinsheng
Zhuhai

Kaiping

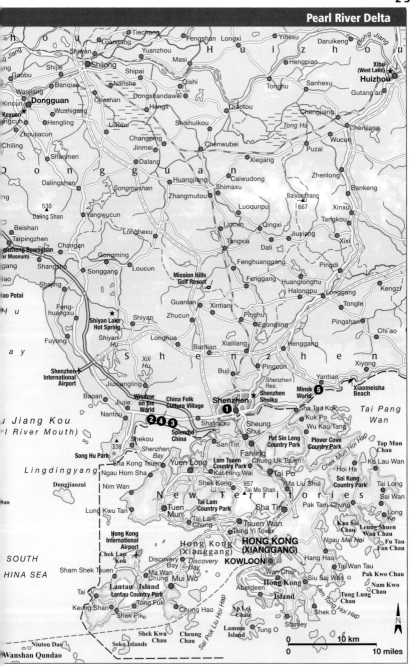

Recommended Restaurants, Bars, Pubs & Clubs on page 245

SHENZHEN AND THE PEARL RIVER DELTA

Just over the border from Hong Kong, the booming city of Shenzhen and the Pearl River Delta region are spearheading China's remarkable economic growth

The past two decades' stupendous growth in the Pearl River Delta (PRD) – with the Special Economic Zone (SEZ) of Shenzhen at the forefront – has been a key part of the transformation of modern China. Occupying around 40,000 sq km (15,500 sq miles) from Jiangmen along the coast to Huizhou and running inland as far as Guangzhou and Zhaoqing, the Delta is a major manufacturing centre, home to more than 55 million people and responsible for around 30 percent of China's total exports.

The Delta's transfiguration from paddy fields to stocks and shares deals, described by *The Economist* magazine as "so huge as to transform global trading patterns and investment flows", began in earnest in 1992. The then paramount leader Deng Xiaoping toured China's southern provinces, passing on the message that to get rich was glorious. SEZS with looser regulations and taxation started up in Shenzhen and Zhuhai shortly after. Investors from Taiwan and Hong Kong hurtled in, putting their international marketing savvy to prime use, to be swiftly imitated by their mainland counterparts.

The PRD produces a large proportion of the world's electronics, motor parts, shoes, toys, furniture, textiles, clocks, watches, lighting and ceramics. There are at least 200,000 factories here, almost half of which are owned by Hong Kong companies, whose workers are largely drawn from the less industrialised inland areas of China. These migrant workers typically live in dormitories

Main attractions
LO WU COMMERCIAL CITY
WINDOW OF THE WORLD
SPLENDID CHINA
OPIUM WAR MUSEUM, HUMEN
ZU MIAO TEMPLE, FOSHAN
SHIWAN (CERAMICS)

PRECEDING PAGES: in the heart of Shenzhen's shopping district.
LEFT: the city is growing at an incredible rate.
RIGHT: Deng Xiaoping made Shenzhen China's first Special Economic Zone.

TIP

The new Shenzhen subway links the city centre with the theme parks. Tickets are cheap, with fares ranging from Rmb 2 to 5. There are also plenty of taxis, as well as buses, either from the bus station past Lo Wu Commercial City shopping mall at the border, or from a stop along Jianshe Lu, the main street leading north from Lo Wu.

ABOVE RIGHT: Lo Wu Commercial City.
BELOW RIGHT: the Shenzhen Development Centre Building.

on site at factories, sending money back to their families at home.

SHENZHEN AND ENVIRONS

Shenzhen ❶, slap bang next to the Hong Kong border, was always going to do well. This is the new face of the PRC, where capitalism has been given pretty much a free hand after decades of communism. Nowadays its Mission Hills Golf Club, which embraces a dozen 18-hole championship courses (designed with help from the likes of Jack Nicklaus, Nick Faldo and Vijay Singh) stands in the *Guinness World Records* as the world's largest. Shun Hing Square, some 384 metres (1,260ft) tall, is the 14th-highest

building in the world. Yet at the end of the 1980s, there was little here except for a farming community.

Shenzhen Bao'an International Airport lies to the west of the city and has good ferry and coach links to Hong Kong. There is talk of creating a "mega-metropolis" comprising Hong Kong and Shenzhen, but for now there are six land borders between the two; most visitors from Hong Kong take the MTR to the Lo Wu border crossing and walk across to enter mainland China.

Shenzhen offers a (rather unrepresentative) glimpse of the People's Republic to Westerners visiting Hong Kong, while Hong Kongers themselves visit in search of inexpensive

The Rise and Rise of Shenzhen

The creation of Special Economic Zones (SEZs) during the 1980s, with their modern and relaxed business and tax regulations, kickstarted the transformation of the Pearl River Delta, and nowhere was this more pronounced than in Shenzhen. Pell-mell, the factories and skyscrapers grew almost overnight, immigrants from all over China poured into the burgeoning city to make their fortunes, highways were rolled out, airports and railways constructed, and arable land smothered in concrete. The few hundred peasants who once eked out a living here dispersed in a phenomenon that was to become a byword for fast living, cheap shopping and a no-holds-barred race to the future.

Two decades later and Shenzhen is the second-richest city in China. Per capita income is around eight times the national average, and the population has risen from 700,000 to 11 million in 25 years. Between 1992 and 2004, the city's GDP increased ten-fold, from Rmb 32 billion to 342 billion. Of course, the relentless growth has its downside. As inequality rises, so does crime: you are around nine times as likely to be mugged in Shenzhen as in Shanghai, and the pollution is notorious – on average, the air is classed as hazardous 130 days of the year.

Recommended Restaurants, Bars, Pubs & Clubs on page 245

dining, nightlife and recreation, not to mention the shopping bargains at the emporia where the goods are "inspired by" major fashion companies like Prada and Chanel.

What to do in Shenzhen

One of the most extensive retail romper rooms is the exhausting **Lo Wu Commercial City** Ⓐ (Luo Hu in pinyin), on the right after you exit the customs hall. Jewellery, clothes,

leather goods, knick-knacks and a cornucopia of other merchandise are packed one atop the other here – although shops selling the same sort of items tend to cluster together. The cardinal rule is to bargain fiercely. Offer less than a third of the asking price and settle for no more than half. Stallholders will calculate the price in Renminbi or HK dollars, but you will get a better deal if you use the former.

Shenzhen's other main shopping areas are **Dongmen** Ⓑ, with a wide range of shops and some good tailors, and at **Huaqiang Lu** Ⓒ, where electronics goods stores can be found. There is little difference in price compared to Hong Kong as far as mainstream electronics brands are concerned: the bargains lie in goods manufactured for the domestic market, although the price is a fair indication of the quality and life expectancy of any item. *(For more details on Shenzhen shopping, see page 273.)*

Minsk World, a former Soviet aircraft carrier turned fun day out.

LEFT: wall sculpture at the Beijing Quadrangle, Splendid China theme park.

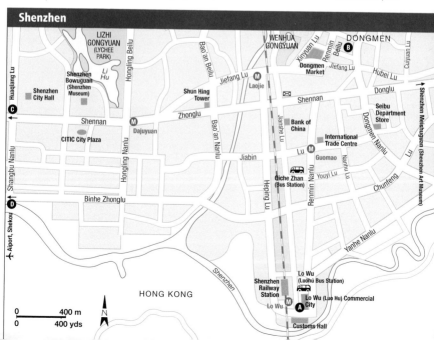

Map: Shenzhen

Shenzhen's nightlife is lively and raucous, with plenty of bars to choose from.

Even half a day's shopping in Shenzhen is likely to take it out of you, so take time out to enjoy some inexpensive grooming. Lo Wu Commercial Centre has dozens of low-key nail bars and well priced – if a tad spartan – massage parlours and beauty salons.

If Shenzhen has a wild west vibe during the daytime, wait until the evenings. International hotels are a safe bet unless you are partying with locals. The main bar areas are International Bar Street in Futian and **Shekou** , a more expat-friendly residential area.

The theme parks

It's tempting to regard Shenzhen as one enormous wacky theme park, and there's certainly no shortage of the real thing. The three main parks are clustered together in the Nanshan District, about 12km (8 miles) west of the downtown area. There are combination tickets available if you wish to see more than one park.

Window of the World ❷ (daily 9am–10.30pm; charge) showcases facsimiles of everything from Thai palaces and Japanese teahouses to

ABOVE RIGHT: Window of the World brings Europe to China.
BELOW: re-enactments of historical events are part of the Splendid China experience.

European monuments – none more spectacular than the impressively large scale model of the Eiffel Tower.

In a rather similar vein, **Splendid China** ❸ (daily 9am–9.30pm; charge) packs the whole country into one park, while the **China Folk Culture Village** ❹ (daily 9am–9.30pm; charge) presents 56 different ethnic perspectives; and – from the sublime to the incredulous – **Minsk World** ❺ (daily 9am–7.30pm; charge), on the other side of Shenzhen, is a 40,000-tonne former Soviet aircraft carrier.

Recommended Restaurants, Bars, Pubs & Clubs on page 245

TRANSPORT TO/FROM SHENZHEN

Hong Kong–Shenzhen

Trains: Every 6–8 minutes (5.30am–10.20pm) from Kowloon to the border terminus of Lo Wu (40 mins). Shenzhen station is located just over the border.

Ferries: 20+ daily ferries between Hong Kong/ Kowloon and Shekou port (50 mins); 11–13 daily between Hong Kong Airport and Shekou (30 mins); 5–8 daily between Hong Kong Airport and the Fuyong Ferry Terminal (Shenzhen Airport; 45 mins).

Buses: Frequent shuttle buses (typically every 30 mins) run from several locations around Hong Kong, including Central, Tsim Sha Tsui and the airport, to downtown Shenzhen, Shekou and Shenzhen Airport.

Shenzhen–Macau

Ferries: 3 daily to/from Shekou port (80 mins). Also hourly Shekou–Zhuhai (1 hr).

Shenzhen–Guangzhou

Trains: 3–5 express per hour (55–70 mins), plus slower trains (1½–2 hrs).
Buses: frequent departures (1½ –2 hrs).

THE SHENZHEN METRO

Shenzhen's metro system opened in 2004. There are currently two lines: line 1 runs from Lo Wu to the central Dongmen area and then through Futian district out to the theme parks; line 4 is shorter and runs north–south. Trains run every 6–8 minutes 6.30am–11pm. Shekou and the airport will be linked to the network by 2010.

TIP

The Mission Hills golf course in the hills north of Shenzhen is a testament to the New China. The superb 12-hole course is surrounded by spas, upmarket shops and the odd mansion. Membership fees can be in excess of US$100,000.

The **Shenzhen Museum**, on Fuzhong 3rd Road in Futian District (Tues–Sun 10am–6pm; free), is home to more than 20,000 cultural relics, with permanent exhibitions on the history of the Pearl River Delta. Exhibitions on folk history include Hakka culture and Hakka roundhouses.

AROUND THE DELTA

Away from Shenzhen, much of the Pearl River Delta is a mix of sprawling industrial parks, odd swathes of farmland and occasional golf courses interspersed with a few less developed hilly areas. The areas to the west of the river delta itself are, on the whole, more attractive than those to the east.

Humen and the Opium Pits

While international trade is now all the rage in the Delta, early attempts by Western traders to introduce opium to China in the 19th century met with stiff official resistance, commemorated at both a park and a museum in the town of **Humen**, right on the river delta, around 25km (15 miles) northwest of Shenzhen Air-

port. It was at Humen that Commissioner Lin Zexu *(see page 36)* contaminated several thousand chests of opium with quicklime in 1839, then deposited the haul in the so-called opium pits on the shore to the south of town. The British retaliated, sparking the First Opium War, and Lin was exiled. In the **Opium War**

BELOW: park bench slumber.

On the eastern side of Shenzhen, the resort area of Dameisha is going more upmarket. A 5-star Sheraton resort has opened on the beachfront and, in typically quirky Shenzhen style, there is now a luxurious 5-star hotel modelled on the Swiss village of Interlaken set in the hills above Dameisha.

BELOW: the Pearl River Delta is a major centre for textiles and manufacturing.

Museum (Yapan Zhanzheng Bowuguan; daily 8.30am–5pm; charge) in Zhixin Park, much is made (and rightly so) of the perfidiousness of foreign merchants who started the conflict that ended with the Chinese forces vanquished and the ceding of Hong Kong in 1841. On the coast some 5km (3 miles) south of Humen town, the original **opium pits** and the **fortress of Shajio** (Shajiao Potai) are worth a visit (8am–5pm; charge).

Foshan and Shiwan

The busy city of **Foshan** ❻ lies southwest of Guangzhou. It's a dusty centre of ceramics and textile production, but hidden away from the grids of factories is the 1,000-year old **Zu Miao Temple complex** (21 Zumiao Lu; daily 8.30am–7.30pm) The temple is well preserved, with many finely sculptured friezes made from limestone, ash of shells, paper, rice, straw and sand. The once colourfully painted friezes depict fables and scenes of Foshan's history. Many of the friezes have faded to an antique tone, which adds to the temple's charm.

Shiwan ❼, just 2km (1¼ miles) southwest of downtown Foshan, has been making ceramics for centuries, and is home to many porcelain factories that these days welcome tour groups. The fires at the **Nanfeng Ancient Kiln** (daily 8am–6pm; charge) are said to have been alight and firing pottery since the Ming era. The four-day firing process is explained by way of a series of English-language signs.

In the Nanhai district of Foshan, **Xiqiao Shan** ❽ is a hilly area with villages that have retained some of their 19th-century flavour. Xiqiao is one of the more peaceful areas in Guangdong, one that still thrives on its local produce and river trade. From the town, it's possible to travel by cable car to visit the statue of Guanyin on the crest of the nearby hill and walk along stone paths that wind through even smaller villages, rocky plateaux and waterfalls, including **Feiliutian Chi**, which is reckoned to be the most picturesque.

South to Macau

Shunde ❾, on the road from Guangzhou to Zhuhai, is renowned for its Qing garden, and has some photogenic back lanes and canals. Further south, the large town of **Jiangmen** ❿ is eminently missable, although the Ming-era villages in the surrounding countryside – centred round a watchtower – are a pleasant reminder of architectural whim in former days. Closer to Zhuhai, and on the coast, the memorial garden at **Cuiheng** ⓫ pays tribute to its best-known son, Dr Sun Yat-sen, China's first republican president. **Zhuhai** ⓬ is the last major city before Macau, and is steadily growing in importance as a Special Economic Zone. ❑

BEST RESTAURANTS, BARS, PUBS AND CLUBS

Restaurants

Average price for a meal for one, with one drink:

$ under US$12 (under Rmb 100)
$$ US$12–20 (Rmb 100–160)
$$$ over US$20 (over Rmb 160)

Being an international business centre, Shenzhen has a wide range of restaurants. Regional Chinese cuisines are well represented and there are many options in all price ranges, from cheap canteens and street food to upmarket hotel restaurants. The downtown area around Jianshe/Shennan Lu and Heping Lu is well supplied, as is Lo Wu (Luohu). Futian district's shopping area further west has plenty more, and also numerous bars.

Cantonese

Laurel Restaurant

Shop 5010, Lo Wu Commercial City 0755 8232 3668 L & D daily. $
Innovative Cantonese food. Try the marbled beef or the drunken chicken hotpot.

Phoenix House

2/F, The Pavilion Hotel, 4002 Huaqiang Donglu, Futian 0755 8207 8888 L & D daily. $$$
Hankering for dim sum? This is the place, very "Hong Kong" and with a great ambience.

Other Chinese

Lao Yuan

2/F, Qi Che Building, intersection of Zhenhua and Yan'an rds 0755 8332 8400 L & D daily. $$
Super-spicy Sichuanese, and a touch of theatre, as trad-garbed waiters wield long-necked teapots.

International

Cabin BBQ

Honey Lake Holiday Village Amusement City, Futian District Tel: 0755 8305 1942 D only. $
One of a chain of semi-outdoor barbecue joints owned by Mark Ndesandjo, half-brother to President Obama. Once you've got your head round this, enjoy the plentiful Asian-style barbecue.

Grange Grill

25/F, The Westin Shenzhen Nanshan, 9028-2 Shennan Rd Tel: 0755 2698 8888 L & D only. $$$
The Westin's top-floor steakhouse is a show-stopper with its open kitchen and city views.

360 at the Shangri-La

Shangri-La Hotel, Jianshe Lu, Lo Wu Tel: 0755 8396 1380 L & D daily. $$$
Views are top-notch, ditto the cuisine and decor.

Italian

Prego Italian Restaurant

2/F, 3018 Nanhu Lu, Landmark Hotel, Lo Wu 0755 8217 2288 D only, daily. $$$
This relaxing Italian is one of the best hotel restaurants in town.

Bars, Pubs and Clubs

Captain's Club Wine and Cigar Bar, Minghua Boat, Sea World Square, Taizi Lu, Shekou. Shenzhen's new-found love affair with grape and leaf meets its full measure here, amid a slightly irrational nautical theme.

Champs, Level 2, Shangri-la Shenzhen, 1002 Jianshe Rd, Luohu District. Tel: 0755 8396 1387. Friendly hotel sports bar, American-style bar food and popular with all kinds of expats.

Coko Club, Shenzhen International Bar St, Zhongxin Citic Plaza, Shennan Zhonglu, Futian. Tel: 0755 2598 9998. The largest of the establishments on International Bar St, with a lively office crowd.

The Galleon, InterContinental Shenzhen, Overseas Chinese Town, Nanshan. Tel: 0755 3399 3388. Live music, micro-brew beers and a mix of international food. The terrace looks out across Shenzhen Bay.

Ibiza, 1024 Huafu Lu. Tel: 0755 8326 6996. If it's not quite as wild as its island namesake, it's still fun.

In Club, L5, 001 King Glory Plaza, Renmin Nanlu, Lo Wu. Tel: 0755 8261 1111. The In – famous for its drinks specials – is very much on the party people's circuit.

V Bar, Crowne Plaza Shenzhen, 9026 Shennan Dadao, Overseas Chinese Town. Tel: 0755 2693 6888. A crescent-shaped stage draws everyone into the action, at this upmarket joint.

Vegetarian

Dengpin

3/F, Jun Ting Ming Yuan, Bao'an Nanlu, Lo Wu 0755 2590 8588 L & D daily. $
A rarity in carnivorous Shenzhen, Dengpin has a fine range of well-priced veggie dishes.

GUANGZHOU

One of the first Chinese cities open to the outside world, Guangzhou has long had economic modernisation as its goal. Still, despite the usual urban bustle, some of old Canton remains

BELOW: going shopping in Guangzhou.

n Guangzhou ⑬ – always one of China's more dynamic cities – there is a palpable sense of the energy fuelling the country's rapid transformation. This is a boisterous urban centre with all the blemishes one associates with modern cities, air pollution and traffic jams included. The greater metropolitan area – with countless factories and accompanying migrant workforce – is home to around 11 million. For tourists, the main interest lies in coming face to face with the new China, rather than in the traditional tourist sights themselves – although the city is fairly well endowed in this respect.

Guangzhou is thought to have been founded in the third century BC as an encampment by the armies of the Qin emperor, Qin Shi Huangdi. During the Tang dynasty (618–906), the city was already an international port, although for centuries it remained second to Quanzhou, (Marco Polo's Zaytun, up the coast in Fujian province). Trade with Europe began after the Portuguese established themselves in the region after 1514, and from 1757 to 1842, Guangzhou was the only Chinese port open to foreigners and was at the centre of the build-up to the First Opium War *(see pages 36–37)*. It later became one of China's four treaty ports.

Following the overthrow of the Qing dynasty in 1911, the city attracted reformers and revolutionaries. Sun Yat-sen established the headquarters of the Guomintang (Nationalist Party), the first modern political party in China. Later, Mao Zedong and Zhou Enlai worked and taught in Guangzhou during a brief period of cooperation between the two political groups. During the Mao era, while the rest of China was closed to foreign trade, Guangzhou resumed its role as China's trading

window on the word, continuing to do business at the international Canton Fair. In recent years, even though it has lost ground to the economic miracle that is modern Shanghai, the city has consolidated its prosperity and is a magnet for migrant workers.

AROUND THE CITY

Guangzhou is defined by the Pearl River (Zhu Jiang), which flows through the centre of the city from west to east. Places of interest are scattered around a wide area.

Shamian Island **Ⓐ**

The most attractive neighbourhood to explore is around **Shamian Island**, a preserved relic of colonial times in the southwest of the city. Originally a sandbar on the northern bank of the Zhu Jiang, the small island was reclaimed and expanded, then divided in 1859 into several foreign concessions, primarily French and British. A canal was dug, and after ten o'clock in the evening two iron gates and narrow bridges kept the Chinese off the island.

Shamian is compact and feels very much like a resort area, in sharp contrast to the hustle of the rest of the city. A programme of gentrification has renovated a number of old colonial buildings and nurtured open-air restaurants and riverside cafés, whilst former Catholic and Anglican churches have been reopened for worship.

Qingping Market

To the north of Shamian Island, along Qingping Lu, is **Qingping Market Ⓑ** (Qingping Shichang), long known for selling every imaginable animal for food. It has changed in recent years – in part because of SARS – and there are fewer exotic mammals on display. However the sight of live scorpions and turtles, or live fowl, cats and rabbits kept in small dirty cages still shocks. The nearby streets of pet shops offer some new conflicts to puzzle over. Stalls lining Dishipu Lu and Daihe Lu sell jade, jewellery, old timepieces and Mao paraphernalia.

Around 1km (⅔ mile) to the north, the parallel streets of Xiajiu

As the capital of Guangdong, "workshop of the world", Guangzhou has become one of the most prosperous cities in China, and attracts migrant workers in huge numbers.

BELOW: the Pearl River flows through the heart of the city.

There are 12 daily trains between Guangzhou and Hung Hom Station in Kowloon. Journey time is just under two hours.

ABOVE RIGHT: Tianhe Plaza, one of the city's main shopping malls.

Lu and Changshou Lu form the centre of a lively shopping and dining area. Behind the Guangdong Restaurant, a narrow side alley called Shangxia Jie leads to **Hualin Si ©**, said to have been founded by an Indian monk in 526, although the existing buildings date from the Qing dynasty. There are 500 statues of *luohan*, pupils of the Buddha, in the main hall.

The waterfront

The **Bund** (Yanjiang Lu) runs eastwards along the waterfront from Shamian to **Haizhu Qiao ◐**, built in 1933 and the oldest steel bridge across the Pearl River. Around 2km (1½ miles) east of the bridge on Er-Sha Island is the **Guangdong Museum of Art ©** (Guangdong Meishuguan; 38 Yanyu Lu; Tue–Sun 9am–5pm; charge). Its dozen exhibition halls display some of the more avant-garde examples of Chinese art, with exhibitions of work by local students and an outdoor sculpture area.

A cathedral and a mosque

To the northwest of Haizhu, the 50-metre (160-ft) double towers of the **Sacred Heart Catholic Cathedral ©** (Shishi Jiaotang) are plainly visible. Built in the early 1860s it holds services under the auspices of the Patriotic Catholic Church.

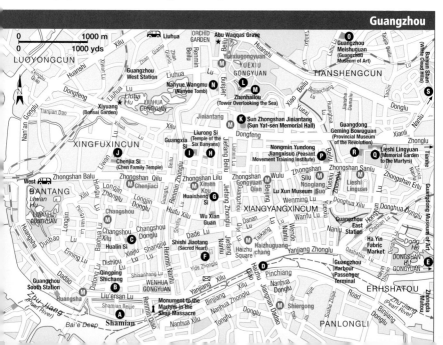

Recommended Restaurants, Bars, Pubs & Clubs on pages 252–3

CITY TRANSPORT

Guangzhou's **metro system** (www.gzmtr. com/en) is extensive, and the network connects most places of interest. Trains are clean and run every few minutes from 6am to midnight. Tickets (actually a disc which is inserted in the turnstile) cost from Rmb 2, and stored-value cards are an option. Stations are marked by red signs with a split Y symbol, and signage and ticket machines are bilingual. **Taxis** fill in the gaps that the metro has yet to reach; ask your concierge to write your destination in Chinese, as few drivers speak any English. All cabs have meters. The **bus** network is comprehensive, but slow and crowded. There are fewer **bicycles** these days, but this can still be a good way of getting about – bike hire is available on Shamian Island.

TIP

A cruise on the Pearl River (Zhu Jiang) is a pleasant way of seeing Guangzhou, particularly in the evening when the city looks at its best – all the bridges along the way, and many of the skyscrapers on either bank, are imaginatively festooned with lighting displays. Boats depart from Tianzi Pier on the north bank, and most cruises last for 90 minutes, with the option of dining aboard. The Guangzhou Passenger Ship Company (tel: 020 8333 0397) operates several cruises each evening; buy tickets at Tianzi Pier.

BELOW: colonial architecture on Shamian Island.

Further north is the onion-shaped dome of **Huaisheng Si** Ⓖ, dating back to 627 and founded by a trader said to be an uncle of the Prophet Mohammed. The 25-metre (82-ft) minaret, the **Guang Ta Pagoda** (Naked Pagoda), dominates an area where high-rises are competing to capture the skyline. The mosque functions as a cultural centre for Guangzhou's Hui Muslims, who comprise about 5 percent of the city's population.

Liurong Si Ⓗ

✉ 87 Liurong Lu Ⓒ daily 8.30am– 5pm Ⓢ charge Ⓧ Ximen Kou

North of Zhongshan Lu, one of the city's main east–west thoroughfares, a narrow street leads to the **Liurong Temple** (Temple of the Six Banyan Trees). It was built in 1097 together with the **Hua Ta Pagoda** (Flower Pagoda), although a temple has stood here since the sixth century. Each storey has doorways and an encircling balcony – climb to the top to be rewarded with a great view of Guangzhou's urban sprawl.

Guangxiao Si Ⓘ

✉ 109 Guangxiao Lu Ⓒ daily 8.30am– 5pm Ⓢ charge Ⓧ Ximen Kou

Guangxiao Temple (Temple of Bright Filial Piety) was preserved during the Cultural Revolution on orders from Premier Zhou Enlai.

The temple is believed to date back to sometime around AD 400, although most buildings are of 19th-century vintage. The entrance is marked by a brightly painted laughing Buddha, and the main hall is notable for its ceiling of red-lacquered timber, while the rear courtyard has some of the oldest iron pagodas in China.

The **Dongtie** and **Xitie pagodas** (Western and Eastern Iron pagodas) date back to the city's earliest beginnings. There is a 10th-century stone pagoda behind the main hall with sculptures of the Buddha placed in eight niches.

In its earliest times, Guangzhou was called Panyu, and the name Guangzhou first appeared during the period of the Three Kingdoms (AD 222–280). The city was formerly known to Westerners as Canton. From the provincial name "Guangdong", the Portuguese somehow derived the name of Cantão. From Cantão came Canton.

Chenjia Si ❶

✉ Zhongshan Lu ⓒ daily 8.30am–5.30pm ⓢ charge Ⓚ Chenjia Si

Chenjia Si (Chen Family Temple), located on the western end of Zhongshan Lu close to the eponymous subway station, is one of China's more whimsical temples. The temple, built in 1894, has six courtyards and a classical Chinese layout, and is decorated with friezes crafted in Shiwan, near Foshan *(see page 244)*. The largest frieze depicts scenes from the epic *Romance of Three Kingdoms*, with thousands of intricate figures against a backdrop of ornate houses, grandiose gates and pagodas. There is a giant altar of gold-leaf plating and additional wood, brick and stone friezes along the rooftops.

The temple houses the **Guangdong Folk Arts Museum** with displays from all over China, including embroidery, ethnic minority costumes, porcelain figures and jade carvings.

Around Jiefang Lu

The **Sun Yat-sen Memorial Hall** (Sun Zhongshan Jiniantang) Ⓚ, set within a lush 6-hectare (15-acre) park, is easy to spot with its eye-catching blue roof tiles. The octagonal hall, built shortly after the death of Sun Yat-sen in 1925 and completed in 1931, now houses a large theatre and lecture hall.

Guangzhou's largest park, **Yuexiu** Ⓛ, is beautifully landscaped with three artificial lakes, rolling hills, rock sculptures and lush greenery. Its centrepiece is the **Tower Overlooking the Sea** (Zhenhailou) Ⓜ, a memorial to the seven great sea journeys undertaken by the Muslim eunuch admiral Zheng He to East Africa, the Persian Gulf and Java between 1405 and 1433. Today, the tower houses a **municipal museum** showcasing the history of Guangzhou (Tue–Sun 9am–4pm; charge).

Nearby is the marble and granite **Sun Yat-sen Monument**, which sits on a hill above the Sun Yat-sen Memorial Hall.

On the other side of Jiefang Beilu from Yuexiu Park is the **Nanyue Tomb** Ⓝ (Xihan Nanyue Wangmu; daily 9.30am–5pm; charge), the tomb of the Nanyu emperor. In 1983, bulldozers uncovered the tomb of the emperor Wen Di, who ruled southern China from 137 to 122 BC. Now an underground museum, the site houses the skeletons of the emperor and 15 courtiers, including concubines, guards, cooks and a musician, who were buried alive with the emperor. Thousands of funeral objects from jade armour to bronze music chimes are displayed in adjoining rooms.

Eastern districts

East of Yuexiu Park, on the edge of Luhu Park, is the **Guangzhou Museum of Art** Ⓞ (Guangzhou Meishuguan; 13 Luhu Lu; Tue–Fri 9am–5pm, Sat–Sun 9.30am–4.30pm; charge), with an impressive collection of ancient and contemporary art and sculpture (including genuine terra-

BELOW: whimsical figures at Chenjia Si.

cotta warriors from Xi'an).

Close to the junction of Yuexiu and Zhongshan Lu is the former Kongzi Miao, or Confucius Temple, which lost its religious function during the "bourgeois revolution" of 1912. In 1924, the **Peasant Movement Training Institute ℗** (Nongmin Yundong Jiangxisuo; daily 8.30–11.30am, 2–5pm; charge) was opened here as the first school of the Chinese Communist Party. The elite of the Party taught here: Mao Zedong (his work and bedroom are on show), Zhou Enlai, Guo Moruo and several others.

After the collapse of a workers' uprising in 1927, the communists were forced to retreat from the cities. A park and memorial, **Lieshi Lingyuan ℚ** (Memorial Garden to the Martyrs) situated just to the east of the Peasant Training Institute,

was created in 1957 in memory of the uprising and its nearly 6,000 victims. Nearby is the **Guangdong Geming Bowuguan ℝ** (Provincial Museum of the Revolution; daily 9am–5pm; charge), a reminder of the role of the Guomintang (Nationalist Party) and its predecessors since the First Opium War.

Baiyun Shan

An easy half-day trip to the north of the city leads to **Baiyun Shan ⓢ** (White Cloud Hills), a series of hills overlooking Guangzhou. To get there take a taxi or, if you feel up to it, bus no. 24 from the south side of Renmin Park – journey time is 30 minutes. A cable car ascends to the top, where you can walk to several other peaks. Souvenir stands and teahouses are found at various peaks and precipices in the area, ideal places to sit back and take in the surrounding hills. If you prefer to walk up to the peak, there is a paved road as well as stone paths that wind up through the trees. ❑

Zhaoqing is a scenic resort 110km (70 miles) west of Guangzhou, and can be accessed directly from Hong Kong on a daily jetfoil (4 hours). Frequent trains and buses to Guangzhou take 1½–2 hours.

ABOVE LEFT: the Sun Yat-sen Memorial Hall.
BELOW: Yuexiu Park.

BEST RESTAURANTS, BARS, PUBS AND CLUBS

Restaurants

Average price for a meal for one, with one drink:
$ under US$12 (under Rmb 100)
$$ US$12–20 (Rmb 100–160)
$$$ over US$20 (over Rmb 160)

Guangzhou is a great place for eating out. The city is the home of Cantonese cuisine, with hundreds of good restaurants in which to sample it, and prices are relatively low. There is also a good supply of dining options from elsewhere in China and, reflecting Guangzhou's cosmopolitan nature, from around the world.

There are numerous restaurants on Shamian Island and in the nearby streets north of Qingping Market, but overall they are spread quite evenly around the city.

Cantonese and other Southern Chinese

Banxi
151 Long Jin Xilu ☎ 020 8181 5777 ◉ L & D daily.
$–$$
One of three garden-style restaurants remaining in Guangzhou, the Banxi (or Panxi) consists of several linked dining rooms with views overlooking Liwan Lake. The 100-year-old institution claims to serve over 1,000 varieties of dim sum.

Dongjiang Seafood Restaurant
276 Huanshi Zhonglu, Tinahe District ☎ 020 8322 9188 ◉ L & D daily. **$$**
Downtown and downright excellent. There are non-seafood choices, but regulars sing the praises of the stuffed giant crabs and other seafood specialities.

Guangzhou Restaurant
2 Wenchang Nanlu, Shangxiajiu Lu ☎ 020 8138 0388 ◉ L & D daily. **$$**
Ranged over several floors, signature dishes include Wenchang chicken and double-boiled shark's fin soup with black chicken. Very popular with local residents for dim sum.

Lai Heen
3/F The Ritz-Carlton, 3 Xing An Road, Pearl River New City, Tianhe District ☎ 020 3813 6888 ◉ L & D daily.
$$$
Cantonese fine dining in a sumptuous setting. Choose from dim sum, classic and modern Cantonese cuisine. Tea and wine pairings enhance the experience.

Tao Tao Ju
20 Dishipu Lu, Liwan District ☎ 020 8139 6111 ◉ L & D daily. **$$$**
Historic establishment that makes the most of its location and reputation. The dim sum is excellent, and its menu runs to 200 items.

Chinese Muslim

Nur Bostan
43 Guangta Lu ☎ 020 8187 4919 ◉ L & D daily. **$**
Good Uighur-style halal food – with lamb predominating – at this inexpensive reminder of the city's sizeable muslim *(hui)* population.

Other Chinese

Dong Bei Ren
36 Tianhe Nanerlu ☎ 020 8750 1711 ◉ L & D daily. **$$**
Dong Bei Ren is one of Guangzhou's most popular restaurants, renowned for its myriad Manchurian *jiaozi*, or mini dumplings, and its sweet red wine.

European

Silk Road Grill Room
White Swan Hotel, Yi Shamian Lu, Shamian Island ☎ 020 8188 6968 ext. 18

Ⓒ L & D daily. **$$$**
Sophisticated establishment with a price tag to match, and service that would not be out of place in a capital city.

Indian

Haveli

2 Aiguo Lu Ⓒ 020 8359 4533 Ⓒ L & D daily. **$**
Haveli's fulsome Indian fare tastes even better beneath the trees of its picturesque garden. Very well priced.

Jewel of India

123 Huangpu Dadao Xi, Tianhe Ⓒ 020 3846 6955 Ⓒ L & D daily. **$**
Great for a classic curry house feast, the Tianhe branch is one of a chain of authentic Indian-owned restaurants, with others in Dongguan, Foshan and Zhuhai.

International

1920

183 Yanjiang Zhonglu Ⓒ 020 8333 6156 Ⓒ L & D daily. **$$**
A charming, emphatically German riverside café that's just the place for lunch, Sunday brunch, or somewhere to listen to live jazz of an evening.

Backstreet Restaurant

Guangdong Museum of Arts, 38 Yanyu Lu, Ersha Island Ⓒ 020 8735 3960 Ⓒ L only (daily). **$$$**
Arty ambience, as might be expected given the location, and plenty of

platters from around the planet dished up in chic surroundings.

Lucy's

3 Shamian Nanjie, Shamian Island Ⓒ 020 8121 5106. **$$**
A menu that embraces the world, and smiles that embrace all diners, pretty much sums up this Shamian stunner. Tables and chairs outside on the banks of the Pearl River make this one of the most popular places to hang out on Shamian.

Italian

Prego

40/F The Westin Guangzhou, 6 Lin He Zhong Lu, Tianhe District – Guangzhou, Guangdong Ⓒ 020 2886 6868 Ⓒ L & D daily. **$$$**
Upscale rooftop Italian restaurant, with authentic cuisine, exceptional pasta and an extensive wine menu.

Thai and Vietnamese

Cow & Bridge

54 Shamian Da Jie Ⓒ 020 8185 8288 Ⓒ L & D daily. **$$**
The Cow is well into its second decade of serving consistently good Thai dishes to very satisfied customers. Great atmosphere.

Vietnamese Lemon House

Ground Floor, 11 Jianshe Liu, Ma Lu/507 Huifu Donglu

Ⓒ 020 8375 3600 Ⓒ L & D daily. **$$**
There are some Thai dishes on the menu,

but you should concentrate on the Vietnamese, especially the range of *pho*.

Bars, Pubs and Clubs

Guangzhou has a buzzing nightlife scene, with a range of clubs and other late-night options, as well as more standard bars. For more detailed information, see www.guangzhouhotel. com/bardisco.htm.

African Bar, 2/F, Zi Dong Hua Building, 707 Dongfeng Zhonglu. Tel: 020 8762 3336. Beats from around the world and not just the African continent keep this place throbbing till the small hours.

Baby Face, 83 Changti Lu. Tel: 020 8335 5771. A high-decibel club that really gets going as the night wears on. Can be very busy – getting served at the bar might take a while.

China Box Bar, 3 Heping Lu, Overseas Chinese Village. Tel: 020 8359 6868. One of several bars at the Overseas Chinese Village, the Box attracts mainly young professional types.

Elephant and Castle Bar, 363 Huanshi Donglu. Tel: 020 8359 3309. The Elly's two

bars and pool table blend sports and socialising nicely, pulling in the after-work crowd on a nightly basis.

Hare and Moon, White Swan Hotel, Yi Shamian Lu, Shamian Island. Tel: 020 8188 6968. A very relaxing bar, not least for the riverine panoramas beyond the picture windows.

Hill Bar, 367 Huanshi Donglu. Tel: 020 8359 0206. An old favourite, and deservedly so. There's usually something going on in this straightforward drinking den every night of the week.

The Paddy Field Irish Pub, Central Plaza Grd Floor, 38 Huale Lu. Tel: 020 8360 1379. Excellent craic guaranteed in this first outpost of Erin in Guangzhou. Plus, of course, Guinness and Jameson's.

Tang Club, 1 Jianshe Liu Malu. Tel: 020 8384 1638. This place is fun – not least for its maze of floors and lounges. At weekends, elbow room only at the bar and adjacent dance floor.

LEFT: a typical large Cantonese restaurant.

INSIGHT GUIDES

HONG KONG
Travel Tips

TRANSPORT

GETTING THERE AND GETTING AROUND

Arriving at Hong Kong's sleek airport gives most people an immediately positive impression, bolstered by first encounters with the straightforward (and inexpensive) public transport system. The trams and the Star Ferry are tourist attractions in themselves, and taxis are cheap and easy to find. It is possible to explore most of the major sites and areas by foot, but if the weather is hot and humid you will welcome the choice of taxis, buses, ferries, trains and trams to break up the journey.

GETTING THERE

By Air

Hong Kong Airport

Hong Kong is a major international air-traffic hub for the region, handling just under 50 million passengers in 2009. The impressive Hong Kong International Airport (HKIA) is located at Chek Lap Kok, on the northern shore of Lantau and about 34km (21 miles) from Central. The Y-shaped building is highly efficient. With two runways and two terminals, at peak times HKIA handles 59 flights per hour. Aircraft are received at a plethora of gates; moving walkways and an Automated People Mover speed arrivals to Immigration, where queues are dealt with swiftly. Suitcases are usually circling the carousel when you reach the baggage hall, and there is a large shopping mall, left-luggage office, post office, plus plenty of

food and beverage outlets. A 1,100-room hotel is connected to Terminal 1, while a new Marriott and 9-hole golf course are accessed via SkyPlaza, a giant entertainment and retail complex alongside Terminal 2. Enquiry hotline: 2181 0000; www.hkairport.com.

The **Airport Express** (tel: 2881 8888) railway, which runs from right inside the terminal building, is the easiest and quickest way to get into town – trains reach Hong Kong Island in just 23 minutes, with stops at Tsing Yi and Kowloon stations. Single fares cost HK$90–100, returns HK$160–180. Many hotels operate free shuttle buses to and from the Airport Express stations.

Numerous **buses** link the airport with the city. Airbus services (prefixed "A") run at regular intervals to Hong Kong Island, Kowloon and the New Territories, and most run from 6am to midnight. The fare to Central is around HK$35. Slower "commuter" buses (pre-

fixed "E") run at similar times. There are night buses, and shuttle buses to Tung Chung MTR station.

The **taxi fare** to Kowloon should work out at about HK$300, and just under HK$400 to Central District on Hong Kong Island. There are direct **ferry services** from the airport to Macau and Shenzhen, as well as a fleet of **buses to destinations in Guangdong**.

Other airports

Macau International Airport (tel: 598 8888, or see www.macau-airport.gov.mo) provides a convenient gateway for travellers from many points in Asia. A number of **low-cost airlines** now operate out of Macau, so it can be economical to fly to destinations in Southeast Asia and China from here. The airport is on the east side of Taipa Island, and is linked by bridges to the downtown area. Taxi fares are about 40 Patacas

MAJOR AIRLINE OFFICES IN HONG KONG

Air Canada
Rm 1612, Tower 1, New World
Tower, 18 Queen's Road Central.
Tel: 2867 8111. www.aircanada.ca

Air China
2/F, CNAC Group Building,
10 Queen's Road Central. Tel:
3102 3030. www.airchina.com.cn/en/

Air New Zealand
17/F, Jardine House,
1 Connaught Road Central.
Tel: 2862 8988. www.airnz.co.nz

American Airlines
2907 Central Plaza, 18 Harbour
Road, Wan Chai. Tel: 2507
9288. www.aa.com

Asiana Airlines
34/F, The Landmark, Central.
Tel: 2523 8585. www.flyasiana.com

British Airways
24/F, Jardine House, Central.
Tel: 2822 9000. www.ba.com

Cathay Pacific Airways
1808, Tower 6, The Gateway,
Harbour City, 9 Canton Road,
TST, Kowloon. Tel: 2747 1888.
www.cathaypacific.com

Delta Air Lines
703 Central Plaza, 18 Harbour

Road, Wan Chai.
Tel: 2117 7488. www.delta-air.com

Dragonair
1808, Tower 6, The Gateway,
Harbour City, 9 Canton Road,
TST, Kowloon. Tel: 3193 3888.
www.dragonair.com

Emirates
11/F, Henley Building, 5
Queen's Road Central. Tel:
2526 7171. www.emirates.com

Finnair
2312 Cosco Tower, 183
Queen's Road Central.
Tel: 2117 1238.

Garuda Indonesia
101, 68 Yee Woo Street,
Causeway Bay. Tel: 2840 0000.
www.garuda-indonesia.com

Gulf Air
2508 Caroline Centre, Yun Ping
Road, Causeway Bay.
Tel: 2769 8337. www.gulfairco.com

KLM Royal Dutch
22/F, World Trade Centre, 280
Gloucester Road, Causeway Bay.
Tel: 2808 2111. www.klm.com

Korean Air
11/F, Tower Two, South Seas

Centre, Tsim Sha Tsui East.
Tel: 2733 7111.
www.koreanair.com

Lufthansa
10/F Guangdong Investment
Tower, 148 Connaught Road
Central. Tel: 2868 2313.
www.lufthansa.com

Malaysia Airlines
23/F, Central Tower, 28 Queen's
Road Central. Tel: 2521 8181.
www.malaysia-airlines.com

Qantas Airways
24/F, Jardine House, Central.
Tel: 2842 1438. www.qantas.com

Singapore Airlines
17/F, United Centre,
95 Queensway, Admiralty.
Tel: 2520 2233 (res); 2216
1088 (info). www.singaporeair.com

Thai Airways International
24/F, United Centre, Admiralty.
Tel: 2876 6888 (res); 2769
7421 (info). www.thaiair.com

Virgin Atlantic Airways
8/F Alexander House, 15–20
Chater Road, Central.
Tel: 2532 3030.
www.virgin-atlantic.com

(written as MOP\$40). The regular
AP1 bus serves major hotels, the
Ferry Terminal and the border
gate – the fare is MOP\$3.30.

Shenzhen Baoan International
Airport (www.szairport.com/eng) is
not (yet) a major port of entry
into China. If you are planning
onward travel to other mainland
cities, it is cheaper to fly from
Shenzhen than from Hong Kong.
The airport is linked to Hong
Kong by a ferry and bus service,
and is situated northwest of the
city on the Delta coast.

Guangzhou's new Baiyun
International Airport, which
opened in 2004, is 28km (18
miles) and a 45-minute drive
from downtown. There are international flights to various Asian
cities as well as to Paris, Los
Angeles, Melbourne and Sydney,
and domestic flights to most
large Chinese cities. For flight
information, tel: 020-3606

6999, www.gahco.com.cn/
index_e.htm. Buses and taxis shuttle passengers to and from the
airport. Expect to pay around
RMB120 by taxi.

By Rail

MTR operates direct intercity
trains from Shanghai and Beijing
to Hung Hom Station, Kowloon
on alternate days (www.it3.mtr.
com.hk). Journey time is 20 hours
to/from Shanghai and 24 hours
to/from Beijing. Note that Hong
Kong usually appears as "Jiu-
long" – putonghua for Kowloon –
on Chinese pinyin timetables,
noticeboards and tickets. If travelling by train from other destinations in China, Guangzhou is the
main rail hub, and 12 direct intercity through trains run between
Hung Hom and Guangzhou East
daily. Alternatively you can head
to Shenzhen and walk across the

border at Lo Wu, then catch an
MTR train south to Kowloon once
you have cleared customs.

By Sea

Numerous cities in Guangdong
province are connected by sea
with Hong Kong, and it is also
possible to take a ferry from
Xiamen in Fujian province.
*See page 259 for details on
regional transport.*

GETTING AROUND

Hong Kong is an easy city to get
around, once you are armed with
a bilingual map, and have worked
out where Hong Kong Island, the
harbour and the the Kowloon
peninsula are in relation to one
another. Public transport is
excellent, but be aware, however,

that since this is such a densely populated city, trying to navigate your way around in the rush hour is challenging – even impossible at times – for the uninitiated. Travelling at this time of day may also make you feel less than charitable towards the local population, and mystified when people push to get onto buses, trains and trams before everyone has got off. If you're waiting for a taxi on the street away from a taxi rank, it's everyone for themselves, don't expect anyone to acknowledge whether you have been there 10 seconds or 10 minutes. If you think it's your turn, just take the taxi.

Public Transport

Rail: the MTR

Hong Kong has a fast and efficient rail system with clear signage in English and Chinese. All trains are air-conditioned and operate from around 6am until just after midnight.

Following a merger between the KCR (Kowloon–Canton Railway) and **MTR** (Mass Transit Railway) in 2007, all trains in Hong Kong are now operated by the MTR (tel: 2881 8888, www.mtr.com.hk), in a network now comprising nine railway lines serving Hong Kong Island, Kowloon, North Lantau and the New Territories. An additional Light Rail line serves Tuen Mun and Yuen Long. The MTR also runs the Airport Express *(see page 256)*.

Adult single fares range from HK$4–26, and there is a 10 percent discount if you use an Octopus card *(see panel, below)*. There are also ticket deals for tourists: a HK$50 one-day tourist pass allows unlimited travel on the Island, Tsuen Wan, Kwun Tong, Tseung Kwan O, Tung Chung and Disneyland Resort lines. For HK$220/300 you can get one or two Airport Express journeys and three consecutive days unlimited travel on the MTR.

Ferries

The 12-strong Star Ferry fleet crosses the harbour between Central and Wan Chai on Hong Kong Island and Kowloon side from 6.30am–11.30pm every day, (top deck HK$2.50, lower deck HK$2 Mon–Sat, top deck HK$3, lower deck HK$2.40, weekends and public holidays). There are also routes from Hung Hom to both Central and Wan Chai. Departures are every 6–12 minutes depending on the time of day, and the journey takes about eight minutes Central–Tsim Sha Tsui, and around 15 minutes Wan Chai–Tsim Sha Tsui.

Ferries to the Outlying Islands – Lamma, Lantau (including 24-hour service to Discovery Bay), Cheung Chau and Peng Chau – leave from the ferry piers to the north of the IFC tower on Hong Kong Island. Fares start from HK$11. Fast ferries cost more.

Buses

Six different bus companies provide services in Hong Kong, covering all the major areas as well as speedy connections to and from the airport. Routes are reduced at night. Fares range from HK$1.20 for short journeys in the city to HK$45 for longer trips into the New Territories. Final destinations are marked in English and Chinese on the front top panel. Drivers rarely speak much English, but timetables and route maps are posted at bus stops. Exact change is needed, or use an Octopus Card *(see panel, left)*. **Enquiries**: Citybus (tel: 2873 0818) and New World First Bus (tel: 2136 8888), which run on Hong Kong Island, Kowloon and the New Territories, are owned by the same company (http://www.nwstbus.com.hk). Other operators are Kowloon Motor Bus (KMB; tel: 2745 4466; www.kmb.hk); Long Win Bus Co.

OCTOPUS CARDS

Visitors staying more than a few days should buy an Octopus stored-value card, which permits travel on the rail systems, buses, some minibuses and ferries at reduced fares. It can also be used at many public phones, photo booths, vending machines and for purchases at a number of retail outlets such as 7-Eleven, Starbucks and local supermarkets. Octopus cards are sold at service counters at Airport Express and Mass Transit Railway stations. The minimum price is HK$150, which includes a refundable HK$50 deposit. Children and seniors pay reduced fares. For enquiries, tel: 2266 2222. www.octopuscards.com.

(tel: 2261 2791), which serves the airport; Discovery Bay Transportation Services (tel: 2987 0208); and the New Lantao Bus Co. (tel: 2984 9848; www.newlantaobus.com) on Lantau Island.

Minibuses/Maxicabs

These 16-seater passenger vans, coloured cream with either a red or green side-stripe, run on fixed routes but will stop anywhere except on double yellow lines. They are usually faster than regular buses, but not as cheap. Destinations are usually written in English at the front of the van. Call out clearly when you want the driver to stop. Fares vary from HK$1.50–20. Vans with a green stripe (maxicabs) take Octopus Cards or exact change only. Those with a red stripe do not take Octopus Cards but do give change.

Taxis

It is usually easy to hail a taxi on the street, although at busy times you may need to join a queue at a taxi rank – best at a hotel. Taxis in Hong Kong and Kowloon are coloured red and, in theory, can take you anywhere in the territory apart from non-airport destinations on Lantau. However, sometimes you will come across taxis on Hong Kong

STREET SIGNS

All street signs are in both English and Chinese. Hong Kong street maps usually have both English- and Chinese-language sections in the back to make it easier to find your destination. Be aware that while sometimes the English name of a street or district is a transliteration of the Chinese, at other times the Chinese name is totally different and seemingly bears no relation to the English name.

Man Wa Lane
文 華 里

Island which are so-called "Kowloon taxis": otherwise identical, these will only take passengers across to Kowloon – which can be frustrating. Green taxis operate in the New Territories, and blue cabs on Lantau Island. All taxis can carry passengers between the airport and the rest of Hong Kong.

The initial fare is HK$18 for red taxis, HK$14.50 for green, HK$13 for blue. There are additional charges for heavy luggage, animals and travelling via tunnels, which are all posted inside the taxi. Passengers must wear a seat-belt (when available) whether sitting in the front or rear.

Many taxi drivers can speak some English and know the main hotels and tourist spots in Hong Kong, but to avoid problems, take your destination written down in Chinese. If you encounter difficulties, all cabs are equipped with a radio telephone, and somebody at the control centre should be able to translate.

Taking passengers for a ride by a circuitous route is not unknown, and drivers will sometimes refuse a fare, usually if the journey will take them out of their way as they are about to finish work. You may call a police officer or phone the complaint hotline, tel: 2527 7177, but to save time it is probably better to walk off and find another taxi. If you lose something in a taxi you can call 1872 920 to try and trace it. You will need to pay a charge for them to search for you whether or not you get your belongings back.

REGIONAL TRANSPORT

By Rail

Guangzhou–Hong Kong

Twelve daily trains link Guangzhou's East Railway Station and Hunghom Station in Kowloon. Travelling time is just under two hours. There is also a

TRAMS

A picturesque and inexpensive way to get around on Hong Kong Island is by tram. The tramlines run across the north of Hong Kong Island west and east. Stops are frequent, and you can simply hop on and off as you please. The flat fare is HK$2, or $1 for under-12s and over-65s (exact change required or use an Octopus Card), and the service operates between 6am and 1am. Sit on the top deck for the best views (see also page 123).

The **Peak Tram** is a funicular railway and has been running since 1888. It takes eight minutes to reach the upper terminus from the terminus on Garden Road, Central, running every 15 minutes, between 7am and midnight daily.

The Peak tram adult return fare is HK$36, single $25, children $16 and $9.

daily train between Foshan and Hong Kong via Guangzhou, with a travelling time of just over two hours. See also Getting There, pages 256–7.

In Guangzhou, away from the station itself, most hotels and the CTS (China Travel Service) office can help with train tickets. In Hong Kong, tickets can be purchased through travel agents, hotels, CTS offices and at Hunghom Station (tel: 2947 7888). If tickets to Guangzhou are sold out, take the MTR to the border terminus of Lo Wu (a 40-minute journey, with departures roughly every 10 minutes). Shenzhen Station is a few minutes walk across the border.

There are dozens of trains daily between Shenzhen and Guangzhou. Travelling time is two hours. Trains arrive in Guangzhou either at the central station or at Guangzhou East Railway Station (Guangzhou Dong), in Tianhe, a 30-minute taxi ride from the city centre.

ACCOMMODATION

SHOPPING

ACTIVITIES

A – Z

LANGUAGE

All trains between Kowloon and Guangzhou are air-conditioned, but not all between Shenzhen and Guangzhou offer this service. Ask for the air-con class when buying a ticket – it's worth the extra money when temperatures soar in summer.

By Boat

Hong Kong–Macau

There are numerous ways to travel from Hong Kong to Macau by sea. Fares for sea crossings vary between services and the class of ticket, the time of the day, and the day of the week you travel. First Ferry runs its high-speed catamarans from the China Ferry Terminal in Tsim Sha Tsui. Turbojet services are slightly more expensive and more frequent, and they leave from the Macau Ferry Terminal at the Shun Tak Centre in Sheung Wan, Hong Kong Island. Tickets range between HK\$134 and HK\$176 for economy class one way. For the most up-to-date information on fares, check with the company providing the service or the Hong Kong offices of the Macau Government Tourist Office, tel: 2857 2287; www.macautourism.gov.mo.

Shun Tak Holdings' Turbojets carry the largest percentage of passengers between Hong Kong and Macau, and take about an hour. Refreshments are provided on board, with complimentary newspapers, coffee and tea on the first-class top deck. Departures are every 15 minutes from 7am until 1am, and then roughly one an hour. Turbojets also operate a route direct from Hong Kong Airport to Macau, although there are only seven departures daily. Contact Turbojet on tel: 2859 3333, www.turbojet.com.hk.

The New World First Ferry "flying cats" are two-deck catamarans that carry 400 passengers. They leave every half-hour between 7am and midnight from China Ferry Terminal TST [only]. Contact First Ferry on tel: 2131

8181, www.nwff.com.hk. You can also go straight from Hong Kong to Taipa on Cotai Jet Ferries (tel: 2859 1588; www.cotaijet.com.mo), which depart for the new Taipa Ferry Terminal on the hour 7am–5am from the Macau Ferry Terminal at the Shun Tak Centre on Hong Kong Island. From Taipa they depart on the half-hour from 9.30am–5.30pm. Tickets cost from HK\$134 on weekdays and from HK\$146 at weekends. This is a good option if you are heading straight for the Cotai casinos or for Taipa/Coloane.

It is wise to buy your return ticket in advance, especially if you are travelling at the weekend or during a public holiday, as tickets can sell out.

Baggage

Baggage is limited to 9kg (20lb), and there is not much space on board for large suitcases. The Left Luggage Service Centre, G/F Shop G02, Shun Tak Centre (6.30am–12.30am) charges HK\$50 per piece for the first three hours and then HK\$15 per hour.

Hong Kong–Guangdong

Ferries ply between Hong Kong and several Guangdong cities including Zhuhai, Shekou (for Shenzhen Airport) and even all the way to Zhaoqing, but there is no longer a Guangzhou service. Most leave from Hong Kong's China Ferry Terminal on Canton Road, Tsim Sha Tsui. Tickets can be bought from the ferry pier or CTS offices.

By Helicopter

SkyShuttle (in HK, tel: 2108 9898; www.skyshuttlehk.com) operate a **helicopter** service between Hong Kong and Macau. There are flights every 30 minutes from 9am until 10.30pm. The flights use helipads on the Macau Ferry Terminal in the Shun Tak Centre in Hong Kong and the Macau Ferry Terminal in Macau. One-way fares are HK\$2,600 on weekdays, and HK\$2,800 at weekends and on Fri-

days. Journey time is around 20 minutes. There is also a less frequent helicopter service between Macau and Shenzhen.

Macau Transport

The huge rise in visitor numbers to Macau has resulted in traffic problems, and taxis are often difficult to find away from hotels, casinos, the ferry pier or the border crossing. Many casinos operate free shuttle buses from the ferry terminal.

Buses

Buses and minibuses are easy to use in Macau, with the English destination written on the front along with the Chinese. Bus stops have routes and numbers clearly marked. Exact change is needed. A battalion of buses wait at the ferry terminal and stop at most major hotels, casinos and tourist sites. Fares are cheap, ranging from MOP\$2.50 for anywhere on Macau peninsula to MOP\$5 for Hac Sa on Coloane.

Taxis

The former Portuguese colony has a fleet of black or yellow taxis. The initial fare is MOP\$13. Drivers here speak less English than those in Hong Kong, and many carry a list of tourist sites written in English and Chinese in their cab. There is a small surcharge for large items of luggage.

Pedicabs

As an echo of the quieter colonial past, there are a small gaggle of pedicab drivers who wait for custom at the jetty terminal. You will need to bargain with the driver – a typical price is around MOP\$150 per hour, but note that a lot of Macau is hilly, with the roads being congested and unsuitable for these two-seater bicycle cabs.

For information on public transport in Shenzhen and Guangzhou, see pages 243 and 249.

ACCOMMODATION

SOME THINGS TO CONSIDER
BEFORE YOU BOOK YOUR ROOM

Hong Kong has some of the world's best hotels, but they are also among the most expensive. Service standards are high, and the rooms, restaurants and ambience at the city's five-stars are hard to beat. There are some excellent mid-range hotels, too, although budget accommodation is limited. Macau's recent push to become Asia's leisure capital has brought world-class resort hotels to the formerly sleepy enclave, and the hotel situation in Shenzhen and Guangzhou is also vastly improved in the past few years.

Hotel Areas

Hong Kong's relatively small size means that you are never much more than an hour from the city centre and harbour. Most hotels are suitable bases for business or sightseeing. The majority of tourists stay in Tsim Sha Tsui, although Wan Chai and Causeway Bay are increasingly making headway into this lucrative market.

Business travellers' choice of hotel is determined by the purpose of their trip. There are plenty of top hotels close to the main financial and business districts on Hong Kong Island. If an event at the Hong Kong Convention and Exhibition Centre is the focus of the trip, then a hotel within walking distance in Wan Chai is useful. For business people using Hong Kong as a base for travel to southern China, hotels in Kowloon and the New Territories may be best.

The low level of personal crime in Hong Kong means that there are

no districts to avoid. If you would like to escape the more dense urban areas it is perhaps worth investigating the handful of hotels located in the New Territories and the Outlying Islands; travel times into Central will be between 30 minutes and one hour.

In Macau, the choices range from the brand new Las Vegas style casino resorts on the Macau peninsula or Cotai to quiet escapes on Coloane. If you are not in Guangzhou for business then Shamian Island is probably the most interesting and pleasant place to base yourself. Shenzhen, Shekou and Dameisha have well-equipped resorts, and any hotel within 15 minutes of Lo Wu is ideal for shopping.

Prices and Booking

The hotel industry is enjoying high occupancy rates, and several new hotels have opened in recent years. Prices are generally high. In the following listings pages, hotels

are grouped according to the maximum "rack rate" published by the hotel for a standard double room in peak season – ie during trade fairs and local public holidays. At these times booking ahead is essential. If you plan to stay for a week or more, it's worth enquiring about longer-stay packages.

Rooms at the best hotels start at more than US$200, but reductions are often available. Good hotels in the moderate to expensive category are often reduced by 50 percent. Check with the hotel's website, travel agents or hotel-booking websites for the best time to take advantage of bargain rates – reliable hotel-booking websites with a good selection of hotels include Asia Travel, ww.asiatravel.com, Asia Hotels, www.asiahotels.com, C-Trip, www.ctrip.com, and Wotif www.Wotif.com.

Visitors arriving at the airport without hotel bookings can make reservations at a booth operated by the Hong Kong Hotels Association (open 6am and 1am) in the arrivals area. Travel agents at Macau Ferry Terminal display hotel rates clearly and offer ferry and room deals.

There is no sales tax in Hong Kong; however hotels add a 10 percent service charge to bills.

In Macau, prices are significantly higher at weekends and often fully booked on Saturdays and around major public holidays.

In Shenzhen and Guangzhou you can usually get a double room in a five-star hotel for under US$100 (less than 50 percent of the official maximum price) unless there is a trade fair on at the time.

For more details about hotels, check with the Hong Kong Hotels Association (tel: 2375 3838), or try the Hong Kong Tourist Board at www.discoverhongkong.com.

Many Chinese tourists are chain smokers. If you are not a smoker, insist firmly on a non-

smoking floor when booking, and double check your request has been met before you arrive.

A C C O M M O D A T I O N   L I S T I N G S

HONG KONG ISLAND

HOTELS

Luxury

Conrad Hong Kong
Pacific Place
88 Queensway, Admiralty
Tel: 2521 3838. Fax: 2521 3888
[p307, E3]
www.conrad.com.hk
Towering above the Pacific Place complex in Admiralty, this elegant, modern business hotel is located on floors 40 to 61. Spacious and luxurious. 510 rooms.

Four Seasons Hotel Hong Kong
8 Finance St, Central
Tel: 3196 8888. Fax: 3196 8899
[p307, C1]
www.fourseasons.com
Glamorous hotel using light and harbour views to maximum effect. French and Cantonese restaurants have already won international acclaim. 399 rooms.

Grand Hyatt
1 Harbour Rd, Wan Chai
Tel: 2261 0222. Fax: 2802 0677
[p308, A2]

www.hongkong.grand.hyatt.com
The high-rollers' hotel of choice on Hong Kong Island, this glitzy five-star hotel is adjacent to the convention centre and popular with business-people and delegates. Features an amazing 7,000-sq metre (80,000-sq ft) spa. 556 rooms.

Hotel LKF
33 Wyndham St, Central
Tel: 3518 9688. Fax: 3518 1699
[p306, C3]
Chic hotel that now lords it over Lan Kwai Fong from the LKF Tower, with spacious rooms and huge suites. No hotel restaurant, but there are half a dozen in the same building and hundreds nearby. Make sure your taxi takes you to Wyndham Street entrance.

Island Shangri-La
Pacific Place
Supreme Court Rd, Central
Tel: 2877 3838. Fax: 2521 8742
[p307, E3]
www.shangri-la.com/island
Regularly acclaimed as one of the best hotels

in Hong Kong, the Shangri-La is a perfect retreat from the bustle of the city. Exceptional restaurants add to its deserved reputation. 565 rooms.

J.W. Marriott Hotel
1 Pacific Place
88 Queensway, Admiralty
Tel: 2810 8366. Fax: 2845 0737
[p307, E3]
www.marriotthotels.com/hkgdt
Classic modern luxury hotel with Marriott's signature clear in the high standards of service and smart decor. 602 rooms.

Mandarin Oriental
5 Connaught Rd, Central
Tel: 2522 0111. Fax: 2810 6190
[p307, D2]
www.mandarinoriental.com
A Hong Kong institution for the last four decades, the Mandarin holds its own in the face of stiff competition. A wonderful combination of impeccable service, grand atmosphere and beautiful decor. Major renovations were completed in 2006. 502 rooms.

Expensive

Excelsior
281 Gloucester Rd,
Causeway Bay
Tel: 2894 8888. Fax: 2895 6459
[p309, D2]
www.mandarinoriental.com/excelsior
A very popular hotel managed by Mandarin Oriental. Great location in Causeway Bay overlooking the yacht club. 883 rooms.

Fleming Hotel
41 Fleming Rd, Wan Chai
Tel: 3607 2288. Fax: 3607 2299
[p308, B2]
In the heart of Wan Chai, the Fleming focuses on providing simple, stylish and spacious rooms. Endless dining and entertainment options nearby. 66 rooms.

Hotel Jen
508 Queen's Rd West,
Sai Ying Pun
Tel: 2974 1234. Fax: 2974 0333
[off p306,A1]
www.hoteljen.com
This former Novotel property had a make-over and was renamed Hotel Jen in 2008, and is now very hip. Views from the rooftop pool. 280 rooms.

Lanson Place Hotel
133 Leighton Rd,
Causeway Bay
Tel: 3477 6888. Fax: 3477 6999
[p309, D2]
www.lansonplace.com/
Modern, boutique-style hotel with kitchenettes in many rooms for longer-staying guests. Small gym, attractive library-style lounge and wireless Internet throughout. 204 rooms.

Le Meridien Cyberport
100 Cyberport Rd, Pok Fu Lam
Tel: 2980 7788. Fax: 2980 7888
[off p306,A2]
www.lemeridien.com
Located in the Cyberport development near Aberdeen, with good amenities and use of technology. 173 rooms.

Park Lane Hong Kong
310 Gloucester Rd,
Causeway Bay
Tel: 2293 8888. Fax: 2576 7853
[p309, D2]
www.parklane.com.hk
A tourist favourite near Victoria Park and right in the thick of the shopping district. 802 rooms.

Renaissance Harbour View Hotel
1 Harbour Rd, Wan Chai

Tel: 2802 8888. Fax: 2802 8833
[p308, B2]
www.renaissancehotels.com/hkghv
A road bridge connects this luxury hotel to the Hong Kong Conference and Exhibition Centre. 860 rooms.

Moderate

Bishop Lei International House
4 Robinson Rd, Mid-Levels
Tel: 2868 0828. Fax: 2868 1551
[p306, C3]
www.bishopleihtl.com.hk
Small, hospitable hotel with an extremely convenient Mid-Levels location. Budget rate is offered for the most basic rooms. 215 rooms.

Cosmopolitan Hotel
387–397 Queen's Rd East,
Wan Chai
Tel: 3552 1111. Fax: 3552 1122 [p308, C3]
www.cosmopolitanhotel.com.hk
Opened in 2004, the Cosmopolitan is a 20-storey four-star hotel with a contemporary feel. Guests booking with the hotel are guaranteed a full 24 hours for their money, regardless of check-in time. 454 rooms.

Courtyard by Marriott
167 Connaught Rd West,
Sai Ying Pun
Tel: 3717 8888. Fax: 3717 8228
[off p306,A1]
www.marriott.com/
Located close to the Western waterfront, an easy 10 minutes from Central and close to Macau Ferry Pier. Well equipped rooms and Wi-fi (charges) throughout. 245 rooms.

East
29 Taikoo Shing Rd,
Island East
Tel: 3968 3968; www.east-hongkong.com [off p309, E1]

Funky business hotel in Quarry Bay that is a fun place to stay no matter why you are visiting. Tech-savvy rooms, free Wi-fi and cool rooftop bar. 345 rooms.

Emperor (Happy Valley)
1 Wang Tak St, Happy Valley
Tel: 2893 3693. Fax: 2834 6700
[off p308, B4]
www.emperorhotel.com.hk
Tucked away in a residential part of Happy Valley, close to the racecourse. Good value – if you can bear to be more than five minutes from the heart of things. 150 rooms.

Holiday Inn Express
33 Sharp St, Causeway Bay.
Tel: 3558 6688 [p309, C3]
If you are in HK to shop, then this hotel puts you in the heart of the action. Rooms are large, with big comfortable beds and contemporary decor. No restaurants on site, but there are hundreds within five minutes walk. 282 rooms.

Novotel Century Hong Kong
238 Jaffe Rd, Wan Chai
Tel: 2598 8888. Fax: 2598 8866
[p308, B2]
www.accorhotels-asia.com
A good-value choice in this price bracket. Undistinguished, but a convenient good-quality hotel. 512 rooms.

The Wesley
22 Hennessy Rd, Wan Chai
Tel: 2866 6688. Fax: 2866 6633
[p308,A3]
www.hanglung.com
A location between the shopping centres of Admiralty and the Wan Chai nightlife is a big plus for this hotel. Monthly and weekly packages are good value. Bright, welcoming lobby. 251 rooms.

Wharney Guangdong Hotel
57–73 Lockhart Rd, Wan Chai
Tel: 2861 1000. Fax: 2865 1010
[p308,A3] www.gdhhotels.com
Business hotel located in the heart of Wan Chai. 358 rooms.

Budget

Alisan Guest House
5/F, Flat A Hoito Court,
275 Gloucester Rd,
Causeway Bay
Tel: 2838 0762. Fax: 2838 4351
[p309, C–D2]
Small guesthouse with clean, basic accommodation on three floors of a commercial building. Free Internet access. 21 rooms.

Ibis North Point
138 Java Road, North Point
Tel: 2588 1111. Fax: 2204 6677
[off p309, E1]
www.accorhotels-asia.com/
A clean, no-frills modern hotel popular with tourists. 275 rooms.

Mount Davis Youth Hostel
Mount Davis, Western District
Tel: 2788 3105. Fax: 2788 1638
[off p306,A1] www.yha.org.hk
Basic accommodation with a hilltop location and wonderful harbour views. Free shuttle bus to/from Central (Shun Tak Centre; runs approximately every two hours). Dormitory accommodation for 171 and self-catering facilities. Also triples,

PRICE CATEGORIES

Luxury: over US$200
Expensive: US$120–200
Moderate: US$60–120
Budget: under US$60
Prices are for a standard double room at peak season. Price reductions are usually possible at off-peak times.

twins, just three double rooms and a few family rooms.

Jia
1–5 Irving St, Causeway Bay
Tel: 3196 9000. Fax: 3196 9001
[p309, D2]
www.jiahongkong.com
Sleek Philippe Starck-designed serviced apartments in Causeway Bay. 54 apartments.

Ovolo
2 Arbuthnot Rd, Central
Tel: 2165 1080. Fax: 2868 6717
[p306, C3]
www.ovolo.com.hk
Smart and spacious

one-bedroom serviced apartments located just above Central. 20 apartments.

Shama
52 Hollywood Rd, Central
Tel: 2103 1713. Fax: 2103 1700
[p306, C2]
www.shama.com
Smart designer apartments, handily located next to the Mid-Levels escalator in SoHo.

Moderate

Ice House
38 Ice House St, Central
Tel: 2836 7333. Fax: 2836 7000
[p307, C3]
www.icehouse.com.hk
Modern boutique studio apartments in a handy Central location next to Foreign Correspondents' Club, close to Lan Kwai Fong. 64 apartments.

KOWLOON

Harbour Grand
20 Tak Fung St, Hung Hom
Tel: 2621 3188. Fax: 2621 3311
[off p305, E2]
www.harbourgrand.com
Hotel of choice for China's political and business leaders, located away from downtown Kowloon. Contemporary decor with the odd ostentatious touch. 411 rooms.

InterContinental
18 Salisbury Rd, Tsim Sha Tsui
Tel: 2721 1211. Fax: 2739 4546
[p305, C4]
www.interconti.com
Formerly the Regent, this is the most glamorous modern hotel on the Tsim Sha Tsui waterfront. Delightful rooms, wonderful harbour views, exceptional restaurants and a superb spa. 495 rooms.

Kowloon Hotel
19–21 Nathan Rd,
Tsim Sha Tsui
Tel: 2929 2888. Fax: 2739 9811
[p304, C4]
www.thekowloonhotel.com
Across the road from The Peninsula, this is a

good hotel in an excellent location. 736 rooms.

Kowloon Shangri-La
64 Mody Rd,
Tsim Sha Tsui East
Tel: 2721 2111. Fax: 2723 8686
[p305, D3]
www.shangri-la.com/kowloon
Superb luxury hotel on Tsim Sha Tsui waterfront. Excellent restaurants and views. Short walk to the MTR and Star Ferry. 700 rooms.

Langham Hotel
8 Peking Rd, Tsim Sha Tsui
Tel: 2375 1133. Fax: 2375 6611
[p304, B4]
www.langhamhotels.com
Solid five-star hotel with a handy location close to Star Ferry, China Ferry and cruise terminal. 490 rooms.

Langham Place Hotel
555 Shanghai St, Mong Kok
Tel: 3552 3388. Fax: 2384 3670
[p302, B2]
www.langhamhotels.com/
langhamplace/
This plush hotel is leading the revival of Mong Kok with five-star class. Rooms feature the latest technology, which contrasts with striking art, sculpture and architecture reflecting Chinese tradition. 665 rooms.

The Mira
118 Nathan Rd, Tsim Sha Tsui
Tel: 2368 1111. Fax: 2369 0972
[p304, C3] www.themirahotel.com
After a US$65 million makeover in 2009, The Mira was reborn as a design-conscious hotel with fresh attitude. Enjoying a great location in the heart of Tsim Sha Tsui, some rooms look towards Kowloon Park. Superb restaurants and a spacious spa.

The Peninsula
Salisbury Rd, Tsim Sha Tsui
Tel: 2920 2888. Fax: 2722 4170
[p304, C4] www.peninsula.com
Established in the 1920s, The Pen is Hong Kong's only historic hotel and arguably still the best. Potted palms and string quartets in the lobby; world-class restaurants and bars, plus a Clarins spa – this place oozes class and elegance. 300 rooms.

Sheraton Hong Kong Hotel & Towers
20 Nathan Rd, Tsim Sha Tsui
Tel: 2369 1111. Fax: 2739 8707 [p304, C4]
www.sheraton.com/
hongkong
Lively five-star hotel close to Star Ferry,

MTR and Nathan Road. Some great restaurants and bars. 782 rooms.

Expensive

Holiday Inn Golden Mile
50 Nathan Rd,
Tsim Sha Tsui
Tel: 2369 3111. Fax: 2369 8016
[p304, C4]
www.goldenmile.com
Ever-popular tourist hotel in the middle of Nathan Road – the tourist golden mile of Tsim Sha Tsui. 585 rooms.

InterContinental Grand Stanford
70 Mody Rd,
Tsim Sha Tsui East

ACCOMMODATION ◆ **265**

TRANSPORT

ACCOMMODATION

SHOPPING

ACTIVITIES

A–Z

LANGUAGE

Tel: 2721 5161. Fax: 2732 2233
[p305, D3]
www.hongkong.intercontinental.com
Luxurious and fully
equipped five-star business hotel in Tsim Sha
Tsui East. 579 rooms.

Marco Polo Gateway
Harbour City, 13 Canton Rd,
Tsim Sha Tsui
Tel: 2113 0888. Fax: 2113 0022
[p304, B3]
www.marcopolohotels.com
A good-quality tourist
hotel, part of the
Harbour City shopping
centre and cruise
terminal. 433 rooms.

Marco Polo Hong Kong Hotel
Harbour City, 3 Canton Rd,
Tsim Sha Tsui
Tel: 2113 0088. Fax: 2113 0026
[p304, B4]
www.marcopolohotels.com
Largest of the three
Marco Polo hotels on
Canton Road, with harbour views from many of
its spacious rooms.
644 rooms.

Marco Polo Prince
Harbour City, 23 Canton Rd,
Tsim Sha Tsui
Tel: 2113 1888. Fax: 2113 0066
[p304, B4]
www.marcopolohotels.com
Proximity to the China
Ferry Terminal and
relaxed restaurants distinguishes this Marco
Polo from its sibling
hotels. 394 rooms.

New World Renaissance Hotel
22 Salisbury Rd, Tsim Sha Tsui
Tel: 2369 4111. Fax: 2721 2105
[p305, C4]
www.renaissancehotels.com/hkgnw
A modern and efficient
hotel on the Tsim Sha
Tsui waterfront. 549
rooms.

Novotel
348 Nathan Rd, Yau Ma Tei
Tel: 3965 8888.
[p304, C1]
This superb, newly renovated contemporary
four-star hotel (formerly
the Majestic) is packed
with neat design
touches and has a great
location. 389 rooms.

Moderate

BP International House
8 Austin Rd, Tsim Sha Tsui
Tel: 2376 1111. Fax: 2376 1333
[p304, B2]
www.bpih.com.hk
Owned by the Boy
Scouts Association, but
operated by a hotel
management company,
this is a modest midrange hotel. Great location on the edge of
Kowloon Park compensates for unexciting
interiors. 529 rooms.

Hotel Metropark Mongkok
22 Lai Chi Kok Rd, Mong Kok
Tel: 2397 6683. Fax: 2397 6440
[p302, B1]
www.metroparkhotel.mogkok.com
Large, moderately priced
hotel in gritty, vibrant
Mong Kok. 430 rooms.

Hotel Nikko Hongkong
72 Mody Rd, Tsim Sha Tsui East
Tel: 2739 1111. Fax: 2311 3122
[p305, D3]
www.hotelnikko.com.hk
A four-star hotel that is
especially popular with
Japanese tour groups.
462 rooms.

Kimberley Hotel
28 Kimberley Rd,
Tsim Sha Tsui
Tel: 2723 3888. Fax: 2723 1318

[p305, C3]
www.kimberleyhotel.com.hk
Reliable three-star
hotel, two minutes from
bustling Nathan Road.
There's a good choice of
restaurants and bars in
nearby Knutsford
Terrace. 546 rooms.

The Minden
7 Minden Ave, Tsim Sha Tsui
Tel: 2739 7777. Fax: 2739 3777
[p305, C3]
www.theminden.com
Small, friendly boutique
hotel with a European
feel enhanced by a
terrace bar-restaurant.
60 rooms.

Nathan Hotel
378 Nathan Rd, Jordan
Tel: 2388 5141. Fax: 2770 4262
[p304, C1]
www.nathanhotel.com
Close to the night market
and shopping district, a
mid-range hotel with 30
years of experience. 192
rooms.

The Salisbury YMCA
41 Salisbury Rd, Tsim Sha Tsui
Tel: 2268 7000. Fax: 2739 9315
[p304, B4] www.ymcahk.org.hk
Book ahead at this
upmarket YMCA. Rooms
are hotel-style, and many
enjoy panoramic views of
the harbour. Large indoor
pool, good restaurant
and a range of sports
and child-friendly facilities. 363 rooms.

Stanford Hillview Hotel
13–17 Observatory Rd,
Tsim Sha Tsui
Tel: 2722 7822. Fax: 2723 3718
[p305, C2]
www.stanfordhillview.com
High-quality three-star
hotel tucked away from
the hustle of Nathan
Road. 163 rooms.

Budget

Anne Black Guest House (YMCA)
5 Man Fuk Rd, Ho Man Tin
Tel: 2713 9211. Fax: 2761 1269

[p303, C/D2]
www.ywca.org.hk
Clean, simple rooms.
Ten minutes' walk from
the Ladies' Market and
Mong Kok MTR station.
A safe, reliable and
inexpensive option.
169 rooms.

Chungking House
4&5/F, Block A, Chungking
Mansions, 40 Nathan Rd,
Tsim Sha Tsui
Tel: 2366 5362. Fax: 2721 3570
[p304, C4]
There are plenty of
cheaper deals in the
area, but within the
dark corridors and grim
stairwells of Chungking
Mansions this is the
only establishment
approved by the HKTB.
75 rooms.

New Garden Hostel
13/F, Mirador Mansions, 58
Nathan Rd, Tsim Sha Tsui
Tel: 2311 2523. Fax: 2368 5241
[p304, C3]
One of the better of Tsim
Sha Tsui's hostels, but
still strictly backpacker
accommodation, with
dormitories or private
rooms. 60 rooms.

Rent-A-Room
2/F, Flat A Knight Garden,
7–8 Tak Hing St, Jordan
Tel: 2366 3011. Fax: 2366
3588. [p304, C2]
www.rentaroomhk.com
Popular budget hostel in
Jordan, immediately to
the north of Tsim Sha
Tsui. Doubles and
singles available. 28
rooms.

PRICE CATEGORIES

Luxury: over US$200
Expensive: US$120–200
Moderate: US$60–120
Budget: under US$60
Prices are for a standard
double room at peak
season. Price reductions
are usually possible at
off-peak times.

NEW TERRITORIES AND OUTLYING ISLANDS

HOTELS

Expensive

Regal Airport Hotel
9 Cheong Tat Rd, Chek Lap
Kok, Lantau
Tel: 2286 8888. Fax: 2286 8686
www.regalhotel.com
Award-winning hotel
connected to Hong
Kong's airport by an
air-conditioned foot-
bridge. Short- and long-
stay rates available.
1,103 rooms.

Moderate

Concerto Hotel
28 Hung Shing Yeh,
Lamma Island
Tel: 2982 1668. Fax: 2982 0022
www.concertoinn.com.hk
Small guesthouse, a
15-minute walk from the
ferry pier, with a beach-
side location. 8 rooms.

**Harbour Plaza
Resort City**
18 Tin Yan Rd, Tin Shui Wai,
New Territories
Tel: 2180 6688. Fax: 2180 6333

www.harbour-plaza.com
A good-value option for
longer stays if you don't
mind the location in a
rather bland residential
centre in the northwest
New Territories. 1,102
rooms.

Panda Hotel
3 Tsuen Wah St, Tsuen Wan,
New Territories
Tel: 2409 1111. Fax: 2409 1818
reservations@pandahotel.com.hk
The Panda tries hard to
overcome its unlikely
location in the large
New Town of Tsuen
Wan. Convenient for the
airport and ferries.
Large number of rooms
assures availability, and
prices are always rea-
sonable. 1,026 rooms.

Silvermine Beach Hotel
DD2 Lot 648, Mui Wo (Silvermine Bay), Lantau
Tel: 2984 8295. Fax: 2984 1907
www.resort.com.hk
Close to the ferry pier on
Lantau Island, this low-
key beach hotel offers
an alternative to the city.
Outdoor swimming pool
and adequate accommo-
dation. 128 rooms.

APARTMENTS

Budget

Horizon Suite Hotel
29 On Chun Street, Ma On
Shan, Sha Tin
Tel: 3157 8888. Fax: 2123 2128
www.horizonsuitehotel.com
Competitively priced
New Territories complex
of serviced apartments
with easy access to
country parks. Facilities
include 65-metre (213-
ft) pool. For longer
stays, rates start under
US$1,000 per month.
831 apartments.

Sunrise Holiday Resort
Jackson Property Agents, 15

Main Street, Yung Shue Wan
Tel: 2982 2626. Fax: 2982 0636
www.lammaresort.com
Experience village life in
a self-contained holiday
apartment on Lamma
Island. Five minutes
from the ferry pier, this
is a pleasant alternative
to cramped city-centre
budget accommodation.
Surcharges on Satur-
days and public holi-
days. 10 apartments.

MACAU

HOTELS

Luxury

Altira Macau
Avda de Kwong Tung, Taipa,
Macau
Tel: 2886 8888. Fax: 2886 8666
www.crown-macau.com
The classiest of all the
casino hotels, with
beautifully designed
guest rooms, and con-
stant attention to detail.

Stunning views of
Macau peninsula from
the pool and many
restaurants. 216
rooms.

Pousada de São Tiago
Avda da Republica
Tel: 2837 8111. Fax: 2855 2170
www.saotiago.com.mo
This piece of Macanese
history includes part of a
17th-century Portuguese
fortress built for its commanding views. Dark
wood, marble, chande-
liers and white linen add

to the historic ambience.
Good restaurants, an
outdoor swimming pool
and a delightful terrace.
12 suites.

The Venetian
Cotai Strip
Tel: 2887 1111. Fax: 2887 1122
www.venetianmacao.com/en
The Venetian's suite-only
hotel is a spectacular
addition to the burgeon-
ing Macau resort scene.
Over 3,000 suites and
luxury suites.

Westin Resort

1918 Estr. de Hac Sa, Coloane
Tel: 2887 1111. Fax: 2887 1122
www.westin-macau.com
Located on the quiet
island of Coloane, the
Westin is a luxury hotel

overlooking the sea. Guest rooms terrace down towards the beach, and the extensive recreation facilities include an 18-hole golf course on the resort's roof, and a spa. 208 rooms.

Expensive

The Grand Lapa
956–1110 Avda Amizade
Tel: 2856 7888. Fax: 2859 4589
www.mandarinoriental.com/grandlapa/
Former Mandarin Oriental property, The Grand Lapa is a charming hotel with five-star facilities and a superb spa in garden setting. 435 rooms.

Rocks Hotel
Macau Fisherman's Wharf
Tel: 2878 2782. Fax: 2872 8800
www.rockshotel.com.mo/
Victorian-style boutique hotel situated on the tip of the Fisherman's

Wharf entertainment area on the water's edge. French windows and balconies allow you to take in the views of the harbour and South China Sea. 72 rooms and suites.

Moderate

Grand View Hotel
142 Estr Governador Albano de Oliveira, Taipa
Tel: 2883 7788. Fax: 2883 7777
www.grandview-hotel.com
De luxe hotel in the heart of Taipa Island. Great value, and fascinating views of Macau Jockey Club's race track. 407 rooms.

Hard Rock Hotel
City of Dreams
Estrada do Istmo, Cotai.
Tel: (853) 8868 3338.
www.hardrockhotelmacau.com
Live like a rockstar in the City of Dreams. The smallest of the three

COD hotels, Hard Rock's rooms are oversized and extravagant, and you are close to all the action. 366 rooms.

Hotel Royal
2–4 Estr. da Vitoria
Tel: 2855 2222. Fax: 2856 3008
www.hotelroyal.com.mo
Convenient mid-range hotel at the foot of the Colina da Guia, in a quiet area close to central Macau. Spacious, comfortable rooms. Facilities include an indoor pool. 380 rooms.

Pousada de Coloane
Praia de Cheoc Van, Coloane
Tel: 2888 2144. Fax: 2888 2251
www.hotelpcoloane.com.mo/
A long-time favourite with Hong Kong residents, recent renovations have greatly brightened up this family-run hotel that provides a peaceful retreat. 22 rooms.

Pousada de Mong Ha
Colina de Mong-Ha
Tel: 2851 5222. Fax: 2855 6925
www.ift.edu.mo/pousada
Tucked away on a green hillside below 19th-century ruins, this romantic boutique hotel has beautifully decorated rooms with attractive Portuguese and oriental style. 20 rooms.

Regency Hotel
Estr. Almirante Marques Esparteiro, Taipa
Tel: 2883 1234. Fax: 2883 0195
www.regencyhotel.com.mo/
A spacious and conveniently located property, with large pool. 326 rooms.

SHENZHEN

HOTELS

Luxury

Interlaken OCT Hotel Shenzhen
OCT East Dameisha
Yantian District
Tel: 8888 3333. Fax: 8888 3331
www.cityinn.com.cn
A few thousand miles and a small leap of the imagination from Switzerland, this luxury lakeside hotel is 30 minutes east of downtown Shenzhen. A huge spa, two golf courses and acres of green hills with a tea plantation to explore. 299 rooms.

Mission Hills Resort
1 Mission Hills Rd
Tel: 2801 0888. Fax: 2801 1111
www.missionhillsgroup.com
In the hills north of Shenzhen, China's No. 1 golf club boasts a record 12 championship courses comprising 216 holes. Luxurious rooms and suites with balconies overlooking the greens. Non-golfers can enjoy the scenery, 51 tennis courts, pools, spas and extensive recreation and kids facilities. 315 rooms.

The Ritz-Carlton
116 Fuhua San Rd,
Futian District
Tel: 0755 2222 2222
Luxury all the way at the fabulous Ritz-Carlton

Shenzhen, which is near the Shenzhen Convention & Exhibition Center and a metro station. Rates can be a steal for this level of quality. 282 rooms.

Shangri-La Hotel Shenzhen
East Side, Railway Station, 1002 Jianshe Lu
Tel: 8233 0888. Fax: 8233 9878
Leading five-star hotel close to the Lo Wu border crossing. High standards and spa. A popular meeting place for tourists and business travellers. 553 rooms.

Expensive

Nan Hai Hotel
1 Gong Ye 1 Lu,

Shekou Industrial Zone
Tel: 2669 2888. Fax: 2669 2440

PRICE CATEGORIES

Luxury: over US$200
Expensive: US$120–200
Moderate: US$60–120
Budget: under US$60
Prices are for a standard double room at peak season. Price reductions are usually possible at off-peak times.

TRANSPORT · ACCOMMODATION · SHOPPING · ACTIVITIES · A – Z · LANGUAGE

www.nanhai-hotel.com
A low-rise resort hotel in Shekou, west of Shenzhen, with ferry connections to Macau and Hong Kong. 396 rooms.

Moderate

Century Plaza Hotel
1 Chunfeng Road,
Luohu District.
Tel: 0755 82320888

www.centuryplazahotel-shenzhen.com
Great location close to Lo Wu shopping malls and business district. Rooms are comfortable, with the more expensive – such as those on the Japanese floor – worth the extra. Laurel, a fine Chinese restaurant, is on site. 401 rooms.

Four Points by Sheraton
5 Guihua Lu, Futian District
Tel: 8359 9999. Fax: 8359 2988
This business hotel is located in the Futian Free Trade Zone. Full five-star-quality and facilities. 446 rooms.

Budget

City Inn Zhuzilin

Haitian Building,
2038 South Caitian Lu,
Futian District, Shenzhen
Tel: 8346 0888. Fax: 8346 1090
www.cityinn.com.cn
One of a new homegrown chain. Contemporary design, clean rooms with TV, bathroom and free Internet. Self-service laundry room and vending machines, but no restaurant.

GUANGZHOU

HOTELS

Luxury

China Hotel
122 Liu Hua Lu
Tel: 8666 6888. Fax: 8667 7288
www.marriott.com
This five-star Marriott hotel complex includes serviced apartments. Convenient location just across the street from the trade-fair grounds, which makes it a favourite with business travellers. 890 rooms.

Garden Hotel Guangzhou
368 Huanshi Dong Lu
Tel: 8333 8989. Fax: 8335 0467
www.thegardenhotel.com.cn
Spectacular hotel that claims to have the largest lobby in Asia. 828 rooms.

White Swan Hotel
1 Shamian Nan Lu
Tel: 8188 6968. Fax: 8186 1188
www.whiteswanhotel.com
Well-known hotel with a prime location on Shamian Island, with top-class boutiques and restaurants as well as two pools, a health centre and massage facilities. 843 rooms.

Expensive

Dong Fang Hotel
120 Liu Hua Lu
Tel: 8666 9900. Fax: 8666 2775
www.hoteldongfang.com
Large luxury hotel complex situated just opposite Liu Hua Park and the trade-fair headquarters. 900 rooms.

Phoenix City Hotel
Xintang Section,
Guangyuandong Road
Tel: 8280 8999. Fax: 8280 8288
www.phoenixcityhotel.com
This sprawling five-star European-influenced city hotel has luxurious hillside villas, as well as townhouses and apartments. There are Vietnamese, Chinese and Japanese restaurants. Recreation facilities include an amusement and nature park. 621 rooms.

Ramada Plaza Guangzhou
1 Qingyung Street, 313 Shougouling Lu, Guangyuan East, Tianhe District
Tel: 8720 6888. Fax: 8720 6999
www.ramadaplazagz.com
Close to Tianhe, the Ramada's rooms are equipped with all the required amenities, including broadband internet. There is a swimming pool, gym and table tennis facilities. 214 rooms.

Moderate

Guangdong Hotel
309 Dongfeng Zhong Rd
Tel: 8333 9933. Fax: 8333 9723
www.guangdong-hotel.com
Convenient location, well equipped, comfortable and good value. 490 rooms.

Landmark Hotel Canton
8 Qiao Guang Lu, Haizhu Sq
Tel: 8335 5988. Fax: 8333 6197
www.hotel-landmark.com.cn
Next to the Pearl River, a facelift has improved standards in decor and comfort. 566 rooms.

Landsman Hotel
111–118 Liu Hua Lu
Tel: 3622 2988. Fax: 3622 2680
www.landsmanhotel.com
Business hotel situated next to the trade-fair centre and close to Liu Hua Lake. 243 rooms.

Budget

Guangdong Shamian Hotel
52 Shamian Nan Lu
Tel: 8121 8288. Fax: 8121 8628
www.gdshamianhotel.com

Small hotel on Shamian Island with comfortable rooms. 47 rooms.

Guangdong Victory Hotel
53 Shamian Bei Lu
www.vhotel.com
Great-value three-star hotel with Old-World architecture, pleasant rooms and good facilities. 330 rooms.

Guangzhou Youth Hostel
No. 2, Shamian San Lu
Tel: 8121 8606. Fax: 8121 8298
Bargain accommodation on historic Shamian Island. Clean and comfortable. 50 rooms.

PRICE CATEGORIES

Luxury: over US$200
Expensive: US$120–200
Moderate: US$60–120
Budget: under US$60
Prices are for a standard double room at peak season. Price reductions are usually possible at off-peak times.

SHOPPING

BEST BUYS

Hong Kong loves to shop, and it wants its visitors to shop, too. International brand names are everywhere, but there are still plenty of stores and open-air street markets that are unique. Luxury goods abound and the scale of these exclusive shops is amazing. Top souvenirs are Chinese handicrafts and art, traditional clothing, reproduction and genuine antiques and collectables, Chinese tea, gold and designer fashion. Look out for VIP discount voucher booklets from the HKTB counter at the airport.

SHOPPER'S PARADISE

Hong Kong has frequently been called a shopper's paradise, and it is certainly true that most Hong Kong citizens are insatiable shoppers. Shopping ranges from colourful night markets and glitzy shopping malls to multi-storey department stores and bustling narrow streets full of antiques and bric-a-brac. These days, Hong Kong may not be the bargain basement it once was, but shopping may nonetheless prove one of the most compelling activities of any trip to the territory for many visitors. There is certainly no shortage of supply.

SHOPPING ADVICE

The Hong Kong Tourism Board (HKTB) offers straightforward advice for shoppers:

● Shop around and compare prices before you make any decision to buy, particularly for an expensive purchase.

● Always deal with reputable establishments, such as members of the Hong Kong Tourism Board's Quality Tourism Services Scheme, identifiable by the logo of a red junk, with the Chinese character for quality written in black inside. The sign should be displayed prominently on the premises. Shops that have joined the QTS scheme are supposed to provide genuine products, display prices clearly, provide product information and offer good customer service.

● When buying electrical goods, consider whether you need an international guarantee and not just a local Hong Kong version. Sometimes goods that seem suspiciously cheap are only guaranteed for the local area, and repairs or replacements will have

to be carried out by the manufacturer's Hong Kong agent.

● The problem of retailers cheating tourists was rife a few years ago, but has been brought under much greater control. However, if you do have a problem you should contact the HKTB or the **Consumer Council** (tel: 2929 2222). Both organisations are keen to protect Hong Kong's shopping reputation, and will offer whatever assistance they can.

● Shopkeepers are sometimes accused of being rude and impatient – although the situation has improved. Sometimes foreigners misunderstand the abrupt sound of Hong Kong English, and what they perceive as rude and abrupt is just the normal Hong Kong way of trying to do things quickly.

WHERE TO SHOP

Hong Kong's malls are destinations in themselves for the happy shopper, and are full of cafés and restaurants in which to take a break. Many also house cinemas and entertainments such as ice-skating rinks. Shopping hours vary, but generally continue until late every day of the week. Even during public holidays most shops are open, the exception being during the week of Chinese New Year. As a guide, shops in Central close around 7pm, but the other main areas tend to stay open until 10pm, sometimes even later. The sales start in mid- to late June and December.

Shopping Malls

Malls are landmarks in Hong Kong. Taxi drivers will recognise their names rather than the street they are on, and most are part of an MTR station development.

Hong Kong Island

IFC Mall (www.ifc.com.hk) Hong Kong MTR. Over 200 international brands, smart restaurants and a cinema.
The Landmark (www.centralhk.com) Central MTR. Over 250 shops focusing on famous names from fashion, leather goods and jewellery.
Pacific Place (www.pacificplace. com.hk) Admiralty MTR. Broad range of menswear, children's and womenswear outlets, jewellery and watches, sports goods, antiques, gourmet supermarket and upmarket food court, department store and cinema.
Prince's Building (www.centralhk.com) Central MTR. Exclusive mall for antiques, homeware, jewellery, expensive gifts and a deluxe delicatessen.

Kowloon

Elements (www.elementshk.com) By

WATCHES

Note that if you are not buying from a reputable outlet, and if the price of the watch seems to be a bargain, it's extremely likely that it will be a fake.

Kowloon MTR (airport express line) in the West Kowloon reclamation, Elements is the newest mall in town, with trendy design touches and plenty of space to browse – plus an ice rink and 12-screen cinema.
Harbour City (www.harbourcity.com.hk) Star Ferry, or TST MTR. With 700 shops, 50 restaurants and two cinemas, this giant mall stretches the almost the entire length of Tsim Sha Tsui.
Langham Place (www.langhamplace. com.hk) Mongkok MTR. Over 100 boutique stores, a handful of international brands and a six-screen cinema.
Festival Walk (www.festivalwalk. com) Kowloon Tong MTR. Huge fashion and lifestyle mall with an ice rink and cinema.

New Territories

Citygate Outlets (www.citygateoutlets. com.hk) Tung Chung MTR. End-of-season fashions from major brands.
SkyPlaza, Terminal 2, Hong Kong Airport (www.hongkongairport. com/eng/skyplaza/). Three floors of shopping, dining, a "4D" cinema (charge), iSports sports simulators (charges) and a PlayStation centre (free).

Markets

Cat Street, Upper Lascar Row, off Hollywood Road in Central, is a flea market offering inexpensive trinkets and bric-a-brac. The surrounding area is famous for its antiques. Open 11am–6pm.
Pottinger Street in Central is lined with small stalls selling fancy-dress costumes, wigs, inexpensive accessories, shoes and party decorations. Open 10am–7pm.

Stanley Market, on the south side of the island, is famous for sports and casualwear, linen, tableware, silk and leather garments. Open daily 10am–7pm.
Temple Street Night Market, Hong Kong's most popular night market runs from Jordan to Yau Ma Tei in Kowloon. Cheap clothing, watches, pens, sunglasses, CDs, electronic gadgets, luggage and numerous fakes are available in its colourfully lit stalls. There are also fortune-tellers and Chinese opera singers practising. Open 6pm to midnight.
Ladies' Market on Tung Choi Street is a busy street market in Mong Kok and is less tourist-oriented than Temple Street. Specialities include local women's fashions, jewellery and accessories. Open 3–10pm.

Jewellery fans may like to check out the **Jade Market**, located under the flyover near Kansu Street in Yau Ma Tei. Open daily 10am–6pm.

WHAT TO BUY

Antiques and works of art

The network of antique shops located around **Hollywood Road** offers an extraordinary range of Asian antiquities and artworks at a very wide range of prices. The half-dozen **Chinese Arts & Crafts** (www.crcretail.com/CR_CAC/) department stores scattered around Hong Kong also offer inexpensive traditional ceramics, textiles, clothes and handicrafts from mainland China. The largest stores are located at Star House, 3 Salisbury Road, Tsim Sha Tsui, and at Pacific Place. With the huge global interest in contemporary Chinese art, Hong Kong's art scene is booming. Hong Kong also hosts regular art **auctions** for the likes of Christie's and Sotheby's, and there are hundreds of small independent galleries. The Hong Kong

Commercial Art Galleries Association has a useful map and up-to-date listings at www.hongkonggalleries.org.

Ivory

For many years, Hong Kong was the international centre of carved ivory. However, the ban imposed by the Convention on International Trade in Endangered Species (CITES) means that you now have to obtain an import licence from your country of residence in order to take any ivory out of Hong Kong.

Bookshops

Bookazine, 3/F, Prince's Building, 10 Chater Rd, Central; 1/F, Star Ferry Pier 8, Central.
Commercial Press, 3/F, Star House, 3 Salisbury Road, Tsim Sha Tsui.
Dymocks, Level 2, IFC Mall, Central; G/F, The Peak Galleria, 118 Peak Road, The Peak.
Flow, 1/F, 40 Lyndhurst Terrace, Central. Second-hand books.
Page One, Shop 3202, Zone A, Harbour City, Canton Rd, Tsim Sha Tsui; 9/F, Times Square, 1 Matheson St, Causeway Bay. Shop LG 1-30, Festival Walk, 80 Tat Chee Avenue, Kowloon Tong (with café). Large selection of design books.
Swindon, 13–15 Lock Rd, Tsim Sha Tsui; 310 Ocean Centre, Harbour City, Tsim Sha Tsui.

Clothing

For international brands and designer names head to any of the large malls and department stores (see opposite). Local brands include Giordano, Bossini and Esprit; they now have competition from global brands like Zara and H&M, which have opened huge stores in Hong Kong.

For young local designers and imported Japanese and European fashions try Causeway Bay. Close to the MTR station on Great George Street, the Island, Beverley, Causeway

Place and Delay No Mall arcades all sell youthful clothes and accessories. Fashion Island and Style House, also on Great George Street, have more upmarket brands like Armani, Calvin Klein, Max Mara, Agnès b and Vivienne Tam.

Traditional Chinese clothing can be found at all price points. **Chinese Arts & Crafts** department stores have a good range of styles and prices, while **Shanghai Tang** has styles with a designer edge and price. You will find inexpensive silk and nylon pyjamas, cheongsams and padded jackets in many street markets (see page 170).

Shops selling seconds and factory over-runs are scattered throughout the city. There are bargains to be had, but often you cannot try the clothes on before you buy. As a starting point, look out for outlets in The Lanes (Li Yuen Street East and West) in Central, Johnston Road in Wan Chai, and the streets between Jardine's Bazaar and Percival Street in Causeway Bay. In Tsim Sha Tsui, have a

look in the shops along Granville Road and Cameron Road, then – if you still have the stamina – head north to Fa Yuen Street in Mong Kok.

Computers

China and Hong Kong are the top two exporters of computer components and accessories in the world. Hong Kong also has the second-highest level of computer ownership.

Depending on the exchange rate, you may find some bargain prices. Some of best retailers are found on the tenth and eleventh floors of Windsor House in Causeway Bay, and in Star House near Tsim Sha Tsui's Star Ferry pier. There are a number of arcades devoted solely to selling computers and accessories, which, if you know your stuff, are treasure troves. Try the always crowded **Golden Computer Centre** in Sham Shui Po or **Wan Chai Computer Centre**, 130 Hennessy Road. Make sure the operating system and keyboard are in the language you use, and check everything that goes in the box before you take it away!

Custom Tailors

Having a suit made to measure is still a popular luxury for many visitors, and something of a Hong Kong tradition: immigrant Indian tailors set up shop here

BARGAINING

The practice of bargaining for goods in Hong Kong has been declining for years, and price differences are usually so marginal that it is hardly worthwhile trying to bargain. It is still de rigueur in markets, but remember – if you buy from a market there are no guarantees and there's no possibility of exchanging goods. Even in street markets, it is highly unlikely that

you'll be able to reduce the asking price by much more than about 10 to 20 percent.

Shopkeepers who are not used to bargaining will probably react rather impatiently to your efforts. If you settle by cash you may get a slightly better deal than if you use a credit card – in many cases, shops will add an extra few percent to the price if you pay with plastic.

TRANSPORT

ACCOMMODATION

SHOPPING

ACTIVITIES

A – Z

LANGUAGE

CAMERAS AND ELECTRICALS

Cameras and electrical items can still be good buys in Hong Kong, but it pays to research prices at home first. Many camera and electronics stores Causeway Bay, Tsim Sha Tsui and Mong Kok seldom have price tags on the items, so compare prices before you buy.

Citywide chains Broadway (www.broadway.com.hk) and Fortress (www.fortress.com.hk) are reliable options. Professional and keen photographers recommend the long-established Photo Scientific, Stanley Street, Central, tel: 2525 0550, and Hing Lee Camera Company, 25 Lyndhurst Terrace, Central, tel: 2544 7593. Staff are friendly, the goods are reasonably priced. When buying electronic goods, remember to check for correct voltage, adaptors, etc.

in the late 19th century, and after 1949, the city became home to some of the legendary tailors of old Shanghai.

The speed and quality of craftsmanship and the range of fabrics here are all excellent. Such personal tailoring is no longer such a notable bargain, but it can still prove worthwhile. A few establishments can produce your suit within 24 hours, but you won't usually see the best-quality results – expect your tailor to take about a week if you want a genuinely high-quality garment.

Raja Fashions, Bespoke Tailor, 34-C Cameron Road, Tsim Sha Tsui. Tel: 2366 7624
Sam's Tailor, Burlington Arcade, 94 Nathan Road, Tsim Sha Tsui. Tel: 2367 9423
Shanghai's Tailor, 35 G/F, Far East Mansion, 5–6 Middle Road, Tsim Sha Tsui. Tel: 2739 6165
Taipan Tailor, Shop 5 & 6, 1/F, Tower 1, Admiralty Centre, Hong Kong. Tel: 2529 8861.

Jewellery

Hong Kong is the world's fourth-largest exporter of jewellery, and there is a wide range of designs available in retail outlets throughout the territory. Because Hong Kong is a free port and there is no tax on the import or export of precious metals, prices are good, and tourists from mainland China are major buyers.

Popular jewellery includes jade items (though you should avoid buying expensive pieces without expert advice) and bright-yellow 24-carat gold, called *chuk kam* in Cantonese. Jewellery stores specialising in *chuk kam* are usually very crowded, and the atmosphere is more akin to that of a betting shop than an exclusive store. These items are sold by the weight of the gold only, so you pay no premium for the design. There are many fine jewellery stores selling a vast range of gem-set designs – here, you pay for the craftsmanship as well as the materials.

Another good buy in Hong Kong are pearls, which come in all shapes, sizes and colours. The practice of bargaining is much less common in jewellery stores now, but you can certainly try your luck by asking for a discount.

WATCHES

After Switzerland, Hong Kong is the largest exporter of clocks and watches in the world; most are now produced at factories in Guangdong. Many of the major Swiss watchmakers now have stores in Hong Kong, but if you buy a brand-name watch away from one of these glamorous stores, never doubt that it is a fake. However, there is a good selection of timepieces in the city, from inexpensive fun watches in the markets to fashionable brands that do not cost multiples of HK$100K.

Leather Goods

Hong Kong's malls all have innumerable shops selling leather goods from international brands. Elsewhere, in the street markets and side streets around Central, Tsim Sha Tsui and Causeway Bay there are plenty of small stalls selling wallets and bags inspired by such brands. If you need something in which to carry all your extra shopping, street markets sell inexpensive suitcases and backpacks. For something longer-lasting without a logo, try mid-range departments stores like Wing On.

Sportswear

Hong Kong has many chain stores selling inexpensive sportswear and sports shoes (try Marathon Sports, Gigasports or Royal Sporting House). In Mong Kok, parts of Fa Yuen, Nelson and Shantung streets east of the Ladies Market are known as "Sneaker Street", and are devoted to sports stores.

MACAU

Macau is a good place to buy well-crafted Chinese antique and reproduction wooden furniture. Many Hong Kong expats have "repro" furniture made to order and have it delivered to Hong Kong, so shops are used to shipping abroad.

Antique and furniture stores cluster along Rua de São Paulo, the busy lane which leads up to the facade of São Paulo. You are free to bargain hard here. The backstreets of Taipa and Coloane near their village squares also hide a few antique and crafts shops, and Taipa has a flea market on Sundays. Tourists from the mainland are packing out designer handbag and jewellery shops at the MGM Grand and Wynn Macau's fancy arcades, but the largest retail area is now The Grand Canal Shoppes at The Venetian, with over 350 stores open 10am–11pm Sunday to Thursday and until midnight on Friday and Saturday, where painfully titled "Streetmosphere" is created by international street performers and gondoliers singing Italian opera.

SHENZHEN

Shenzhen is a major shopping destination for Hong Kongers. There is a wide variety of merchandise at prices much lower than you will ever find in Hong Kong. Designer clothing and accessories can be bought for less than a fifth of the price in Europe or North America.

Lo Wu Commercial City, immediately on the right as you emerge from customs, is the place everyone heads to for cheap fashion, handbags, wallets and shoes. It's not for the fainthearted: everyone will want to try and do business with you.

Most tailors' shops are grouped around the fabric market on the fifth floor. Tailoring costs can be less than HK$100 for a simple dress, skirt or tailored trousers. The second floor of Lo Wu Commercial City is well endowed with jewellery shops, and there can be amazing bargains. The main focus is on pearls (mostly of the freshwater variety), but jade and various precious and semi-precious

stones are easy to find, too. Stalls will help you create your own design.

Shops are generally open seven days a week from about 10am until 8 or 9pm. Most people venture no further than Lo Wu, but there are also some great bargains to be had in Dongmen (central Shenzhen; take the new subway, or find a taxi).

Whatever you are buying, remember to bargain hard!

Art

A short cab ride from Lo Wu, in Baoan, Danfen Art Village (www.dafenart.com) is home to dozens of artists who can copy any style of art you suggest or create an oil-painting based on a photograph.

Clothing and Textiles

Lo Wu Commercial City also has plenty to offer those looking for a tailor-made suit or other custom-made clothing. Most tailors' shops are around the fabric market on the fifth floor. There are literally hundreds of clothing, footwear and accessories shops spread throughout the complex.

The best tailors in Shenzhen cluster together in **Bu Cheng** – Fabric City – in the Dongmen district. Customers are welcome to choose their fabrics in one shop and then get them made up by the tailor of their choice. A pair of trousers, for example, can be made in a week and should cost less than RMB80. The Dongmen Fabric Market on Hu Bei Lu is also worth visiting.

Jewellery

Lo Wu Commercial City is also well endowed with jewellery shops, and there can be amazing bargains. The main focus is on pearls (mostly of the freshwater variety), but jade and various precious and semi-precious stones are easy to find, too.

Electronics

Shenzhen's main electronic-goods stores are gathered around a single block on Huaqiang Lu, with names like Electronic City and Aihua Computer City – take a taxi or bus 101 from Lo Wu. The first floor of Lo Wu Commercial City also has plenty of electronics shops. The major bargains are in items manufactured for the domestic market.

GUANGZHOU

Don't expect the glitz and variety of goods available in Hong Kong to be on offer here, although Guangzhou does still have interesting shopping and good bargains. The main shopping areas are Beijing Lu, Zhongshan Wulu, Renmin Nanlu, Zhongshan Silu and Xiajiu Lu-Shangjiu Lu. Xin Da Xin, at the corner of Beijing Lu and Zhongshan Wulu, offers a good range of Chinese goods, including silk. The main open-air market is Qingping Market (see page 247), selling everything under the sun.

Antiques

The largest private market for antiques is the Daihe Lu Market, which sprawls over several lanes just north of Qingping Market, near Shamian Island.

Antiques that date from before 1795 may not be legally exported. Any antique over a century old must carry a small red wax seal or have one affixed by the Cultural Relics Bureau before it can be taken out of China.

Beware of fakes, as the production of new "antiques" complete with "official" seal is a thriving industry in China. Despite the pitfalls, there is still much to buy: kam muk (gilded sculptured wood panels), vintage watches, tiny embroidered shoes for Chinese women with bound feet and beautiful Shiwan porcelain.

ACTIVITIES

THE ARTS, NIGHTLIFE, FESTIVALS AND SPORTS

Hong Kong has a lively arts scene which is further stimulated by a series of cultural festivals through the year. These days it is also far more of a venue for international performers and exhibitions than was the case just a decade ago. Nightlife is exciting and accessible. Colourful Chinese festivals provide another twist to this cosmopolitan cocktail, and there is plenty to occupy the sports enthusiast, too.

THE ARTS

Art Galleries and Exhibitions

The **Hong Kong Museum of Art** houses the territory's largest collection of traditional Chinese painting and calligraphy. A wider variety of work is displayed in the

WHAT'S ON LISTINGS

Listings and reviews are given in the freebies – *HK Magazine* and *BC Magazine* – available in bars and cafés. The fortnightly *Time Out Hong Kong* also has listings for Macau. See "The Planner" pages in the *South China Morning Post* for cinema and arts listings every day. The tourism websites have calendars of events and festivals – try www.discoverhongkong.com and www.macautourism.gov.mo.

Hong Kong Heritage Museum in Sha Tin. As well as traditional Asian paintings and sculptures, the museum has held funky exhibitions on subjects as diverse as poster art and Tibetan treasures. Local artists and photographers have a space at the **Hong Kong Arts Centre** and the **Fringe Club** to showcase their work. There are also dozens of small commercial art galleries, mainly concentrated around Hollywood Road in Central.

City Hall
1 Edinburgh Place, Central
Tel: 2921 2840
Fringe Club
2 Lower Albert Road, Central
Tel: 2521 7251
www.hkfringe.com.hk
Open Mon–Sat noon–10pm.
Hong Kong Arts Centre
2 Harbour Road, Wan Chai
Tel: 2582 0200
www.hkac.org.hk
Temporary exhibitions only –
mainly local artists. Open
10am–8pm during exhibitions.

Hong Kong Heritage Museum
1 Man Lam Road, Sha Tin
Tel: 2180 8188
www.heritagemuseum.gov.hk
Open Mon, Wed–Sat 10am–6pm,
Sun 10am–7pm.
Hong Kong Museum of Art
10 Salisbury Road, Tsim Sha Tsui
Tel: 2721 0116
Open Fri–Wed 10am–6pm.
University Museum and Art Gallery
94 Bonham Road, Mid-Levels
Tel: 2241 5500
www.hku.hk/hkumag
Open Mon–Sat 9.30am–6pm,
Sun 1.30–5.30pm.

Commercial galleries

Connoisseur Art Gallery
1 Hollywood Road, Central
Tel: 2868 5358
www.connoisseur-art.com
Open Mon–Sat 10.30am–7pm,
Sun noon–6pm.
Schoeni Art Gallery
21–31 Old Bailey Street, Central

MUSEUM PASS

A museum pass allows free access to six museums for a week – the Heritage Museum, Museum of Art, Science Museum, Space Museum, Museum of History and the Coastal Defence Museum. The HK$30 pass is available from these six museums or HKTB information centres.

Tel: 2869 8803
www.schoeni.com.hk
Open Mon–Sat 10.30am–6.30pm.
Good collection of contemporary Asian artists.

Wattis Fine Art
20 Hollywood Road, Central
Tel: 2524 5302
www.wattis.com.hk
Open Tue–Sat 10am–6pm, Sun 1pm–5pm.
Specialises in historical paintings, prints and maps.

Macau

The severe, steely grey building of the Macau Museum of Art has five floors of exhibition space, mainly given over to traditional Chinese painting, calligraphy and ceramics, but there is also room for international visiting exhibitions. For an overview of Macau's art scene, there is a useful website at www.macauart.net.

Macau Museum of Art
Avda. Xian Xing Hai
Tel: 87919814
www.artmuseum.gov.mo
Open 10am–6.30pm.
Tap Seac Gallery
95 Avda. Conselheiro Ferreira de Almeida
Tel: 2833-5140
Open Tue–Sun 10am–6pm.

Guangzhou

Gallery of Guangzhou Painting Academy
3 Zhongshan San Lu
Tel: 8384 3949
Open Tues–Sun 10am–5pm.

Guangdong Museum of Art
38 Yan Yu Lu, Ersha Island
Tel: 8735 1468
www.gdmoa.org/english/
Open Tues–Sun 10am–5pm.

Concerts

Classical

The Hong Kong Philharmonic Orchestra, chief conductor Dutchman Edo de Waart, and the Hong Kong Chinese Orchestra, principal conductor Yan Huichang, perform regularly when they are not on world tour. They, the Hong Kong Sinfonietta and visiting orchestras, hold concerts at the Hong Kong Cultural Centre and urban theatres. Recitals (sometimes free) are held at the Hong Kong Academy for Performing Arts and Hong Kong University's historic Loke Yew Hall (www.hku.hk/music).

Pop, rock etc.

Despite the lack of a world-class concert venue, Hong Kong periodically attracts some big-name acts from the world of pop, rock and jazz, as well as many fading stars, including the hairy-chested Englebert Humperdinck. As a taster, Santana, Elton John, My Chemical Romance and Plácido Domingo played here in 2008. Tickets are expensive, though – generally ranging between HK$500 and HK$900. You can also catch local Cantopop bands and Taiwanese pop stars – both are hugely popular. International acts tend to play at the Hong Kong Convention and Exhibition Centre, while Cantopop stars favour the Hong Kong Coliseum.

AsiaWorld-Expo
Hong Kong International Airport, Lantau. Tel: 3606 8888
www.asiaworld-expo.com
Hong Kong Academy for Performing Arts (HKAPA)
1 Gloucester Road, Wan Chai
Tel: 2584 8500
www.hkapa.edu
Hong Kong Convention and

Exhibition Centre (HKCEC)
1 Expo Drive, Wan Chai
Tel: 2582 8888
www.hkcec.com.hk
Hong Kong Coliseum
9 Cheong Wan Road, Hung Hom
Tel: 2335 7234
www.lcsd.gov.hk/CE/Entertainment/Stadia/HKC/

Hong Kong Cultural Centre
10 Salisbury Road
Tsim Sha Tsui
Tel: 2734 2009
www.lcsd.gov.hk/CE/CulturalService/HKCC
Rockschool and the **Fringe Club** (see page 279). The suitably-named **Underground HK** (www.undergroundhk.com) plus **Shazza Music** (www.shazzamusic.com) promote independent artists and a new generation of would be rockstars and musicians.

BUYING TICKETS

You can buy tickets for shows, concerts and some sporting events from any of the venues' box offices or Tom Lee music stores (noticeable by their bright yellow sign). If you have a credit card you can buy tickets over the phone via Urbtix (tel: 2111 5999) or HK Ticketing (tel: 3128 8288). Urbtix will also allow you to reserve tickets free of charge for three days (tel: 2734 9009 to book). You can also pay for tickets on the Internet at Cityline – www.cityline.com.hk or HK Ticketing – www.hkticketing.com. You are required to register (free) first.

Venues in Macau

The Venetian on the Cotai Strip has raised the bar for entertainment in the region. Its 15,000 seat stadium has already brought some big names to Macau.
www.venetianmacaotickets.com

Macau Cultural Centre
Av. Xian Xing Hai South
Tel: 700 699
www.ccm.gov.mo/en/intro.htm
Large venue for performances, with a 1,000-seat auditorium.

Dance/Ballet

There is a vibrant dance scene in Hong Kong, with performances by the home-grown Hong Kong Ballet, Hong Kong Dance Company and the offbeat City Contemporary Dance Company. Dance troupes from around the region, particularly from the mainland, can also be seen – perhaps the most spectacular are the Shaolin Monks who leap and tumble elaborate kung fu moves. Shows are usually held at the City Hall, urban theatres or the Fringe Club *(see page 279).*

Film

Hong Kong's movie industry was once the third-largest in the world after Hollywood and Bollywood, but the studios that once churned out kung fu action films and soppy romantic comedies have been in decline for the last decade or so. At the same time the influence of the Hong Kong industry is more widely recognised than ever, thanks to the recent Hollywood success of director John Woo, actors Michelle Yeow, Chow Yun-fat and the irrepressible Jackie Chan.

Oscar wins for Martin Scorsese's remake of *Andrew Law* and Alan Mak's Hong Kong crime-thriller *Infernal Affairs,* and period kung fu *Crouching Tiger, Hidden Dragon* (a joint-production between Hong Kong, mainland China, Taiwan and the US) plus the continued appeal of Bruce Lee's movies all keep the city's

movie industry in the spotlight. For a taste of modern Hong Kong movies look up anything by art-house director Wong Kar Wai (*Chungking Express, In the Mood For Love, 2046*) or the outrageous Fruit Chan (*Little Cheung, Made in Hong Kong, Durian Durian*).

Look out, too, for Hong Kong's amusing actor-director Stephen Chow *(Shaolin Soccer, Kung Fu Hustle).* Recent homegrown hits include *Echoes of the Rainbow,* which depicts daily life of a street in 1950s Hong Kong.

Cinemas

There are dozens of cinemas and multiplexes in Hong Kong that show a mixture of the latest Hollywood releases, local offerings and big-budget Japanese, South Korean and Thai movies. There are also several good art-house theatres with European and Asian productions. Almost all non-English films will come with English subtitles, but beware of cartoons dubbed into Chinese. As evening shows tend to sell out quickly, it's best to buy in advance by a few hours. Tickets cost around HK$60–70, while discounts of around HK$20–30 are offered on tickets all day Tuesday and for morning and matinée shows.

Broadway Circuit
Tel: 2388 3188
You can book tickets for the following Broadway cinemas via www4.cinema.com. The **Palace IFC** in the IFC mall is a luxurious cinema with big comfy armchair

seats, but tickets are standard price. It shows art-house movies as well as mainstream films, and has a DVD store and café. **Cinematheque**, 3 Public Square St, Yau Ma Tei, near Temple Street market, shows art-house movies and has a DVD shop and café.

AMC Cinemas
(www.amccinemas.com.hk) has multiplexes in Pacific Place and Festival Walk.

UA Cinemas runs nine multiplexes including the UA Times Square, Causeway Bay and UA Langham Place Mong Kok. Tel: 2317 6666.

Multiplex Cinema Limited
(www.mclcinema.com) runs the "4D" cinema at the airport's Sky Plaza, the state-of-the-art Grand Cinema at Elements Mall, with 12 theatres and "infrasonic" sound.
Theatre, Macau Tower, tel: 2893 3339.

Film Festivals

Every spring, Hong Kong holds its two-week **International Film Festival** (www.hkiff.org.hk). It's advisable to book ahead as tickets sell out fast. You can buy online on their website. **Le French May** (www.frenchmay.com), held in May, is a festival of French culture, and usually offers a run of French movies. Throughout the year various **mini-film festivals** are held. Check freebie magazines and the local press for details.

There are numerous small festivals throughout the year. The Hong Kong Film Archive (50 Lei

King Road, Sai Wan Ho, Hong Kong. Tel: 2739 2139) runs short seasons at the archive near Chai Wan. See www.filmarchive.gov.hk for details.

Museums

Hong Kong has some world-class museums. The Museum of History and the Heritage Museum offer great hands-on displays of life in the city in days gone by. The Space and Science Museums are fun places for children and often have superb visiting exhibitions. The Space Museum also has an Omnimax theatre. See the Places section of the book for full details.

Theatre

Most theatre productions are in Cantonese or Mandarin – although some of the larger theatres will put on English subtitles. The professional Hong Kong Repertory Theatre always provides subtitles to its shows. There are also local English-language drama troupes, but the quality is variable. Performances are usually held at the Fringe Club, the Hong Kong Arts Centre

KARAOKE

Many bars and even restaurants have private rooms where groups get together to sing Chinese songs. There are TV screens showing music videos and the words to the song in Chinese. Words are highlighted when you are supposed to sing them. Some karaoke bars also employ "hostesses" to sing together with the customers, who are usually rowdy groups of Asian businessmen. A night out in one of these establishments will prove extremely expensive. Westerners unaccompanied by local Chinese will probably not be made very welcome.

or the Hong Kong Cultural Centre. Big-name musicals like *Mama Mia* and *Les Misérables* periodically make it to Hong Kong.

The Hong Kong Arts Festival (www.hk.artsfestival.org), which runs for about a month at the beginning of every year, features opera, concerts, musicals, ballet and drama by artists from all over the world.

Regular performances of **Cantonese opera**, shunned by the younger generation but loved by the over-fifties, are held at the Sunbeam Theatre, 423 King's Road, North Point, tel: 2563 2959, and at other urban theatres. While the elaborate costumes, shocking make-up and slow-motion dance look and sound exotic, the strangled singing, atonal music and difficulty in following the story often make it impossible for foreigners to sit through an entire performance.

Macau

As Macau strives to broaden its entertainment options, Broadway-style shows like *CATS* and *The Sound of Music* have been staged at the Macau Cultural Centre. *Zaia*, a permanent Cirque du Soleil show, has its own theatre at The Venetian. See www.cirquedesoleil.com/zaia. City of Dreams has invested

US$250 million in a theatre for *The House of Dancing Water* spectacular.

NIGHTLIFE

Hong Kong has an extremely lively nightlife scene. There are plenty of Western-style bars and clubs that attract a mix of locals and expats. Note that smoking is now banned inside most bars and restaurants.

There are three districts in which most bars and clubs likely to appeal to visitors are located: Central, Wan Chai (including Causeway Bay) and Tsim Sha Tsui. Central draws the after-work crowd to the chic bars and restaurants of Lan Kwai Fong and SoHo. Wan Chai has a grungier drinking scene interspersed with girlie bars and tacky basement discos that keep going throughout the night. On Kowloon side, Tsim Sha Tsui's nightlife tends to be split between bars that are exclusively for locals and those aimed mainly at tourists, with Knutsford Terrace attracting a mix of the two.

Bars in Central and the swankier Causeway Bay and Tsim Sha Tsui joints are the most expensive, with drinks costing HK$60 upwards. The grittier Wan

MACAU'S CASINOS

Casino Lisboa
Avenida de Lisboa
Tel: (853) 8297 7111
www.hotelisboa.com
Casino Oceanus no Pelota Basca
Avenida do Dr. Rodrigo
Rodrigues No.1470 1526
Tel: (853) 8801 3388
www.oceanus-macau.com
Casino Kam Pek
1–2/FL Rua Da Foshan,
No.51, A Andar, Edf, Centro
Comercial, San Kin Yip
Tel: (853) 2878 6945
Casino Jimei
956–1110, Avenida Da
Amizade
Tel: (853) 2822 8811
www.jimeihotels.com
Casino New Century
Avendia Padre Tomas Pereira
No. 889, Taipa
Tel: (853) 2883 6011
www.newcenturyhotel-
macau.com
Casino Diamond
Hotel Holiday Inn, Rua De
Pequim 82–86
Tel: (853) 2878 5645
Casino Casa Real
Avenida do. Dr. Rodrigo
Rodrigues 1118
Tel: (853) 2872 7791
www.casarealhotel.com.mo
Casino Taipa
Regency Hotel, 2 Estrada
Almirante Marques
Esparteiro, Taipa

Tel: (853) 2883 1537
Casino Lan Kwai Fung
Rua De Luis Gonzaga
Gomes 230
Tel: (853) 2880 0888
www.macaulkf.com
Club VIP Legend
3–5/FL, Macau Landmark,
Avenida Da Amizade
Tel: (853) 2878 6233
www.landmarkhotel.com.mo
Casino Grandview (Macau Jockey Club)
142 Estrada Governador
Albano De Oliveira, Taipa
Tel: (853) 2883 2265
www.grandview-hotel.com
Casino Marina
Pousada Marina Infante,
Avenida Olimpica, Taipa
Tel: (853) 2883 3623
Casino Fortuna
No.63, Rua de Cantão
Tel: (853) 8982 1301
Casino Golden Dragon
Rua de Malaca
Tel: (853) 8982 6201
www.goldendragon.com.mo
Casino Emperor Palace
No.288 Avenida Comercial
De Macau
Tel: (853) 8981 6803
www.grandemperor.com
Casino Babylon
Macau Fisherman's Wharf
Avenida Dr. Sun Yat-sen
Tel: (853) 2823 2233
Casino Grand Lisboa
Avenida de Lisboa

Tel: (853) 2828 3838
www.grandlisboa.com
Casino Ponte 16
Rua do Visconde Paço de
Arcos, Ponte 16
Tel: (853) 8861 8888
www.ponte16.com.mo
Casino President
355 Avenida Da Amizade
Tel: (853) 2878 8198
www.hotelpresident.com.mo
Casino StarWorld
Avenida Da Amizade
Tel: (853) 2838 3838
www.starworldmacau.com
Casino Sands
Largo de Monte Carlo, No. 203
Tel: (853) 2888-3388.
www.sands.com.mo
Casino Venetian
The Venetian Macau-Resort-
Hotel, Estrada da Baía de N.
Senhora da Esperança, s/n,
Taipa
Tel: (853) 2882-8888.
Wynn Casino
Rua Cidade de Sintra, NAPE
Tel: 8986 9966

Chai bars are the cheapest, with HK$40 beers as a rule.

For a list of bars and club nights check *HK Magazine* and *BC Magazine*. You can also try www.hkclubbing.com for guest DJ nights and party dates.

Recommended pubs, bars and clubs are listed at the end of each relevant chapter in the Places section of the book.

Gay/Lesbian Nightlife

Hong Kong has a small but thriving gay scene, though lesbians

are stuck with a few local-style karaoke bars in Causeway Bay office blocks. The bars and clubs that are the most welcoming to foreigners are mainly located in Central.

On Fridays **Club 97**'s gay happy hour (6pm–9pm) is a cornerstone of the scene, and welcomes a mixed crowd to mingle in the 'fong'. 9 Lan Kwai Fong, Central. Tel: 2810 9333.

T:me, B/F, 65 Hollywood Rd, Hong Kong. Tel: 2332 6565 Stylish new bar attracts a mixed crowd (next door to Club 71).

Propaganda, 1 Hollywood Rd, Central. Tel: 2868 1316.
Long-running gay club, packed at weekends, with great music.

Live Music Venues

Most hotel bars will have a resident band to warble out some golden oldies, an instrumentalist or a jazz band. Many bars also have cover bands that play dance and pop. See live music listings in *HK Magazine, Time Out Hong Kong* or the *South China Morning Post* to find out who's playing.

Dusk Till Dawn, 76 Jaffe Rd, Wan Chai. Tel: 2528 4689. Rowdy bar with a resident cover band playing rock, indie and pop tracks.

Fringe Club, Live music in the Main Bar every Friday and Saturday, ranging from young energetic rock bands to slick jazz quartets. Tel: 2521 7251. www.hkfringe.com.hk

Gecko, 15–19 Hollywood Rd, Ezra's Lane (alley next to the escalator), Central. Tel: 2537 4680. Funky lounge and wine bar with live jazz during the week.

Peel Fresco Music Lounge, 49 Peel Street, Central. Tel: 2540 2046. Bohemian-style lounge bar with live jazz most nights of the week.

SPORT

Facilities

Top **hotels** in Hong Kong generally have **swimming pools**, **gyms** and **tennis courts** available free to their guests. A few allow non-guests to use their facilities for a fee – for example, the Marriott in Admiralty charges HK$2,500 for a one-month membership.

There are also scores of **gyms**, including international chains like Fitness First with a large gym at G/F, Cosco Tower, Grand Millennium Plaza, 181–183 Queen's Road, Central (tel: 3106 3000, www.fitnessfirst.com.hk), and California Fitness, whose flagship gym is at 1 Wellington Street, Central (tel: 2522 5229, www.calfitnesscenters.com).

Yoga and **pilates** are big business in Hong Kong. Classes are run at major gyms, and there are now dozens of studios close to offices and shops. *HK Magazine* is packed with their ads. By posing as a resident, you can usually pick up a free introductory class, but be prepared for a hard sell afterwards.

The government-run Leisure and Cultural Services Depart-

ment (LCSD) has **sports centres**, with tennis, badminton and squash courts and swimming pools all over the city. Visitors to Hong Kong can use their sports facilities, but you must go in person to the centre to book a court (bring your passport). You should be able to walk in and find an available court during the daytime on weekdays, but evening and weekend slots are usually booked days in advance. For a list of centres see www.lcsd.gov.hk/leisurelink/en/ ls_booking_1.php.

The **Hong Kong Squash Centre** is at 23 Cotton Tree Drive, Admiralty, tel: 2521 5072. For **tennis** try King's Park Tennis Court, Jordan, tel: 2385 8985, Victoria Park Tennis Court, Causeway Bay, tel: 2570 6186 and Causeway Bay Sports Ground, tel: 2890 5127. Hourly rates are around HK$50.

There are good LCSD **swimming pools** in Victoria Park, Causeway Bay (tel: 2570 4682), and Kowloon Park, Tsim Sha Tsui (tel: 2724 3577). Entry fee is HK$19 per person. Most pools – which are unheated – are closed between November and March.

There are **ice-skating rinks** at numerous shopping malls. Price, including skate hire, is between HK$45 and HK$60.

The most convenient **bowling alleys** for tourists are the Olympian Super Fun Bowl, tel: 2273 4772 (Olympic MTR station), and the South China Athletic Association Bowling Centre, 88 Caroline Hill Rd, Causeway Bay, tel: 2890 8528.

The only public **golf course** in Hong Kong is the Jockey Club Kau Sai Chau course on an island off Sai Kung in the southeastern New Territories (tel: 2791 3388; www.kscgolf.com/eng/course.html). There are also a handful of private members' clubs which are open to non-members on weekdays. Try Hong Kong Golf Club, which has three 18-hole courses in Fanling in the northern New Territories (tel:

2670 1211; www.hkgolfclub.org/golf/index.jsp) and three nine-hole courses at Deep Water Bay at 19 Island Rd (tel: 2812 7070), on the south side of Hong Kong Island.

There are **bicycle trails** around Tai Mei Tuk reservoir in the New Territories, from Sha Tin to Tai Po market, around Shek O village and on Cheung Chau. Bikes can be hired for around HK$40 per day at all these places. You will have to leave your passport as deposit.

Spectator Sports

During the **horse-racing** season (September to June), locals swarm to the city's two big racing stadia, in Happy Valley on Wednesday nights and Sha Tin at weekends. Come in March for the Hong Kong Derby, April for the Queen Elizabeth II Cup and December for the Hong Kong International Races. *See pages 136–137 for more details.*

The city's single biggest sporting event is arguably the **Hong Kong Rugby Sevens** – three days of heavy drinking, silly hats and manic singing in the stands while teams from all over the world fight it out on the pitch *(see page 132).* The tournament is held at the Hong Kong Stadium in Causeway Bay (www.hksevens.com.hk). Tickets sell out quickly.

More demure is the **Hong Kong Cricket Sixes** (www.cricketsixes.hk), held in November at the Kowloon Cricket Club.

The **Macau Grand Prix** (http://gp.macau.grandprix.gov.mo) is held every November; hotels get booked out, so plan ahead. Races – car, motorbike and formula cars – are exhilarating since they take place along a 6.2-km (3¾-mile) street circuit, so for one weekend normality is suspended, with tens of thousands of racing fans crowding into this tiny enclave. Buy tickets online at www.macauticket.com.

Hiking and Rock Climbing

An oft-quoted "little-known fact" is that around three-quarters of Hong Kong is actually countryside, and if you have the time there are plenty of great hikes on well-marked trails, including circling or descending The Peak, mountain climbs on Lantau Island and spectacular coastal walks in the wilds of Sai Kung. The Country and Marine Parks Authority lists walks on its website(http://parks.afcd.gov.hk/newparks/ eng/hiking/index.htm), otherwise there's a good series of hiking guides by Pete Spurrier, for all levels of fitness. For your own safety bring maps, water and a mobile phone. Walk Hong Kong (www.walkhongkong.com) organises hiking tours all over Hong Kong, while Kayak and Hike (www.kayak-and-hike.com) runs hiking, biking and kayaking trips to the most remote parts of the New Territories.

Every November, teams race to complete the 100-km (62-mile) **MacLehose Trail**, which runs east–west across the New Territories in the Oxfam Trailwalker. The record to date is held by a Gurkha team in 2004 – they finished in 11 hours 57 minutes.

If you are into rock climbing there are at least 19 sites dotted around country parks, from headland crags at Shek O to Lion Rock in Kowloon. See www.hongkongclimbing.com for a good overview as well as a list of indoor climbing walls. The most convenient climbing wall for tourists is at the YMCA in Tsim Sha Tsui, which has two U-shaped walls.

Diving and Watersports

While certainly no match for what's on offer in nearby Thailand and the Philippines, Hong Kong does have a fair few diving schools which brave the territory's murky water. Pollution and overfishing have taken their toll, but octopus and barracuda are sometimes spotted (www.hk-fish.net), and there are several wreck and reef dives. There is even a small amount of coral in Mirs Bay in the northeastern New Territories. Email the Hong Kong Underwater Club at sec@hkuc.org.hk to book a dive. They go out every fortnight. A day's diving with all equipment hire costs around HK$550.

Windsurfing is popular. You can hire boards at Cheung Chau's Kwun Yam Wan Beach. Windsurfing and wakeboarding are also available at beaches at Stanley and Sai Kung, amongst others.

OTHER ACTIVITIES

Cultural Tours

The HKTB runs free "meet the people" and "Nature Kaleidoscope" tours, which provide more than the usual shopping-and-skyscrapers look at the city. You can join an early-morning tai chi class at 8am at the Avenue of Stars in Tsim Sha Tsui on Monday, Wednesday, Thursday and Friday. Other "classes" include an architecture tour, how to shop for pearls and jade, how to taste Chinese tea, an antiques lesson and guided tours of Mai Po Wetland and a Ngong Ping Fun Walk. All classes are free. See the HKTB for times and booking.

Boat trips & tours

The distinctive diamond-shaped junk with bright red sails, emblematic of Hong Kong, was replaced long ago by container ships and sleek turbojets. The last remaining authentic junk, the *Duk Ling*, is owned by the HKTB, visitors can book a one-hour cruise on the boat for HK$50. There are four departures every Thursday afternoon leaving from Tsim Sha Tsui and Central. You must register first with the HKTB visitor centre in person.

Aqua Luna (tel: 2116 8821 , www.aqua.com.hk) is a more sophisticated craft than the HKTB junk. This newly-built red-sailed junk has a bar and canapés, and the price includes one drink. Two 45-minute cruises every afternoon (HK$150) and six sailings in the evening (HK$180). Cruises depart from Tsim Sha Tsui at half-past, and Central Pier 9 a quarter to the hour. Booking ahead online or by phone is essential.

Star Ferry (tel: 2118 6201,

www.starferry.com.hk) runs various circular harbour tours throughout the day and tickets are available at the Star Ferry piers in Central, Tsim Sha Tsui, Hung Hom and Wan Chai. The Symphony of Light Harbour Tour (HK$150 adult, HK$135 children), takes you on two harbour circuits for two hours and leaves Central at 7pm. Its other evening cruises last one hour and cost HK$110 and HK$99.

Junks and boats can be hired from **Saffron Cruises** (tel: 2857 1311 (http://www.saffron-cruises.com) Saffron also has a Category Four rescue boat for high-powered 30-minute trips around Hong Kong at breathtaking speeds on board the powerboat *Seafari*.

For a unique Hong Kong experience, take to the water to see the rare **pink dolphins** that live in the Pearl River Delta. Hong Kong Dolphinwatch Ltd (tel: 2984 1414, www.hkdolphinwatch.com) runs tours every Wednesday, Friday and Sunday morning. A coach collects visitors from Central and Tsim Sha Tsui for a two- to three-hour junk trip. Adults HK$360, children (3 to 11 years) HK$180.

Children's Activities

There is a great deal on offer for children in Hong Kong. Travelling on its public transport is adventure enough for some, with its trains, trams, taxis, minibuses, double-decker buses, ferries and junks.

Hong Kong now has two large theme parks. The new kid on the block is **Disneyland** (Lantau, tel: 1 830 830, www.hongkongdisney land.com), which is at or near the top of most children's must-see list. Just 30 minutes by MTR from Central, the 126-hectare (310-acre) site includes four themed areas – Main Street USA, Fantasyland, Adventureland and Tomorrowland. Entrance fees are HK$350 for adults, HK$250 for children aged 3–11, and HK$170 (HK$200) for over-65s.

Ocean Park (Aberdeen, tel: 2552 0291) is a home-grown

theme park located on the south side of Hong Kong Island. Its animal collections include giant pandas, sea lions, birds, butterflies and dolphins. The coral-reef-themed aquarium includes a dramatic shark tunnel. There are also various stomach-churning rides. Admission charges are: adults HK$250, children (3–11) HK$103.

A must-see for most visitors, including kids, is the tram ride up **The Peak** and the view from the Peak Tower. There are family-friendly restaurants, and an expanded Madame Tussaud's (Shop P101, Level P1, www.madame-tussauds.com.hk, open daily). Charges on weekdays are: adults HK$160, children (3–11) and seniors (65 plus) HK$90.

A good few Hong Kong museums are particularly child-friendly. In Kowloon, visit the highly interactive **Science Museum** (2 Science Museum Road, Tsim Sha Tsui East, tel: 2732 3232, closed Thurs). On the ground floor, the Children's Zone under-fives make giant bubbles and experiment. Among 17 other galleries, older children are drawn to transport simulators and a computer lab.

The **Museum of History** (100 Chatham Road, Tsim Sha Tsui, tel: 2724 9042, closed Tue) is a modern museum that recreates the "Hong Kong Story". Younger kids love the volcano simulation and life-size examples of the mammals that once roamed Kowloon. The walk-through Hong Kong street scenes are excellent.

The **Space Museum** (10 Salisbury Road, Tsim Sha Tsui, tel: 2721 0226, closed Tue) has exhibitions, but best of all is its dome-shaped cinema screen, which shows Omnimax films and the Sky Show (adults HK$32, children HK$16).

Perhaps an unlikely hit with kids, the Hong Kong Jockey Club's **Racing Museum** (2/F, Happy Valley Stand, Happy Valley Racecourse, tel: 2966 8065, closed Mon) focuses on horses instead of gambling – dress up as a jockey,

and try out the horse simulators.

Adventurous types love clambering around the battlements and tunnels at the extremely well-designed **Museum of Coastal Defence** (175 Tung Hei Road, Shau Kei Wan, tel: 2569 1500, closed Thurs). Explore 600 years of coastal history and walk around the hillside at this historic fort that once protected the eastern approach to the harbour.

If it's raining or very hot, you will need a few indoor activities on your itinerary. **Ice-skating** is a cool option, and several large malls have decent-sized rinks.

For space in the city, head to the free public parks and playgrounds. In Causeway Bay there's **Victoria Park** (tel: 2890 5824), with mini-playgrounds, boat pond, small roller-skating rink and outdoor swimming pool. Cross the road bridge to the **Central Library** (66 Causeway Road, Causeway Bay, tel: 3150 1234, closed Wed a.m.) for air-conditioning, children's books, a playroom, readings and information about what's on for children.

Connecting Admiralty to Central, **Hong Kong Park** (tel: 2521 5041) is good for a few hours of fun. Enjoy its large children's playground, water features, aviary and open-air restaurant.

Kowloon Park (tel: 2724 3344) is a haven in the heart of Tsim Sha Tsui. Its playground, maze, swimming pools and sculpture park are useful diversions.

The **outlying islands** are an easy day out with children. Take a ferry to Cheung Chau or Lamma and set your own pace. The tanks of live fish outside the islands' renowned restaurants will fascinate. Enjoy a stroll to the beach, hike in the hills or hire bikes and explore the traffic-free islands.

For a day on the **beach** on Hong Kong Island visit Deep Water Bay, Repulse Bay and Chung Hom Kok. The beaches are kept clean and are patrolled by lifeguards *(see page 146)*.

All sights are detailed in full in the Places section of the book.

AN ALPHABETICAL SUMMARY OF PRACTICAL INFORMATION

Admission Charges

Government-owned museum and gallery admissions are good value in Hong Kong. Average charges are around HK$10 for adults and HK$5 for seniors and students. Children under three are free, and many museums are free to all on Wednesdays. To make your money go further, the HK$30 Museum Pass gives one week's unlimited access to seven of the city's most popular museums.

Privately owned venues are more expensive. Adults pay HK$160 at Madame Tussaud's, while children aged 3 to 11 years cost HK$90. A day of fun at Ocean Park is HK$125 for children and HK$250 for adults. At cinemas, tickets average HK$70 for adults with a small reduction

for children. Admission to all parks and beaches is free.

Budgeting for your Trip

Having stayed steady for most of the past decade, prices are slowly starting to rise. The Hong Kong dollar is pegged to the US dollar, so how far your money goes in Hong Kong and China will always be relative to the strength and weakness of the greenback.

Hotel prices can vary throughout the year. The busiest times at Hong Kong hotels are during the main public holidays in China and the large trade fairs in April and October. Outside these times prices can drop considerably. Researching your options will pay off, as many hotels have regular promotions on their websites, and

travel agents and online hotel-booking sites negotiate special rates (see hotels, page 261).

Once in Hong Kong, transportation is a bargain. For HK$15 (US$2) you can travel up to 10 stops on the MTR or cross Hong Kong Island by public bus. It costs HK$2 to ride the length of the island by tram and on Hong Kong's other iconic transportation, the Star Ferry, you will spend next to nothing crossing the harbour.

Discovering the range of food in Hong Kong is part of the experience, and prices can vary dramatically. You can expect to pay US$15 or less per person at a very reasonable Chinese restaurant. A meal for two in a mid-range restaurant can cost upwards of US$100 with wine. At the best restaurants diners expect to pay

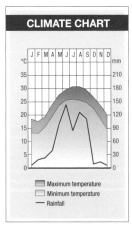

CLIMATE CHART

Maximum temperature
Minimum temperature
— Rainfall

US$250 plus for two.

To stretch the budget further, look out for special menus and budget set menus at cafés and restaurants. "Business lunch" set menus are great value.

There are bargains to be had at the best hotels. The hotel buffet is an institution and a great way to sample a huge variety of cuisine, or satisfy different tastes within a group for a reasonable price. It's an event in itself and a treat for gastronomes.

Standard drinks in Hong Kong cost around US$8 and can be double in luxury hotel bars and the trendiest venues. Look out for Happy Hours.

Business Hours

Office hours in Hong Kong are 9am to 5.30pm or 6pm. Small shops, grocers and markets are open before 8am, but major stores and shopping centres generally open around 10am. Banks open between 8.30am and 4.30pm, but times may vary between branches and banks.

While shops in Central close by 7 or 8pm, elsewhere it's late-night shopping every night. In particular, many shops in Causeway Bay, Tsim Sha Tsui and Mong Kok stay open until 10 or 11pm seven days a week, including public holidays.

Bars and restaurants are free to choose their own opening times. Things start to quieten down in the main entertainment districts after 1am. If you want to drink and party all night you will find venues.

In Macau, restaurants and bars are open late, but after midnight most of the action is centred around the 24-hour casinos. In Shenzhen and Guangzhou shops and shopping centres are open in the evening, and although locals like to dine early, there are many places to eat and drink late at night.

C limate

Hong Kong has a humid subtropical climate. There are, however, four distinct seasons. The ideal time for travelling to Hong Kong is from the end of September to early December, when the weather is warm, the air is relatively dry and it seldom rains. The average daytime temperature is around 24°C (75°F), with humid-ity around 70 percent.

Despite the latitude, winter (late December to early March) temperatures can be slightly chilly, especially in the rural areas, so it is advisable to bring light woollens and sometimes a coat. The average daytime temperature is 17°C (63°F), with humidity around 75 percent.

Temperatures and humidity rise abruptly in spring, when daytime temperatures shoot up from 20°C (68°F) in March to 28°C (82°F) in May. In summer, which lasts until early September, temperatures hover around 30°C (86°F) and humidity is consistently above 70 percent. Even at night it is rare for the temperature to dip below 26°C (79°F), and even when it doesn't rain you will quickly be dripping with sweat. Wear light clothes, but bring something with long sleeves for the summer – because many restaurants and shops have very effective air-conditioning.

Macau's climate is the same as Hong Kong's. Temperatures in

TYPHOONS

From June to early September, it is not uncommon for Hong Kong to experience tropical storms or typhoons (the name derives from *dai fung* – big wind). If you are in Hong Kong when a typhoon hits, you will find that virtually everything comes to a complete standstill.

The Hong Kong Observatory has standard typhoon warnings that vary according to how close a typhoon is to Hong Kong. Usually, this begins with a typhoon number one (T1) signal, which may shortly escalate to a number three. When the number eight signal is raised, it means Hong Kong may suffer a direct hit. Schools, offices and shops close immediately and everyone goes home. A rare typhoon number ten is almost certain to mean serious damage, as the storm sweeps through the territory causing floods and sometimes deaths. Watching typhoon news bulletins can be dramatic and exciting, but when everything closes you will be stuck for anything to do. Hotels, however, do continue to operate. In fact, locals often go to hotel restaurants as they are the only places likely to be open during a typhoon. Stay inside during a typhoon, as fatalities have been known to occur in both urban and rural areas, mainly due to objects and structures that fall in the strong winds.

The frequency of direct hits is erratic: of the thirteen since 1946, only one (typhoon York in 1999) has occurred in the past twenty years. In April 2008, typhoon Neoguri passed close to Hong Kong, the earliest storm for over 50 years.

Guangzhou are slightly higher in summer, slightly lower in winter, and there is rather more rain through the year.

Crime & Safety

One of the great joys of Hong Kong is the low level of crime and the resultant freedom from fear of crime. In the main commercial and entertainment areas you are safe to walk alone at any hour of the day, and most of the night. Tourists are more obvious targets for pickpockets in the busiest areas, but normal precautions should suffice.

Both Guangzhou and Macau are considered safe destinations for tourists. Avoid touts, and do not be tempted to pursue goods and services offered to you on the street.

More caution is required in Shenzhen. Hong Kong residents have reported muggings. Dress down for a visit to Shenzhen and leave your jewellery behind. Stick to busy public areas. When shopping, do not let the lure of a bargain make you forget your common sense.

Customs Regulations

Hong Kong is a free port, so you can bring as many gifts as you like in and out of the territory. Wine and beer are now duty-free, too. Firearms must be declared and handed into custody until departure. Duty-free allowances for visitors are 20 cigarettes (reduced from 60 in 2010), a single cigar or 25g tobacco, and 1 litre of alcohol over 30% proof.

Departure tax

Hong Kong imposes a HK$120 Air Passenger Departure Tax on all passengers aged 12 years and above departing Hong Kong International Airport or by helicopter at the Hong Kong Macau Ferry Terminal. This is normally included in the price of the airline ticket.

D isabled Travellers

The Hong Kong Council of Social Services has compiled a useful accessibility guide for buildings and tourist attractions, www.hkcss.org.hk/rh/accessguide.

Taxis are often the best way to get about in Hong Kong, and reasonably priced. The train networks have a very inconsistent level of access. Station announcements are in Cantonese, Mandarin (Putonghua) and English.

Easy-Access Travel is a subsidiary of the Hong Kong Society for Rehabilitation, and has a fleet of specially adapted buses so it can cater for visitors with limited mobility. Day trips, full itineraries and advice are available. Email: enquiry@easyaccesstravelhk.com, tel: 2772 7301, www.easyaccesstravelhk.com.

E mbassies & Consulates

Australia, Harbour Centre, 21–4/F, 25 Harbour Rd, Wan Chai. Tel: 2827 8881.
Canada, One Exchange Square, 11/F, 8 Connaught Place, Central. Tel: 2810 4321.
France, Admiralty Centre, Tower II, 26/F, 18 Harcourt Rd, Admiralty. Tel: 3196 6100.
Germany, 21/F, United Centre, 95 Queensway, Admiralty. Tel: 2105 8712.
Japan, 46/F, One Exchange Square, 8 Connaught Place, Central. Tel: 2522 1184.
New Zealand, Rm 6505, Central Plaza, 18 Harbour Rd, Wan Chai.

ELECTRICITY

The voltage in Hong Kong is 200/220 volts, 50 cycles. For a place of such international standing, it is surprising that Hong Kong still does not seem to have standardised plug fittings. However, hotels will certainly have adaptors to make any appliance work.

Tel: 2877 4488.
Singapore, Unit 901, 9/F, Tower 1, Admiralty Centre, 18 Harcourt Rd, Admiralty. Tel: 2527 2212.
South Africa, 27/F, Great Eagle Centre, 23 Harbour Rd, Wan Chai. Tel: 2577 3279.
United Kingdom, 1 Supreme Court Rd, Admiralty. Tel: 2901 3000.
United States, 26 Garden Rd, Central. Tel: 2523 9011.

Entry Requirements

Visas and passports

Nationals of most developed countries do not require a visa for entry to Hong Kong or Macau, but you will need one if you plan to visit mainland China (see panel, opposite).

For those taking up employment in Hong Kong, it is necessary to obtain a work permit from the Immigration Department, usually in advance of entering the territory. Your company should be able to assist with the necessary paperwork. Hong Kong residents should carry a Hong Kong identity card, which is issued by the Immigration Department.

All other visitors are supposed to carry photographic identity such as a passport with them, but it is unlikely that you will be stopped by police officers and asked to produce identification.

G ay & Lesbian Travellers

Hong Kong's gay scene may not yet have come of age, but it had

CHINESE VISAS

Visas for China are issued at the Office of the Commissioner of the Ministry of Foreign Affairs, 5/F Lower Block, China Resources Bldg, 26 Harbour Rd, Wan Chai; tel: 3413 2300 www.fmcoprc.gov.hk/eng/. Visa applications are made on the seventh floor. Two photos are required. Single-entry visas cost from HK$250 to HK$400 (depending on nationality), and are processed in about three days. China visas can also be obtained through all the Hong Kong Offices of the China Travel Service (CTS). The two main offices are at 78 Connaught Road, Central; tel: 2853 3888, and at 1/F, Alpha House, 27 Nathan Road, Tsim Sha Tsui, tel: 2315 7106, 24-hor hotline 3413 2300. www.ctshk.com, Finally, visas can be obtained through most Hong Kong travel agents.

If you plan on visiting Hong Kong as a side trip from the mainland, make sure that you have a double- or multiple-entry China visa.

its long-overdue coming-out party with its first Pink Parade in October 2004, and the city's Gay and Lesbian Film Festival has become part of the alternative arts calendar. For information on events and happenings, look for *HK Magazine*.

To sample the local scene, visit Hong Kong's self-proclaimed "first Internet gay bar". New Wally Matt Lounge, G/F, Humphrey's Avenue, Tsim Sha Tsui, is open from 5pm to 4am daily, and is a friendly pub with free computers. On Hong Kong side, try Club 97 in Lan Kwai Fong on a Friday night.

H ealth & Medical Care

No vaccinations are required for Hong Kong, but it is advisable to consider inoculations against Hepatitis A. Tap water is safe in

Hong Kong, but you may find bottled water more palatable. The most important thing is to keep well hydrated in the heat and humidity. Eat in licensed cafés and restaurants, and avoid eating food from street stalls.

Medical services
Hong Kong
Adventist Hospital, 40 Stubbs Rd, Happy Valley. Tel: 2574 6211.
Central Medical Practice, 1501 Prince's Bldg, Central. Tel: 2521 2567.
Hong Kong Central Hospital, 1B Lower Albert Rd, Central. Tel: 2522 3141. (24-hr GP outpatient).
Prince of Wales Hospital, 30–32 Ngan Shing St, Sha Tin, New Territories. Tel: 2632 2211.
Queen Elizabeth Hospital, 30 Gascoigne Rd, Kowloon. Tel: 2958 8888.
Queen Mary Hospital, Pokfulam Rd, Hong Kong. Tel: 2816 6366.

Macau
Kiang Wu Hospital, Estr. Coelho do Amaral. Tel: 2837 1333.
S. Januário Hospital, Estr. do Visconde de S. Januário. Tel: 2831 3731.

Shenzhen
Shenzhen People's Hospital, Dongmen Bei Lu. Tel: 2553 3018.
Guangzhou
Guangzhou Can Am International Medical Centre, 5/F, Garden Hotel, 368 Huanshi Dong Lu. Tel: 8386 6988.
Guangzhou No. 1 People's Hospital, 602 Renmin Bei Lu. Tel: 8108 2090.

I nternet

Most hotels offer broadband connections in their rooms, and many offer wireless internet in public areas. Internet cafés are not common in Hong Kong, but free Internet access is available at many coffee shops around the SAR. Branches of chains Pacific Coffee, Starbucks and Mix offer two or three computers for free

use by their customers – although you may have to wait at busy times. Free Government Wi-fi hotspots are springing up around the city.

L eft Luggage

Facilities are available at Hong Kong Airport, and in Kowloon at Hung Hom Station and the Hong Kong China City Building.

Lost Property

To report lost or stolen property, contact the Hong Kong Police. Call 2860 2000 to find out the location of the nearest police station. If you are think you left your property in a taxi, it may be worth contacting the taxi lost property line which will – in theory at least, and for a charge – inform all taxi drivers. Tel: 1872 920.

To report a lost credit card, call American Express on 2811 6122, MasterCard on 800-966-677 and Visa on 800-900-782.

M aps

There are numerous maps available in Hong Kong. The Hong Kong Tourist Board provides welcome packs which include maps at airport, seaport and border crossings from mainland China. The laminated Insight Fleximaps to Hong Kong, Macau, Shenzhen and Guangzhou are durable, detailed and easy to use, and each has a full street index. If you are travelling into China, maps with place names in both English and Chinese are useful. If you can point at a place name written in Chinese with a friendly smile, many a misunderstanding can be avoided.

EMERGENCY NUMBERS

For police, fire and ambulance services in Hong Kong and China, dial 999. In Macau call 999 for emergencies, or 919 for police.

Media

Newspapers & magazines

Hong Kong has a large number of newspapers and magazines, most of which are published in Chinese. Hong Kong continues to enjoy a free press despite being part of China, and the territory is noted as a media centre for the region.

By far the most influential newspaper in Hong Kong is the daily English-language *South China Morning Post*. A second English daily is *The Standard*, handed out free on the streets. Two of the most popular Chinese-language dailies are the rather sensationalist *Oriental Daily News* and the *Apple Daily News*.

Listings magazines worth looking out for are the weekly English-language *HK Magazine*, which is published every Friday and distributed free at most popular bars, restaurants and bookshops in the territory, and the new *Time Out Hong Kong* magazine, published every fortnight. Tourists who want an opinionated insider's view will find the restaurant, club and entertainment reviews worth a read. *Time Out* also includes reviews of events in Macau. *BC* is another free listings magazine, published every fortnight.

Radio & television

Over a dozen radio stations are broadcast in Hong Kong, though there is now only one dedicated English-language channel, RTHK. Some other stations offer an element of programming in English. The BBC World Service is available 24 hours a day. For local news, Hong Kong's two TV stations, TVB and ATV, each broadcast one English-language channel and one Chinese-language channel. If you are staying in a hotel you should have access to a selection of regional and international broadcasters in English via cable and satellite.

PUBLIC HOLIDAYS

The fact that many Hong Kong residents work a five-and-a-half-day week and have short periods of annual leave is compensated by a relatively large number of public holidays every year – 17 in total. These are as follows:

1 January: New Year's Day
January/February: Lunar New Year (three-day holiday)
March/April: Good Friday and Easter Monday; Ching Ming Festival (5 April)
May/June: Dragon Boat Festival; Buddha's Birthday (lunar); Labour Day (1 May)
1 July: SAR Establishment Day
September/October: The day following the Mid-Autumn Festival
1 October: National Day
October: Chung Yeung Festival
25 December: Christmas (two days).

Money

The Hong Kong dollar is the standard unit of currency and comes in denominations of HK$1,000, $500, $100, $50, $20 and $10 notes plus HK$10, $5, $2 and $1 coins. The dollar is divided into 100 cents, and there are coins of 50¢, 20¢ and 10¢ denominations. The dollar rate fluctuates against most major international currencies but it is pegged to the US dollar at approximately 7.8 Hong Kong dollars to the US dollar.

There are three note-issuing banks in Hong Kong: Hongkong and Shanghai Bank, Standard Chartered Bank and the Bank of China. Most banks will exchange foreign currency and generally display exchange rates on digital boards. They usually offer better rates than the money-changers in the major tourist areas, there's usually a HK$50 charge for a single transaction. Cash machines are plentiful in the urban areas,

Macau

As for Hong Kong, but with some additional days:
National Day (1 October) is a two-day holiday in Macau. There are public holidays for **All Souls' Day** in **November**, the **Feast of the Immaculate Conception** on **8 December** and the **Winter Solstice** on **22 December**. The Macau Special Administrative Region Establishment Day (**20 December**) replaces Hong Kong's 1 July holiday.

China

Official state holidays are:
1 January: New Year's Day
Lunar New Year: officially three days (Jan/Feb). Most shops and offices close for a full week
1 May: Labour Day, plus two following days
1 October: National Day, plus two following days.

and allow the withdrawal of local currency with most major credit cards.

Macau's official currency, the pataca (MOP$), is divided into 100 avos. There are banknotes in denominations of 1,000, 500, 100, 50, 20 and 10 patacas and 10, 5, 2, and 1 pataca coins. The pataca is linked to the Hong Kong dollar, which is accepted as currency in Macau.

Hong Kong dollars are also widely accepted in Guangzhou and Shenzhen, but if you are staying more than a day in mainland China it is worth changing your money to Chinese currency, renminbi (RMB). The basic unit is the yuan, often called kuai. One yuan is worth 10 jiao. Banknotes come in 100, 50, 10, 5 and 1 yuan denominations: plus 5, 2 and 1 jiao.

Tipping

Tipping is customary in Hong Kong in bars, restaurants and

hotels. A 10-percent service charge is added to the bill in many restaurants, but it is still customary to add a further 5 percent to go direct to the staff. Taxi drivers do not expect to be tipped, but rounding up the fare to the nearest dollar or two is appreciated.

In places frequented by tourists in Macau, Shenzhen and Guangzhou tipping is increasingly common practice; follow the same guidelines as Hong Kong.

P ostal Services

Airmail stamps are available from convenience stores and vending machines outside post offices. The General Post Office in Central, 2 Connaught Road, also sells a selection of cards and gifts.

Most post offices are open 9.30am to 5pm Monday to Friday and 9.30am to 1pm on Saturday. On Kowloon side, the main post office is located at 10 Middle Road, Tsim Sha Tsui, and is also open on Sundays, 9am to 2pm.

If you choose to mail presents and purchases rather than carry them home, Hong Kong Post is cheap, efficient and can also courier documents and parcels. In Hong Kong, Macau, Shenzhen and Guangzhou hotels will assist guests with posting mail and packages.

In Macau, the main post office is located in picturesque Senado Square. If you are tempted by antique and reproduction furniture, shops can assist in arranging shipping. Shenzhen shoppers rely on the post office on the ground floor at the Lo Wu shopping centre to ease their burden after bargain-hunting. In China it is probably much simpler to use the postal services at business and tourist hotels.

Public Toilets

Toilet facilities at tourist attractions in Hong Kong are generally clean, well maintained and always free of charge. Public toilets in other locations are of a variable standard, and soap and paper may be absent. Shopping centres and restaurants usually have clean facilities. To be on the safe side, always carry a small pack of tissues.

There are few public toilets to be found in Macau, and clean public toilets are a rarity in Shenzhen. However, in recent years Guangzhou has opened some acceptable new public toilets, complete with star rating. Patrons must pay a small fee of one or two yuan at these new public conveniences.

S tudent Travellers

Students over the age of 11 years do not benefit from many travel discounts in Hong Kong, Macau and the mainland. Some cultural events offer slightly reduced ticket prices for students with identification.

T elecommunications

Hong Kong is well known for having one of the most advanced telecommunications systems in the world. Virtually the entire network consists of fibre-optic cabling with digital switching, which means a whole host of advanced telecommunications services are available to local users.

Local telephone calls are free of charge, so if they still have a landline, it is acceptable to use telephones in shops, bars and restaurants. Using a public telephone booth usually costs HK$1 for five minutes, and calls can be paid by phone card or coins. Stored-value phone cards are available from retail stores of telephone companies and convenience stores. All hotels offer international direct-dial services at an inflated price and charge for local calls from guest rooms.

Mobile Phones

Hong Kong has one of the highest rates of mobile-phone ownership – at 140 percent there are more phone subscribers than residents. Mobile phones can be rented at Hong Kong International Airport. To avoid roaming changes, you can buy pre-paid SIM cards with a Hong Kong number and a fixed number of minutes from convenience stores or the telephone companies' shops. These cards are compatible with tri-band and dual-band phones. Mobiles can be used on the MTR subway system.

International dialling codes:
● **Hong Kong: 852**
● **Macau: 853**
● **Shenzhen: 86-755**
● **Guangzhou: 86-20**

In Hong Kong:
● **Directory Assistance:** 1081 (in English)
● **Collect Calls:** 10010

TRANSPORT

ACCOMMODATION

SHOPPING

ACTIVITIES

A – Z

LANGUAGE

• **International directory enquiries /Overseas numbers:** 10013
International access codes:
AT&T: 800 96 1111
MCI: 800 96 1121
Sprint: 800 96 1877.

Time Zone

Hong Kong, Macau, Shenzhen and Guangzhou all operate on the same time zone (Beijing time). This is GMT +8 hours (EST +13 hours). There is no daylight savings time, so from early April to late October, when Europe and America put their clocks forward by one hour, Hong Kong is seven hours ahead of London and twelve hours ahead of New York.

Tourist Information

The Hong Kong Tourism Board (HKTB) is the official government-sponsored body representing the tourism industry of Hong Kong, and offers many useful services and helpful publications. HKTB also provides information packs for tourists arriving at the airport and the land crossing at Lo Wu. Out-of-hours computer terminals provide 24-hour access to the www.DiscoverHongKong.com website.

At the HKTB's Visitor Information and Services Centres you can pick up useful publications including the weekly *Hong Kong Diary* and the monthly *Official Hong Kong Map. A Guide to Quality Shops and Restaurants* is a handy (but dense) book that lists all establishments that have been accredited by the HKTB's QTS scheme, and includes special offers and vouchers that are exclusive to visitors. The centres also provide a tour-reservation service

for selected tours, and stock an interesting selection of souvenirs.

HKTB visitor centres

• **International Airport**: (only accessible to arriving visitors), 7am–11pm daily
• **Lo Wu Terminal Building**: Arrival Hall, 2/F, 8am–6pm daily
• **Hong Kong Island**: Causeway Bay MTR station (Near Exit F), 8am–8pm daily. There is also an office at the Peak Piazza (between The Peak Tower and The Peak Galleria), 9am–9pm daily
• **Kowloon**: Star Ferry pier, Tsim Sha Tsui, 8am–8pm daily
Visitor Hotline (multilingual): 2508 1234 8am–6pm daily
Tourist information is available at www.DiscoverHongKong.com.

CTS offices

China Travel Service (CTS) is China's state travel agency and can arrange tours, tickets and visas for travel to the mainland, although CTS offices do not provide a tourist information service.
Hong Kong: G/F, CTS House, 78–83 Connaught Road, Central. Tel: 2853 3533.
Kowloon: 1/F, Alpha House, 27 Nathan Road, Tsim Sha Tsui. Tel: 2315 7106.

Macau

The Macau Government Tourist Office runs offices at the Macau ferry terminal in Hong Kong and upon arrival in Macau. There is also a **tourist information centre** on the Largo do Senado square, open 9am–6pm daily. Visitors

can contact the tourist hotline (853) 2833 3000 or view the website www.macautourism.gov.mo.

Tourist offices overseas

Hong Kong is the most visited city in Asia, and the HKTB has offices in Sydney, London, Paris, Frankfurt, Los Angeles, New York, Toronto, Tokyo, Osaka, Seoul, Singapore and Taipei. There are also HKTB offices in Beijing, Shanghai, Chengdu and Guangzhou.
www.DiscoverHongKong.com
Australia
Level 4, Hong Kong House, 80 Druitt Street, Sydney, NSW 2000
Tel: 61 2 9283 3083
Fax: 61 2 9283 3383
Canada
Ground Floor, 9 Temperance Street, Toronto, Ontario M5H 1Y6
Tel: 1 416 366 2389
Fax: 1 416 366 1098
United Kingdom
6 Grafton Street, London W1S 4EQ
Tel: 44 20 7533 7100
Fax: 44 20 7533 7111
United States
115 East 54th St, 2nd Floor, New York, NY 10022-4512
Tel: 1 212 421 3382
Fax: 1 212 421 8428.

W eights & Measures

Imperial, metric and traditional Chinese measures are all legally accepted weights and measures in Hong Kong. Distance is most often measured in kilometres. Clothes and shoes also mix Asian, European, British and US sizings.

VITAL STATISTICS

Area: The Hong Kong Special Administrative Region covers a total area of 1,103 sq km (426 sq miles), comprising Hong Kong Island, the Kowloon peninsula, the New Territories and 262 outlying islands.
Geography: Hong Kong lies on a latitude of 22° 15 North (similar to Kolkata and Havana) and a longitude of 114° 10 East.

Population: Hong Kong's population is just over 7 million, and population density is 6,300 people per sq km (2,400 per sq mile). Of the half a million or so non-Chinese living in Hong Kong, the three biggest groups are the approximately 131,000 people from the Philippines, 96,000 Indonesians and 32,000 US passport-holders.

LANGUAGE

A BRIEF INTRODUCTION TO CANTONESE

Hong Kong's official languages are Chinese and English. The main Chinese dialect is Cantonese, spoken by more than 90 percent of the population and an inseparable part of the sound and rhythm of the city. Mandarin Chinese *(Putonghua)*, the official language of the People's Republic of China, is gaining in popularity. This reflects the importance of doing business with the mainland and inbound tourism rather than government directives.

There are eight dialects or varieties of Chinese that share some similarities and a writing form, but they are not mutually intelligible. The written form of Chinese was originally derived from pictures or symbols that represented objects or concepts, so there is no correlation between the apperance of Chinese characters and the sound that they represent.

Cantonese is spoken in Hong Kong, Macau and the southern provinces of Guangdong and Guangxi. Outside China, Cantonese is the most widely spoken form of Chinese due to the history of worldwide migration from Hong Kong and its neighbouring provinces.

Hong Kong people use a standard form of Cantonese when they write, or in a business situation,

but speak colloquial Cantonese in everyday conversation. Colloquial Chinese is rich in slang, and some spoken words do not have characters.

To confuse the Chinese learner further, Hong Kong (like Taiwan) uses a slightly different style of characters to the rest of China. During reforms initiated by Mao in the fifties to increase literacy, the PRC simplified its characters. Hence the characters used on the mainland are referred to as Simplified Chinese while Hong Kong's more complex characters are called Traditional Chinese.

Tones

If all this was not enough to master, many an enthusiastic linguist has been defeated by Cantonese tones. Tone is not used within a sentence to indicate stress as in many European languages; instead, each word has a distinct pitch that goes higher, lower or stays flat within each word. Among the Cantonese there is no real agreement as to how many tones there are – some say as many as nine – but most people use six in daily life (which makes Putonghua's four tones seem more accessible).

The Jyutping transliteration system devised by the Linguistic

Society of Hong Kong classifies the six main tones as: 1, high falling/high flat; 2, high rising; 3, middle; 4, low falling; 5, low rising; 6, low. For the new learner, just hitting three tones to boost their intelligibility is a triumph.

Each word has one syllable, and is represented by one distinct character. A word is made up of three sound elements. An initial e.g., "f", plus a final sound e.g. "an", plus a tone.

Tone is an essential part of each word. A few rare words just have a final sound and a tone, e.g. "m" in "m goi" (thank you).

Therefore, when combined with a tone, "fan" has seven distinct and contradictory meanings: to divide (high rising 1); flour (high falling 2); to teach (middle flat 3); fragrant (high flat 1); a grave (low falling 4); energetic (low rising 5); and a share (low flat 5).

The wealth of sound-alike words (homonyms) that can be easily mispronounced play a part in many Cantonese traditions and the development of slang. However, for the visitor or new learner tones mean that utter bafflement is a common reaction to your attempt simply to say the name of the road you wish to visit. Persevere and attempt to mimic the way a Cantonese speaker says each part of the phrase.

Pronunciation

j as in the "y" of **y**ap
z is similar to the the sound in bei**g**e or **j**ar or the zh in Guang**zh**ou
c as in **ch**ip
au as in h**ow**
ai as in b**uy**
ou as in n**o**
i as in h**e**

Numbers

one	jat
two	ji
three	saam
four	sei
five	ng
six	luk
seven	cat
eight	baat
nine	gau
ten	sap
eleven	sap jat
twelve	sap ji
twenty	ji sap
twenty-one	ji sap jat
one hundred	baak
zero	ling
140	jat sei ling
235	ji saam ng

Common words and phrases

Good morning	zou san (joe san)
Good afternoon	ng on
Good night	zou tau
Goodbye	bai bai
Hello (on phone)	wai!
Thank you (service)	m goi
Thank you (gift)	do ze
You're welcome	M sai m goi
No problem	mou man tai
How are you?	Nei hou maa? (neigh ho marr)
Fine, thank you	gay ho, yau sum
Have you eaten?	sik zou faan mei a?
yes	hai
no	m hai
OK	hou aa
so-so	ma ma
My name is...	ngor geeu
yesterday	kum yut
today	gum yut
tomorrow	ting yut

Nouns

hotel	zau dim
key	so si
manager	ging lei
room	haak fong
telephone	din wa
toilet	ci so
bank	ngan hong
post office	yau jing guk
passport	wu ziu
restaurant	zaan teng
bar	zau ba
bus	ba si
taxi	dik si
train	fo ze

Questions

Questions are often followed by "a"

Who?	bin go a?
Where?	bin do a?
When?	gei si a?
Why?	dim gaai a?
How many?	gei do a?
How much does that cost?	gei dor chin a?
Do you have...?	yau mo ... a?
What time is the train to Guangzhou...?	Guangzhou ge for che, gay dim hoy a?

People

mother	maa maa
father	baa baa
son	zai
daughter	neoi
baby	be be
friend	pang jau
boyfriend	naam pang jau
girlfriend	neoi pang jau
husband	lou gung
wife	lou po

Adjectives

small	sui
big	dai
good	ho
bad	mm ho
expensive	gwai
cheap	peng
thin	sau
fat	fei
slow	maan
fast	faai
pretty/beautiful	leng
hot	jit

cold	dung
very...	hou ...
very cold	hou dung
delicious	ho sick

Taxis

taxi	dik si
Please take me to	m goy chey ngor hur-ee.
straight on	jick hur-ee
left	hai jor bin
right	hai yau bin

Health and Emergencies

I have (a) ...	ngo...
headache	tau tung
stomach ache	tou tung
toothache	nga tung
cough	kau sau
fever	faat sui
flu	gam mou
I have a headache	ngo tau tung
I am sick	ngo jau beng
doctor	ji sang
nurse	wu si
ambulance	gau surng che
police	ging chaat

Food and drink

breakfast	zou caan
lunch	ng caan
dinner	maan caan
eat	sik faan
rice	faan
boiled rice	baak faan
fried rice	cau faan
noodles	min
vegetables	coi
meat	juk
beef	ngau juk
pork	zyut juk
lamb	joeng juk
chicken	gai
prawn	ha
fish	jyu
tea	ca
coffee	gaa fei
water	sur-ee
beer	be zau
white/red wine	baak/hung zau
I am a vegetarian	ngo sik zaai
My bill, please!	maai daan, m goi!
a little	seeu seeu
enough	gau la

GLOSSARY

Amah bag – large blue, red and white bag favoured by elderly women who can carry more than their body weight inside one stripy bag, also popular with anyone moving house.

Astronaut – someone who travels between different family members, work etc in different countries.

Cha Chaan Teng – aka Hong Kong Café. Serves up comfort food that includes the local take on foreign cuisines. Milk is always of the condensed or evaporated variety.

Chinese Tea - green or black tea without milk.

Chop – self-inked stamp used for signing documents.

Dai Pai Dong – literally means "big licence place", a reference to the size of the licence. Outdoor seating expands simply by

adding more plastic stools and fold-up tables. Serves inexpensive Cantonese fare from enormous woks in the ultimate no-frills environment.

F.I.L.T.H. – Failed In London, Try Hong Kong.

Godown – a warehouse.

Gweilo – white devil, foreigner.

Hawker – someone selling goods from a stall, sometimes licensed sometimes not.

Helper – always means a domestic helper or maid. The term "amah" is rarely used except in reference to hold-alls.

Lai See – luck money, given at weddings and Lunar New Year.

Junk – traditional square-sailed Chinese vessel. The term is also used for any vessel hired for a "junk party".

Kaido (Gaido) – small cargo boat or ferry.

Kowloon taxi – a taxi whose driver claims no knowledge of

streets or major buildings on Hong Kong Island.

Legco – Hong Kong's governing body, only partially elected.

Lunchbox – not filled with a packed lunch from home, but a polystyrene box of food delivered to the workplace.

Mark 6 – the lottery, a chance to win millions for just HK\$20.

MTR – mass transit railway – Hong Kong's train system.

Octopus card – pre-paid transport card, also used as a debit card.

Pseudomodels – women with no modelling experience who will strip for photographers.

Sampan – small boat, with motor at the back, usually driven by a senior citizen.

SAR – Special Administrative Region (of China).

Tai Tai – housewife, a married woman, especially ladies who lunch.

FURTHER READING

Fiction

Clavell, James. *Taipan*. Atheneum & Dell, 1966. The rise of an influential 19th-century British merchant family in Hong Kong.

Gao, Xingjian. *One Man's Bible*. Flamingo, 2002. Nobel Prize-winning author's tale about a man in Hong Kong recalling his youth in Mao's China.

Gardam, Jane. *Old Filth*. Abacus, 2005. Poignant and at times amusing tale of a Hong Kong judge who retires to the UK and recalls his life in the law in Hong Kong, and as a Raj orphan.

Mason, Richard. *The World of Suzie Wong*. 1957, Pegasus Books, 1994. An English artist falls in love with a local lass in this, the book that made Wan Chai famous.

Mo, Timothy. *The Monkey King*. Paddleless Press, 2000. A brilliant account of a dysfunctional family living in colonial Hong Kong.

Morris, Jan. *Hong Kong*. Vintage, 1997. Wonderfully insightful text from the doyenne of modern travel writers.

Row, Jess. *The Train to Lo Wu*. Dial Press, 2005. Highly acclaimed philosophical short stories about Hong Kong,

this book is unusual and thought-provoking.

History and Current Affairs

Booth, Martin. G*weilo: Memories of a Hong Kong Childhood*. Bantam, 2005. A thoroughly enjoyable memoir, amusing and affectionate.

Chamberlain, Jonathan. *King Hui: The Man Who owned all the Opium in Hong Kong*. Blacksmith, 2007. This biography spans most of Hong Kong's 20th century with the adventures of a sometime playboy, brigand, gambler, smuggler, businessman, teacher and spy. Hui King certainly led an interesting life.

Coates, Austin. *Myself a Mandarin*. OUP, 1988. Evocative memoirs of 1950s Hong Kong.

Keay, John. *The End of Empire in the Far East*. John Murray, 1997, 2005. Explores the legacy of the British Empire in Asia with some fascinating detail, and a new afterword on the remarkable development of the Chinese economy.

Sinclair, Kevin. *Tell Me a Story: Forty Years of Newspapering in Hong Kong and China*. SCMP, 2007. Plenty of bar room tales and the inside story of how the recent history of Hong Kong unfolded, from the SAR's best-known journalist.

SEND US YOUR THOUGHTS

We do our best to ensure the information in our books is as accurate and up-to-date as possible. The books are updated on a regular basis using local contacts, who painstakingly add, amend and correct as required. However, some details (such as tele-phone numbers and opening times) are liable to change, and we are ultimately reliant on our readers to put us in the picture.

We welcome your feedback, especially your experience of using the book "on the road". Maybe we recommended a hotel that you liked (or another that you didn't), or you came across a great bar or new attraction we missed.

We will acknowledge all contributions, and we'll offer an Insight Guide to the best letters received.

Please write to us at:
Insight Guides
PO Box 7910
London SE1 1WE
Or email us at:
insight@apaguide.co.uk

Tsang, Steve. *A Modern History of Hong Kong*. (Tauris, 2007). This detailed, up-to-date history of the territory has become the most authoritative general history yet published.

Vines, Stephen. *Hong Kong: China's New Colony*. Texere Publishing, 2000. A thorough overview of the economy, media and political set-up of modern Hong Kong.

Welsh, Frank. *A History of Hong Kong*. HarperCollins, 1997. A social, economic and political history of the territory.

Wordie, Jason. *Streets*. (Hong Kong University Press, 2002). A fascinating guide to the history of individual streets on Hong Kong Island.

Nature/Walking Guides

Spurrier, Pete. *The Leisurely Hiker's Guide to Hong Kong*. FormAsia, 2007. Easy walks around Hong Kong's hills. A guide for more serious hiking is also available.

Stokes, Edward. *Exploring Hong Kong's Countryside: A Visitor's Companion*. HKTB, 1999, 2001, 2002; *The Wilson Trail: Hiking Across Hong Kong*. HKCP Foundation, 2003; *Hong Kong's Wild Places: An Environmental Exploration*. OUP, 1995. These books explore the scenic beauty of the Hong Kong countryside.

Williams, Martin. *Hong Kong Pathfinder*. Asia, 2000, 2004. 23 walks in rural Hong Kong.

Macau

Jackson, Annabel. *Portuguese Cuisine on the China Coast*. Hong Kong University Press, 2003. The best book on Macau's unique fusion cuisine, with 62 recipes.

Porter, Jonathan. *Macau : The Imaginary City : Culture and Society, 1577 to Present*. Westview Press, 2000. Recommended to anyone who is interested in learning more about Macau.

China

Becker, Jasper. *The Chinese*. OUP, 2002. Fine analysis of con-temporary China and what makes the country tick.

Simons, Rowan. *Bamboo Goalposts*. Macmillan, 2008. The entertaining story of one man's quest to teach the PRC to love football, written by a UK-born Beijing television presenter.

Studwell, Joe. *The China Dream: The Elusive Quest for the Greatest Untapped Market on Earth*. Grove Press, 2003. Salutary observations and cautionary tales for those doing business in China.

Other Insight Guides

Other *Insight Guides* to China include: *Southern China* (covering the southern provinces from Fujian to Yunnan), *China*, *Beijing* and *Shanghai*.

The *Insight Step by Step* series uses an itinerary-base approach to assist the traveller with a limited amount of time. Titles include *Beijing* and *Hong Kong*.

Insight Select Guides are inspirational city guides that offer a selection of hip, fresh and quirky ideas. Stylishly designed with evocative photography, the listings for atmospheric bars, one-of-a-kind shops, really good food and places to relax are compiled by writers who know the city inside out. Titles include *Hong Kong*.

Insight Smart Guides offer the traveller a highly portable encyclopedic A–Z guide packed with detailed listings, photographs and maps. Titles include *Beijing* and *Hong Kong*.

Insight Fleximaps combine clear, detailed cartography with a laminated finish. Titles include *Beijing, Xi'an, Shanghai, Nanjing, Guangzhou, Shenzhen, Hong Kong* and *Macau*.

HONG KONG STREET ATLAS

The key map shows the area of Hong Kong covered by the atlas section. An index of street names and places of interest shown on the maps can be found on the following pages. For each entry there is a page number and grid reference

Map Legend

══╤══	Motorway with Junction
═ ═ ═	Motorway (under construction)
════	Dual Carriageway
────	Main Road
────	Secondary Road
────	Minor Road
▬ ▬ ▪	International Boundary
─ ─ ─	Province Boundary
─ ● ─	National Park/Reserve
─ ─ ─	Ferry Route
✈ ✈	Airport
† ⛪	Church (ruins)
†	Monastery
🏰 🏚	Castle (ruins)
Ω	Cave
★	Place of Interest
※	Viewpoint
⚑	Beach
────	Motorway
────	Dual Carriageway
──── ⎫	Main Roads
──── ⎬	
──── ⎭	
──── ⎫	Minor Roads
──── ⎬	
──── ⎭	
────	Footpath
▬▬─▬	Railway
▭	Pedestrian Area
▬	Important Building
▭	Park
❌Ⓜ	Metro
🚌	Bus Station
❶	Tourist Information
✉	Post Office
🉐	Cathedral/Church
✡	Synagogue
𝟏	Statue/Monument

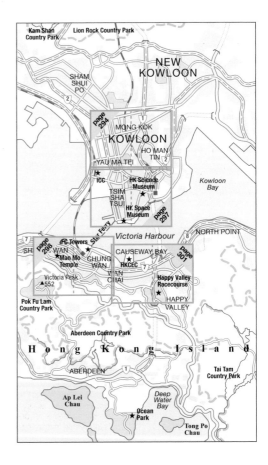

A   B

Sycamore

Maple St.

← Sham Shui Po, Cheung Sha Wan

Willow

Foursquare Gospel Church

Lai Chi Kok Road

Tai Cedar St.

Nan Street

KT Lung St.

Portland

Nathan

Playing Field Road

Fa

Flower Market Rd

Bir
Mark

Flower Market

Edward

Prince Edward

Cheung Lo Church

Man On St

Tai Kok Tsui Rd

Bedford

Tung

Larch

Walnut

Chau Street

Mi Street

Tsuen Lime Street

Fuk Street

Street Road

Tung

Prince

St

Yuen

Road

Nullah Rd

Sai Yee Street

Goldfish Market

Reclamation

Street

Sai Yeung Choi St South

Bute Street

Street

Street

Grand Century Place

Mong Kok KCR Station

Golden Crown Theatre

Hung Shin Temple

Canton

Arran

Street

Shanghai

Mong Kok Church

Asse
o
Ch

Tai Tsun St

Ivy

Elm Street

Street

Fir

Ash St

Bute

Portland

Street

Kok

Wan Road

Li Tak St

Street

Pine St

Street

Mong

Hong Lok St

Argyle Ctr. Tower II

Street

Fuk Chak St

Anchor Street

Oak

Anchor St.

Fife

Argyle Ctr. Tower I

Sincere

Sai

Hak Po St

Ka Shin St

Trt Shiu St

Beech

Palm St.

New Kowloon Plaza

ANCHOR PARK

Bute St.

Hang Seng Bank Bldg

Mong Kok

Shacombank Bldg

Wayfoong Plaza

Yuen

Fa

Nelson Street

Yin Chong

MACPHERSON GARDENS

Tung Choi St

Cherry Street

HSBC Mong Kok Building

Hoi King St

Chung Wing St

Bulky Road

Argyle Street

CHERRY STREET RECREATION GROUNDS

Langham Place

Grand Tower

Ladies Market

Kun

MONG

Nelson

Thistle St

Street

Shantung

Street

First

Soy Street

All Sa
Chu

Olympic

Olympian City

KOK

Hoi Wang Road

Hoi Fu Court

Hoi Ting Road

Ferry

Kam Lam St

Soy

Kam Fong St

Street

Changsha St.

Yin Chong Street

Nathan Centre

Dundas Street

Kwong Wah Hospital

The
Me
Me
Chu

Waterlo

Lin Cheung Road

Hoi Ting Road

2

Dundas

Reclamation Road

Canton

Street

Portland

Peniel Church

Chun Y Ln

YAU MA TEI

Lee Yip St

Tung On St

Hamilton

Street

Street

YMCA International House

Truth Lutheran Church

Pitt

Street

Yau Ma Tei

Tak Cheong Ln.

Waterloo Road

Yunnan Ln.

Arthur St

Nathan Road

KING'S PARK

Lai Cheung Road

Shek

Lung

Reclamation

Man Ming Lane

Ngo Cheung Road

King's

Cliff Rd

0   400 m

Ching

Tung Kun St

Canton

Street

Prosperous Gardens

Temple Street Night Market

Temple

0   400 yds

Pong

Street

Public

Square

St

Tin Hau Temple

Market St.

Jade Market

······· Aerial Walkway

|||||||| Steps or Escalator

↑ Wong Tai Sin Temple

Kowloon Hospital

Kadoorie Ave

Circuit

Braga

Waterloo Road

Kowloon Rehabilitation Centre

St John's Ln.

Argyle Street

Baptist Church

Lomond Rd

→ Walled City Park

MA TAU WAI

Tin

san Boys chool

Kadoorie Avenue

Street

Kwong Road

Farm Road

Argyle

Staffa Ave

Julia Ave

Emma Ave

Metropole

Man Fuk Rd

Dunbar Road

Perth Street

Shek

Ko St

King Tak

St Mark's Church

Mormon Church

Sheung Hong St

Sheung Shing St

Tin Kwong Road

Kau Pui Lung Rd

YWCA

Pentecostal Tabernacle

wloon Chamber Commerce

Kowloon Central Library

Man Wan Rd

Princess

Sheung Shing Street

Sheung Hin St

Pui Ching Road

Ho Man Tin Estate

Foo St

Sheung Wo St

Sheung Lok Street

Chinese Church of Christ

Ho Man Tin Street

Tin Hill Rd

Rd

Man

Tin Hill

Ho

Tin

Chung

Hau

Fat Kwong

Good

Shepherd St

Sheung Street

HO MAN

Wylie

Margaret

Chung Man St

Village St

Carmel St

TIN

Hau Man St

KO SHAN ROAD PARK

Ko Shan Theatre

Sheung Lok Street

Ko Shan Road

Yung St

East Kowloon Corridor

Oi Man Shopping Centre

Chi Man St

Road

Sports Centre

Chung Yee St

Shun St

Wo Chung St

King's Park Rise

Wylie Road

Fat Kwong Street

Hau St

Yan Fung St

Valley Rd

Queen Elizabeth Hospital

PARK

Chung

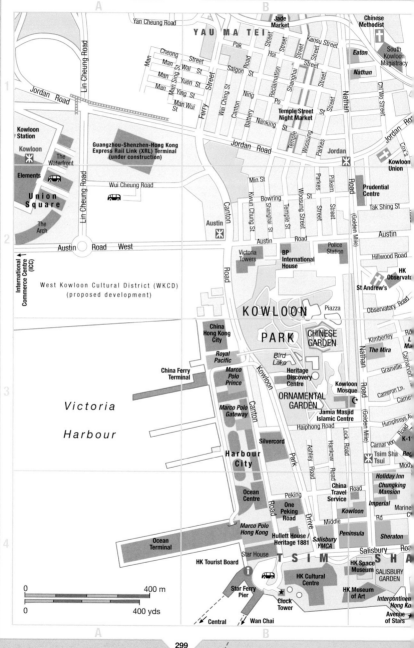

A · B

Yan Cheung Road

Jade Market

Chinese Methodist

YAU MA TEI

Pak · Street · Street · Kansu Street

Eaton

South Kowloon Magistracy

Cheong · Street

Man · St · Wal · St · Saigon · St · Hoi · St · Shanghai · Street · Street

Nathan

Man · Man St · Yuen · St

Man · Man Ying St

Man Wui St

Ferry · Street

Wai Ching St · Canton · Ning · St · Battery · Nanking · St · Reclamation · Po · St · Street · Street · Woosung · Parkes · Street

Chi Wo Street

Jordan · Road

Temple Street Night Market

Kowloon Station

Kowloon

The Waterfront

Elements

Lin Cheung Road

Guangzhou-Shenzhen-Hong Kong Express Rail Link (XRL) Terminal (under construction)

Jordan · Road

Temple · Street · Woosung · Street

Jordan

Cox's

Jordan Ro

Kowloon Union

U n i o n
S q u a r e

Wui Cheung Road

Min St

Parkes

Pilkem

Road

Prudential Centre

The Arch

Lin Cheung Road

Canton

Bowring · Shanghai St · Temple St · Woosung · Street · Street

(Golden Mile)

Tak Shing St

Austin

Austin · Road · West

Austin

Victoria Towers

BP International House

Austin · Road

Police Station

Hillwood Road

International Commerce Centre (ICC)

West Kowloon Cultural District (WKCD) (proposed development)

Canton · Road

Nathan

HK Observato

St Andrew's

Observatory · Road

KOWLOON

Piazza

Kimberley · Ro
L
Ma

China Hong Kong City

PARK

CHINESE GARDEN

The Mira

Granville

Carnarvon

Royal Pacific

Bird Lake

Kowloon

Nathan

Cameron Ln.

Came

China Ferry Terminal

Marco Polo Prince

Heritage Discovery Centre

Kowloon Mosque

Road

Humphreys Av

Road

Victoria

Marco Polo Gateway

ORNAMENTAL GARDEN

Jamia Masjid Islamic Centre

(Golden Mile)

K-1

Harbour

Canton

Haiphong Road

Lock Road

Carnarvon

Silvercord

Park

Ashley Road

Harkow Road

Tsim Sha Tsui

Mody

Reg

Harbour City

China Travel Service

Road

Holiday Inn

Chungking Mansion

Peking

Imperial

Marine

Ocean Centre

Road

Kowloon

C

One Peking Road

Middle

Rd

Marco Polo Hong Kong

Drive

Hullett House / Heritage 1881

Peninsula

Sheraton

Ocean Terminal

Star House

Salisbury YMCA

T S I M · S H A

Salisbury · Roa

HK Tourist Board

HK Cultural Centre

HK Space Museum

SALISBURY GARDEN

Star Ferry Pier

HK Museum of Art

Intercontin Hong Ko

Clock Tower

Avenue of Stars

0 · 400 m

0 · 400 yds

Central · Wan Chai

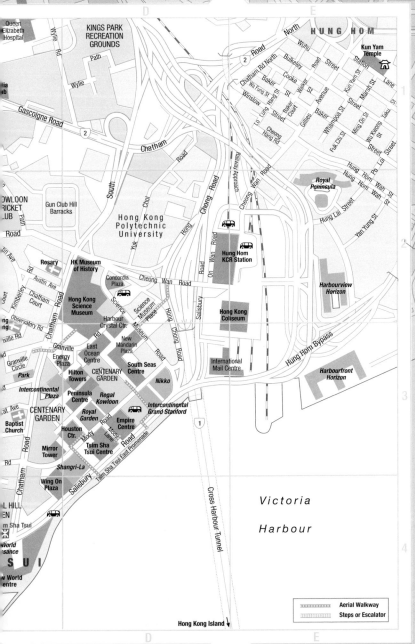

Queen Elizabeth Hospital

KINGS PARK RECREATION GROUNDS

Wylie Rd

Wylie

Path

Gascoigne Road

Chatham

North Road

Wuhu

Kun Yam Temple

Kun Yam Street

Lane

Chatham Rd North

Bulkeley

Cooke

Walker St

Avenue

Marsh St

Wa Fung St

St

Baker St

Street

Winslow

Lo Lung Hang St

Baker Court

Baker Street

Gillies

Whampoa St

Ming On St

Wu Kwong Street

Taku St

Street

Cheong Hong Rd

Fuk Chi St

Po Lai Street

KOWLOON CRICKET CLUB

Gun Club Hill Barracks

South Road

Chui Rd

Hong

Chong Road

Cheong Wan Road

Railway Approach

Hung Hom Wah St

Hung Hom Wah St

Royal Peninsula

Hung Lai Street

Yan Yung St

Hong Kong Polytechnic University

Rosary

HK Museum of History

Austin Ave

Rd

On Wan Road

Hung Hom KCR Station

Harbourview Horizon

Kimberley

Chatham Court

Concordia Plaza

Cheong Wan Road

Science Museum Place

Salisbury

Observatory Rd

Hong Kong Science Museum

Science Museum Rd

Hong Chong Road

Hong Kong Coliseum

Harbourfront Horizon

Granville

Harbour Crystal Ctr.

New Mandarin Plaza

Granville Circle

Park

East Ocean Centre

South Seas Centre

Energy Plaza

CENTENARY GARDEN

Nikko

International Mail Centre

Hung Hom Bypass

Hilton Towers

Intercontinental Plaza

Peninsula Centre

Regal Kowloon

Intercontinental Grand Stanford

CENTENARY GARDEN

Royal Garden

Empire Centre

Baptist Church

Houston Ctr.

Mody Road

Tsim Sha Tsui Centre

Mody Lane

Chatham Road

Mirror Tower

Shangri-La

Tsim Sha Tsui East Promenade

Wing On Plaza

Salisbury

Hong Kong Island ↓

Rd

AL HILL EN

m Sha Tsui

World sance

SUI

w World entre

Chatham Road

Victoria

Harbour

Cross Harbour Tunnel

	Aerial Walkway
	Steps or Escalator

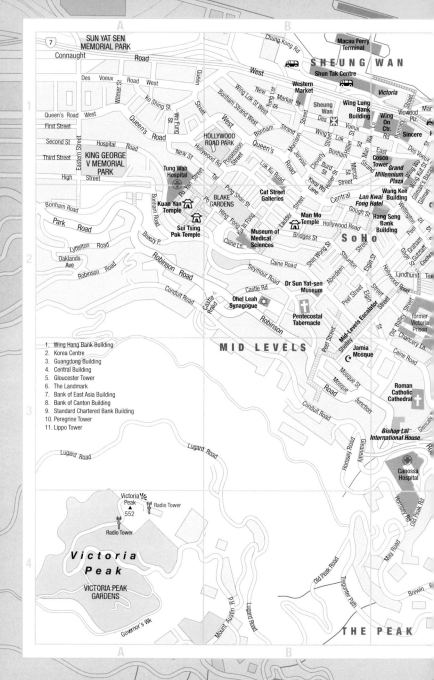

1. Wing Hang Bank Building
2. Korea Centre
3. Guangdong Building
4. Central Building
5. Gloucester Tower
6. The Landmark
7. Bank of East Asia Building
8. Bank of Canton Building
9. Standard Chartered Bank Building
10. Peregrine Tower
11. Lippo Tower

↗ Kowloon

Pier 1
Pier 2
Pier 3
Pier 4
Pier 5
Pier 6
Pier 7
Pier 8

Outlying Islands
Ferry Piers

Star Ferry
Pier

Pier 9

Pier 10

Victoria

Harbour

0   400 m
0   400 yds

Man
Man
Man
Po
Kwong
Kwong
Street
Street
Street

Finance Street

Four
Seasons
Hotel

IFC Mall

International Finance Centre (ifc)

1ifc

2ifc

Central
Station

Hong
Kong

Harbour View Street

Central Reclamation
Project
Phase 3

Central Reclamation Project
Phase 3

Lung Wo Road

Connaught

Jubilee St

Hang Seng
Bank
Building

The
Forum

Road

1

Douglas St

2

Exchange
Square

Connaught
Pl.

General
Post Office

Jardine
House

Edinburgh

City
Hall

Place

CENTRAL

Lung Wui Road

Tamar
Development Project
(under construction)

Pottinger

Chiu Lung St.

Douglas Ln.

Central

St George's
Building

Theatre Lane

Voeux

Pedder St

Chater

Mandarin
Oriental

Central

Ice House St.

Prince's
Building

LegCo
Building

Chater

Club St

Murray

AIG
Tower

Road

Lambeth

Harcourt

Bank of
America
Tower

Walk

Tim Wa Avenue

Tim Mei Avenue

Citic
Building

Shell
House

4

5

Landmark
Mandarin
Oriental

Des Voeux Road

STATUE
SQ.

Jackson

**CHATER
GARDEN**

Far East
Finance
Centre

Zetland St.

New
World
Tower

Ice House St.

8

HSBC
Bldg

9

Bank's St.

Bank of
China

Duddell St.

Battery Path

Queen's Rd C.

Cheung Kong
Centre

Fairmont
House

Cotton Tree Drive

Harcourt

10

11

Tamar St

Admiralty
Centre

Admiralty

Rodney St.

Road

7

**HARCOURT
PARK**

St Paul's

HK Central
Hospital

HK Diamond
Exchange
Building

Government
House

Albert

Road

St John's
Cathedral

Bank of
China
Tower

Citibank Plaza
ICBC Tower

Cotton Tree Drive

Flagstaff
House
Museum of
Tea Ware

Supreme
Court

Government
Offices

Queensway

Queensway
Plaza

United
Centre

May
House

Albert Rd

American
Embassy

St Joseph's
Cathedral

Garden

Peak Tram
Terminus

**HONG KONG
PARK**

Sir Edward
Youde Aviary

Supreme Court Rd

Pacific
Place Two

Pacific
Place One

**Pacific
Place**

*J.W.
Marriott*

*Pacific
Place Three*

The Upper House

Cotton Tree Dr.

Kennedy Road

Visual Arts
Centre

Kennedy Road

*Island
Shangri-La*

Conrad

Justice Drive

Mounmon
Path

Star
Street

Union

First Church of
Christ Scientist

Hong Kong
Design Centre

Macdonnell Road

*Regent on
the Park*

Borrett Road

Kennedy Rd

**ZOOLOGICAL &
BOTANICAL
GDNS**

Peak Tram Funicular

Magazine Gap Rd

May Road

Bowen

Road

Bowen

Borrett Road

Drive

Bowen

Magazine

Gap Rd

Magazine Gap

k Tower

Aerial Walkway
Steps or Escalator

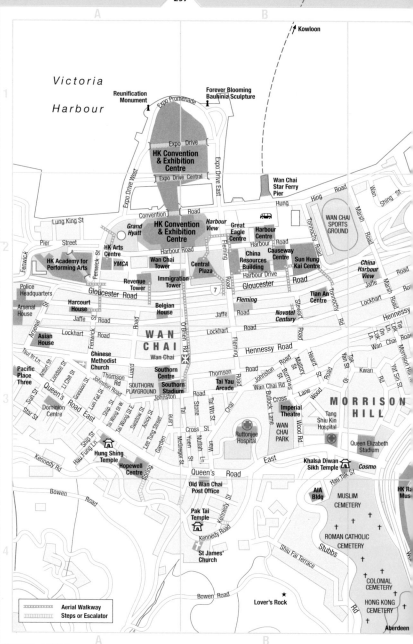

Victoria

Harbour

↑ Kowloon

Reunification
Monument

Forever Blooming
Bauhinia Sculpture

Expo Promenade

Expo Drive

**HK Convention
& Exhibition
Centre**

Expo Drive Central

Expo Drive West

Expo Drive East

Wan Chai
Star Ferry
Pier

Hung Hing Road

Marsh Road

Wan Shing St

WAN CHAI
SPORTS
GROUND

Convention Road

Harbour View

Great Eagle Centre

Lung King St

Grand Hyatt

**HK Convention
& Exhibition
Centre**

China Resources Building

Harbour Centre

Causeway Centre

Sun Hung Kai Centre

China Harbour View

Pier Street

HK Arts Centre

Harbour Road

Harbour Road

Fleming Road

Tonnochy Road

Jaffe Road

Marsh Road

Fenwick St

**HK Academy for
Performing Arts**

YMCA

**Wan Chai
Tower**

Central Plaza

Harbour Drive

Gloucester Road

Tian An Centre

Lockhart Road

Hennessy Road

Police
Headquarters

**Revenue
Tower**

**Immigration
Tower**

Gloucester Road

7

Fleming

Stewart Rd

Wan Chai Rd

Arsenal House

**Harcourt
House**

**Belgian
House**

Jaffe Road

*Novotel
Century*

Fenwick St

Arsenal St

**Asian
House**

Lockhart Road

Lockhart Road

Fleming Rd

Morrison Hill Rd

Tsui In Ln

Luard Rd

Jaffe Rd

Hennessy Road

Heard St

Yan Tak

Kwan

Yat Sin St

W A N
C H A I

Hennessy Road

Landale St

O'Brien Rd

Wan Chai

Johnston Road

Mallory St

Burrows St

**Pacific
Place
Three**

**Chinese
Methodist
Church**

Thomson Rd

Thomson Road

Wan Chai Rd

Cross Lane

**MORRISON
HILL**

Queen's
Road East

Dominion
Centre

Li Chit St

Gresson St

Tai Wong St W.

Tai Wong St E.

Swatow St

Lee Tung Street

**Southorn
Centre**

**Southorn
Stadium**

**Tai Yau
Arcade**

Bullock Lane

Tang
Shiu Kin
Hospital

Queen Elizabeth
Stadium

Star St

SOUTHORN
PLAYGROUND

Johnston

Road

Cross St

Tai Wo St

Stone Nullah Ln

Cross St

**Imperial
Theatre**

**WAN
CHAI
PARK**

Wood Rd

Ship St

Hau Fung Ln

Lun Fat St

Ruttonjee
Hospital

Queen's Road

East

Cosmo

**Hung Shing
Temple**

Garden Rd

McGregor St

**Khalsa Diwan
Sikh Temple**

Kennedy Rd

**Hopewell
Centre**

Ship St

Spring Gdn

Hau Tak St

**AIA
Bldg**

**HK Ra...
Mus...**

Bowen Road

**Old Wan Chai
Post Office**

Kennedy St

Kennedy Road

**MUSLIM
CEMETERY**

**Pak Tai
Temple**

✝ ✝ ✝

**ROMAN CATHOLIC
CEMETERY**

**St James'
Church**

Shiu Fai Terrace

Stubbs

Road

✝

✝ ✝

**COLONIAL
CEMETERY**

Bowen Road

Lover's Rock ★

**HONG KONG
CEMETERY**

Aberdeen

Aerial Walkway
Steps or Escalator

299

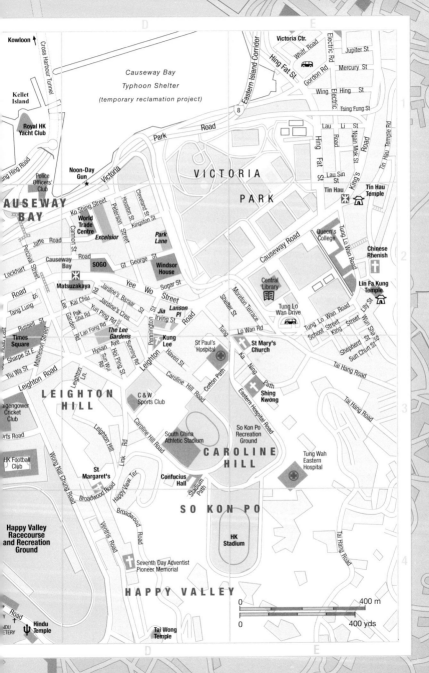

Kowloon ↑

Kellet Island

Royal HK Yacht Club

Cross Harbour Tunnel

Causeway Bay Typhoon Shelter
(temporary reclamation project)

Eastern Island Corridor

Victoria Ctr.

Whitf. Road

Electric Rd

Jupiter St

Hing Fat St

Gordon Rd

Mercury St

Wing Hing St

Electric

Tsing Fung St

8

Lau Li St

Hing Fat St

Ngan Mok St

S's Bury

Tin Hau Temple Rd

Park Road

Lau Sin St

Tin Hau

Tin Hau Temple

AUSEWAY BAY

Police Officers' Club

Noon-Day Gun ★

Victoria

VICTORIA PARK

ng Hing Road

Jaffe Road

Ko Shing Street

Cleveland St

Paterson Street

Houston St

Kingston St

World Trade Centre

Excelsior

Park Lane

Causeway Road

Tung Lo Wan Road

Chinese Rhenish

Queen's College

Percival Street

Cannon St

Causeway Bay Road

SOGO

Gt. George St

Lockhart Road

Yee Wo Street

Windsor House

Sugar St

Moreton Terrace

Central Library

Lin Fa Kung Temple

Tang Lung St

Matsuzakaya

Jardine's Bazaar

Kai Chiu Rd

Jardine's Cres.

Pak Sha Rd

Yun Ping Rd

Jia

Lanson Pl

Shelter St

Lily St

Tung Lo Wan Road

School Street

King Wun Sha St

Street

Road

Russell St

Lee Garden Rd

Lan Fong Rd

The Lee Gardens

Irving St

Kung Lee

Tung Lo Wan Drive

Lo Wan Rd

St Paul's Hospital

St Mary's Church

Shepherd Sun Chun St

Tai Hang Road

Sharpe St E.

Matheson Street

Hysan Ave

Sun Wui Rd

Ho Ping St

Sunning Rd

Haven St

Ka Ning Path

Tai Hang Road

Yiu Wa St

Times Square

Leighton Road

Caroline Hill Road

Cotton Path

Eastern Hospital Road

Shing Kwong

LEIGHTON HILL

Leighton Ln.

Leighton Hill Rd

C&W Sports Club

aigengower Cricket Club

orts Road

Leighton Hill Rd

Caroline Hill Road

South China Athletic Stadium

So Kon Po Recreation Ground

Tung Wah Eastern Hospital

HK Football Club

Wong Nai Chung Road

St Margaret's

Tai Wan Ter.

Tung St

CAROLINE HILL

Confucius Hall

Stadium Path

Happy View Ter.

Broadwood Road

SO KON PO

Tai Hang Road

Happy Valley Racecourse and Recreation Ground

Ventris Road

Broadwood Road

HK Stadium

Seventh Day Adventist Pioneer Memorial

HAPPY VALLEY

Road

Hindu Temple

NDU ETERY

Tai Wong Temple

0   400 m
0   400 yds

Sham Shui Po, Cheung Sha Wan

Sycamore

Willow

Maple St.

Tai

Ki Lung St.

Cedar St.

Nam Street

Portland

Nathan

Sai Yeu St.

Playing Field Road

Fa

Tung

Flower Market Rd

Prince Edward

Bird Market

Flower Market

Edward

Ro

Man On St.

Tung

Bedford

Street

Chau

Street

Walnut

Street

Road

Mr

Reclamation

Canton

Prince

Reed

Nullah

Cho

Yuen

Street

Sai Yee Street

Cheung Lo Church

Ro
Ple

Tai Kok Tsui Rd.

Fuk

Larch

Street

Foursquare Gospel Church

Lai Chi Kok Road

Golden Crown Theatre

Hotel Metropark Mongkok

Goldfish Market

Grand Century Place

Hung Shin Temple

Tsuen Lime

Street

Fir

Street

Arran Road

Arran La.

Shanghai

Street

Portland

Mong Kok Church

Sai Yeung Choi St South

Bute

Street

Mong Kok KCR Station

Tai Tsun St

Ivy

Street

Street

Bute

Street

Mong

Portland

Road

Luen

Assem of C Chu

Li Tak St

Elm St

Street

Pine

St

Ash St.

Anchor St.

Fife

Argyle Ctr. Tower II

Argyle Ctr. Tower I

Street

Sincere

Sai Yee

Hak Po St.

Fuk Chak St

Beech

Anchor

Street

New Kowloon Plaza

Tit Shu St

Oak

Palm St.

Wong Road

Hang Seng Bank Bldg

Shacombank Bldg

Fa

Yuen

Tim Po Fong St.

Ka Shin St

ANCHOR PARK

Argyle Street

Mong Kok

Wayfoong Plaza

Nelson Street

MACPHERSON GARDENS

Kun Ya

Lin Cheung Road

Hoi Kwong Rd

Cherry Street

CHERRY STREET RECREATION GROUNDS

The Place

M Garden

Ladies' Market

Ling Chik St.

All Saint Church

MONG

Nelson

Street

Langham Palace

Grand Tower

Yin Chong Street

Olympic

Olympian City

KOK

Thistle St.

Shantung

Street

First

Soy Street

Hoi Fu Court

Kam Lam St.

Kam Fong St.

Changsha St.

Nathan Centre

Dundas

Street

Kwo

Hoi

Wang

Road

Hoi Ting Road

Ferry

Soy

Street

Shanghai

Street

Nathan

Kwong Wah Hospital

Waterloo R

The W Memo Mettho Chur

YAU MA TEI

2

Dundas

Lee Yip St

Tung On St

Hamilton

Portland

Street

Peniel Church

Street

YMCA International House

Chor Y Lin

Truth Lutheran Church

Ferry

Street

Pitt

Street

Street

Tak Cheong Ln.

Yau Ma Tei

Yuman

Arthur

Nathan Road

KING'S PARK

Lai Cheung Road

Waterloo

Road

Shek

Lung

Reclamation

Man Ming Lane

 Arthur

King's

Ngo Cheung Road

Ching

Canton

Temple Street Night Market

0 ——— 400 m

0 ——— 400 yds

Tung

Kun

St

Prosperous Gardens

Temple Street Night Market

Square

Tin Hau Temple

Cliff Rd

Pong

Public

Market St.

Jade Market

Hotel

Restaurant

Aerial Walkway

Steps or Escalator

Wong Tai Sin Temple

Kowloon Hospital

Kowloon Rehabilitation Centre

Walled City Park

Baptist Church

MA TAU WAI

san Boys chool

St John's Ln.

Waterloo Road

Kadoorie Ave

Braga

Circuit

Argyle

Street

Tin

Kwong

Road

Gillies Rd

Tweed Rd

Dunbar

Road

Kadoorie Avenue

Street

Perth

Shek Ku St

Hop Yat Church

St Mark's Church

Mormon Church

Farm Road

Tin Kwong Road

Kau Pui Lung Rd

Sheung Hong St

Sheung Shing St

Sheung Wo St

Argyle

Sports Ave

Julia Ave

Emma Ave

Metropole

Man Fuk Rd

King Tak St

Anne Black Guest House (YMCA)

Pentecostal Tabernacle

Kowloon Central Library

Man Wan Rd

Princess

Sheung Shing Street

Sheung Lok Street

Chinese Church of Christ

wloon Chamber Commerce

Pui Ching Road

Ho Man Tin Estate

St

Sheung Lok Street

Sheung Hin St

Fat

Kwong

Ho Man Tin Street

Tin Hill Rd

Rd

Ho Man

Good

Chung

Hau St

Shepherd St

Ego St

Sheung Street

Wylie

Road

Margaret

Tin Hill

HO MAN

TIN

Chung Man St

Carmel Village St

Hau St

KO SHAN ROAD PARK

Ko Shan Theatre

Ho Man

St

Sheung Lok Street

Ko Shan Road

Oi Man Shopping Centre

Sports Centre

East Kowloon Corridor

King's Park Rise

PARK

Wylie Road

Chi Man St

Road

Chung Yee St

Fat Kwong Street

Shun Yung St

Yan Fung St

Valley Rd

Wo Chung St

Queen Elizabeth Hospital

Chung

A   B

Yan Cheung Road

Jade Market

Chinese Methodist

YAU MA TEI

Kansu Street

South Kowloon Magistracy

Pak

Cheong

Man St

Wai St

Man

Salgon St

Hoi

Reclamation Street

Shanghai Street

Street

Eaton

Nathan

Man St

Yuen St

Street

Ning

Novotel

Man St

Ying St

Canton

Battery

Nanking St

Temple Street Night Market

Nathan

Man Wui St

Ferry

Wai Ching St

St

Woosung St

Parkes

Street

Jordan

Jordan Road

Lin Cheung Road

Jordan Road

Temple St

Kowloon Rd

Kowloon Station

Guangzhou-Shenzhen-Hong Kong Express Rail Link (XRL) Terminal (under construction)

Jordan

Corb's

Kowloon Union

Kowloon

The Waterfront

Min St

Parkes

Pilken

Road

Prudential Centre

Olive
Elements

Wui Cheung Road

Bowring

Woosung Street

Street

Rent-A-Room

El Pomposo

Kwun Chung St

Shanghai St

Temple St

Tak Shing St

Union Square

Peking Restaurant

The Arch

Austin

Road

Austin

PRIME STEAKHOUSE and Wine Bar

Victoria Towers

(Golden Mile)

Hillwood Road

Austin Road West

Austin

BP International House

Police Station

HK Observate

International Commerce Centre (ICC)

Canton Road

St Andrew's

Observatory Road

West Kowloon Cultural District (WKCD) (proposed development)

KOWLOON

Piazza

Heaven on Earth

China Hong Kong City

PARK

CHINESE GARDEN

Nathan

Kimberley

Rd

Royal Pacific

Bird Lake

The Mira

Granville

Victoria

China Ferry Terminal

Marco Polo Prince

Heritage Discovery Centre

Kowloon Mosque

Road

Car

Super Star Seafood Restaurant

Harbour

ORNAMENTAL GARDEN

Golden Mile

Canton

Jamia Masjid Islamic Centre

Humphreys

Marco Polo Gateway

Haiphong Road

Misocool

Hyatt Regency

Silvercord

Park

Ashley Road

Hankow Road

Lock Road

Tsim Sha Tsui

New Garden Hostel

Victoria Harbour

Harbour City

Branto

Holiday Inn Golden Mile

T'ang Court

Langham Hotel

Chungking House

Ocean Centre

Hutong

Peking Road

Delhi Club Mess

Imperial

Aqua

Kowloon Hotel

Marco Polo Hong Kong Hotel

Canton Road

Salisbury YMCA

Middle Road

Sheraton HK Hotel & To

Arirang

Cucina

Hullett House Heritage 1881

The Peninsula

Oyster an Wine Bar

Ocean Terminal

Star House

Salisbury Dining Room

Gaddi's

Salisbury

HK Tourist Board

Star Ferry Pier

HK Cultural Centre

TSIM

SHA

SALISBURY GARDEN

HK Space Museum

Clock Tower

HK Museum of Art

InterContinen Hong Ko

Central

Wan Chai

Avenue of Stars

0   400 m

0   400 yds

A   B

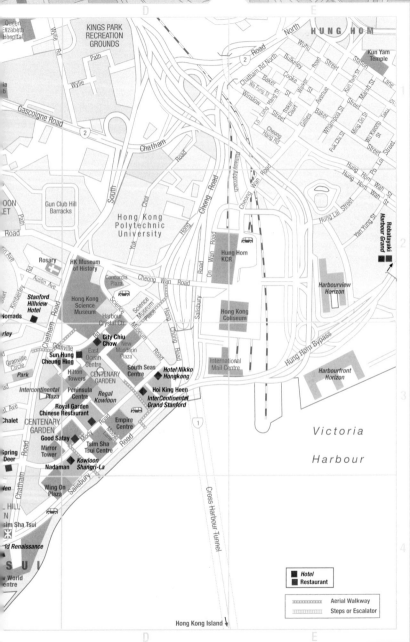

Queen
Elizabeth
Hospital

KINGS PARK
RECREATION
GROUNDS

North Road

HUNG HOM

Wylie Rd

Wylie

Path

Kun Yam Temple

Wuhu

Station

2

Chatham Rd North

Bulkeley St

Cooke St

Baker St

Wakes St

Kun Yam St

Marsh St

Lane

Gascoigne Road

2

Chatham Road

South Chatham Road

Chu Road

Winslow Street

Lo Lung Hang St

Gillies Avenue

Cheong Hang Rd

Whampoa St

Baker St

Fuk Chu St

Mau On St

Wuhu

Nu

Taku

Lai

Street

Street

GOON
LET

Gun Club Hill
Barracks

Path

Hong Kong
Polytechnic
University

On Wan Road

Salisbury Road

Chai Wan Road

Cheong Wan Road

Railway Approach

Hung Hom Po

Hung Hom Wan St

Hung Hom Wan St

Hung Lai Street

Yan Tung St

Robatayaki
Harbour Grand ■

Rosary

HK Museum
of History

Austin Ave

Kimberley Rd

Austin Ave

Stanford
Hillview
Hotel ■

Nomads ■

Concordia
Plaza

Hong Kong
Science
Museum

Hung Hom
KCR

Harbourview
Horizon

Harley

Granville
Circle
Park

Granville Rd

Hilton
Towers

Science Museum Rd

Science Museum Place

Harbour
Crystal Ctr

City Chiu
Chow ■

New
Mandarin
Plaza

Hong Kong
Coliseum

Sun Hung
Cheung Hing ■

South Seas
Centre

Hotel Nikko
Hongkong ■

Hung Hom Bypass

Harbourfront
Horizon

Intercontinental
Plaza

Mody Road

CENTENARY
GARDEN

East
Ocean
Centre

Peninsula
Centre

Regal
Kowloon ■

Hoi King Heen ■

InterContinental
Grand Stanford ■

International
Mail Centre

1

Royal Garden
Chinese Restaurant ■

Chalet

CENTENARY
GARDEN

Empire
Centre

Victoria

Spring
Deer

Good Satay ■

Mirror
Tower

Tsim Sha
Tsui Centre

Chatham Road

Nadaman ■

Kowloon
Shangri-La ■

Harbour

Wing On
Plaza

Salisbury Road

den

HILL
N
sim Sha Tsui

d Renaissance

SUI

w World
entre

Cross Harbour Tunnel

■ Hotel
■ Restaurant

▨▨▨▨▨ Aerial Walkway
▥▥▥▥▥ Steps or Escalator

Hong Kong Island ↓

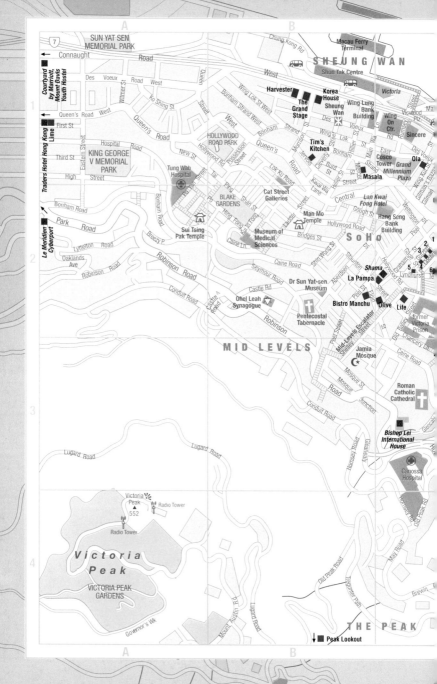

A

B

7

Connaught

SUN YAT SEN
MEMORIAL PARK

Road

Chung Kong Rd

Macau Ferry
Terminal

SHEUNG WAN

West

Shun Tak Centre

Courtyard by Marriott, Mount Davis Youth Hostel

Des Voeux Road West

Wilmer St

Ko Shing St

Queen

Queen's Road West

First St

Third St

High Street

Hospital

Road

Bonham Strand West

Wing Lok St West

Bonham Strand West

Harvester

The Grand Stage

Korea House Sheung Wan

Victoria

Wing Lung Bank Building

Wing On Ctr.

Sincere

Traders Hotel Hong Kong Lime

Eastern Street

KING GEORGE V MEMORIAL PARK

Bonham Road

New St

Hollywood Rd

HOLLYWOOD ROAD PARK

Possession Street

Bonham Strand

Des Voeux

Wing Lok

Bonham

Queen's

Jervois

Cleverly St

Burd St

Hillier St

East Cosco Tower

Ola

Grand Millennium Plaza

Des Voeux Rd

Tim's Kitchen

Masala

Le Meridien Cyberport

Park

Road

Tung Wah Hospital

Sui Tsing Pak Temple

BLAKE GARDENS

Cat Street Galleries

Man Mo Temple

Kwai Wa Lane

Central

Lan Kwai Fong Hotel

Hang Seng Bank Building

SoHo

Lyttelton Road

Oaklands Ave

Robinson Road

Breezy P.

Hollywood Road

Museum of Medical Sciences

Bridges St

Caine Ln

Ladder Street

Staunton

Wellington

Graham

Gough St

Peel

1
2

Shama

3

5

6

Conduit Road

Castle Road

Seymour Road

Caine Road

Dr Sun Yat-sen Museum

La Pampa

Aberdeen St

Hollywood Rd

Lyndhurst Te

Ohel Leah Synagogue

Pentecostal Tabernacle

Bistro Manchu

Olive

Life

Robinson

Peel St

Mid Levels Escalator

Shelley Street

Former Victoria Prison

MID LEVELS

Elgin St

Old Chancery Ln

Jamia Mosque

Mosque St

Junction

Caine Road

Roman Catholic Cathedral

Conduit Road

Road

Bishop Lei International House

Glenealy

Lugard Road

Lugard Road

Canossa Hospital

Old Peak Rd

Victoria Peak
▲552

Radio Tower

Radio Tower

May Road

Old Peak Road

Tramitter Path

Brewin

Victoria Peak

VICTORIA PEAK GARDENS

Governor's Wk

Mount Austin Rd

Lugard Road

THE PEAK

Peak Lookout

A

B

304

→ Kowloon

0 _____ 400 m
0 _____ 400 yds

■ Hotel
■ Restaurant

1. Habibi Cafe
2. Between Wu Yue
3. Ser Wong Fun
4. Yellow Door
5. Tandoor
6. Pizza Express
7. Nha Trang
8. Mak's Noodles

Pier 1
Pier 2
Pier 3
Pier 4
Pier 5
Pier 6
Pier 7
Pier 8
Pier 9
Pier 10

Outlying Islands
Ferry Piers

Man Man
Man Kwong Street
Man Po Kwong Street
Finance Street
Street

Four
Seasons
Hotel

Watermark
Star Ferry
Pier

Red
IFC Mall
International Finance Centre (ifc)
ifc
2ifc   Harlan's

Central
Station
Hong
Kong

Harbour View Street

Hang Seng
Bank
Building

The Forum

Exchange
Square

Jardine
House

General
Post Office

Connaught

Central

St George's
Building

Mandarin
Oriental

Prince's
Building

STATUE
SQ.

Chater Road

Ice House Street

Chater Road

Dot Cod
LegCo
Building

Landmark
Mandarin
Oriental

New
World
Tower

Ice
House

Di
Vino

HSBC
Bldg

Bank
of
China

CHATER
GARDEN

M at the
Fringe

Queen's Rd C.

Battery Path

HK Diamond
Exchange
Building

Cheung Kong
Centre

Bank
of China
Tower

St John's
Cathedral

Citibank Plaza
ICBC Tower

Flagstaff
House,
Museum of
Tea Ware

Supreme
Court

Government
Offices

Government
House

American
Embassy

St Joseph's
Cathedral

Peak Tram
Terminus

Peak Tram Funicular

HONG KONG
PARK

Visual Arts
Centre

Hong Kong
Design Centre

Sir Edward
Youde Aviary

Pacific
Place One

Pacific Place Two

Union

First Church of
Christ Scientist

Macdonnell Road

Magazine Gap Rd

Bowen

Road

Bowen

May Road

Magazine Gap Rd

Victoria

Harbour

Central Reclamation
Project
Phase 3

Lung Wo Road

Central Reclamation Project
Phase 3

City Hall
Chinese
Restaurant

City
Hall

CENTRAL

AIG
Tower

Bank of
America
Tower

Fairmont
House

Harcourt
Road

Tim Wa Avenue

Tamar
Development Project
(under construction)

Far East
Finance
Centre

Admiralty Centre

Admiralty Road

Admiralty

Citic
Building

HARCOURT
PARK

May
House

Queensway
Plaza

United
Centre

Ye
Shanghai

Queensway

Cafe Grey
Deluxe

J.W.Marriott

The Upper House

Pacific
Place

Conrad

Island
Shangri-La

Regent on
the Park

Kennedy Road

Borrett Road

Bowen

Borrett Road

Kennedy Rd.

May Road

Magazine Gap

⬡⬡⬡⬡⬡ Aerial Walkway
▨▨▨▨▨ Steps or Escalator

Luk Yu
Teahouse

Yung Kee

St Paul's

Government
House

ZOOLOGICAL &
BOTANICAL
GDNS

Cotton Tree Dr.

308

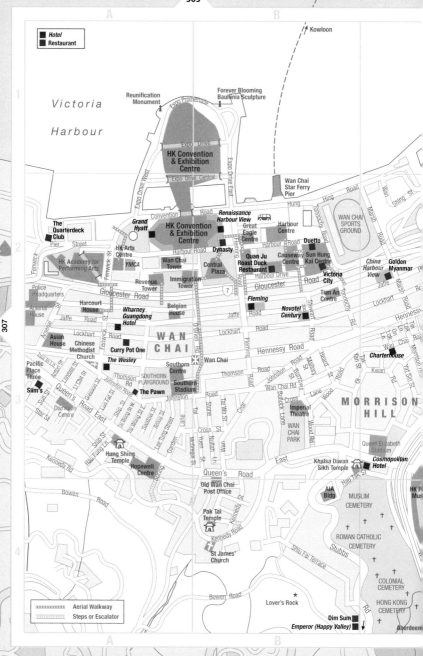

Hotel
Restaurant

Victoria

Harbour

Kowloon

Reunification
Monument

Forever Blooming
Bauhinia Sculpture

Expo Promenade

Expo Drive

HK Convention
& Exhibition
Centre

Expo Drive Central

Expo Drive East

Wan Chai
Star Ferry
Pier

Convention   Road

Hung

Hing   Road

Tonnochy

Wan   Shing   St

Marsh

WAN CHAI
SPORTS
GROUND

The
Quarterdeck
Club

Grand Hyatt

Renaissance
Harbour View

HK Convention
& Exhibition
Centre

Great
Eagle
Centre

Harbour
Centre

Duetto

Pier   Street

HK Arts
Centre

Fenwick   St

HK Academy for
Performing Arts

YMCA

Wan Chai
Tower

Dynasty

Central
Plaza

Quan Ju
Roast Duck
Restaurant

Causeway
Centre

Sun Hung
Kai Centre

China
Harbour
View

Golden
Myanmar

Police
Headquarters

Revenue
Tower

Immigration
Tower

Harbour   Road

Harbour   Road

Gloucester   Road

Victoria
City

Jaffe

Marsh   St

Tian An
Centre

Lockhart

Hennessy

Arsenal
House

Harcourt
House

Gloucester   Road

7

Fleming

Novotel
Century

Stewart

Wan   Chai

Morrison   Rd

Asian
House

Jaffe   Road

Belgian
House

Jaffe

Road

Fleming   St

Kwan

Tat   Sin   St

Wharney
Guangdong
Hotel

Lockhart   Road

Lockhart   Road

Hennessy   Road

Charterhouse

Chinese
Methodist
Church

Curry Pot One

O'Brien   Rd

WAN
CHAI

Burrows   St

Mallory   St

Heard   St

Marsh   St

Luard   Rd

Wan   Chai   Rd

MORRISON
HILL

Pacific
Place
Three

The Wesley

Thomson
Rd

Johnston   Road

SOUTHORN
PLAYGROUND

Southorn
Centre

Wan Chai

Thomson

Johnston   St

Wan   Chai   Rd

Cross

Lane

Wood

Imperial
Theatre

Queen Elizabeth
Stadium

Slim's

Queen's   Road   East

Dominion
Centre

Star   St

Southorn
Stadium

The Pawn

Johnston

Cross   St

Tai   Yuen   St

Stone   Nullah   St

Tai   Wo   St

Cross   St

Spring   Garden   Lane

McGregor   St

WAN
CHAI
PARK

Wood   Rd

Stone   Nullah   Lane

Cosmopolitan
Hotel

Khalsa Diwan
Sikh Temple

Hung Shing
Temple

Kennedy   Rd

Ship   St

Hopewell
Centre

Queen's   Road

Old Wan Chai
Post Office

Kennedy   Road

East

AIA
Bldg

MUSLIM
CEMETERY

HK R
Mus

Bowen   Road

Pak Tai
Temple

St James'
Church

Shiu   Fai   Terrace

Stubbs

ROMAN CATHOLIC
CEMETERY

COLONIAL
CEMETERY

Bowen   Road

Lover's Rock

Aerial Walkway

Steps or Escalator

Dim Sum

Emperor (Happy Valley)

HONG KONG
CEMETERY

Aberdeen

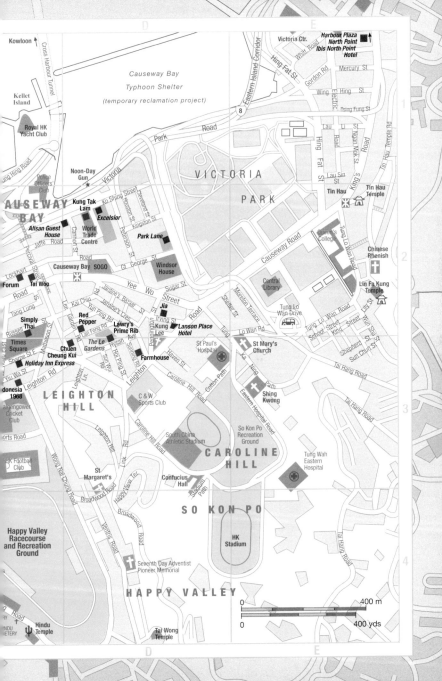

Kowloon

Cross Harbour Tunnel

Kellet
Island

Royal HK
Yacht Club

Causeway Bay
Typhoon Shelter
(temporary reclamation project)

Eastern Island Corridor

Victoria Ctr.

Harbour Plaza
North Point
Ibis North Point
Hotel

Whitfield Road

Hing Fat St.

Gordon Rd.

Mercury St.

Wing

Hing

St

Electric

Tsing Fung St.

Lau Li St.

Ngan Mok St.

Park

Road

8

VICTORIA

PARK

Hing Fat St.

King's

Road

Lau Sin
St

Tin Hau

Tin Hau
Temple

Police
Officers'
Club

Noon-Day
Gun

Victoria

AUSEWAY
BAY

Kung Tak
Lam

Atisan Guest
House

Excelsior

World
Trade
Centre

Park Lane

Causeway Bay SOGO

Forum

Tai Woo

Windsor
House

Queen's
College

Causeway Road

Central
Library

Tung Lo Wan Road

Chinese
Rhenish

Lin Fa Kung
Temple

Ko Shing Street

Cleveland St.

Houston St.

Kingston St.

Patterson St.

Cannon St.

Percival Street

Jaffe Road

Lockhart

Road

Gt. George St.

Yee Wo Street

Sugar St.

Marathon Terrace

Tung Lo Wan Drive

Tung Lo Wan Road

School Street

King St.

Wun Sha St.

Lily St.

Shelter St.

Tang Lung

Simply
Thai

Jardine's Bazaar

Jardine's Cres.

Kai Chiu Rd.

Yun Ping Rd.

Lan Fong Rd.

Jia

Red Pepper

Lawry's
Prime Rib

Kung
Lee

Lanson Place
Hotel

Lo Wan Rd.

Tung

Russell St.

Matheson St.

Lee Garden Rd.

Times
Square

Chuen
Cheung Kui

The Le
Gardens

Holiday Inn Express

Sharp St E.

Yiu Wa St

donesia
1968

Pak Sha Rd.

Hoi Ping Rd.

Sunning Rd.

Sunning

Irving St.

Leighton Lin.

Farmhouse

Haven St.

St Paul's
Hospital

St Mary's
Church

Cotton Path

St Mary's

Tai Hang Road

LEIGHTON
HILL

Leighton Rd.

Leighton Hill Rd.

C & W
Sports Club

Caroline Hill Road

Eastern Hospital Road

Shing
Kwong

aisengower
Cricket
Club

orts Road

HK Football
Club

Wong Nai Chung Road

South China
Athletic Stadium

St
Margaret's

CAROLINE
HILL

Tung Wah
Eastern
Hospital

Tai Hang Road

So Kon Po
Recreation
Ground

Happy View Terr.

Confucius
Hall

Stadium
Path

SO KON PO

Happy Valley
Racecourse
and Recreation
Ground

Broadwood Road

Ventris Road

Broadwood Road

Seventh Day Adventist
Pioneer Memorial

HK
Stadium

HAPPY VALLEY

0   400 m

0   400 yds

Road

Hindu
Temple

NDU

Tai Wong
Temple

STREET INDEX

ART & PHOTO CREDITS

All photography Alex Havret/APA except:
akg-images 39B, 40L, 41T&B
Alamy 100/101T, 114/115B, 124, 131B
AP/PA Photos 49L
The Art Archive/Eileen Tweedy 38TL
Massimo Borchi/4Corners Images 219B
The Bridgeman Art Library 37
CARO/Sorge/Still Pictures 143B
R Celentano/laif/Camerapress 54/55
Corbis 42B, 46T, 51T, 52B, 78/79T, 132TL, 174B
CPA Media 36T, 109TL
Mary Evans Picture Library 35
Alain Evrard 45R, 53T
FormAsia 42T
Getty Images 3, 16/17, 31B, 34, 45L, 46L, 50R, 51B, 53C, 81R, 116/117, 174T
Glyn Genin/APA 217, 219T, 220,/T, 221,/T, 224T, 226/T, 227/TL, 228, 229
Government Information Services 43
Tim Hall/Axiom 98, 209B
David Henley/APA 80T, 242B, 248R
Mark Henley/Panos 33T
Peter Hessel 249
Nigel Hicks 156B, 185TR&B
Jack Hollingsworth 56, 180/181, 250
Hong Kong Museum of Art Collection (Auguste Borget) 38/39T
Hong Kong Tourist Board 6B, 8T, 9TL&CL, 12BL&BR, 13CL, 29CL, 31TL, 44B, 93L&R, 106/107L, 110B, 115BR, 116T, 126L, 128TL, 132TR, 141, 142BL, 142/143T, 143TR, 146T, 150, 152(all), 158TR, 159T, 161BR, 186TL, 187, 188T&B, 191BR, 196B, 197T, 206B, 264, 265, 266, 279, 280
ImagineChina 49R, 70T, 238, 241R, 251TR
iStockphoto.com 13BL, 48T, 70L, 104BL, 108TL&TR, 114T, 126/127T, 146BR, 206TL&TR, 210TL, 214/215, 223T, 224/225T, 251B
Britta Jaschinski/APA 10BR
Gerhard Joren 47T, 244B
Catherine Karnow 20, 22TR, 47B, 76, 202

The Kobal Collection/Shaw Brothers 190B
Taras Kovaliv/APA 1, 7T, 21, 27L, 28, 29TR, 104T, 106B, 115TL, 161BL, 162B, 163B, 175T, 177, 193T, 195, 204TL, 258C, 270
Las Vegas Sands Corp 228/229B, 230T, 278
Olivier Laude 247T
Max Lawrence 82
Mary Anne Le Bas 8CR, 210TR
Tom Le Bas/APA 115TR, 207T, 267
Leonardo.com 225B
Manfred Morgenstern 36B, 50T, 51C
The National Archives/HIP/TopFoto 50B
PA Archive/PA Photos 40R
Paramount/The Kobal Collection 128B
Andrea Pistolesi 159B
Michael Pitts/Nature Picture Library 186B
GP Reichelt 204B
Rex Features 81L
Rick Senley 60
Sinopix 31TR, 32R, 52T, 84L
Sinopix/APA 6T, 11T&BR, 12TR, 13CR, 23, 57, 61R, 62TL, 62/63T, 66, 67, 68TL&TR, 79TR, 80L, 101B, 104BR, 111B, 112BL&BR, 117T, 119, 129T, 130B, 131T, 133, 134, 144T&B, 147T&B, 148TL&TR, 153T, 155T, 156T, 157T&B, 160B, 161TR, 163TR, 164, 175B, 176B, 190TL, 194B, 196T, 198B, 203T, 209TR, 210B, 224B, 230B, 231, 232, 234/5, 239, 240B, 241L, 242TL&TR, 247B, 248L, 251TL, 252, 258T, 273
South China Morning Post 44T
Starworld 216
Ed Stokes 9C, 90/91, 140, 182, 185TL, 193B, 197B
Rick Strange 192B
Sun Hung Kai Properties 53B
Ming Tang-evans/APA 33B
Graham Uden 10T, 18, 26T, 48B, 59T, 69R, 83, 85T, 102B, 113B, 129B, 132B, 243, 246
Bill Wassman 69L
Bill Wassman/APA 7B, 99, 145T, 146BL, 155BL, 158BR, 191BL, 192T, 222, 240T, 287
Ruth Williams 100TL, 244T
Trisha Williams 207B
David Wilkinson 204TR

all Alex Havret/APA except:
64/65: Sinopix/APA 64/65T, 65CL, CR, BL&BR

72–75: Hong Kong Tourist Board 72CR; National Palace Museum 73BR; Sinopix/APA 72/73T; Alain Evrard 75BL; Hong Kong Tourist Board 74TL; Ian Lloyd 75TR; Sinopix/APA 74CR, 75BR

86/87: Taras Kovaliv/APA 87TR; Sinopix/APA 86BL&BR, 87BL&BR; Getty Images 86/87T

122/123: Kevin Cummins 122/123T, 123CL; Hong Kong Tourist Board 123BL; Catherine Karnow 122TL&BL; Sinopix/APA 123TR&BR

136/137: Mike Clarke/AFP/Getty Images 137BR; iSockphoto.com 135TL, 137BL; Rick Senley 136/137T; Sinopix/APA 137CL; Ruth Williams 137TR

168–171: Hong Kong Tourist Board 168CR; Sinopix/APA 169BL; David Henley/APA 171TR

178/179: Hong Kong Tourist Board 178TL, 178/179T, 179CL&B; The Image Bank/Derek Berwin 178BL; Tom Le Bas/APA 179R; Sinopix/APA 178BR

200/201: Nigel Hicks 200TL, 201TR, C&BR; Ed Stokes 200CR&B, 200/201T

212/213: Disney 212CR, BL&BR, 212/213T, 213TR; Hong Kong Tourist Board 213CR; Tom Le Bas/APA 212TL; Ocean Park 213BR

Map Production: Dave Priestley, Stephen Ramsay & APA Cartography Dept.

©2011 Apa Publications GmbH & Co Verlag KG (Singapore Branch)

Production: Tynan Dean, Linton Donaldson, Rebeka Ellam

GENERAL INDEX

RESTAURANTS

Bars, Pubs and Clubs

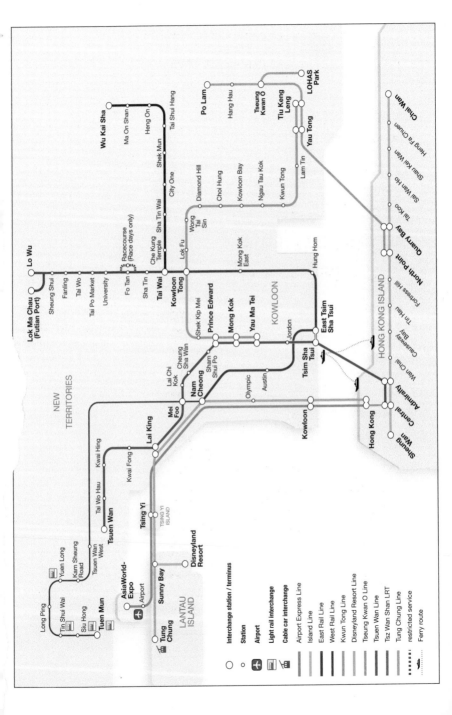

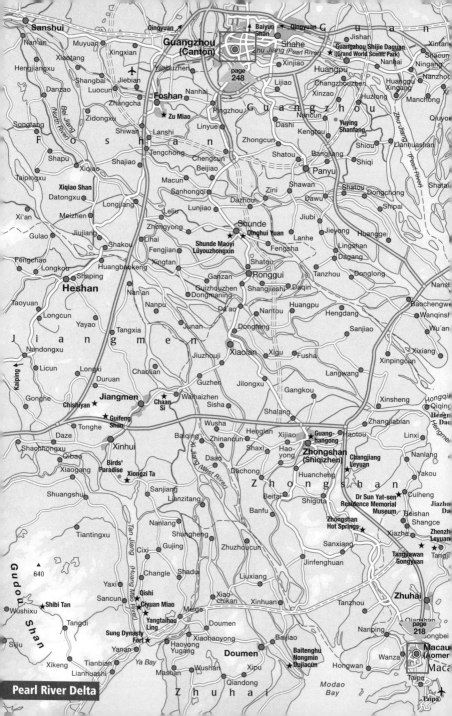